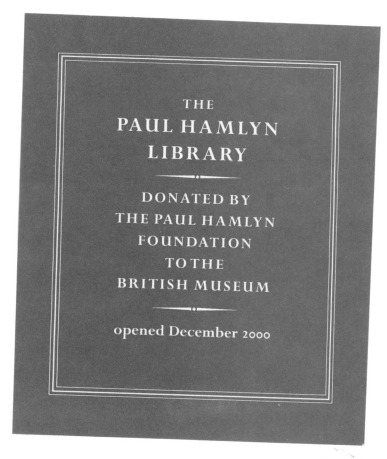

WOODEN SHIP BUILDING AND THE INTERPRETATION OF SHIPWRECKS

WOODEN SHIP BUILDING AND THE INTERPRETATION OF SHIPWRECKS

J. RICHARD STEFFY

TEXAS A&M UNIVERSITY PRESS

COLLEGE STATION

CHATHAM PUBLISHING

LONDON

Copyright © 1994 by J. Richard Steffy
All rights reserved
Second printing, 1998

Published in Great Britain in 1998 by
Chatham Publishing, 61 Frith Street
London W1V 5TA
Chatham Publishing is an imprint of
Gerald Duckworth & Co Ltd

The paper used in this book meets the minimum requirements
of the American National Standard for Permanence
of Paper for Printed Library Materials, Z39.48-1992.
Binding materials have been chosen for durability.

This publication has been supported by a grant from the National Endowment
for the Humanities, an independent federal agency.

Library of Congress Cataloging-in-Publication Data

Steffy, J. Richard (John Richard), 1924–
    Wooden ship building and the interpretation of shipwrecks / J.
Richard Steffy. — 1st ed.
        p.   cm.
    Includes bibliographical references and index.
    ISBN 0-89096-552-8 (alk. paper)
    1. Ships, Wooden.   2. Shipwrecks.   3. Underwater archaeology.
I. Title.
VM 144.S73   1993
623.8'207—dc20   93-30036
                                                                          CIP

British Library Cataloguing in Publication Data
A catalogue record for this book is available from the British Library
ISBN I 86176 104 X
This edition printed in Great Britain

To Lucille

CONTENTS

TABLES

PREFACE

This is a guide to the study of the most marvelous structures ever built by humankind—wooden ships and boats. It is intended for use by nautical archaeologists and those people charged with documenting and interpreting the remains of wrecked or abandoned vessels. I hope it will also be of value to historians, authors, model builders, and others interested in the design and construction of watercraft.

The need for such a book became increasingly apparent over the past several years. Students in my classes on wooden shipbuilding and ship reconstruction expressed a desire for a comprehensive textbook on these subjects that could be taken into the field for guidance in their own projects. Teachers of nautical subjects at other institutions made similar requests. In addition, I received letters from people of various interests asking that I publish my research methodology, a glossary applying to vessels of all periods, and bibliographical lists. This work is a response to those requests, arranged in what I hope will be a convenient format and including as much information as could be compiled within the covers of a single volume of practical size. It is the way I comprehend the discipline of ship and boat research, the way I taught it at Texas A&M University for fourteen years, and the way I practiced it in the field for many more.

The book is divided into three parts. The first introduces the discipline and presents enough basic information to permit the untrained reader to understand the analysis of ship and boat construction that follows. Part II is broken into three chapters that investigate ancient, medieval, and postmedieval shipwrecks and provide supporting documentation. Not all of the world's ship and boat excavations can be included in this single volume; nautical archaeology has progressed too far for that. Instead, these three chapters have been assembled to represent a cross section of shipbuilding technology as seen through the interpretation of a select group of finds. Additional excavation reports and supportive information are noted in the bibliography.

Part III addresses the techniques of recording hull remains, assembling archival information, reconstructing vessels, and converting data into plans and publications. It is by no means a how-to section. Sites, logistics, and the wrecks themselves vary so much that, like wooden shipbuilding, our discipline can never become an exact science. Rather, the third part of the book discusses work done on previous projects and suggests additional methods that might prove helpful to readers in their own endeavors.

An illustrated glossary, specifically designed for archaeological use, may be found in the back of the book. There is a select bibliography, too, annotated where titles do not indicate content and arranged in historical groups to provide sources for most areas of research. Many of the citations were selected for their own bibliographical lists, which will guide the reader to additional source material.

It would be impossible to list all the wonderful people who have shared information or, in some other way, influenced this work, but certainly George Bass, Michael Katzev, and Fred van Doorninck have been the most helpful over the years. A fellowship from the John D. and Catherine T. MacArthur Foundation provided both time and funding, while most of my own projects outlined in this text were possible because of the facilities and generous support provided by Texas A&M University and the Institute of Nautical Archaeology. I am indebted to four people for reading the manuscript and providing valuable suggestions: Fred Hocker and Kevin Crisman of the nautical archaeology faculty at Texas A&M; Paul Johnston, curator of maritime history at the Smithsonian Institution; and Lionel Casson, professor emeritus of classics at New York University. Ole Crumlin-Pedersen and Patrice Pomey were especially helpful with advice and illustrations, while the administrative assistance of Claudia LeDoux, Rebecca Holloway, Clyde Reese, and Robert (Chip) Vincent made my work much easier. Thanks also go to all those who supplied information and illustrations; their names appear in the notes and illustration credits.

None of this would have been possible were it not for Lucille, my wife of forty years. She served as proofreader and critic, and she prevented me from trashing the project on several occasions. Although she didn't live to see the finished product, it was her effort and support over the years that made all my work possible.

Finally, there was the letter from eight-year-old Terry, who neglected to give his last name or address but said, "Please tell me everything you know about ships." Terry, this is for you.

J. Richard Steffy
College Station, Texas

ABBREVIATIONS

The following abbreviations are used for frequently cited works throughout the text:

AJA   *American Journal of Archaeology*

BAR   British Archaeological Reports (British Series)

BAR-S   British Archaeological Reports (International Series)

IJNA   *The International Journal of Nautical Archaeology and Underwater Exploration*

MM   *The Mariner's Mirror*

TAPS   *Transactions of the American Philosophical Society*

Tropis I   *Tropis I: Proceedings of the 1st International Symposium on Ship Construction in Antiquity,* edited by Harry E. Tzalas (Athens, 1985).

Tropis II   *Tropis II: Proceedings of the 2nd International Symposium on Ship Construction in Antiquity,* edited by Harry E. Tzalas (Athens, 1987).

WOODEN SHIP BUILDING AND THE INTERPRETATION OF SHIPWRECKS

PART   I

Fundamentals

1

INTRODUCTION

Most of us envision wooden sailing ships of the past in multifarious, sometimes glamorous roles—on voyages of exploration with Eriksson, Magellan, or Cook; as fighting craft at Actium, Lepanto, or Trafalgar; or as carriers of goods and people between Alexandria and Rome, Spain and the Indies, or New York and the Orient. Although the majority of watercraft must have been something substantially less than our mental images portray them, these wooden vessels made an enormous contribution to what Jacob Bronowski termed "the ascent of man." And yet, how much do we really know about them? Even some of the famous types—the great Roman grain ships or the swift Barbary corsairs, for instance—are but superficial representations in our minds (and on our drawing boards). We could not supply half of the minute details necessary to build one of them authentically.

We have barely begun to uncover the secrets of our maritime past. New archaeological discoveries frequently reveal timbers, techniques, even complete vessel types that were previously unknown. How many more undocumented types were there, how many other strange and unsuspected timber shapes and arrangements, how many other techniques for their design and construction?

Enough information still survives in the remains of countless unexcavated watercraft to increase our knowledge of shipbuilding and shiphandling many times over. To extract that information, however, each wreck must be analyzed as accurately and extensively as possible by means of a controlled discipline; we have come to know this discipline as *ship reconstruction*.

The Scope of Reconstructions

Webster defines reconstruction as the act of rebuilding. Even the secondary definitions seem to provide no broader meaning for the reconstruction of wrecked or abandoned ships and boats than the reassembly of their remains. Were it so limited, this study could be contained within the confines of a journal article. But a wooden ship was, in reality, far more than a lifeless structure. It began as a desire for profit, a hope for victory, or a dream of exploration or conquest in the minds of its originators. The idea moved to the shipyard, where the efforts of shipwrights, carpenters, and smiths—who sometimes left the marks of their tools or the signs of their ingenuity—converted hundreds of trees into a variety of shapes and joined them together. Tons of timber, metal, caulking, paint, rope, and cloth were fabricated into a type of structure that was perhaps the most complex of its time—one that could carry cargoes far heavier than any

other form of transport and travel distances landsmen could only ponder.

Once launched, the ship became host to captain and crew, passengers, port officials, and stevedores of many tongues. In time, seams were recaulked, timbers and planks were replaced, or rigging was restored. The construction and operation of this vessel might have been influenced by hundreds or even thousands of people, some of whom, in some manner, left their marks on its remains.

Reconstructing ships and boats, then, is not merely determining information about the ship's structure. We have tampered with the original definition and turned it into an all-inclusive description of the ship as a venture. Where sufficient information survives, the reconstruction might include a partial reenactment of the final voyage or battle, the dispersion of the hull and cargo on the seabed, or the technological methods of the period, as well as the determination of the original design of the vessel. In fact, there are now so many subjects included in the study of hull remains that specialists in sub-disciplines within the realm of reconstructing ships have surfaced. In most cases, this is because they have been forced to become experts in order to do a good job of interpreting specific parts of a hull. Within a stone's throw of my laboratory, there are authorities on anchors, bilge pumps, figureheads, period rigging, various forms of construction, tools, guns, and hygiene—a dozen of them in all; worldwide the figure must be impressive.

How well must a ship or boat be preserved before a thorough study becomes necessary? There is no lower limit. The success of a reconstruction is largely restricted by the ingenuity of its investigator, not the extent of hull survival. Of course, there is more flexibility and opportunity with a well-preserved vessel. The Kyrenia ship was a merchantman from the fourth century B.C. whose hull was about two-thirds preserved when excavated.[1] The remains of that wreck were physically reconstructed in a castle on Cyprus, and a full-size replica was built and is now undergoing extensive sailing tests. While this study contributed substantially to our understanding of ancient shipbuilding and seafaring, an equally challenging and interesting discovery, the Athlit ram in Israel, was completely counter to

the Kyrenia wreck as far as the extent of preservation is concerned.[2] A bronze ram and sixteen pieces of wood from a classical warship survived, some of them small enough to fit into the palm of a hand. Yet that little pile of wood increased the knowledge of ancient warship construction a hundredfold, and its ram was equally generous in providing information about metallurgy and naval matters.

Most shipwrecks are sparsely preserved, with perhaps 10 percent or less of the hull remaining, but sometimes information can be compiled about a vessel that did not survive at all. I am fascinated by the Sutton Hoo excavation and the means by which the mere earthen impression of a hull has revealed so much.[3] Indeed, one does not need even a mud impression. Cargo arrangement can sometimes indicate hull size, the existence of bulkheads, and hold parameters. Anchor concretions locate bulwarks, ballast defines ceiling, and artifact provenance occasionally reveals living or galley areas. Usually something can be learned about a ship's hull on a wreck-site, even where nothing of the hull itself survived. Frequently it is new information or information that might assist someone on another project. That old phrase, "there wasn't enough of the hull preserved to do a study of it," is seldom accepted anymore.

Terminology

Shipbuilders and sailors talked strangely. They spoke of *futtocks* and *limbers* and *martingales* and *moonrakers*. But are those words any more curious than *megabyte* or *blastoff*? Whether one is discussing computers, spacecraft, or ships, there is a need to establish specific terminology in order to discuss or analyze the subject. Any complex object has components that are not found on other objects, so exclusive verbal designations must be applied to those components. Wooden ships had hundreds of parts, hence the need for technical language is clear, but even simple boats require a strict adherence to proper terminology. If one records a small hull made of only two dozen pieces, the field catalog can be completed successfully with designations such as pieces 1 through 24 or doodads A through X. But the task is not complete until this information is shared with others—until it is published; here is where the proper terminology is required. One compares *keels, frames*, and *scarfs*—not doodads—with others. In addition, it is important to sound professional about one's work. You wouldn't employ a mechanic who called a carburetor a thingamajig, or even a gas passer. It is every bit as unprofessional to call a wale a board as it is to describe an amphora as a clay jug. This language of ships is a fascinating language; furthermore, it's often controversial. That makes it more fun. Learn it.

One can use a good dictionary to find many of the terms that describe a hull's structure, but too often they are helpful only for the later periods of history and do not apply to ancient construction at all. Marine dictionaries are better; I have listed several good ones in the bibliography, along with comments regarding the limits of their coverage. There is a danger in using these technical dictionaries, though. They tend to relate to certain periods and areas; even those written in the past few decades are guilty of this. For instance, one must be cautious when applying eighteenth-century terms to medieval or ancient hulls.

Why can't we adopt one marine dictionary as a standard? Well, it's not that easy. The problem with shipbuilding terminology is that ships have been around for a long time over a large area of the globe. We are studying a subject that represents thousands of years, millions of ships and boats, and probably millions of shipwrights who spoke hundreds of languages. Unlike modern medicine or engineering, in which constant communication automatically adopts a terminology that serves the present, we are dealing with a nearly extinct craft that was influenced by a broad scale of technological development yet was controlled by formal communication during only a small percentage of that time.

Consequently, standardized shipbuilding vocabularies became commonplace only near the end of the industry's lifetime, and then only in a limited and ambiguous state. For instance, when the earliest shipbuilding practices were recorded, *foot-hook* was exactly that: a frame timber that had a hook, or relatively sharp radius, at its lower end. Ship designs changed, and so did the shape of that timber. Its spelling changed somewhat too, although *futtock* still referred to certain parts of a frame. Similarly, the sub-keel, or son of the keel, became *keelson* or *kelson*.

Area and preference had a lot to do with it, too. One boatbuilder may refer to the piece protecting the keel of his boat as a *false keel*, while another might call the same piece a *shoe*. United States naval contracts in the late eighteenth and early nineteenth centuries frequently refer to the shoe at the bottom of the keel, yet *Falconer's Marine Dictionary* of approximately the same period defines *shoe* only as a cover for an anchor fluke.

But what about the ships that came before those first formal publications? We see types and arrangements of timbers on their hull remains that were no longer used in the documented periods. How does one refer to a timber whose proper designation also has not survived? Usually, it is a matter of logic. Like *foot-hook,* there is a logical meaning for each hull part. If it doesn't exist, you may have to name it. Over the years, I have been confronted by at least a dozen hull parts that didn't survive long enough to get into marine dictionaries. Had I been an astronomer or botanist, my own name could have been applied to at least one of them (gussied up in Latin at that), but here logical terms were best applied—*ramming timber, limber ledge,* and so on.

By now you should be sufficiently confused to welcome the fact that an illustrated glossary of ship terms is included in the back of this book. Unlike the marine dictionaries, it lists many of the alternate terms and definitions one is likely to encounter in studying old and ancient vessels. It also goes a step farther than most dictionaries in that processes, such as fastening or scarfing, are identified as well.

This is by no means a complete dictionary; it is intended only to fill the demands of archaeological interpretation. One may still find it necessary to consult additional texts for specialized information on rigging, shiphandling, and other broad subjects.

Some of you will need the glossary to get through the shipbuilding chapters that follow. Terms will seldom be defined in the text. Remember that you need to be able to speak this language as well as read it. If you know what a treenail does but cannot pronounce it properly, you won't convince anyone of your mastery of the subject. It's pronounced *trunnel;* some even spell it that way now. Don't sound like an outsider—say *folks'l* for forecastle, *mains'l* for main sail, *bo'sun* for boatswain.

Before leaving terminology, there is one problem to be discussed that cannot be included in the glossary. Too many people still confuse the nut and bolt words of our field—*boat* and *ship.* A boat is a small, open vessel whereas a ship is a large sailing vessel with a bowsprit and three to five square-rigged masts. But it is more practical, and entirely proper, to classify boats as small vessels designed for operating in sheltered waters and ships as large vessels designed for deepwater navigation. Sometimes duty rather than size controls the designation. One should never call an ocean liner or aircraft carrier a boat; that's like calling the Sears Tower a house. Yet historians often refer to "Columbus's three ships," properly I think, even though all of them were shorter in length than the Staten Island ferry boats. Ships of settlers and explorers were sometimes less than twenty meters in length, but they were deepwater craft designed to take the worst in wind and weather, and they therefore deserve the designation *ship.*

Both terms should be avoided in technical work wherever possible, however. Just as you would avoid the word *aircraft* when you could more specifically refer to wide-bodied jets, fighters, or bombers, so too should you use more specific terms, such as schooner, galleon, or fishing smack. If in doubt, use general terms (vessel, merchantman, etc.). Many well-known projects used such terms because the status of the vessel was in doubt at the start of excavation—The Brown's Ferry vessel, Serçe Limani merchantman, and the Basque whaler, for example. Others could be specific—fifth-rate *Charon,* privateer-brig *Defence,* and gunboat *Philadelphia.*

Enough. We have set our course. Now let's get down to basics.

2

BASICS

First of all, it is necessary to understand what ships and boats of the past really were. Forget the definitions for a moment; we are referring here to their functional characteristics and the roles they played in their respective societies. The reason for their existence was *mobility;* something or someone had to be moved from here to there. This mobility factor is the most important single aspect affecting the study of ships. Indeed, it was the primary factor affecting all maritime-related enterprises. It separated ships from stationary structures, presenting designers and builders with certain advantages and restrictions. It expanded commercial ventures, enabled the harvest of offshore foods, established communications with otherwise isolated locations, populated uninhabited regions, and transported aggression to otherwise unreachable areas.

This study focuses on a specific form of mobility—*aquatic mobility.* The investigation of ships and boats is really the study of the means by which human beings overcame the problems of the aquatic medium and exploited it. And there were problems! Water is not our natural environment; humans are instinctively uncomfortable with it. It is unstable, presenting structural problems. When water is combined with winds and tides, structural problems increase dramatically. Worse yet, when vessels sank in this unfriendly element there was no haven for their occupants; they could not walk away from a disabled ship as

they could from a broken wagon, nor could they come back later and retrieve its payload. It is no wonder that shipbuilders were so cautious with new designs and that global travel evolved so slowly.

On the other hand, there were distinct advantages in the use of this element for transport. Its fluid state permitted it to spread evenly over the immersed part of the hull, supporting the entire surface with the same force. Density was constant, too, so that once an acceptable floating structure was built, it could be moved wherever there was enough water. To do that with terrestrial vehicles one had to construct roads, and no road could be made strong enough to hold the enormous weights that water was capable of supporting. Better still, the resistance of water was low enough to permit very large floating structures to be moved by a natural source of propulsion—wind.

The ways in which these problems were overcome and their advantages were exploited are tributes to the ingenuity of humankind. They tell us a lot about our ancestors, and it is those same people who add the spice to our ship studies and make the subject interesting. But we don't use terms such as *aquatic mobility* and *fluid support.* They are represented by the three physical principles that control the design of all watercraft—*buoyancy, gravity,* and *stability.*

Mechanics

Although Archimedes is credited with first defining the principle of buoyancy, the large cargoes and long voyages of ships before his time indicate that builders had been aware, at least instinctively, of the principle for centuries. Simply stated, a body partially or totally immersed in a fluid is acted upon by a buoyant force equal to the weight of the fluid displaced. Most woods float when not

waterlogged because they are not as dense as water, displacing an amount of water equal to their own weight. An ingot of iron is so dense that it will sink, however, unless its mass is distributed into the form of a thin-skinned vessel. Then its weight will be spread over a much larger surface area, and the equal force of water on that surface will support it.

The surface area permits hulls—wood or iron—to carry heavy cargo and remain afloat. The weight of a ship and all it carries, pushed downward by a force known as *gravity*, is supported at all submerged parts of its hull by an equal force, *buoyancy*. When a vessel is designed properly, the centers of these combined forces will be located as shown in Figure 2–1, where the center of buoyancy is positioned within the submerged portion of the hull, and the center of gravity is located directly above it at a height determined by the distribution of hull and cargo weight. But that is an ideal condition that exists only in still water. As soon as a wave or gust of wind causes the hull to list and thereby changes the area of distribution of water against its surface, the centers of buoyancy and gravity also change, and the hull becomes unstable.

Stability, the tendency of a listing hull to return to an upright position, is directly affected by the locations of the centers of buoyancy and gravity. Naval architects determine the transverse stability of a hull by measuring the distance between the *center of gravity*, G, and the *metacenter*, M, a point situated at the intersection of the centerline of the hull and a vertical line passing through the center of buoyancy, B. If G is below M, as in Figure 2–2, the vessel will return to a stable position, and the greater this distance the more rapidly it will right itself. If G is too far below M, the vessel might snap upright so rapidly that it causes damage to the rigging and cargo or discomfort to the crew. If G is above M, as in Figure 2–3, the vessel is unstable and in danger of capsizing. The distance between G and M along the hull's vertical centerline is known as *metacentric height* (GM). Modern freighters commonly have a small positive stability (GMs of only a few percent of the vessel's breadth); sailing ships

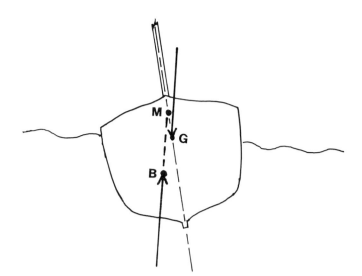

FIG. 2–2. The effects of buoyancy and gravity on a listing hull.

are less predictable due to variations in rig and hull form. A powerful gust of wind can have a devastating effect on a vessel that has not shortened sail sufficiently or is underballasted. Open gunports that are close to the waterline pose an additional problem.

That was a very simple, perhaps oversimplified, explanation of transverse stability. Those who are interested in learning more about the subject should refer to textbooks on naval architecture. In this study, the primary concern is that one does not argue that all the cargo was on the deck of an excavated vessel when such a situation would have placed G so far above M that it could not have sailed there in the first place. Stability and displacement should be considered in any ship reconstruction (related calculations can be found in Appendixes A

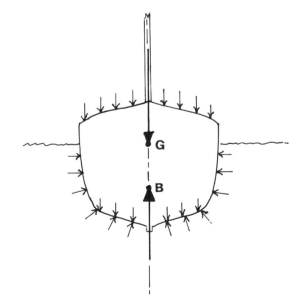

FIG. 2–1. The effects of buoyancy and gravity on a stable hull.

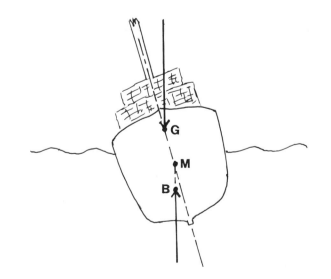

FIG. 2–3. Unstable hull conditions.

and B). These are physical principles that always controlled shipbuilding and, therefore, serve as an accurate check on one's work.

In addition to being buoyant and stable, a vessel had to be strong enough to withstand the worst weather it was likely to encounter. But it wasn't just the storms that tested hull strength; cargo could break loose and place excessive strains on certain hull areas, or the vessel could run aground and concentrate too much of its weight on one part of the keel. Even poor distribution of cargo might cause longitudinal problems—the hull could acquire a permanent hog or sag, which would affect operating efficiency. All

of this had to be taken into consideration when a ship was to be built. Frames were designed to withstand the effects of rolling, wales counteracted distortion, keelsons and stringers resisted longitudinal warpage. Hull strength is the most difficult feature to interpret in reconstructing ships and boats; fortunately, it also is one of the most interesting.

Stability and *strength* must be understood before attempting hull interpretations or reconstructions. One should be aware of them constantly, noting how the shipwright handled them, and questioning whatever seems to ignore them.

Design Fundamentals

Now let's look briefly at hull design. Any wooden ship or boat can be classified into one of four groups: *transport, naval, fishing,* or *utility.* Each of these categories places specific demands on hull design, although only the first two need be discussed here.

Transports—carriers of freight, people, animals, foodstuffs, and the like—were built in a great variety of shapes and sizes. The predominant non-physical factor affecting their design was nearly always economics. Figure 2–4a shows this vessel as the owner or agent saw it: a box or container that could carry whatever required transportation. Owners and agents were not necessarily concerned with stability, structural integrity, decorations, or rigging plans. They were in the business of getting their cargo or passengers from here to there as quickly, safely, and cheaply as was practical in order to make as much profit as possible. However, the aquatic medium they were going to use as a highway demanded compromise, and a rectangular box is a barge, which is good only in sheltered waters and on short, slow routes. The open sea would resist the flat sides of the box and make movement and steering difficult. Storms would twist it and pound away its sharp corners and edges. Just as you must pay for the engine space of your automobile, even though you never occupy it, so the shipowner had to pay for additions and alterations to the cargo box if quickly, safely, and cheaply were to become realities.

Figures 2–4b to 2–4d show the cargo box as it had to be compromised for deepwater transport. The box is still there, but curved ends had to be added so that it could be pushed through the water without much resistance and aimed in a desired direction. Its sides had to be rounded, too, in order to satisfy stability requirements and resist the violence of open water. The area within the heavy lines is the profit area; between them and the lighter lines is only overhead. Naturally merchants wanted the profit area as large as possible and the rest as small as possible. They did not need fancy decorations, unless such additions fostered recognition and improved their

business image. Nor did they provide much in the way of comfort or spaciousness for their crews; even captains suffered a spartan existence when compared to the trappings of people ashore who had similar power and responsibility. Yet seldom was hull strength compromised. Owners and builders realized the power of the sea and the need for construction to withstand it.

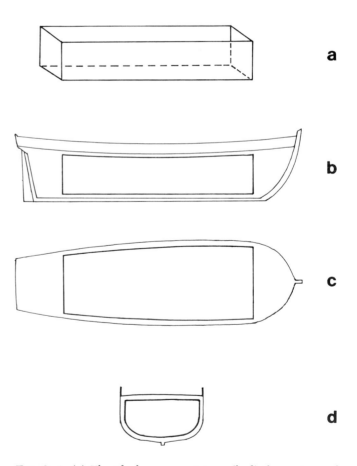

Fig. 2–4. (a) The ideal cargo container; (b-d) three views of cargo box as compromised for sea duty.

The cargo box is essentially that—a box that is mostly repetitious and often not very exciting. Keel, frames, keelson, and ceiling do not change appreciably. The material it housed is equally repetitious. The ends of the ship are different; the crews lived here, and the gear and valuables were stored here. The bows and sterns were the hearts and minds of ships. Personal artifacts, anchors, cable, tools, money, scales, and other items reflecting ownership and operation are normally found in these areas. And the construction is even more impressive. It changes constantly, timber after timber set in different sizes and directions to satisfy the demands of seaworthiness. The best shipwrightery was required here. This is where we can learn about the disciplines, the economics, the technology, and the philosophies of societies. And each society approached these problems in different ways.

If a box seems to be a simple method of illustrating the structural purpose of merchant ships, look what can be done for warships (Fig. 2–5a). A flat surface, a platform, was really the only functional part of a wooden warship; that platform may have had a ram affixed to its forward end or may have supported archers, catapults, or guns. The rest was similar to the merchant's overhead areas; it made the hull seaworthy, housed the troops and ammunition, or contained the propulsion unit in the form of oarsmen. The big difference between transports and warships is that the latter cannot be represented as a single type. Ship designs changed to accommodate new forms of aggression and defense. Figure 2–5 illustrates a few of these basic forms; the overhead areas are again shown with light lines. Ancient warships (Fig. 2–5b) had rams affixed to their bows and a few soldiers on deck. Most of the hull was support area housing the propulsion unit, the dozens or hundreds of rowers required to push the vessel along. The rowers could not be quartered, and the ship had to be kept light enough to be rowed at appreciable speed, so oared fighting ships could not be constructed as strong seagoing vessels in the manner of merchant ships. They were built primarily to facilitate the ramming function as our study of the Athlit ram showed.[1]

Eventually catapults, Greek fire, and guns were developed, and aggressors quickly learned how to mount and use them on their ships. Guns, especially, were more efficient because they could be nastier from a greater distance. During the medieval period, navies reached the advanced stage of placing many guns on the platform (Fig. 2–5c). Soon the platform was too heavy to row, so they turned to using the wind exclusively, as merchantmen had done to move their heavy loads for centuries. As destructive expertise improved, there were several platforms and lots of guns (Fig. 2–5d). You know the rest of the story. What you may not have realized is that these killing machines required design functions that, in some cases, were quite different from those of merchant vessels. Rams needed special backing so that the ramming blow would not destroy the attacking vessel. Guns played

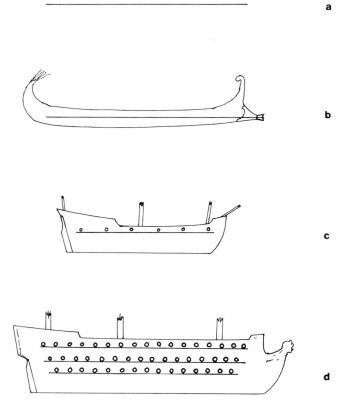

FIG. 2–5. (a) The functional portion of a warship; (b) with ram attached to bow; (c) as a gun platform; (d) as a multi-decked warship.

havoc with stability because they placed so much gravitational force above the waterline. They tended to hog the ends of a ship, too, and all this presented new problems for the shipwright, who dutifully and ably overcame them. We will examine the construction of naval and transport craft, as well as vessels of the other two groups, in the next few chapters.

HULL FORM

Each period of history produced distinctive hull designs in specific geographical areas. Some of these designs survived for centuries, even millennia where civilizations became stable. Individual features, especially the better ones, remained or were adopted in other areas, simply because they were so practical or could not be improved. From an overall point of view, however, each seagoing society produced distinctive design and construction features that changed as the society developed.

Among the major responsibilities of ship reconstructors is the identification of the important features and functions of hull designs. Eventually, scholars will be able to identify sparsely preserved hulls according to nationality and period by interpreting their construction features and hull curvatures, just as some artifact specialists are now recognizing almost precise dates of a ship's sinking. We have already come a long way in doing this, but the techniques must be improved. Many more shipwrecks will have to be excavated in order to establish accurate comparative studies.

Hull-form—the basic shape of a hull—is the primary expression of hull design. It was affected by the extent of technical knowledge, available materials, intended routes, cargoes, economics, environment, social structure, political influences, and a host of other prevalent factors. There is, therefore, a direct relationship between hull forms and historical periods, although it will be shown later that one cannot date shipwrecks exclusively on the basis of hull design.

It is important to be able to understand and describe hull forms, to notice how the various curvatures served the purposes of the type of vessel and the period and geographical area it occupied. Hull form is also directly associated with site distribution of cargo, artifacts, and timbers; it is the boundary description of your shipwreck.

The following four examples of basic hull form span a period of nearly four millennia. They have been selected because they represent widely different, yet very common, designs.

THE DASHUR BOATS[2]

At least four such hulls, similar in shape and size, survive; six were said to have been excavated from the Twelfth Dynasty tomb of Sesostris III at Dashur, Egypt. The shapes indicated here were taken from the hull in the Chicago Field Museum of Natural History; the boat is 9.8 m long, 2.37 m wide, and 0.72 m deep amidships. Although these were funerary craft, they were probably similar in form to Nile River commercial vessels of the period.

Figure 2–6a illustrates the body section at amidships, a cross-sectional shape of the hull at its widest part. It shows a keelless, gently rounded bottom, a soft turn of the bilge, and full sides that become almost flat near the gunwale. Simpler hull forms cannot be found.

The side view (Fig. 2–6b), known as the sheer view in ship drawings, shows an equally simple configuration. The bow and stern are nearly symmetrical, sweeping gently upward from a short flat amidships. The sheer line is also a gentle sweep with approximately the same height at each end.

The top, or breadth, view (Fig. 2–6c) is no more complex. The stern, which is to the right of the drawing, is only slightly fuller than the bow.

The Dashur hulls, known as papyriform hulls, are very primitive in design. Their shapes are about as exciting in form as half of a watermelon rind, which they closely resemble. Yet, as we will consider later, this hull form directly results from available materials and technology, social determinants, and the type of waterway for which they were intended.

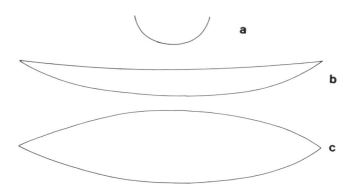

FIG. 2–6. The Dashur boat's hull form; (a) body shape; (b) sheer shape; (c) breadth shape.

THE KYRENIA SHIP[3]

Sixteen centuries after the Dashur boats were entombed, a more interesting craft sank off the northern coast of Cyprus. The Kyrenia ship dates to the late fourth century B.C. and is probably indicative of the small merchantmen that plied Greek trade routes during the reign of Alexander the Great. It had a length of about 14 m, a maximum beam of about 4.5 m, and was capable of carrying more than twenty tons of cargo.

While the simple design of the Dashur hulls seems intended only for quiet Nile waters, the Kyrenia hull's more complex shapes answered the demands of the sea conditions it endured. The body section amidships (Fig. 2–7a) shows a keel and a V-shaped bottom near the centerline of the hull that dampened rolling and resisted lateral drift. The bottom curvature adjacent to the keel is sharp and hollow, turning into a medium deadrise that curves gracefully into a softly rounded bilge. The rounding continues

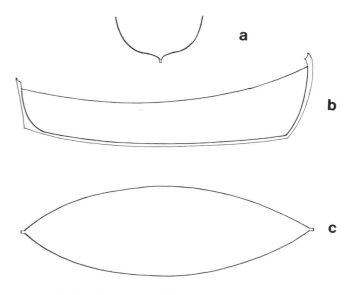

FIG. 2–7. The three views of the Kyrenia ship's hull form.

along the sides; if there is any flatness at all to the sides, it occurs very near the caprail.

Gracefulness was the hallmark of these early Greek designs, and this characteristic is still present in the caïque hulls of the eastern Mediterranean. This is evident in the sheer view (Fig. 2–7b), where even the keel has a sweeping curvature. We will see later that such graceful arcs were intended to provide extra strength rather than aesthetics, but nevertheless the Kyrenia ship was a thing of beauty. The keel is rockered, terminating aft at a curved, raking sternpost. Its junction with the stem is angled more sharply, and the upward sweep of the keel is extreme here, resulting in a comparatively short, forward-raking stem. The line of the sheer is rather steep in the ends of the hull, reaching its lowest point forward of amidships and ending in a stern that is much higher than the bow.

From a seagull's point of view, the Kyrenia ship was not shaped much differently than the Dashur boats. The breadth view (Fig. 2–7c) shows a double-ended, broad hull with maximum breadth occurring at or near the middle of the vessel. The bow was somewhat fuller than the stern, and so the entry into the sternpost rabbet was sharper than it was at the stem.

These are very simple line drawings; however, such shapes must be kept in mind constantly as research progresses, because they represent the fundamental statement concerning the vessel in question. I have not been describing line shapes at all, but rather the differences between Egyptian and Greek technology, between Nile and Mediterranean voyaging. Such simple shapes, distorted on the seabed, become the parameters of wrecks, the boundaries of cargo and artifact containers. Those distorted shapes must be rearranged into the original forms represented in these descriptions. Most important of all, one must learn to examine and describe simple hull forms in a way that prompts the investigation of every detail that such forms might include. It is not unlike the forms of motorcycles and automobiles. Both are wheeled vehicles that can be expressed by three simple line drawings. Those line drawings, however, immediately suggest different uses, capacities, and components. The difference between the Dashur boats and the next hull is as great as that between motorcycles and automobiles.

THE SERÇE LIMANI VESSEL[4]

Serçe Limani means "Sparrow Harbor", the name of the cove along the southern coast of Turkey where this wreck was found and excavated. Artifacts were dated to about A.D. 1025; more than thirteen centuries of shipbuilding experience separated it from the Kyrenia ship. The Serçe Limani vessel carried a mixed cargo that included several tons of glass. It was 15 m long on deck, had a beam of about 5 m, and a cargo-carrying capacity of more than thirty tons. Although its principal dimensions were practically

the same as those of the Kyrenia ship, its hold volume was at least 20 percent greater. The body section (Fig. 2–8a) tells why: the cargo box retained a nearly boxlike configuration. The bottom had very little deadrise, the turn of the bilge was extremely sharp, and the sides were flat with a medium outfall (outward slant). Compared with the wineglass shape of Kyrenia, this was a clumsy hull. Cargo capacity was only one of the reasons it was so built; rig, construction methods, and other factors also dominated this design. The important thing to remember about this body section is that aesthetics had very little to do with hull efficiency. While the Kyrenia section is more pleasing to the eye than that of Serçe Limani, this hull section represents important technological advancements over that of the Kyrenia ship.

The sheer view (Fig. 2–8b) presents a different appearance. Here the configuration was nearly as smooth and graceful as that of the Kyrenia ship. The keel was flat, curving rather sharply into a forward-raking stem and a curved sternpost. The sheer line, which is based on secondary evidence because the uppermost timbers of this hull did not survive, remains that of the caïque form, steep in the ends with a high stern.

Our seagull sees quite a different breadth view (Fig. 2–8c). The sides still entered the stem at rather sharp angles, but they reached nearly full-breadth dimensions within a few meters and maintained that fullness for the length of the hold area. Here, too, the boxlike nature of the hold was maintained. The most radical change was in the stern, where fullness provided a spacious area for storage, crew, or passengers. Here the sheer line entered the sternpost rabbet at a greater angle.

Thus we have seen two ships separated by about thirteen centuries, approximately the same size and operating

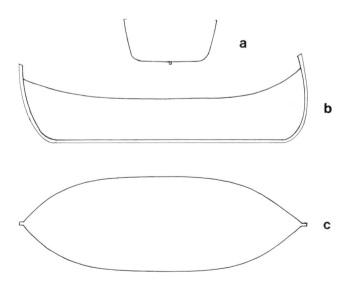

FIG. 2–8. The Serçe Limani vessel's hull form.

in the same waters, whose hulls would have looked very similar when afloat. Yet knowledge of these simple shapes tells quite a different story. These differences will be appreciated even more when we study their construction plans.

THE *CHARON* [5]

Another seven and a half centuries passed before the demise of a much larger and very beautiful ship—the fifth-rate, forty-four gun warship HMS *Charon*. This was the flag vessel of the support fleet for Lord Cornwallis at the close of the American Revolutionary War at Yorktown, Virginia, in 1781. During the battle at Yorktown, the *Charon* was set afire and sank in the York River off Gloucester Point. Although little survived for us to excavate, some of the original drawings were still on file in London. Compared with the three previous hulls, this one was a giant—140 ft (42.7 m) long on the gundeck, a beam of 38 ft (11.6 m), and a tonnage rating of 880. By the eighteenth century, naval architecture was a scientifically controlled discipline. The hull forms shown here are the result of mathematically proportioned projections.

Figure 2–9a shows a full, complex body shape. A slight hollow emanates from the heavy keel into a flat plane, then a reverse curve begins the turn of the bilge. A gentle, sweeping arc brings the body to full breadth near the waterline, where it remains flat and vertical for a few feet before it begins to tumble home in another pair of reverse curves. Tumblehome, that inward direction of the topsides, was the designer's way of combating the heavy and unstable deck loads of guns and ammunition. By reducing the beam above the waterline, the stability of the hull was greatly improved.

The *Charon's* body section illustrates a very full and spacious hull, softly rounded in order to accommodate severe sea conditions. It was a deep hull, yet that depth was countered with tumblehome that permitted it to maintain a high degree of stability. Thus the *Charon's* sectional design retained the best features of the earlier hulls, while advancements in naval architecture provided the technology to facilitate assignments that could not have been handled by those hull forms.

Seven and a half centuries of shipbuilding progress are evident in the sheer plan, too (Fig. 2–9b). The relatively flat sheer line takes on a functional appearance, with its smooth sweep now broken by raised fore and after decks. The sternpost is straight to accommodate the stern-mounted rudder, which is a device not found on the earlier examples. A transom overhangs this area, providing deck and cabin space beyond the line of floatation. The keel is straight and heavy, running into a gently curved, massive stem, which sports a head knee at its upper end.

The sheer view is one of great bulk—depth, fullness, and strength. Such hulls had to possess these

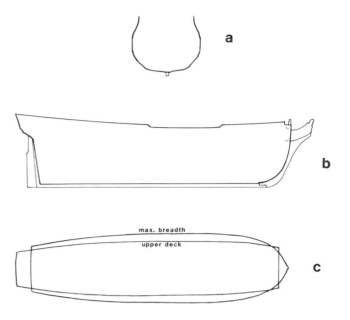

FIG. 2–9. The *Charon's* hull form.

characteristics; they were sent to sea for months at a time with large crews and great burdens. The full appearance applied to large seagoing merchantmen of the period as well as to warships.

Two breadth lines are shown in Figure 2–9c. One illustrates the shape of the upper deck as viewed from above, the other a maximum breath shape a few feet above the waterline. Now you can see the value of the transom stern and tumblehome. The maximum breadth line shows a broad hull with a roomy stern and a relatively full bow that curves gently into the stem (the bow was sharper at the waterline). But the upper gundeck line is a different story. Since it did not have to push water ahead of it, it was made square in the bow as well as in the stern to better accommodate guns and working room for the crew. It was narrower, too, so that the heavy loads were kept well within the line of floatation, greatly improving stability.

Even these simple line drawings indicate the great progress made by shipbuilders during the seven and one-half centuries separating the Serçe Limani vessel and the *Charon*. At first glance, it would appear that this progress was remarkable compared with nearly twice that length of time separating the earlier hulls. Hull forms do not tell the whole story, however. Our later analyses of these vessels will show that there were important advances made in all periods. It must also be noted that we are comparing a funerary boat, two Mediterranean hulls, and a large oceangoing vessel. Nevertheless, shipbuilding progress did accelerate in the later periods and, in part, this was due to ocean travel and the expanding burdens such routes placed upon ships.

Hull Lines

The following chapters contain many types of drawings that are used to illustrate the design and construction features of wooden ships and boats. All should be understood easily with one exception; the uninitiated may have trouble interpreting lines drawings. Lines drawings are graphic descriptions of the shapes of hulls. They are the means by which one can illustrate the design of a ship or boat. For the nautical archaeologist, they are one of several ways by which a jumbled pile of rotted timbers can be reconstructed to its original configuration. In final form, hull lines are one method of illustrating the results of research.

The hull lines we employ are relatively modern. Contemporary manuscripts indicate that comparatively simple line projections were used in the design of ships as early as the sixteenth century, and probably long before that. Most modern ship and boat plans are expressed in systems that date no earlier than the eighteenth or nineteenth centuries. Standards of layout and nomenclature differ somewhat among various draftsmen and nationalities. Tradition plays a role in ship drafting, too; some purists insist that a hull should always be shown on its starboard side, with its bow pointing to the right of the drawing, or that specific symbols be used for this or that.

Hull lines drawn by the nautical archaeologist cannot adhere precisely to the methods followed by naval architects. The architect designs; we interpret. Architects' lines show perfection—the hull as they hope it will be built. Ours show something less—the hull as it actually turned out, including asymmetry, distortion, repairs, and structural weaknesses.

Our projects often involve only partially preserved hulls, and so our lines drawings emphasize the areas that are most strongly supported by excavated evidence. Tradition must make way for accuracy; our plans should always show the side of the hull that has been preserved most extensively, because that is where the substantiating information lies. And lastly, our drawings must follow a standard adaptable to all periods of history. It is important that the same system of drafting be applied to a clipper ship designed by a master architect as to a Bronze Age boat that was literally carved to shape millennia before hull lines were projected geometrically.

Ships are three-dimensional structures; therefore, a minimum of three views is necessary to illustrate their shapes. Once again we will consider the four vessels used as examples for hull form. The Dashur boat's lines and the Kyrenia ship's lines are in chapter 3, those for the Serçe Limani vessel are found in chapter 4, while the *Charon's* lines are in chapter 5. Look at each of them briefly, then come right back to this page.

By now you realize that the shapes of ship's hulls are rather complex and, consequently, difficult to illustrate. Most watercraft consist of an infinite series of graceful curvatures; properly arranged, a lines drawing can become a work of art. But art is not our goal, and these lines are not nearly as complicated as they first appear.

BASICS

To begin with, lines drawings are made with the assumption that both sides of the hull are identical. They seldom are, but they are usually similar enough that the lines of one side are reasonable indicators of those on the other. Earlier, I stated that shipwrecks are normally drawn to illustrate the most extensively preserved side of the hull. For well-preserved wrecks, or for the interpretation of models, other factors may determine which side is to be represented by the drawings. In any case, all three views must represent the same side of the hull drawn to the same scale.

Hull lines usually define the molded shape of a hull, that is, its shape along the inner surfaces of the planking. This is because planking thicknesses vary in some hulls, there are thick wales at or above the waterline, and often there are various external attachments. It would be difficult, often impossible, to express external hull shapes in the form of free-flowing lines. Except for lapstrake-planked hulls, however, the inside surfaces of planking are necessarily smooth, regardless of their thicknesses. Thus hull lines normally describe the inner surface of the planking (or the outer faces of the frames to which they are attached); to find the extreme dimensions of a portion of the hull, the planking thickness must be added at that location.

The three views, or plans, used to describe hull designs are similar in concept to those just discussed. The side view is called the *sheer plan.* Sometimes it is referred to as the elevation plan or the profile plan. Both are acceptable, although sheer plan is more traditional and practical; the other two terms can become confusing in archaeological descriptions. The sheer plan presents the broadside view of the geometry of the hull. It can be as elementary or as sophisticated as the draftsman deems necessary to explain the design.

The top view is known as the *half-breadth plan* because only half of the hull is shown, as if it had been sawn right down through the centerline. On some drawings this view is called the waterline plan or level-line plan. This shows the hull contours as seen from above or beneath one-half of the hull.

The *body plan,* sometimes called the section plan, reveals the cross-sectional shapes of the hull as seen from afore or abaft.

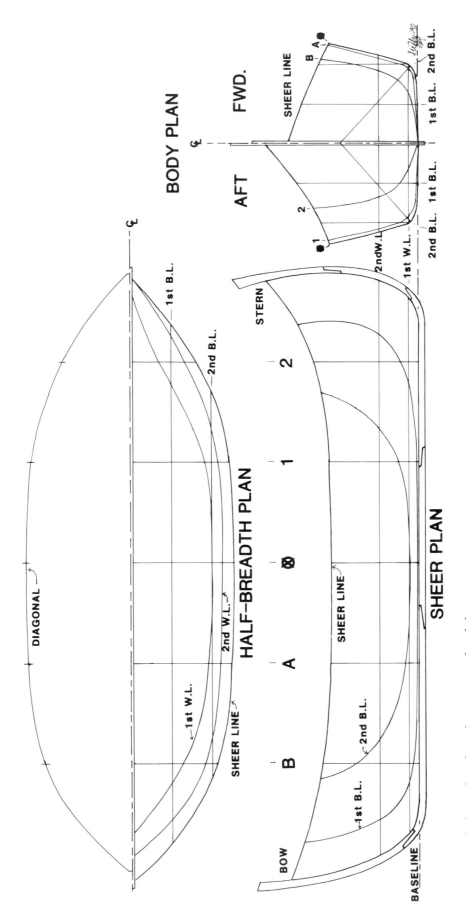

FIG. 2–10. The lines of an eleventh-century medieval ship.

THE LINES OF A MEDIEVAL HULL

The functions of these plans are illustrated first with the lines of a hull with features similar to those of the Serçe Limani vessel (Fig. 2–10). The port side is shown; the bow is to the left of the sheer plan and the stern to the right. The thickest lines on the sheer plan represent the outline, or extreme profile, of the hull (the same lines were used to illustrate hull form). If the hull were sawn downward along the longitudinal centerline and one half discarded, the resulting extreme profile would follow the thickest lines on the half-breadth plan when viewed from above or below. If the full hull were seen from either end of the ship, the extreme profile would look like the thickest line on the body plan. This is the same drawing as in Figure 2–8a. But this is the only line on the body plan that shows up as a full-hull shape. Like the other two plans, the body plan represents only the port half of the hull. The dashed vertical centerline indicates this limit. When the hull is viewed from the bow end, the various curvatures forward of its widest part are seen to the right of the centerline; when viewed from the stern, only the curvatures aft of the widest part can be seen, and they are to the left of the centerline.

Summarily, lines drawings represent only the half of a hull on one side or the other of its longitudinal centerline (the dashed line marked ₵), including half of the widths of the keel, stem, and sternpost. All three views represent the same side; all show the hull shapes to the inside of the planking; all are to the same scale. Let's add another rule; except for reasons of clarity or other special circumstances, all lines shown on one plan must be shown on the other two as well. But what about all those other curved lines on the drawing? Elementary, really. They reveal the hull shapes at selected horizontal, vertical, or transverse planes. Wherever such a curved line is shown on one plan, it can be represented by straight lines on the other two plans. The beauty of all this is that each plan serves as a check on the accuracy of the other two. You can refer to Table 2–1 as you study the medieval ship's (or any other vessel's) lines. The table simply shows which lines are straight and which are curved on the various drawings.

Station lines are also known as section lines, although the former term is more traditional and certainly more convenient for archaeological research. They are placed at selected intervals deemed necessary to best represent the changing body shapes throughout the length of the hull. The midship bend, the name for the widest part of the hull (although it does not always occur at the middle of the hull), is designated here by the symbol ⊗. Forward of this point, the various stations are designated consecutively with capital letters; aft of the midship bend, they are numbered consecutively. They are shown as vertical lines on the sheer plan, as transverse lines on the half-breadth plan, and as sectional shapes on the body plan. If the hull were cut transversely at these stations, the resulting maximum hull profile would take the curved shapes shown in Figure 2–11a. Another way to comprehend such shapes is illustrated in Figure 2–12, where eleven full-body stations of a Byzantine ship are spaced at their proper intervals along the keel and posts of a research model.

Waterlines (marked W.L.), sometimes referred to as level lines, are the horizontal lines on the sheer and body plans and the curved lines on the half-breadth plan. These are construction lines, and they should not be confused with the load waterlines to be discussed later. If the hull were cut horizontally at each of the numbered level lines on the sheer plan, the resulting segments would be shaped as shown by the curved lines on the half-breadth plan and illustrated in Figure 2–11b.

Buttock lines (marked B.L.) are the longitudinal lines on the half-breadth plan, the vertical lines on the body plan, and the curved lines on the sheer plan. They reveal the longitudinal shapes of the hull at these intervals as seen on the sheer plan and in Figure 2–11c.

That's all there is to expressing hull curvatures in lines drawings. Essentially, if one wants to learn the contour of a hull at a certain location, that location is identified on two of the plans in the form of straight lines and the resulting contour is projected on the third plan. Sheer plans show longitudinal vertical shapes, half-breadth plans show horizontal (breadth) curvatures, and body plans indicate transverse vertical profiles. The intervals at which these construction lines are spaced varies with the purpose of the drawings. For convenience in calculating displacement, as described in Appendix A,

TABLE 2–1. Hull line relationships

Plan	Station Lines	Waterlines	Buttock Lines
Sheer	straight	straight	curved
Half-breadth	straight	curved	straight
Body	curved	straight	straight

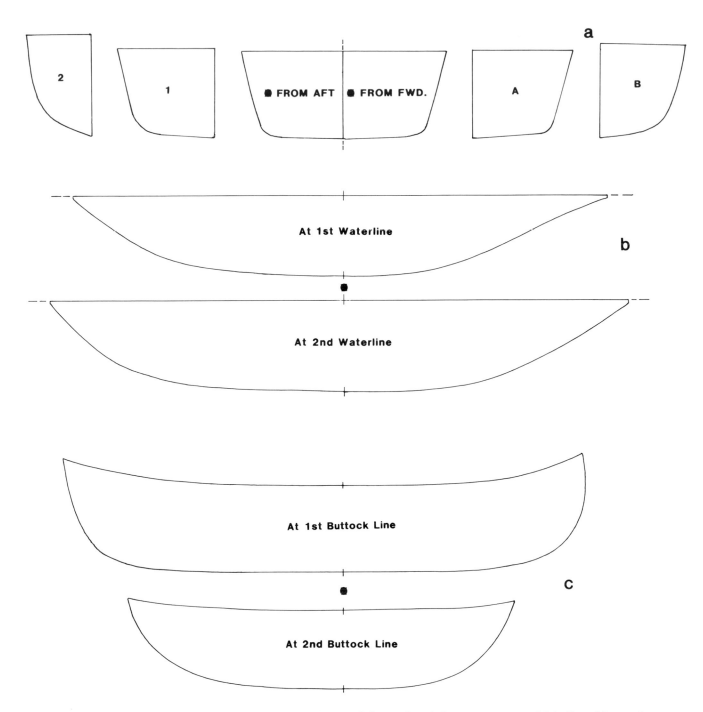

FIG. 2–11. The segregated vertical and horizontal hull shapes of the medieval ship in Fig. 2–10: (a) hull profiles at the separate stations; (b) hull profiles at the separate waterlines; (c) hull profiles at the separate buttock lines.

it is advantageous to space the station lines at regular intervals. Naval architects usually space their lines to provide the best overall descriptions of the shapes of their hulls. But an archaeologist who has only the bottom of a shipwreck preserved may space lower waterlines closely together, while those at upper elevations might be spaced widely or eliminated completely. Reasons for

intermediate or irregular hull line spacing will be considered in chapter 9.

Lines drawings are also used in reconstructing shipwrecks. Here the process is altered in many ways; the lines in such cases are actually used to locate missing timbers or correct distorted areas. But that is a different story. For the moment it is necessary only to understand

FIG. 2–12. Segregated stations of a research model of a Byzantine ship, shown here in the form of thin pressboard.

the relatively simple lines drawings used to describe ships and boats in the next few chapters.

DIAGONALS

You may have observed one set of lines in Figure 2–10 that has not yet been discussed. *Diagonal lines* cross the body plan as straight lines and are shown in curved form in what appears to be a separate half-breadth plan at the top of the drawing. While they are not absolutely essential (and sometimes do not appear in contemporary drafts), *diagonals* are marvelous projections that are used in creating and checking ship drawings. Recently we found a different use for them in archaeology, so that they have become equally important reconstruction aids. There will be more about the mechanics of diagonals later; for the present it is necessary only to know what they are and what they mean. Figure 2–10 shows only one pair of diagonals on the body plan; they are identical lines that start at the same place on the centerline and run across the body lines at precisely the same angle to the baseline. This is important because these two diagonals actually represent a single line. Imagine that you sawed this hull at the angle of the diagonal, starting at the bow and coming out the stern at the same angle. The cut would appear as a pair of angled lines similar to the diagonals shown, one cut being viewed from the

bow and one from the stern. Viewed from the side or above, such a cut would appear as meaningless longitudinal curved lines; therefore, diagonals are never placed in the same context with waterlines or buttock lines. Instead, they are projected either from a common centerline on the half-breadth plan, as in Figure 2–10, or from a separate longitudinal centerline, as in the drawing we will examine next. The intersecting points are determined in the same manner as the other curved lines. The distances between the intersection of the diagonal with the vertical centerline and the point at which the diagonal intersects each body station, as well as the diagonal distances between the centerline and the sides of the posts, are marked on the diagonal plan for the respective stations. Then the points are connected with a drafting spline or computer plotter stylus.

Ship drawings usually employ from one to four diagonals, depending on the size and configuration of the hull. Their angular displacement is selected according to the purpose they must fulfill. For the person creating the drawings, several well-distributed lines serve as accuracy checks; errors made in the projections of any of the three sets of construction lines will usually show up as an unfair (wavy) diagonal. In most cases, they should intersect the station lines on the body plan as near to perpendicular as possible. They can also be used to illustrate various design features, such as fullness of holds, or to confirm that the hull can be planked properly. In archaeology they are employed in a variety of ways, but they most frequently illustrate hold or structural parameters. Diagonals will be used to illustrate hull and reconstruction features infrequently throughout this book.

PRACTICAL LINES DRAWINGS

Figure 2–10 was simplified to illustrate the basics of lines drawings. One does not usually designate buttock and water lines, although stations are frequently numbered or lettered. Title block, scale, and other necessary items were also omitted for clarity. Contemporary draftsmen sometimes showed rudders, gunports, head knees and figureheads, mast and bowsprit locations, and other topside details on their lines drawings. Such amenities were often limited to the sheer plan, the spar locations sometimes being indicated on the half-breadth plan as well. An excellent example of lines drawings developed from a combination of archaeological and archival research are those of the *Eagle* (Fig. 5–61), which Kevin Crisman has represented in contemporary fashion. We will examine the *Eagle*'s lines in chapter 5.

Normally it is faster and more convenient to develop a lines drawing by placing the body plan on a common baseline with the sheer plan. For vessels as long and narrow as the *Eagle*, however, that would result in a long, narrow draft, creating a publication problem unless foldouts were possible. Here Crisman has placed the body plan above the after part of the sheer plan and spaced the title and dimension blocks along the rest of the open space, resulting in a rectangular format that permits a much larger publication scale for a given page size. A similar expeditious use of space involves lapping the two diagonals over the half-breadth plan, their centerline being aligned with the outermost buttock line.

Transom and counter are necessarily shown on all three views, but the sheer plan additionally reveals gunport locations, rail and caprail, a cathead for handling the anchor, hawse holes, the rudder, and spar locations. The deck location is indicated with long-dashed lines on two of the views, but it has been omitted on the half-breadth plan for purposes of clarity. The estimated load waterline is indicated at each end of the hull on the sheer plan. It is higher at the stern end than at the bow, which is a common feature of small vessels of the period. Such a ship was said to "sit by the stern," meaning that the stern drew more water than the bow.

Short-dashed lines reveal the principal dimensions of the hull, which are also listed numerically in the space above the bow. On the body plan, they drop to a baseline to indicate molded beam, which is the width of the hull between the inner surfaces of the side planking at the hull's maximum breadth. Hull length between perpendiculars, the distance between the points where the deck intersects with the planking rabbets on the posts, is indicated directly on a scale that runs the full length of the hull. Such scales were commonly used on nineteenth-century drawings and are convenient in measuring

distances between various features of the vessel. The boxes on the ends of the scale permit one to determine dimensions to the inch by measuring between the angular line and one of the vertical sides. Thus the after perpendicular coincides with the point at which the angular line crosses the third (or 3-inch) line, resulting in a length between perpendiculars of 117 ft, 3 in.

Crisman has made his body plan attractive and easy to interpret without sacrificing information by including only those stations vital to his published interpretation. The use of frequently spaced water and buttock lines, on the other hand, is important to his description of the various longitudinal shapes in defining the differences between oceangoing warships and these men-of-war designed for use in shallower fresh water. Buttock and water lines are not numbered, and stations are identified by frame number or letter (for comparisons with his text) only below the sheer plan. That is all that is necessary, since each line can quickly be identified by comparing the locations of its extremities on each of the plans. Note the way in which the tumblehome of the upper sides affects the outer buttock lines on the sheer plan, making them curve back in the opposite direction as they approach the sheer line. This feature becomes quite interesting on vessels with extreme tumblehome.

Methods of drafting, additional projection lines, the use of scales and symbols, and other important aspects of ship drafting will be dealt with in chapter 9 or as they are presented throughout the remainder of the book. But first, let us briefly examine the history of shipbuilding technology.

PART II

A Brief History of Shipbuilding Technology

3

THE ANCIENT WORLD

Ships and boats were conveyances. Regardless of our elaborate eulogies for them, they were nothing more than structures for conveying someone or something from one place to another. They might have been the only means of reaching a faraway land or the most practical vehicle for transporting weapons and warriors to wherever the enemy was located. Perhaps they were simply faster, safer, or cheaper than alternate land transport along rivers and coastal regions, but ships and boats were always the means to an end, and usually that end was profit, convenience, security, or victory.

It is important that we understand this practical explanation for the existence of watercraft. Far too often they are placed on historical pedestals that tend to segregate them from fact, which clouds accurate interpretations of their true value to society. Ships and boats were merely objects used to accomplish specific ventures—nothing more, nothing less. What really segregated most of them from other forms of transport was the complexity their structures required in order to meet the demands of their assignments.

In the next few chapters we will examine a number of ship and boat types and the various methods by which they were constructed. This will be a rather brief study, largely based on archaeological examples and condensed from much more elaborate work. Space does not permit the inclusion of all excavated wrecks, but those selected provide a comprehensive sampling of the broad spectrum of activity in the shipyards of the world.

The Bronze Age

Ideally, our investigation of shipbuilding technology and its profound impact on civilization should start at the beginning, but we know nothing of the beginning. The forms of watercraft that evolved between the introduction of the first primitive boats or rafts and the oldest surviving vessels are speculative. There are clues; models, paintings, carvings, a few pieces of wood suspected to be boat remains, and the boatbuilding habits of primitive peoples in our own age all provide some understanding of earlier hull forms. But such knowledge is peripheral at best, and technological details are virtually nonexistent. Several millennia of information still elude us and extend an open invitation to excavators and researchers. Certainly there must have been some interesting examples of watercraft in these periods, because boatwrightery was already a sophisticated procedure in Old Kingdom Egypt. Presently, the oldest surviving vessel to be documented is the Fourth-Dynasty Royal Ship of Cheops, dated to about 2650 B.C.

THE ROYAL SHIP OF CHEOPS

The vessel known as the Royal Ship of Cheops was discovered in 1952 in a limestone pit beside the Great Pyramid at Giza. Nearly thirty years of excavation, conservation, and reconstruction followed, and the reassembled craft now can be seen in its own museum near the Great Pyramid. Most of the technical information below results from the excellent study made by Paul Lipke.[1]

This is a large hull: 43.63 m long overall, a maximum beam of 5.66 m, and a depth (sheer line above bottom planking) amidships of 1.78 m. A deckhouse 9 m long stood aft of amidships, and the entire hull was closed with removable panels of decking. Hull weight has been estimated at 38.5 tons. Most of the vessel was made from

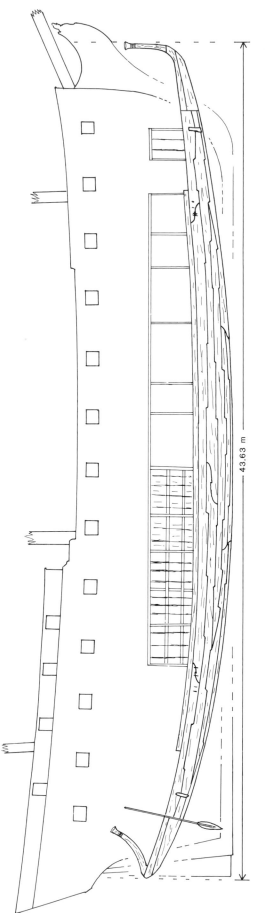

43.63 m

Fɪɢ. 3–1. The length of the Royal Ship of Cheops can be appreciated when its hull is superimposed over the outline of the 32-gun Continental Navy frigate *Raleigh*, built in 1776. (The drawing of the Cheops hull was made from various sketches and dimensions in Paul Lipke, *The Royal Ship of Cheops*; the *Raleigh* outline is after Plan 3 in H. I. Chapelle, *The History of the American Sailing Navy*.)

Lebanese cedar, although there are 467 tenons of sidder as well as small quantities of hornbeam, juniper, sycamore, acacia, and other North African and tropical woods. The wood was remarkably well preserved.

Profile and sectional views of the Cheops hull are shown in Figures 3–1 and 3–2. Figure 3–3 illustrates the planking shapes, Figure 3–4 the run of the bilge strakes, and Figure 3–5 the arrangement of beams. Lipke suggests the following sequence of construction.

1. The bottom was assembled first. This consisted of eight cedar planks, averaging 13 m in length and 13 cm in thickness, arranged so that there were two in the forward section and three each in the middle and after sections of the hull (Fig. 3–3). At each end of this assemblage were two short pieces that Lipke calls backing pieces; these are part of a cluster of short timbers used to secure the sides and bottom together and to support the papyriform stem and sternposts. The planks were aligned with free-standing tenons that were inserted into mortises in the plank edges (several examples can be seen in the plank edges in Figures 3–2 and 3–5) and lashed together at key locations. The ends of the assembly were then raised to the desired longitudinal curvature and supported by shores.

2. The sides were installed next. There were eleven cedar planks on each side varying in length from 7 to 23 m and in thickness from 12 to 15 cm. The lowest strakes were erected first, with their lower edges riding atop the bottom planks for most of the hull's length. Where the angles of these side planks became flatter near amidships, their edges were rabbeted to the bottom planks, finally butting edge-to-edge against them at the widest part of the hull (Fig. 3–4). Each side plank was then installed in logical succession; the two sides were probably worked simultaneously to maintain mechanical balance. Scarfs, joggled edges, and edge angles had to be shaped carefully, as there does not appear to be accommodations for caulking in any of the seams. The watertight integrity of the hull was probably maintained by careful

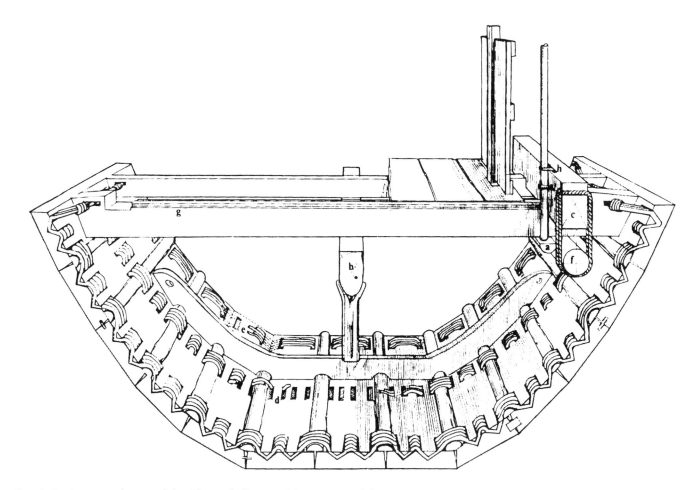

FIG. 3–2. A sectional view of the Cheops hull at amidships. Some of the more important features include the central girder (b), the side girders (c), V-shaped holes for lashings (d and e), and a deck beam (g). (courtesy Paul Lipke, *The Royal Ship of Cheops*, fig. 48; drawing by Peter Schmid)

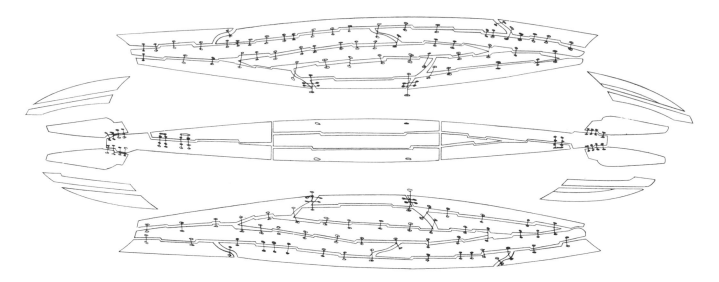

FIG. 3–3. A planking diagram showing the locations of the 277 strategic lashing holes of the Cheops vessel. The bow is to the left of the drawing. (courtesy Paul Lipke, *The Royal Ship of Cheops,* fig. 42; from a drawing by A. Y. Moustafa)

joinery and by the battens pressing against the insides of the seams. As in the bottom, the side planks were kept in alignment with small tenons and held together with lashings. None of the tenons were locked in their mortises with transverse pegs as they were in vessels of the classical period. Such methods will be discussed later in the chapter.

3. A few strategically placed deck beams were installed after the sheer planks were in place in

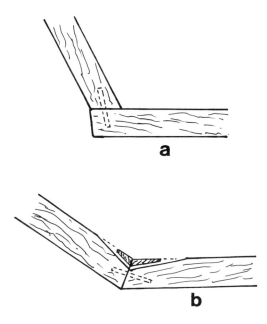

FIG. 3–4. The changing shapes of the lower edge of the first side strake. Throughout most of the hull's length, the side plank rides atop the bottom plank as in (a). Near amidships, however, the edges make a gradual transition to that shown in (b) at amidships. Not to scale. (after Lipke, fig. 65; original drawings by Peter Schmid)

order to stiffen and support the hull. The forward beams were 10 cm square, those in the central part of the hull were as much as 12 cm square, and the beams in the after part of the hull averaged 11 cm square. They fit into notches in the sheer strakes (Fig. 3–2).

4. Hundreds of battens were cut and fitted to the planking seams. The cedar frames, sixteen of them in all, were cut to match the hull shapes at their various locations; each frame had to be notched to seat over each of the batten locations. Planks, the several extant deck beams, frames, and battens were lashed into place, the lashings running continuously from sheer to sheer.

5. The so-called spine, perhaps better described as a central girder, was notched to receive the standing deck beams and installed beneath them with the support of sixteen stanchions.

6. The remaining deck beams (there were 66 in all) were fitted into notches in the sheer strakes and the central girder, the side girders added, and all final hull lashings completed (Fig. 3–5).

7. Decks and superstructure were added last; this appears to have been a relatively elementary procedure.

I have left out many details of this progression as a matter of simplicity; the reference cited should be consulted for more specific information.

Lipke's suggested sequence of assembly seems logical and accurate. Of course, there are the usual arguments that the frames or temporary molds had to be installed first and the rest of the hull built around them. Considering the relative weakness of the frames and the thickness and shapes of the planking, however, such procedures

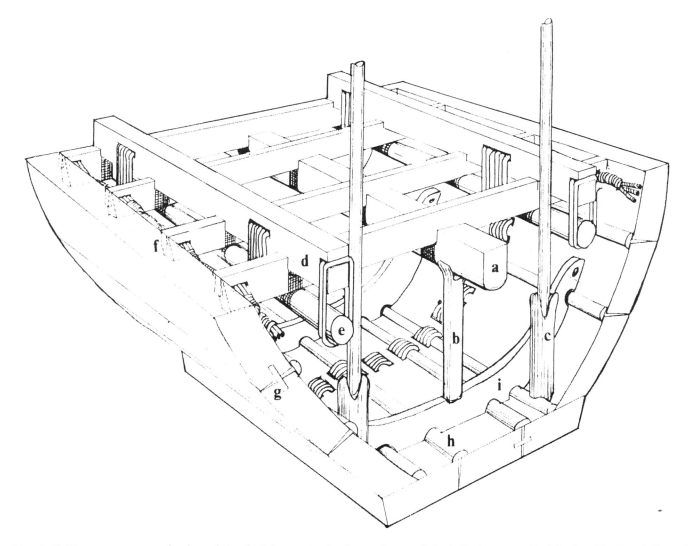

FIG. 3–5 The arrangement of a few of the deck beams in the forward part of the hull. (courtesy Paul Lipke, *The Royal Ship of Cheops,* fig. 11)

seem unlikely, if not impossible. Certainly the most convenient and accurate sequence would have been bottom, sides, initial beams, frames, girders, more beams, and superstructure.

I believe that these builders had the expertise, acquired through many generations of boatbuilding experience, to shape each successive plank and plank edge to exactly the proper configuration in order to arrive at the desired hull form and dimensions. The method will be discussed in more detail in the analysis of the Kyrenia ship below.

Now let us take stock of what the Cheops vessel reveals. First of all, it is large. At more than 43 m in length, it is longer than some eighteenth-century frigates, although its breadth and depth dimensions are very small in comparison. And it is heavy; nearly thirty-eight tons of cedar alone went into the hull, which says a lot. Considerable amounts of waste had to be cut away to shape planks such as these, so that perhaps fifty or more tons of cedar

logs had to be imported from Lebanon to build this one vessel. Cedar is light, strong, easy to work, and resistant to biological attack. No comparable wood could be found in Egypt, and it was impossible to do a good job of so large a hull with what was available locally, and so cedar had to be obtained. The Palermo stone hints at the magnitude of such imports, mentioning one instance of forty shiploads of cedar arriving from Lebanon and another of a ship somewhat larger than the Cheops vessel being built for the king.[2]

The hull was not built entirely of cedar, however. There were tenons of sidder, a very hard wood. The function of mortise-and-tenon joints will be discussed at length in the study of the Kyrenia ship. Here it will suffice to say that these boatwrights already knew the value of using tenons that were harder than the wood surrounding them. They also knew how to configure these woods for maximum strength and minimum leakage. Lipke quotes Ahmed Youssaf Moustafa, the man who masterminded the restoration and reassembly of the timber: "Though other dynasties and periods have their high points, none of these compete with the Fourth Dynasty for beauty and for knowing when to stop."[3] Knowing when to stop. What a marvelous statement! That is precisely the hallmark of good shipwrightery, and the Cheops vessel illustrates this vividly. Many of the structural components that would stiffen and support later hulls had obviously not been invented or developed in this period. Instead, boatwrights of this period used planking strength and wood joinery to accomplish these results. For instance, keel, keelson, stringers, wales, clamps, knees, solid decking, and all the other components that would eventually provide longitudinal ship strength were missing here. Instead, tenons, lashings, girders, and the strength of the planking itself were used to provide longitudinal support. But it was the shape of the planking, and especially the locking effect provided by the joggled plank edges, that prevented longitudinal shift and supplied much of the strength required to keep the ends of the hull from sagging. Those knuckled edges are masterpieces of wood joinery. They could have been cut much deeper, but then the problem of excessive pressures along the edges might have resulted in splitting and weakening large areas of planking. Angled and shallow as they were, they still provided sufficient locking strength while insuring the integrity of the planking. It was a good example of knowing when to stop.

In hull form, the Royal Ship of Cheops is similar to the description we have given for the Dashur hulls in chapter 2. Now let's briefly analyze the form of construction. Some authors refer to such bottom planking as a spine, but it does not perform a spinal function. This vessel has no backbone at all. If the sides were released, the bottom planks could not even support themselves. There is no effective stem or sternpost, either; those eight small end pieces in Figure 3–3 were used to join the ends of the hull. The extant stem and sternposts were decorative and non-functional from a structural standpoint.

Longitudinal bottom support came from the planking—the way it was rockered and locked together. Upper longitudinal support was provided by interlocked planking and the three girders. Lateral strength came from the frames, the deck beams, and the shape of the planking and the resulting edge angles.

The planking was the primary structure, supplying the major portion of the hull strength. It was far more than a watertight skin; it was made extra thick for strength, although not too thick because again the builders knew when to stop. Planking was aligned by mortise-and-tenon joints and held together by the lashings. The only metal fastenings used on the hull were copper staples, which had topside assignments except where they were used as lashing stops.

Is the Cheops vessel representative of Fourth Dynasty maritime technology? Yes and no. It seems analogous to the custom-built limousines used to transport present-day heads of state. Those limousines are not indicative of the motor transport of the masses; they are far too expensive, powerful, and luxurious for comparison with the family automobile, and they are too impractical and labor-intensive for commercial use. And yet there are basic features in those limousines that certainly are common to all automobile manufacture. So it must have been with the Cheops vessel. This was a very plush aquatic limousine, whether for use in life or death, but there are indicators within its structure that reveal what must have been standard maritime technology in ancient Egypt.

It would be more informative if we could examine one of the vessels that transported the Cheops hull's cedar from Lebanon. I suspect they were much beamier and more stable, perhaps deeper amidships, and with greater longitudinal strength. Those girders, while sufficiently strong for a yacht-like river craft, seem inadequate for preventing heavily ladened vessels from hogging in the open sea. Other than the planking, no structural components connected the ends of the hull. The famous Eighteenth-Dynasty depictions of Queen Hatshepsut's Punt ships clearly show hogging trusses providing this necessary longitudinal support (Fig. 3–6). A Fifth-Dynasty tomb at Saqqara reveals what might be interpreted as a similar but more primitive form of hogging truss.[4] Whether such was the artist's intention is speculative, but certainly there remains the probability that seagoing vessels of the Fourth Dynasty already employed this form of longitudinal support.

The Royal Ship of Cheops was not a ship at all; it was a very luxurious barge. It seems an unlikely hull for sailing, even on the Nile, and probably was towed by other vessels. All sorts of theories have been presented concerning its operation and utilization; for more information, and a more general understanding of other watercraft of the period, refer to this book's bibliography. This study is more directly concerned with the role the vessel played in the overall picture of shipbuilding technology.

This was a labor-intensive hull. The hundreds of mortises, the complex planking shapes, and the elaborate methods of lashing as a primary fastening system all attest to that fact. And yet it is done so well that such work must have been standard practice in many of the Egyptian hulls at the time.

The Cheops vessel also lacks structural integrity, largely due to the fastening system. Most later hull fastenings both aligned and attached, the latter in a rigid state. Not so with this lashing system, which required help from the unpegged tenons for planking alignment and could not have provided as rigid an attachment as nails or treenails. Such a lashing system, if subjected to constant service, would have required frequent replacement or resetting, making this an even more expensive, labor-intensive form of construction.

Simply stated, the Royal Ship of Cheops reveals that in the third millennium B.C., at least one society could

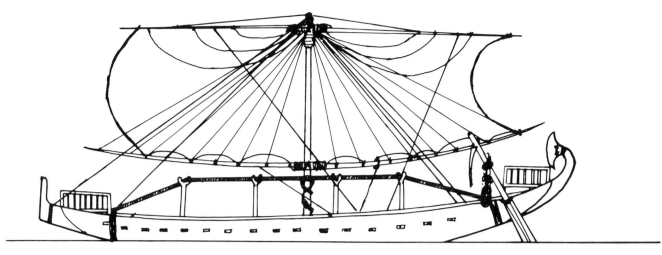

FIG. 3–6. One of Hatshepsut's Eighteenth-Dynasty seagoing ships; note the hogging truss running from bow to stern over crutches. (sketched from part of a relief at Deir-el-Bahari)

build large hulls with good craftsmanship, expeditious use of limited materials, and a thorough understanding of the physical strengths and weaknesses of their construction.

THE BOATWRIGHTS AT SAQQARA

A century or two later, artists provided information about Egyptian boatbuilders at work. Although the hulls are probably out of proportion to the workmen, the paintings on the Fifth-Dynasty tomb of the courtier Ti are detailed and extensive.[5] Only a few significant illustrations are shown here.[6]

In Figure 3–7 (upper panel), two men are hewing a log with axes, while a third seems to be trimming the same timber with an adze. The size of the timber suggests that this may not have been local wood, but one of those large logs imported from Lebanon. In Figure 3–7 (lower panel), mortises are being cut into the edges of a plank or timber by men using club mallets and mortising chisels. Perhaps these mortises are intended to house tenons, but more probably they represent channels for lashings, since the mortises being cut are aligned with those on the side of the timber. Notice that this member is staged on a pair of tree crotches set into the ground for this purpose. Just to the left, a sawyer cuts a small timber into shape, perhaps as a deck beam. It has been set into the earth (or tied to another log set into the earth) and is being sawn downward, not at all curious when one realizes that Egyptian saw teeth were rather random and saws had to be worried or operated as pull saws at best. The device at the top of the log is probably a tensioning arrangement used to keep the cut from opening and thereby helping to prevent the saw from binding or going astray.

Perhaps the Cheops vessel was built in an environment such as is illustrated in Figure 3–8 (upper panel). The bottom of this boat is shored up to its proper curvature, with the center of the hull blocked only slightly above the

ground. Such a vessel would not have been launched, but carried or dragged to the water. A boatwright or official—perhaps Ti himself—stands in the center, directing the construction. The bottom, sides, and ends are being given a final trimming with small adzes, while a long plank is being installed over several protruding tenons. Club mallets and wooden or stone pounders are being used to drive the plank home. A fourth man holds one end of it up with a rope, perhaps to align it with the tenons and keep it level, while a fifth stands outside the hull with a pry bar or stick to control the seating of the timber and prevent its mortises from binding on the tenons. Anyone who has set edge-joined planking will appreciate this scene.

To the left of the hull in Figure 3–8 (lower panel), an overseer or master shipwright stands with a plumb bob and line and measuring staff in his hands. The equipment he is holding illustrates the importance of hull elevations and symmetry to these ancient craftsmen. The vessel in the lower panel of Figure 3–8, which differs in design from that in the upper panel, appears to be in an advanced stage of construction. Notice that the uppermost plank has scarfed ends that resemble some of the scarfs on the Cheops vessel. Men with adzes trim the bottom ends of the hull, while three carpenters are completing the setting of a central strake of planking that has been scarfed to short end planks. Two men are using pounders to drive the strake home, while the third checks or levers the resulting seam with a chisel. Two other carpenters are cutting mortises near the ends of the hull, and the remaining workman is shaping a small timber with an adze.

While the figures, tools, and hulls in Figures 3–7 and 3–8 are out of proportion and often distorted, they do illustrate the relative complexity of Egyptian boatbuilding and the variety of tools used in the process. I disagree with the frequent statements that the boatbuilders on the walls of Ti's tomb are constructing vessels similar to the Cheops barge. The hulls do appear to have a similar

Fɪɢ. 3–7. Boatbuilding scenes from the Fifth-Dynasty mastaba of Ti. (courtesy Institut Française d'Archéologie Orientale au Caire; from Wild, plate CXXIX)

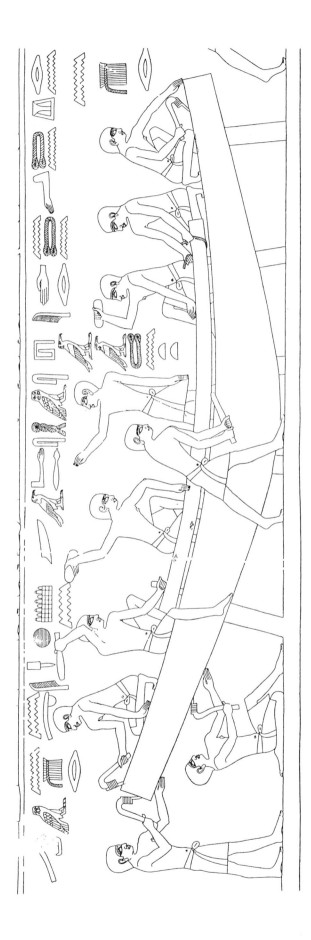

Fig. 3–8. More boatbuilding scenes from the Fifth-Dynasty mastaba of Ti. (courtesy Institut Française d'Archéologie Orientale au Caire; from Wild, plates CCXXIX and CXXVIII)

FIG. 3–9. The reassembled Dashur boat in the Carnegie Museum of Natural History, Pittsburgh. (photo A.N. 1842-1 by Melinda O. McNaugher; courtesy The Carnegie Museum of Natural History)

bottom curvature, but that and a few familiar hull members are the only similarities. These seem more likely to be practical vessels, perhaps commercial boats for the Nile trade. In fact, they appear to be more like the hulls we are about to examine than the previous one.

THE DASHUR BOATS

In 1894 Jean-Jacques de Morgan discovered six boats buried near the Twelfth-Dynasty brick pyramid of Sesostris III at Dashur. Found in two groups of three each and dating to about 1850 B.C., de Morgan's reports leave some confusion concerning the sequence and number of boats excavated.[7] However, it is almost certain that four boats from these excavations are now in museums. Two are in Cairo's Egyptian Museum, one is in the Chicago Field Museum of Natural History, and another is in the Carnegie Museum of Natural History in Pittsburgh. All four are very similar in construction and shape, although the largest (Cairo 4925, 10.2 m long) is nearly a meter longer than the shortest (Pittsburgh).

Scholars have failed to recognize the importance of these boats, sometimes comparing them with the Cheops vessel or declaring them wretched or ill conceived. They are neither; from a practical standpoint they are better conceived than the Cheops vessel. Since their excavation, the first thorough examination of these hulls was made by Cheryl Ward Haldane in 1984.[8] Her analysis revealed many new features, as well as previous misinterpretations. In 1988 and 1989, she conducted a thorough study of the Pittsburgh boat (Fig. 3–9) while it was disassembled and after it was reassembled.[9] The results of that study will be revealed in a forthcoming publication. The following details have largely been extracted from her original report; the conclusions are my own responsibility.

Since all four hulls appear to be very similar in form and construction, only the details of the Chicago hull will be examined. Hull lines are illustrated in Figure 3–10, and the planking arrangement is shown in Figure 3–11. The sheer view shows a papyriform hull shape with a longer bottom flat and less sweep in the sheer line than that of the Cheops vessel. It is also more beamy and fuller throughout, especially in the ends. There is no keel, but there is no lateral flat either; the body shapes are smoothly rounded throughout.

Recent samples of planking have been identified as cedar.[10] The Chicago boat is 9.8 m long and 2.37 m broad; depth at amidships is 72 cm. Its central strake is 10.21 m long and made of three planks butted together and superficially joined by dovetail fastenings. This strake is 39 cm wide amidships and 15 cm wide at its ends; it is 12 cm thick in the forward half of the hull and 9 cm thick over most of its after half. Three vertical mortises at the bow may have been used to attach an end piece or stempost.

There are three planking strakes on each side of the central strake; the lower ones are made of two planks, the second of three planks, and the upper strakes of four planks. They vary from 1 to 4.5 m in length, averaging about 3 m. Their widths range from 10 to 42 cm and average 30 cm. Thicknesses vary from 7 to 11 cm, although scattered humps and hollows of 13.5 cm and 6 cm were recorded.

Generally, planks tend to be wider and thicker in the forward half of the hull. Except for the central strake, planks are widened adjacent to a butt joint, probably to strengthen this otherwise weakened area. Most planks have their lateral curvatures carefully adzed to shape. Inner and outer planking widths are altered by alternating the bevel of the edges, as shown in Figure 3–12. This technique was practiced to a lesser extent by later Greek builders.

All planking was held edge to edge with deep mortise-and-tenon joints and dovetail fastenings. Mortises are 12 cm deep in the forward part of the hull (13 cm deep in the central plank edges) and 8 to 10 cm deep in the after half. They are 7.5 to 8 cm wide and 2 cm thick (Fig. 3–13a). Mortises at butt joins are only 5 cm deep, and each of the joined planks shares half of these mortises. Where plank ends narrow at the ends of the hull, single joints secure several strakes (Fig. 3–13b). Although Haldane is only now evaluating how tightly tenons fit their mortises, it is probable that some of them were as long as 24 cm. Unlike the Cheops tenons, then, these relatively large edge fastenings stiffened the hull in the manner of little internal frames, in addition to keeping the planks aligned.

Dovetail fastenings cross all seams, as well as the butt joins of the upper side strakes, on the inner planking surfaces. They typically measure 14 to 16 cm long—5 cm wide at their ends and half that much at their centers—and are 2 cm deep. They are generally flat, but they curve with the hull contours in the ends of the hull. Although a common form of early Egyptian joinery and usually considered original, Haldane offers very good arguments to establish that further study will be needed to determine whether these fastenings were installed in antiquity or merely added to hold weakened seams after excavation. Metal strapping on the hull exterior is known to have been added for shipment at the beginning of this century.

Gunwales enclose the deck area for a distance of slightly more than 7 m. They are 30 cm wide amidships, 9 cm thick, and composed of three planks lashed together through double holes at the butt joints. Dovetail fastenings, twenty-three mortise-and-tenon joints, and lashings through diagonally placed holes attach each gunwale strake to the upper side planks. The only true scarf on the hull is found at the after starboard butt joint, and this is intended only to place more wood between the joint and the hole for the nearby throughbeam.

There were no frames. Thirteen beams, 12 cm wide and 6 cm high, support the hull laterally. Eleven of them rest in notches cut in the upper side strakes and lower gunwale edges, while the other two rest in shallow grooves at bow and stern. The beams extended only as far as the

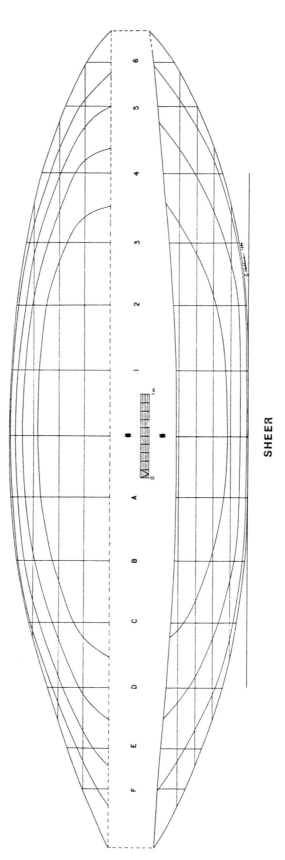

SHEER

Fig. 3–10a. Lines of the Chicago Dashur boat: the sheer and half-breadth plans of the port side. (courtesy C. W. Haldane, "The Dashur Boats," fig. 45)

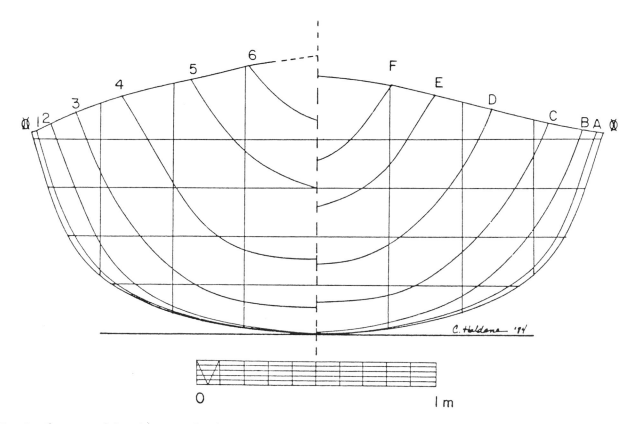

FIG. 3–10b. Lines of the Chicago Dashur boat: the body plan, enlarged to illustrate hull symmetry. (courtesy C. W. Haldane, "The Dashur Boats," fig. 44)

outer hull surface or slightly beyond. They were attached rigidly to the upper edges of the side planks with square treenails. Rabbets were cut into their upper surfaces for the seating of removable deck planks up to 35 cm wide (Fig. 3–14).

The vessel had the typical steering arrangement of funerary vessels of the period; quarter rudders were mounted on large stanchions on each side of the hull. Each stanchion was held in square holes in the throughbeam just inboard of the gunwale, their lower ends resting on

the inner planking surface. The quarter rudders resembled huge paddles and were nearly 4 m long with a blade length of 1.42 m. The boat was decorated colorfully.

Most notably, the Dashur boats did not appear to employ lashings for edge joinery below the waterline, although such may not have been the case originally. Haldane's study revealed that the dovetails may have replaced the remains of shallow mortises on the Pittsburgh boat.[11] The fact that frames were not used seems strange at first, since the dovetail fastenings (if they were originally there at all) might

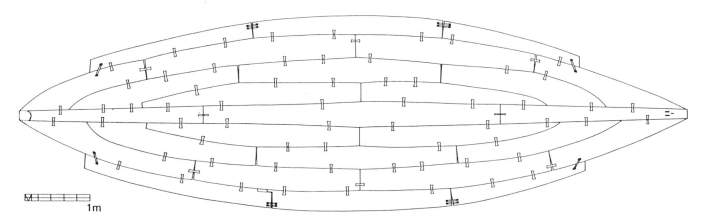

FIG. 3–11. A flattened planking plan of the Chicago Dashur boat. The bow is to the right. (courtesy C. W. Haldane, "The Dashur Boats," fig. 1)

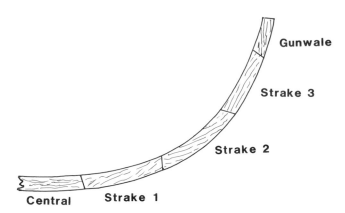

FIG. 3–12. A sectional diagram of the hull, showing the bevels of the planking edges. Not to scale. (after Haldane, fig. 8)

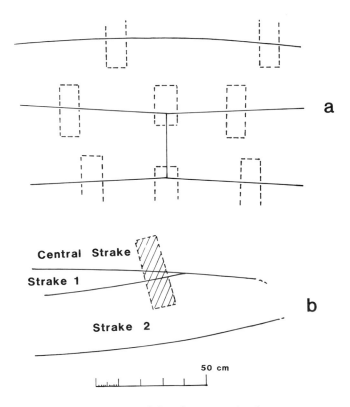

FIG. 3–13. Arrangement of the Chicago Dashur boat's mortise-and-tenon joints: (a) along seams and butts; (b) at the end of a strake. (after Haldane, figs. 8, 9, 11)

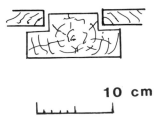

FIG. 3–14. Method of seating deck plank ends in the rabbets of a throughbeam. (after Haldane, fig. 6)

have been accidentally dislodged in some areas, permitting the edges of the planks to pull apart. When one considers the construction carefully, however, there does seem to be enough structural integrity for travel on the Nile. If the tenons fit their mortises tightly, their lengths would assure a substantial amount of bottom support. Water buoyancy would add to this support, although secure dovetail fastenings or lashings still seem necessary internally, because the tenons were unpegged and the planks could separate without them. Two other examples supporting this form of construction should be considered. The first is the oft-quoted description of Herodotus, a fifth-century B.C. historian: "From this acacia tree they cut planks 3 feet long, which they put together like courses of brick, building up the hull as follows: they join these 3-foot lengths together with long, close-set dowels; when they have built up a hull in this fashion [out of planks], they stretch crossbeams over them. They use no ribs, and they caulk seams from the inside, using papyrus fibers" (Herodotus II, 96).[12] Although Herodotus was writing more than a millennium after the Dashur boats were built, the description seems amazingly similar. The construction sequence and the use of crossbeams are the same, but his observation of the lack of frames (ribs) is the most important feature.

Modern examples of this form of construction still survive in Upper Egypt. Although nails now replace tenons, these cargo boats continue to use thick strakes of acacia and similar deck beams; not a frame can be found, and their hull forms are strikingly similar to those of the Dashur boats.[13]

Again, we are examining a funerary boat with no assurance that this was exactly the way commercial craft were constructed in the same period and region. As with the Cheops vessel, however, there are comparative examples; one must assume that some of the technology—perhaps in greater and more sophisticated doses—was applied to seagoing hulls. Is the heavier construction forward a coincidence, or was it meant to strengthen a hull that was hauled bow-first onto beaches and banks? Would seagoing vessels have used the same construction, with perhaps locked tenons and a few frames for larger and stronger hulls? Eventually archaeologists will provide us with a look at such a seagoing hull. At the present time, we have only limited information from the wreck of a slightly later vessel that was a bona fide seafarer.

THE ULU BURUN WRECK

Currently, the Institute of Nautical Archaeology is excavating a Bronze Age wreck off the southern coast of Turkey. Under the direction of George F. Bass and Cemal Pulak, this excavation is yielding an exciting variety of copper and tin ingots, Canaanite amphoras, stone anchors weighing more than two hundred kilograms, and an impressive array of fine artifacts. The wreck, which lies more than 50 m below the surface, is tentatively dated to the fourteenth century B.C.[14] Several more years may pass before we know much about the ship that brought these finds to Ulu Burun, if indeed much of it has survived. We are provided a hint at what may be found, however, and that in itself is new knowledge.

The distribution and weight of the cargo and the size of the anchors suggest that this may have been a large vessel for the period. In one small area, a part of the hull was exposed where an anchor was removed; the following details were recorded. A heavy timber, made from fir and believed to be the keel or a thick central strake, was sided 27.5 cm (Fig. 3–15). Adjacent to it were two strakes of planking tentatively identified as the garboard and second strake. They were 6 cm thick and had widths of 17 and 26 cm. Most important, they were edge-joined to each other and to the keel with mortise-and-tenon joints spaced slightly more than 20 cm between centers. About 4.5 cm on either side of the seams, each tenon was locked with transversely driven pegs having diameters of about 2.2 cm. The tenons were said to be rather thick, perhaps as much as 2 cm, and were cut from oak.

This is all that is known now, but we hope much more information will be forthcoming. Even so, these sparse details have enlightened us. At approximately thirty-four hundred years, this is the oldest seagoing sailing ship yet examined. The anchors alone are impressive, and the cargo will soon reveal tonnage figures that at least will give a minimum size for the ship. Most important of all, now we have extant proof that a few centuries after the Dashur boats were entombed, heavy cargoes were being transported across the Mediterranean in ships whose hulls were stronger and more efficient than those of the Egyptian funerary boats.

THE FERRIBY BOATS

One more example of Bronze Age watercraft must be examined. This one is in England and of an entirely different form of construction.

Three boats with similar structural features were excavated along the Humber River at North Ferriby, Yorkshire, under the direction of E. V. Wright.[15] Only the best preserved one, dated to the middle of the twelfth or thirteenth century B.C., is noted here and is illustrated in Figures 3–16, 3–17, and 3–18.[16] Three bottom strakes and a short piece of a side plank survived; the central bottom plank is over 13.3 m long. This was a laced boat; unlike the Cheops vessel, however, it was laced with a withy of yew—thin branches were pounded and twisted into a flexible state. The center strake, made from two centrally scarfed planks, was 14 cm thick and had a maximum width of

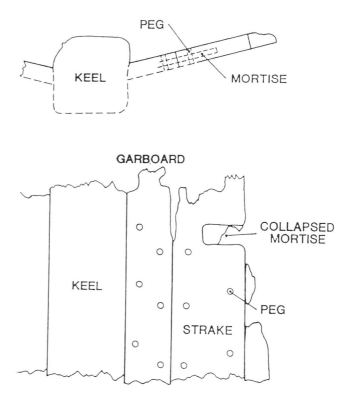

FIG. 3–15. Details of the exposed area of the Ulu Burun hull. (courtesy Cemal Pulak)

65 cm. The bottom planks on each side of it were about half that thickness and were rabbeted into the upper edges of the central plank. Holes and seams were caulked with moss, which was held in place by the battens inside the seams (Fig. 3–17).

Carved from the same bottom planks were a series of cleats (Fig. 3–16), through which horizontal holes were cut and transverse rods inserted. Others are thought to have supported lateral framing or bulkhead members. Similar cleats will resurface in our study of Viking ships in the next chapter. These planks were made from oak, and considering the nature of those cleats and the upturned end, the central strake must have been cut from the center of a log that Mr. Wright has calculated to have been at least 1.1 m in diameter.

A hypothetical reconstruction is shown in Figure 3–18. Like its Egyptian counterparts, such a hull probably would have been paddled. Wright considers these hulls to be examples of seagoing vessels of the period, and he presents interesting descriptions and illustrations of their operation.[17]

The Classical Period

The stage is now set for the comparison of watercraft development in the two widely separated areas of northwestern Europe and the Mediterranean region. Mediterranean builders continued their predominant use of softwood planking for centuries; in the northwest, there was a tendency toward hardwoods and heavier construction.

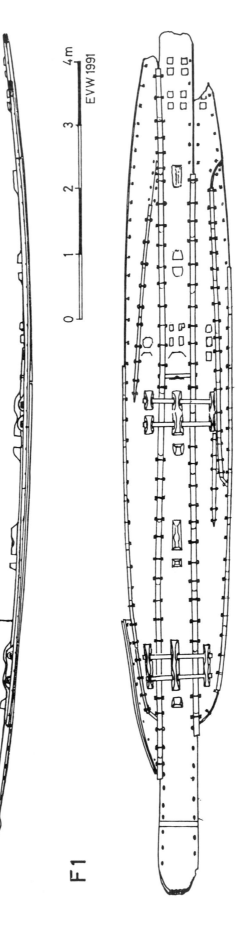

F1

4 m

3

2

1

0

EVW 1991

FIG. 3–16. Ferriby boat No. 1: profile and top views of the surviving hull. (drawing by E. V. Wright, forthcoming)

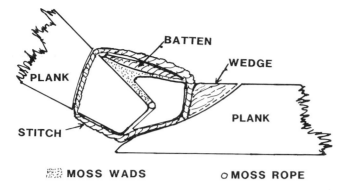

FIG. 3–17. Lacing details on the Ferriby boats, showing a bottom and side plank seam in section. Channel and plank configurations vary with seam locations. (after Wright, 1976, fig. 3)

Southern craft continued to rely on carefully fitted edge joinery and surface applications of pitch as the primary means of preventing water seepage at seams; the northern trend already had begun a strong reliance on internal caulking in coves (luting). But those few differences are only the beginning. The gap will widen considerably, as the next chapter illustrates.

Unfortunately, archaeology has not as yet provided a clear picture of Mediterranean seagoing ships until late in the Greek period. There are plenty of illustrations and there is later literary evidence to whet our appetites. We see and read about long narrow galleys, and it is evident they were subjected to many improvements and increased greatly in size as time progressed. The same might be said about merchant ships. For the present, we can merely hypothesize about the introduction of keels and wales, the increased efficiency of hull structures, the improvement of sails and rigging, and the sophistication of design. For actual evidence, however, our next stop is in the sixth century B.C.

THE BON-PORTÉ I WRECK

The Bon-Porté I wreck, excavated off the southern coast of France near Saint Tropez, has been dated (by amphoras and other objects) to the third quarter of the sixth century B.C. and is almost certainly Etruscan in origin.[18] This is a type of vessel we have come to call, perhaps inaccurately, a sewn boat—a craft whose seams were secured by means of ligatures of one type or another. The Cheops hull was laced transversely, but most sewn boats were laced longitudinally as in this example.

The Bon-Porté I vessel, which was poorly preserved, is believed to have been only 10 m or so in length. Its keel was sided a mere 6.4 cm and molded 9.6 cm; there was no false keel (Fig. 3–19).[19] The few frames that survived were quite large (sided 12 cm and molded 14 cm) and strangely sectioned for so small a vessel, but they were spaced as much as a meter apart. Futtocks were attached to floor timbers by means of diagonal scarfs. Small internal treenails kept them in alignment. The frames did not appear to be attached to the planking.

It is both the planking and its method of assembly, however, that make this hull interesting. Planks, only a little more than 2 cm thick on the average, were aligned with treenails rather than tenons. Seam integrity was accomplished by means of ligatures laced through diagonal holes with triangular openings in the plank surfaces as in

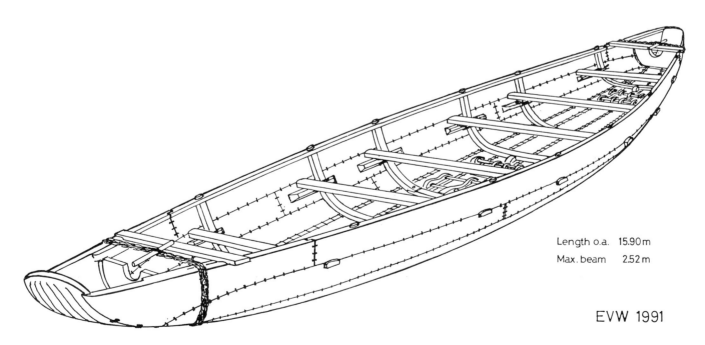

Length o.a.   15.90 m
Max. beam   2.52 m

EVW 1991

FIG. 3–18. A reconstruction of Ferriby boat no. 1, showing frames and thwarts. (drawing by E. V. Wright, forthcoming)

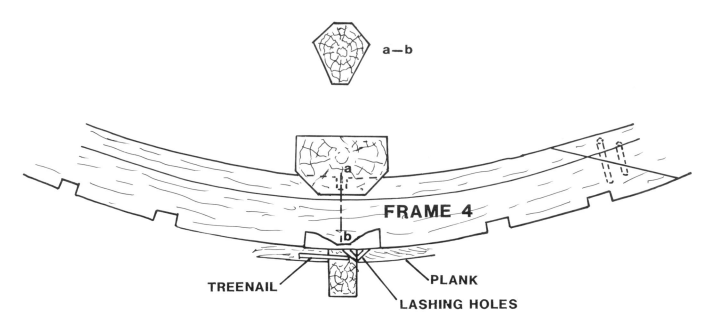

FIG. 3–19. A partial transverse section of the Bon-Porté hull at frame 4. Note the diagonal frame scarf, the treenails securing the scarf, and the curious cross-section of the frame at a-b. Not to scale. (after Joncheray, p. 27)

Figure 3–20. Although the ligatures did not survive, it is assumed they were locked in place with extant pegs found in some of the holes.[20]

Thus there appears to have been an alternate form of construction using treenails and lashings coexisting with mortise-and-tenon joined vessels. Quite a few examples of this technique have been recorded for the classical period; most of them were centered in the Adriatic and westward. There were, in fact, sewn boats in many parts of the world throughout history, including the present century. We will not discuss this building method beyond this chapter because it tended to be localized and has had little effect on the overall progress of shipbuilding technology after the classical period. However, the reader should be aware that it was a more common practice than is generally believed and may, therefore, surface in future archeological discoveries in unsuspected locations. An example follows.

THE MA'AGAN MICHAEL VESSEL[21]

The conservation and analysis of a wreck excavated near the shore of Kibbutz Ma'agan Michael, about 35 km south of Haifa, Israel, is currently still in progress, but enough has been learned to warrant the mention of a few construction details here. Tentatively dated to about 400 B.C., the hull construction and design are similar to that of the Kyrenia ship, whose structural details are described immediately below. To avoid repetition, only the important variations from the Kyrenia ship's structure will be mentioned.

The entire 11.25-m-long bottom of the hull has survived in good condition. The rockered keel, made from a

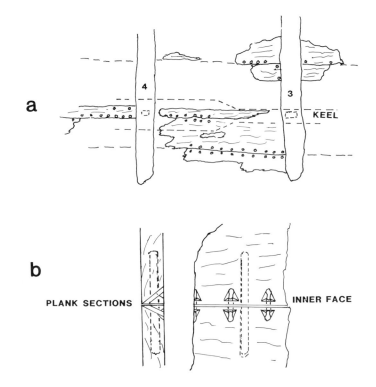

FIG. 3–20. Bon-Porté I wreck: (a) part of the site plan in the area of the mast step; (b) sections and inner surfaces of the planks at this seam, showing the nature of the ligature holes and cavities and a treenail joining the planks. (adapted from Joncheray, pp. 24, 29)

single piece of pine, was intact and had a length of 8.25 m; it was sided 11 cm and molded 16 cm.

Diagonal scarfs and S-scarfs were both used to combine planks into strakes; examples of each will be seen in the Kyrenia and Marsala Punic ships below. The ends of the strakes were lashed to the posts, knees, and a short length of the keel in each end of the ship (Fig. 3–21a). Composition and lacing patterns of the ligatures is currently unknown. Typical mortise-and-tenon joints were 3.5 cm wide, 0.6 cm thick, and spaced on approximate 12 cm centers. The joints were pegged as described for the Kyrenia ship below. Average planking thickness was about 4 cm.

The Ma'agan Michael vessel had a framing system that was reminiscent of the Bon-Porté timbers. The pine floor timbers and futtocks were assembled before installation, and they were joined by scarfs pinned together with small, square treenails. Frames were widely separated; room and space was about 75 cm. Unlike the Bon-Porté vessels, these frames were attached to planks with square, double-clenched iron nails driven through treenails; this is the earliest recorded use of iron as common fastenings on Mediterranean hulls. The floor timbers were not fastened to the keel (Fig. 3–21b).

Stanchions, about 10 cm in diameter and probably used to support deck beams, were stepped into a stringer extending from the mast step to the stern.

Most of the hull remains are in pristine condition, showing no signs of wear or degradation. Among the variety of artifacts found within the hull was a well-stocked carpenter's tool kit and a supply of unused tenons of various sizes. This fortunate discovery should contribute many new facets of information about ancient shipbuilding.

Undoubtedly the most interesting feature of the Ma'agan Michael vessel was the system of ligatures in the ends of the hull only. Was it a transitional step

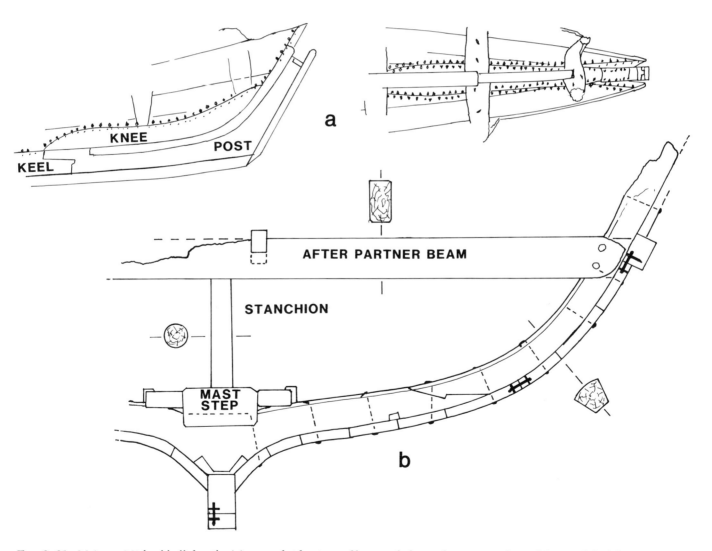

FIG. 3–21. Ma'agan Michael hull details: (a) top and side views of ligature holes in the stern timbers; (b) a simplified drawing of the midship section. The drawings are not to scale. (adapted from drawings by Jay Rosloff)

between the lashed seams of craft, such as the Bon-Porté I wreck, and the non-ligatured hulls described below? Certainly that assumption cannot be ruled out with the limited information at hand, although an equally acceptable argument would opt for the existence of two or more simultaneous disciplines in the classical period in the Mediterranean. Only time and additional excavations will settle such arguments.

Now it is time to examine a slightly larger, non-ligatured merchantman that was preserved and studied extensively.

The Kyrenia Ship

The Kyrenia ship sank during the last decade of the fourth century B.C. near the town of Kyrenia on the north coast of Cyprus, probably the victim of an attack by pirates. It was discovered about 1 km offshore at a depth of 30 m, and it was excavated in 1968 and 1969 by a team of nautical archaeologists under the direction of Michael L. Katzev (Fig. 3–22). Cargo and artifacts included more than four hundred amphoras of eight different types, coarse and fine pottery, hopper-type millstones, coins, tools, a huge copper cauldron, wooden utensils, fishing weights, almonds, and

FIG. 3–22. The Kyrenia shipwreck, with most of the cargo and artifacts removed and initial hull recording underway. (courtesy Kyrenia Ship Project)

dozens of other items defining shipboard life in ancient Greece.[22] For our purposes, however, the most significant part of the wreck was the vessel itself. More than half of the hull had survived in relatively good condition, and those timbers represented at least 75 percent of the original hull structure. Most of the hull remains lay within a 6-by-12 m area, separated along the keel into two major sections (Fig. 3–23). After extensive seabed recording, the wood was raised, preserved in polyethylene glycol, and re-assembled in Kyrenia's Crusader Castle, where it is now displayed with cargo and artifacts from the wreck. An extensive research program implemented the interpretation of the hull, including the construction of numerous models for testing structural theories and sailing characteristics, a sectional replica for studying construction and cargo stowage, and a faithfully executed full-size replica.[23] Here, in abstraction, is what was learned.

HULL CONSTRUCTION

We can only hypothesize the scene of the Kyrenia ship's origin; the scene perhaps included a gentle slope of shoreline near the Aleppo pine forests of the Aegean or eastern Mediterranean, and it most likely occurred during the lifetime of Alexander the Great. Our knowledge of ancient Greek ship contracts and shipbuilding economics is practically nonexistent, but suffice it to say that someone desired a new vessel capable of carrying about four hundred Rhodian amphoras for general trading in the Mediterranean and its neighboring bodies of water. With the exception of concerns about cost and logistical matters, that is probably all the shipwright needed to know to begin construction. A four hundred-amphora vessel would have been about 15 m long, and because design flexibility was limited in the fourth century, it would most likely have been in the form of a square-rigged, broad-beamed sailing craft.

After the details were confirmed, our shipwright began felling the necessary trees, either for curing or to replace an existing stock of cured timber. Selecting the proper trees demanded considerable expertise, as this ship required a lot of naturally grown curvatures for frames, knees, and even some of the planks. Tons of Aleppo pine (*Pinus halepensis*) logs were brought to the site, along with one or two logs of Turkey oak (*Quercus cerrus L.*) needed for tenons, tenon pegs, and a false keel. Now it was time to prepare the bed of logs on which the keel would be laid and to sharpen tools in preparation for the long job ahead.

First, a keel was sawn and hewn from a single log of Aleppo pine, sided 13 cm at the top (12 cm after the rabbets were cut into it) and 10 cm at the bottom, and molded an average of 20.3 cm, becoming more shallow near its ends (Fig. 3–24). Except for a flat section over the middle of the hull, it was rockered over most of its length of 9.33 m. At its forward end a short hook scarf connected it

to a two-piece stem. Although the forwardmost part of the stem did not survive, there is secondary evidence to suggest that the outer post was actually a long knee that angled the stem upward as shown in Figure 3–24.

A knee was nailed to the junction of the keel and sternpost to strengthen that area. While only short pieces of the sternpost and stern knee survived, all of the information at hand suggests an arrangement as shown. However, we have not ruled out the possibility that the knee and post were made from a single piece of pine. In either case, a fixed tenon at the bottom of the sternpost was stepped into a mortise in the after end of the keel and locked in place by means of one or more tapered pegs, as shown in the detail in Figure 3–24 (see also Figure 9–5 for details of the keel as found, and Figure 9–7 for the assembled stem fragments). Then this spinal assembly was checked for alignment and braced rigidly upon the stocks in preparation for the work to follow.

The top of the Kyrenia ship's keel was unblemished except for the sternpost mortise and nails for the knee at its after end. No frames were fastened to, or even touched, the top of the keel. Indeed, the next step was to install the bottom planking. First the garboard rabbets were cut into the upper edges of the keel and stem and part way up the forward edges of the sternpost (Figs. 3–25a, 9–5, and 9–7). Port and starboard garboard strakes, each made of two pine planks joined by a diagonal scarf (Fig. 3–25b), were shaped roughly to both longitudinal and lateral curvature (Fig. 3–25c). The keel and post rabbets and the lower edges of the garboard were then fitted carefully to each other. When the two surfaces were satisfactorily aligned, the shipwright used a sharp awl or scribing knife to make two marks, every 12 cm or so, that defined the parameters of mortise-and-tenon joints. Each of these marks began about 6 cm above the lower garboard edge and continued downward over a third of the keel's side. The builders of Kyrenia II repeated the process in pencil in Figure 3–27. Seventy-eight mortise locations were scribed on each side of the keel. They were then cut with mortising chisels to an average width of 4.3 cm, a thickness of 0.6 cm, and depths that averaged 8 cm but sometimes exceeded 10 cm. Matching mortises were cut into the lower edges of the garboards. Both garboard and keel mortises had to be angled carefully at ever-changing attitudes so the tenons that occupied them could be seated properly (Figs. 3–26a and 3–26b).

Tenons—made of Turkey oak to the same thickness and width as the mortises and to lengths of 15 to 20 cm—were then inserted into the mortises in the keel and stem (Fig. 3–26c). Usually their corners were rounded or angled to fit the mortise bottoms more accurately, because often the carpenters did not cut perfectly square-bottomed mortises. In addition, rounding the corners of the tenons may have reduced the tendency of the tenons to cut into the softer planking. On most, if not all, of the

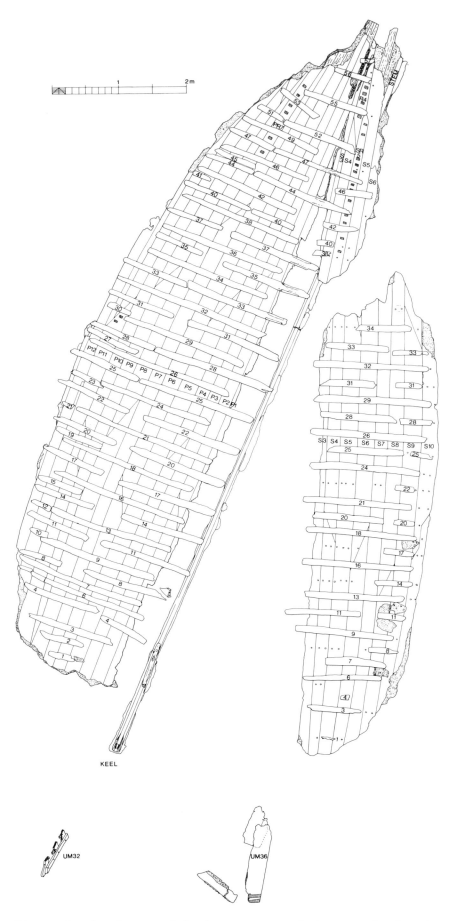

FIG. 3–23. Wreck plan of Kyrenia ship after the removal of ceiling, mast step, and other internal timbers. (revised for reconstruction from an original site plan by Helena Wylde Swiny and Joachim Höhle)

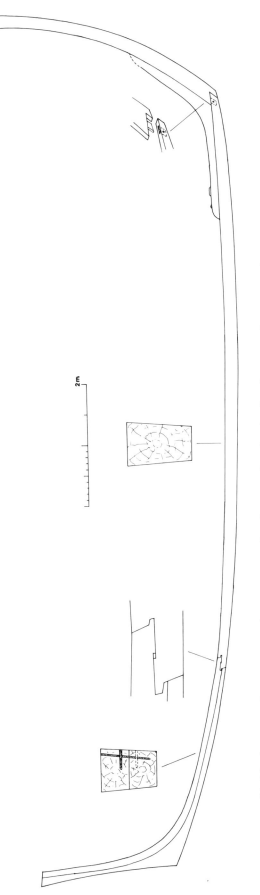

2m

FIG. 3–24. Assembled keel, stem, and sternpost, with cross-sectional and joinery details. The details are not drawn to scale.

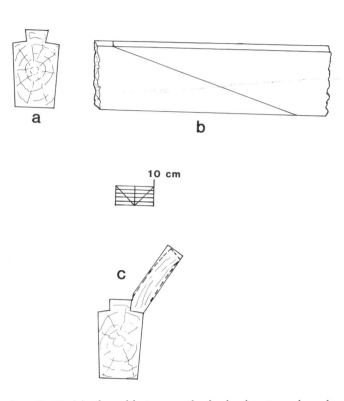

FIG. 3–25. (a) The rabbets gave the keel a keystone-shaped cross-section; (b) a typical diagonal planking scarf; (c) garboards were only roughly shaped at first, their final curvatures (dashed lines) being trimmed off later.

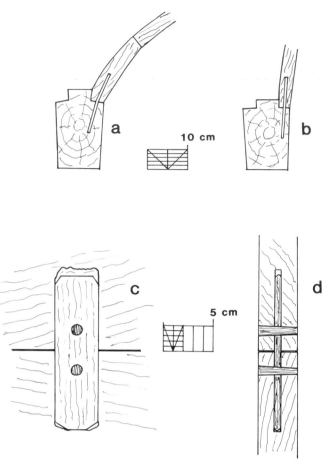

FIG. 3–26. Mortise-and-tenon joint details: mortise attitudes (a) near amidships and (b) near the stern; (c) the interior surface of a typical joint; (d) a cross-sectional view of the same joint.

ancient Mediterranean vessels excavated so far, tenons were as hard or harder than the wood surrounding them; there were mechanical reasons for this. First of all, the tenons had to be thin and as strong as possible. Second, these tenons, at least on the Kyrenia ship, were more than mere seam connectors; they could have been made much shorter were that their only function. But these slips of wood also acted as small internal frames, with their length and close proximity adding considerable stiffness and integrity to the shell of outer planking. And finally, they had to be hard to reduce the possibility of distortion, breakage, or cutting of the tenons as planking seams attempted to shift under the strain of heavy cargoes or turbulent seas.

Mortise and tenon distortion could also be combated by designing hulls so that such strains were minimized. The broad, round hull and soft curvatures of the Kyrenia ship were undoubtedly a result of this knowledge.

The aftermost garboard planks were set first—their mortises were aligned with the protruding tenons in the keel rabbet and the planks were driven over the tenons until their lower edges were seated perfectly in the rabbets (Fig. 3–27). The forward garboard planks were set in similar fashion, which included being secured to three vertical tenons in the diagonal scarfs. When all seams were aligned properly, they were locked with tapered oak pegs. Two cm above and below the seam in the center of each joint, holes with approximate diameters of 6 mm were

drilled through the garboards and at least 5 cm deep into the keel. Oak pegs, tapered so that their diameters decreased about 1 mm for every 1 cm of length, were driven into the holes until they fit snugly and locked the joints in place (Fig. 3–26d). These pegs were multisided rather than perfectly round; they appear to have been tapered with a knife or small hatchet.

One final task was required to complete the installation of the garboards. Holes less than 2 cm in diameter (we can't be certain because of concretion buildup, but they were about 1.5 cm elsewhere in the hull) were drilled laterally through both planks and the knee. Straight-grained wooden treenails of approximately the same diameter were inserted into the holes, and pure, hard-drawn copper nails were driven longitudinally through the centers of the treenails. The treenails expanded, closing the area around the nail tightly and making it waterproof while spreading the pressure of the nail shaft evenly around the surfaces of the holes and reducing the chances of splitting the plank (Fig. 3–28). The knee was nailed into the top of the keel without the treenail housings, because these were internal fastenings, but treenails were used around nails wherever watertight integrity was necessary. All planking nails had round shafts of slightly less than

FIG. 3–27. A garboard being set on the Kyrenia replica. Note the scribed marks for the joint locations. (courtesy Kyrenia Ship Project)

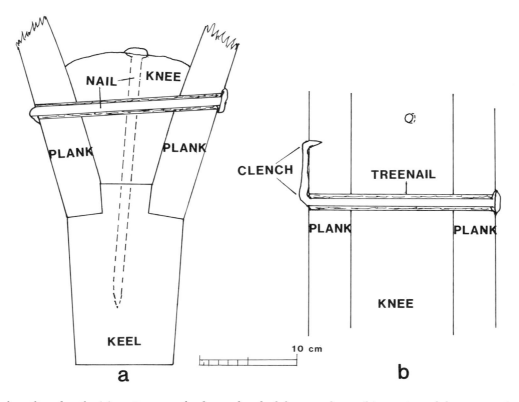

FIG. 3–28. Clench-nailing details: (a) section near the forward end of the stern knee; (b) top view of the same nail.

1 cm diameter and heads of 2 to 2.5 cm diameter. Probably they were drawn and shaped on stone swage blocks, and they were always made 7 cm or more longer than the length of any through-hole. The extra length was needed to double-clench the ends of the nails, as shown in Figure 3–28; the first clench secured the nail and prevented it from pulling out, while the second clench seated the tip and kept the nail from turning or being pried upward accidentally.

Thus the garboards were set, and the shipwright now did a little more surface trimming with small adzes and angled the garboards' upper edges to receive the next strakes.

The second strakes were erected in similar fashion, but in this case the forward planks were set first and the diagonal scarfs were angled in the opposite direction. These scarfs were also located well aft of the garboard scarfs. By separating the locations of adjacent scarfs and varying their directions every few strakes, patterns of shell weakness were avoided. This was important because the Kyrenia ship's planking shell was its primary structure; more than half of the hull's strength was vested in this skin and its reinforcement of closely spaced, tightly locked seam joinery.

Mortise-and-tenon joints along the garboard–strake 2 seams (and at all other seams) were cut approximately midway between the centers of the joints in the seams below (Fig. 3–29); on occasion, joint spacing throughout the hull was varied to avoid knots, concentrations of scarf joints, or other probable complications. Joint spacing between centers averaged 11.7 cm throughout the hull. Mortise depths averaged about 8 cm, although they tended to be somewhat deeper near the keel and more shallow along the flatter parts of the sides. Except at the keel and a few other places, tenon pegs were driven from the inside of the hull. Their inner diameters were about 1 cm, while at the outer planking surface they were 3 mm or 4 mm smaller (Fig. 3–26d). It is estimated that there were about four thousand mortise-and-tenon joints in the hull.

The arrangement of most of the port planking and part of the starboard planking can be seen in the wreck plan (Fig. 3–23). Note the varying strake widths and the distribution and directions of the scarfs. Most of the

planks were installed separately to form strakes, half of a scarf being fitted to a mate that was already in place. In such cases, the attitudes of the joints were necessarily similar to those in the seams, as in Figure 3–30a. Occasionally, the upper scarf tips were held down with one or two small nails until the succeeding strake could be added and the seam secured with tenon pegs.

Sometimes it was more satisfactory to work with long planks, depending on the sweep and curvature of the plank. In such instances, the Kyrenia carpenters assembled two or more planks of a strake before erecting them on the hull. Where that process occurred, the joints were cut perpendicular to the scarf seam, as in Figure 3–30b. On some ancient ships, both scarf tips were also nailed where planks were preassembled.

Figure 3–31 illustrates the construction of the hull in cross section at amidships. There were nine bottom strakes on each side, and each strake consisted of two or three planks joined by diagonal scarfs. Probably the shipwright put in some of the frames as soon as the bottom planking was completed, although he could have erected all of the planking before installing any frames. No permanent frames could have been installed before six strakes were in place on each side and probably not before all nine bottom strakes were completed. Some of the floor timbers spanned the entire bottom, and all of them reached at least as far as strake 6 on each side. Beneath all of the floor timbers were tenon pegs that had been driven from inside the hull. Additionally, it was obvious that the frame faces were fitted to the inside curvature of the planking rather than the planking being fitted to the frame faces. The garboard strakes were at least partially hewn to shape, and the same was probably true for strakes 2 and 3; above that, the strakes were sawn roughly to shape and then trimmed to their

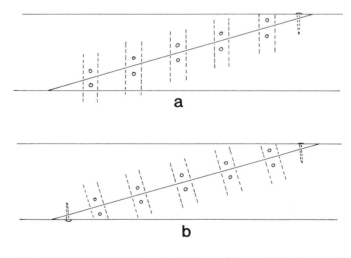

FIG. 3–30. (a) Attitudes of mortise-and-tenon joints in scarf seams where the left plank was installed after the right plank; (b) attitudes of joints in scarfs where both planks were preassembled before installation in the hull.

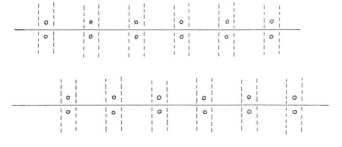

FIG. 3–29. Typical method of staggering mortise-and-tenon joints.

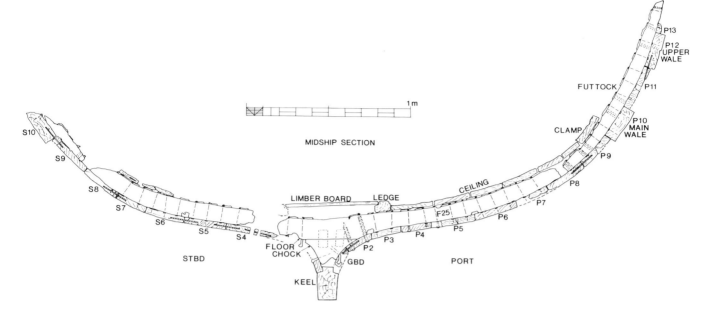

FIG. 3–31. Cross section of the Kyrenia ship's hull at amidships.

lateral curvatures with adzes. These curvatures are smooth, with the frames showing none of the flat surfaces for seating planking as is found on later ships. Since there were no frames present to support the planks being installed, the builders probably used internal and external braces, Spanish windlasses, clamps, and whatever else was needed to retain planking curvatures until the joints were locked with pegs. From the construction of the replica a few years ago, we learned that surprisingly little bracing was required after the tenons were locked in place (Fig. 3–32).

It seems unlikely that the shipwright went beyond the bottom planking before installing floor timbers. It would have been advantageous to use the added rigidity they supplied before setting the heavy wales above and additionally to avoid the extra effort of lifting these heavy timbers over the high sides of a completed hull.

A typical floor timber is shown in Figure 3–31. All frames were made from Aleppo pine and were shaped from compass timber (naturally curved tree trunks and large branches) where required. First, a separate chock was made to fit into the cavity between the lower strakes. Then a floor timber, whose arms spanned most of the bottom of the hull, was aligned with it and the inner planking surfaces. Chock and timber were joined by mortise-and-tenon joints that were about the width and thickness of the planking joints but usually a centimeter or two shorter. These joints were not pegged, since they were intended only to keep the two members aligned during fitting and installation.

When fitting was completed, holes of about 1.5 cm in diameter were drilled through the frame and planking; straight-grained treenails were inserted; and copper nails were driven through the treenails and clenched as explained for the garboard nailing at the stern knee. At the lowest strakes, where the combined thickness of the chock and frame made this process inadvisable, straight nails were driven into the chock or through the chock into the floor timber (Fig. 3–31). As a rule of thumb, there were two nails per frame in planks less than 20 cm wide and three nails where planking was wider than that. It is estimated that there were about three thousand copper nails in the hull, at least three-fourths of them used for attaching frames to planks. Note that I said "frames to planks," because that was the mentality with this form of construction. In the next chapter we will note a reversal of this philosophy.

Nineteen floor timbers were at least partially preserved on the wreck, and the existence of at least four more can be confirmed. They had square cross sections averaging about 9 cm on a side, although they were molded to greater dimensions over the keel and less at their outboard ends. Since they were made from tree trunks and branches, in a few cases retaining patches of bark, they were neither straight nor perfectly square. Figure 3–23 shows the lateral configuration of all the frames. Floor timbers were spaced an average of 50 cm between centers. Most of them had limber holes over the 5-6 and 2-3 planking seams, and a central watercourse was cut in the bottom of the chock directly over the center of the keel.

After the bottom of the hull was completed, the shipwright set about the task of building the sides. The first side strake was the main wale, 21.5 cm wide throughout and twice as thick as the bottom planking, or 8 cm. The wales acted as huge wooden girdles, strengthening the outer hull at its greatest lines of stress. Stress was greatest

FIG. 3–32. The shell of Kyrenia II with floor chocks and a side strake being fitted, but still without frames. Notice the cross-spawls used to stiffen the hull where the planking is being installed. Note also the untrimmed tenon pegs protruding from upper seams and the smoothly trimmed inner surfaces of the lower planking. (courtesy Kyrenia Ship Project)

where the hull was alternately buoyed by the water and unsupported as the ship rolled. Wales helped to counteract the resulting tendency of the sides to flex with the rolling. The Kyrenia ship, because of its body shape and framing plan, required a main wale at the lower part of its side and another whose midship location coincided with the approximate full-load waterline amidships.

The main wales consisted of two pine planks on each side joined together aft of amidships by means of a three-planed scarf (Fig. 3–33). The wales were attached to adjacent planking with mortise-and-tenon joints situated along the inner halves of their edges, but the scarf edges were joined by double rows of joints. Inner scarf joints were pegged from the inside of the hull, while those in the outer rows had pegs driven from the outer wale surfaces. None of the pegs extended completely through the wales.

Broad, 3.5-cm-thick planks separated the main and upper wales. The upper wale was about one and a half times as thick as the bottom planking (6 cm). No scarfs survived within the preserved area of this timber. Although preservation above the upper wale was fragmentary and

sparse, the evidence indicates that only one or two planks originally existed here. The surviving planking fragments are 3 cm thick and contain vertical nails believed to attach a caprail. Above this main part of the hull, there were probably bulwarks or weather screens to ward off choppy seas.

After the wales were installed, perhaps after hull planking was completed, the rest of the frames were inserted. Pairs of half-frames—each extending from a point just above the keel, around the bilge, and upward to the upper wale or above—were inserted about midway between each floor timber. These frames were about 8 cm square and selected from grown curvatures, most of whose grainage followed their assigned irregular arcs rather well. Futtocks, extensions of the floor timbers, were shorter and flatter versions of the half-frames that spanned the sides from bilge to caprail. Both frame types were fastened to the planking in the same manner as the floor timbers. At irregular intervals, top timbers extended from near the upper wale line to an unknown location above the extent of hull preservation; presumably

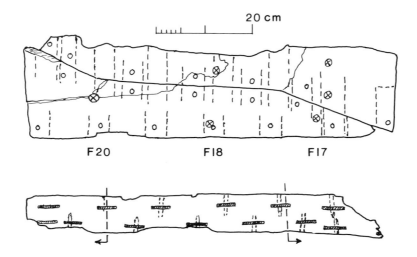

FIG. 3–33. The main wale in the area of the scarf. Note the double row of joints in the scarf.

these represented stanchions for supporting the bulwarks or weather screens above the main hull. None of the timbers were joined together, even though their ends sometimes abutted. Figure 3–34 shows the arrangement of floor timbers, half-frames, futtocks, and top timbers on the Kyrenia ship.

That was the composition of the main hull structure. A shell of pine planking nearly 4 cm thick, stiffened by 15-cm-long oak tenons placed at intervals of about 12 cm, was reinforced longitudinally by a pair of wales and laterally by a framework of pine. The frames, whose room and space averaged about 25 cm, were arranged alternately so

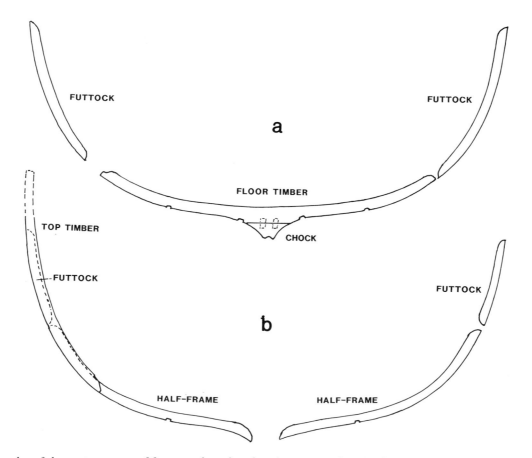

FIG. 3–34. Examples of the various types of frame timbers found in the Kyrenia ship: (a) floor timber and futtocks; (b) half-frames and futtocks; a typical intermediate top timber extends about the left side of the hull. Not to scale.

that one line spanned the entire bottom and sides separately, while adjacent members spanned the turn of the bilge but did not cross the keel. A spine consisting of keel and posts backed the shell but was not directly connected to the framing system.

Internally there was not much to add to the hull's strength. There was no keelson. Instead, lateral limber boards, made from scrapwood, were supported by ledges mounted atop the floor timbers 30 cm on either side of the hull's centerline (see Fig. 3–31). These boards were removable to afford access to the limber holes above the keel. The ceiling was made from 3 cm–thick pine boards that were nailed to the frames infrequently. The only timber that provided longitudinal strength internally was a 5 cm–thick shelf clamp mounted opposite the main wale on the inner frame faces. This clamp, in addition to supporting three rather weak beams, provided limited backing strength to the wales. It was not, however, directly attached to the wales but was straight-nailed to many of the frames that supported it.

Just before launching, the exterior of the hull was covered with a coating of black pitch, which was the only form of caulking used by these builders. The planks had to be shaped very carefully, because watertight integrity of the seams was maintained solely by the pitch and the swelling of the planks. There was no driven caulking in any of the seams.

A bulkhead segregated the after end of the hold and a stern compartment (Fig. 3–35). Our topside reconstruction, based largely on secondary evidence, has short decks fore and aft and an undecked area above the hold. Preserved and hypothesized areas were combined for further study in the form of a sailing replica (Figs. 3–36 and 3–37).

Many of the features found in the Kyrenia hull were obviously the product of a well-established discipline, and most of them were destined to survive for a very long time. The sternpost was stepped and kneed, the keel was protected by a replaceable false keel, and the stem was joined to the keel by a hook scarf. All these features survived throughout shipbuilding history, albeit in greatly improved form. The framing system, while still relatively weak and unconnected to the keel, had a series of floor timbers that would be improved upon and remain forever.

FIG. 3–35. Frames clench-nailed into place, and the stern bulkhead being installed. (courtesy Kyrenia Ship Project)

FIG. 3–36. The Kyrenia replica ready for launching. (courtesy Kyrenia Ship Project)

FIG. 3–37. Kyrenia II sailing in ballast. (courtesy Kyrenia Ship Project)

Planking was edge-joined in a fashion that would be retained in the Mediterranean for centuries; wales would be set higher as overall hull structure improved, but they would survive as long as wooden hulls were built. The method of double-clenching nails in a downward herringbone fashion also would survive for centuries, as would the method of caulking and the steering arrangement. But the internal structure was undeveloped. The lack of a keelson and weaknesses around the keel/chock area were detriments that would soon be corrected.

The design of this vessel is magnificent (Fig. 3–38). It is a graceful hull, although that grace is related mostly to the demands of the structural arrangement. But it is a configuration that has survived the centuries. There are still plenty of fishing boats and interisland vessels in the Aegean and eastern Mediterranean that display this double-ended sweeping sheer, high stern, and soft, full bilges. And they are still praised as being graceful, pleasing, and manageable hulls; after two millennia, that is a tribute to the originators of such a useful design. The use of softwood for construction stayed around for many centuries too, and in a few areas pine is still the preferred timber. I have heard modern boatbuilders criticize this choice of timber, but that is due to their loyalty to hardwoods and their unfamiliarity with the eastern maritime pines. It is a good wood when all the factors are considered—not so

good for the Atlantic, perhaps, but for edge-joined Mediterranean hulls it was most desirable.

THE REPAIRS

We are not finished with the Kyrenia ship yet. What I just told you related only to the original construction. But this was a most revealing artifact, and one of its more important features was its repaired areas. Sections of the false keel had been replaced, leaky seams were patched internally with strips of lead and square lead patches fastened along the seams with small copper tacks, and a new bilge sump was made by cutting away part of a floor timber forward of the mast. These and other minor repairs and alterations were evident in many locations. Of greater concern to ancient shipowners, however, were those frequent and costly damages caused by rot, shipworms, and structural failure. The Kyrenia ship suffered some of each.

A rotten floor timber in the bow was replaced by one that combined the chock and floor in a single piece of pine. At some stage the old ship broke its back. The cracked keel was repaired by the simple insertion of a wooden block spanning the break (Fig. 3–39). Such a solution would have been unacceptable on later seagoing vessels; it was acceptable here only because the keel was unconnected to the framing system and therefore did not function as a proper backbone.

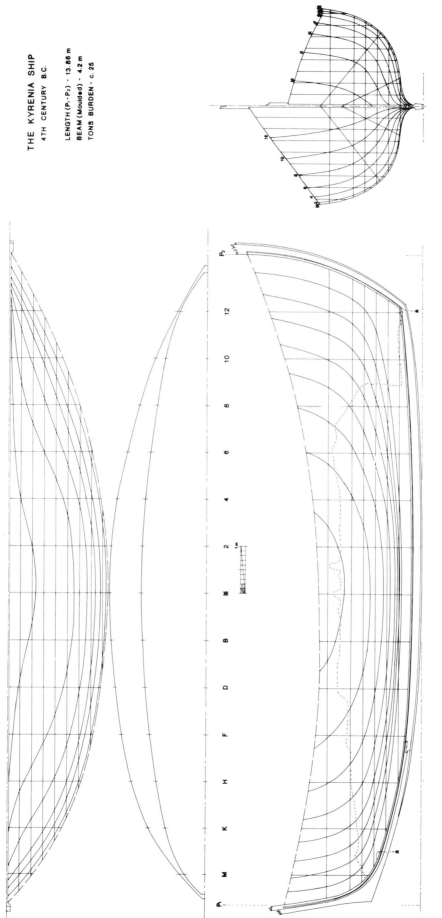

THE KYRENIA SHIP
4TH CENTURY B.C.

LENGTH (P₁-P₂) - 13.86 m
BEAM (Moulded) - 4.2 m
TONS BURDEN - c. 25

Fɪɢ. 3–38. The lines of the Kyrenia ship.

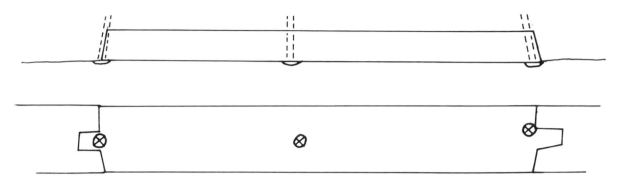

FIG. 3–39. Side and bottom views of the repair block in the keel. Not to scale.

Between the port wales in the after half of the hull and on both sides of the bow, there were rotten strakes that required replacement. Although each area had to be dealt with somewhat differently, a rotten seam between port bow strakes 7 and 8 illustrates the basic procedure best. The rotten sections were removed first by making longitudinal cuts through the approximate centers of both strakes. Old frame nails were extracted, and the edges of the new cuts were flared outward as shown in Figure 3–40. The abbreviated mortises resulting from the cuts were cleared of tenon fragments and—probably with specially shaped mortising chisels—extended to standard depths of 8 cm or so. Next, a plank was shaped to fit the newly formed opening, joint locations were marked on the outer surfaces, and mortises were cut in both edges. It would have been impossible, however, to insert tenons into both edges of this strake in the normal fashion, so square openings were cut into its inner surface for one row of joints. Where the joints coincided with frame locations, the openings were cut into the outer surface of the new plank. Then the replacement strake was lowered onto the protruding tenons of the abbreviated strake 7 and pushed tightly against the frames and lower edge of strake 8, and the special headed tenons we have come to call "patch tenons" were driven through the upper seam from their surface openings. The procedure is illustrated in Figure 3–40.

After all the tenons were inserted and the strake was rigidly in place, peg holes were drilled on each side of the new seams and standard tapered pegs driven to lock the joints. As on the original ship, they were driven from inside the hull except where frames interfered and required exterior installation. Now the shipwright only had to place a drill bit into the existing nail holes in the frames and drill outward through the plank for the new copper nails, which were installed in the manner described previously.

The above method of replacing strakes illustrates far more than an ingenious answer to a mechanical problem, for it reveals a lot about this ancient shipwright's mentality concerning hull structures. Since the frames were already in place, it was only necessary to nail the replacement strake to them to complete the repair; that is what latter-

day shipwrights would have done. Surely such capable carpenters would have recognized this very obvious and seemingly more practical method of plank on frame. Why then did they not take advantage of it? In my opinion, ancient shipwrights did not regard the frames as something that should provide sole support to a plank, even a single repair plank. The planking, including the joinery that connected its edges, was the primary structure and the one that was very carefully and completely replaced. Apparently this was such an important step that it could not be compromised. The frames were used as a secondary support, yes, but not at the expense of the rest of the structure.

There were two kinds of sheathing, too. At some stage the entire bow became so infested with shipworm tunnels and rot that the whole thing had to be stabilized and recaulked. For this the builder chose 1.1-cm-thick pine furring with some unknown caulking material beneath it (Fig. 3–41). The furring deals were simply laid edge to edge, more or less parallel to the run of the lower stem. They were fastened with copper nails having shafts 0.7 cm in diameter and about 10 cm long. To keep the surface as flat as possible, to coincide with frame locations, and to avoid splits, furring nails were driven alongside planking nails. Furring, too, was a construction feature that would still be found on some ships nearly two millennia later.

Immediately after the bow was repaired and furred, shortly before the ship sank, the entire hull was recaulked and sheathed. Figure 3–42 illustrates details. Sheets of lead only a millimeter thick were applied to the hull after it had been coated with thick layers of a mixture of agave leaves and pitch. The edges of the lead sheets were overlapped and fastened with closely spaced copper tacks. It was somewhat similar to the system of coppering latter-day hull bottoms, except that this ship was sheathed well above the waterline and probably all the way to the caprail.

Thus the Kyrenia wreck provided extensive information about its original construction as well as a series of repairs made during an apparently long operating life. Its replica, whose hull is made from pine and fastened with oak and copper as was the original vessel, sports a linen

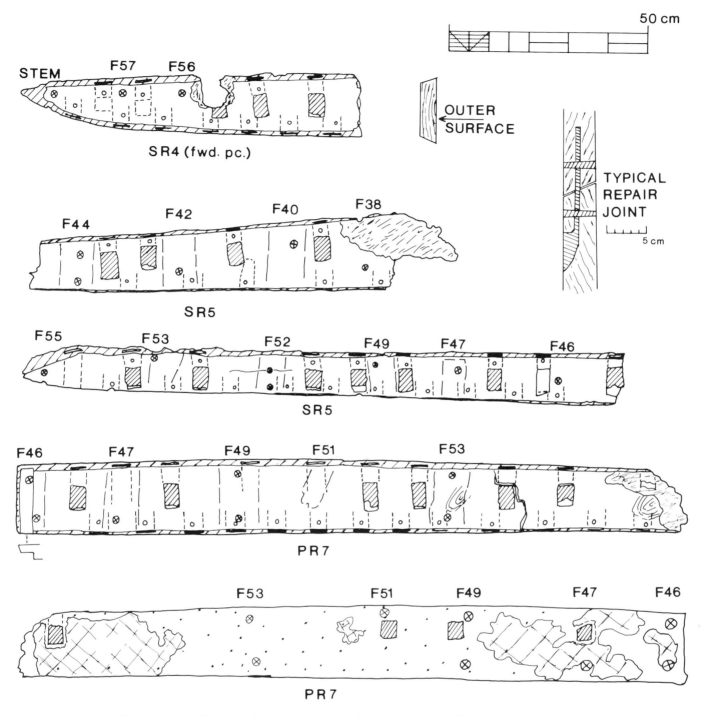

FIG. 3–40. Inner surfaces of two starboard replacement strakes on the Kyrenia ship, and the inner and outer surfaces of port replacement strake 7. The details show the method of inserting the new plank and patch tenons.

sail that is shaped or shortened by means of brailing gear (see Fig. 3–37). It has performed extremely well; it is drier, stronger, faster, and sails upwind better than expected. During one voyage the little ship encountered winds in excess of fifty knots without taking on much water and with insignificant damage to the hull and rig. In most cases, however, Kyrenia II plodded along at two or three knots, sometimes wallowing without forward movement in windless seas. This was probably more indicative of ancient seafaring.

A lot of space has been devoted to a little merchantman that probably never drew a second glance in antiquity. There is a reason—this old ship contains many of the features necessary to understand the ancient methods of ship construction, where much of the hull strength was supplied by the outer planking while the internal structure

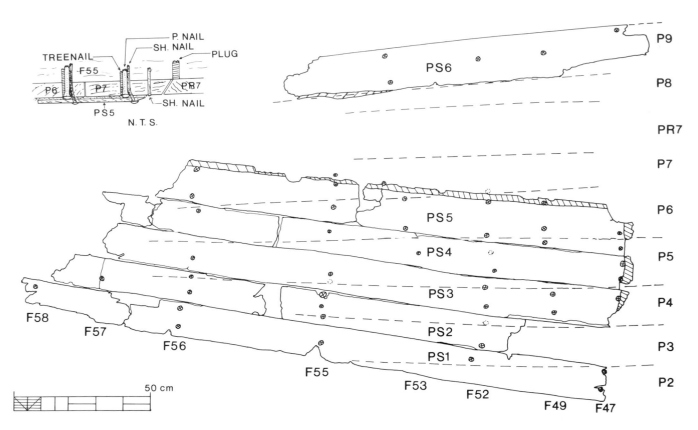

FIG. 3–41. Wood sheathing over ghosted port bow planking on the Kyrenia ship. Detail shows the method of driving sheathing nails alongside planking nails.

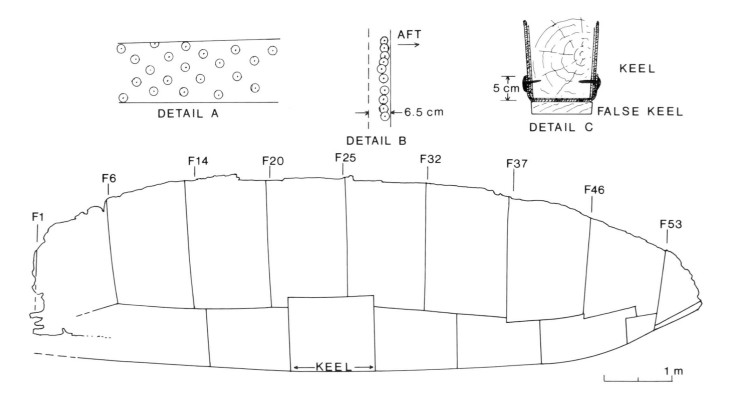

FIG. 3–42. A schematic diagram of the Kyrenia ship's lead sheathing. Details illustrate (A) the typical tack pattern; (B) a typical method of overlapping vertical seams; (C) the method of sheathing the bottom of the keel.

contributed a secondary form of support and was installed only after the planking shell was partially or entirely in place.

THE MARSALA PUNIC SHIP

The Kyrenia ship was a broad, wind-driven vessel with a beam:length ratio of about 1:3. Fifty years or so after it sank, a brand new craft with many similar features sank off Lilybaeum (modern Marsala), Sicily.[24] Unlike the Kyrenia ship, the Marsala vessel was propelled by oars some of the time, for this was a galley with an estimated beam:length ratio of 1:7. In spite of the design differences, however, the two are surprisingly compatible in construction methodology—the cross-sectional shape of the hull, the alternating floor and half-frame pattern, the separation of frames and keel, the keystone shape of the keel, and the edge joinery of the planking, which included sizes and spacings similar to that of the Kyrenia ship. The Marsala ship was also sheathed in lead. And, like the Kyrenia ship, these hull remains have been preserved and reassembled in a museum at Marsala.

Figure 3–43 shows some of the variations from the Kyrenia ship's structure. A different version of kneed stern is shown in (a), where the after end of the keel forms the knee to which the post (or outer sternpost) is attached with mortise-and-tenon joints. The frames were made from oak and maple. Most floor timbers did not

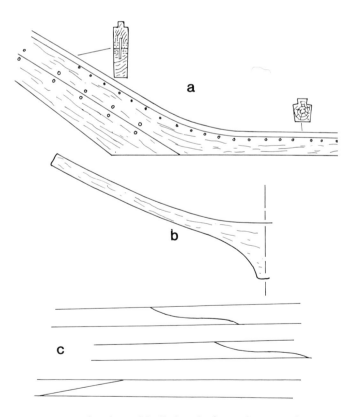

FIG. 3–43. Sketches of hull details from the Marsala Punic wreck. (after Frost, *Lilybaeum:* [a] various drawings; [b] fig. 156; [c] fig. 113)

have separate chocks or watercourses over the keel; the separation between floor timbers and keel was sufficient to permit free flow of bilgewater. Planking utilized both diagonal scarfs and S-shaped scarfs as shown in Figure 3–43c.

THE ATHLIT RAM

Not all galleys were constructed so lightly, however. Early in the second century B.C., what must have been a proud and powerful warship was driven ashore at Athlit, Israel.[25] When discovered in 1980, all that remained was a bronze ram and sixteen bow fragments, yet it is at present the sole example of those magnificent multi-banked warships whose bows were fortified with decorated, three-pronged rams. The bronze ram (Fig. 3–44) is both beautiful and functional. It is ingeniously designed to transfer the striking force of the ship to an enemy's hull, and the compatibility between ram and bow is impressive. The entire bottom of this ship was essentially the weapon; its momentum was transferred to the ram by a pair of thick wales and bottom planking, reinforced at their junction by a ramming timber (Figs. 3–45 and 3–48). Only one of the timbers survived beyond the confines of the ram, making it impossible to determine hull shapes, keel and frame details, or topside arrangements. Nevertheless, what has been preserved is a tribute to the superb craftsmanship of its builders.

The bottom planks and at least two of the side planks were 7.5 cm thick (Figs. 3–46 and 3–48). Waterline wales were 18 cm thick and 24 cm wide. All straddled a ramming timber, which in turn supported a stem whose tenoned bottom was locked into a mortise in the ramming timber with a pair of treenails. A chock and nosing of elm completed the assembly.

Keel, planks, and wales were fashioned from pine, the stem and ramming timber from cedar, and tenons from live oak. The tenons were 1.1 cm thick—twice as thick as those at Kyrenia—and they occupied mortises that averaged 7.7 cm in width and 12 cm in depth. Joint spacing averaged 12 cm between centers. The joints were locked with tapered oak pegs having a maximum diameter of about 1.5 cm. Planks and wales were fastened to the ramming timber (and probably to frames further aft) by means of bronze nails driven through the centers of treenails (Fig. 3–47). Bronze nails also secured the after end of the ram to the bow.

Wales and ramming timber were further secured by means of a large, lateral tenon, which was locked by two vertical treenails (Fig. 3–48). There was no lead sheathing on this hull, although planking surfaces and seams were smeared liberally with pitch.

Preservation was good enough to determine that most, if not all, of the tenon pegs were driven from inside the hull. The bottom planking and main wales must have been assembled before the ramming timber was installed, since their inner surfaces were covered by the ramming

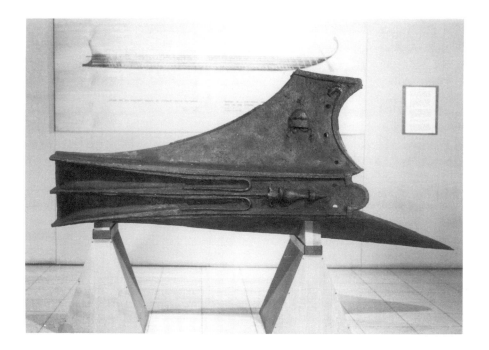

Fɪɢ. 3–44. The bronze ram from Athlit, Israel, on display at the National Maritime Museum, Haifa. (photo by William M. Murray)

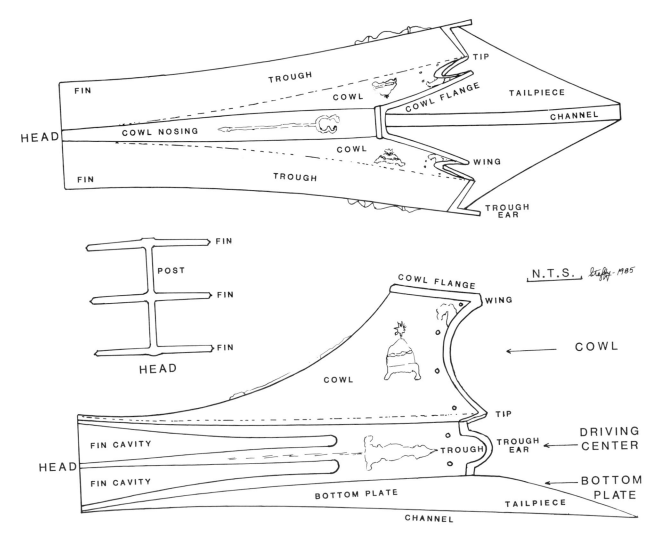

Fɪɢ. 3–45a. Identification of the various parts of the Athlit ram.

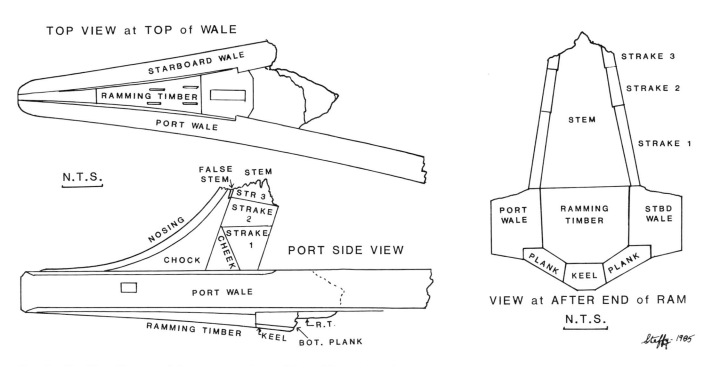

FIG. 3–45b. Identification of the various timbers of the Athlit warship's bow.

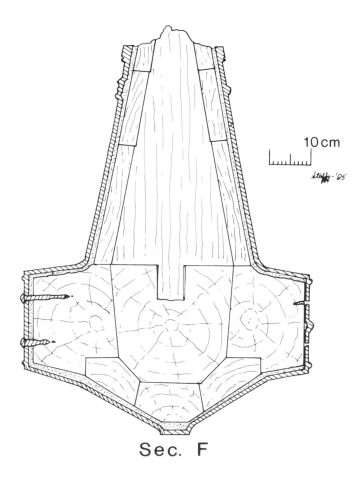

FIG. 3–46. Sectional view of the Athlit bow timbers at the after end of the ram.

timber. Furthermore, the fixed stem tenon was locked into its mortise in the ramming timber with a pair of treenails that passed completely through the ramming timber but did not penetrate the wales. Therefore, the ramming timber and stem must have been lowered into the completed hull bottom as a unit, indicating that the sequence of constructing large warships may have differed from that of merchant ships.

Despite its sparse survival, the Athlit ship revealed many new features about classical warships. Most important of these, from a construction standpoint, was the complexity of the bow structure. Warships apparently demanded the very best in materials and workmanship. It would be most enlightening if one of these monsters could be found in a more extensive state of preservation.

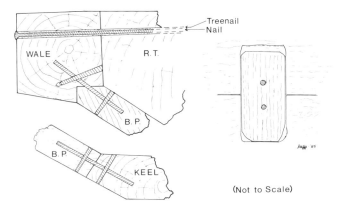

FIG. 3–47. The Athlit warship's fastening systems.

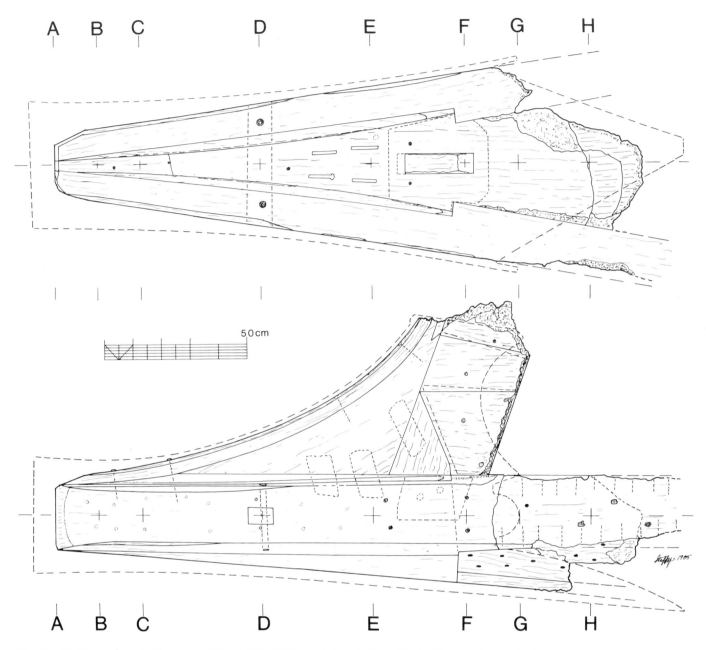

FIG. 3–48. Top and port side views of the Athlit ship's surviving timbers. Dashed lines indicate the bronze ram's perimeter.

THE MADRAGUE DE GIENS SHIP

A number of large, ancient Mediterranean merchant ships have been examined on the seabed, the majority of them dating to the first or second century B.C. One of the more impressive is the Madrague de Giens ship, which was the subject of more than a decade of underwater excavation and many additional years of research by a French team headed by Andre Tchernia and Patrice Pomey.[26] Discovered just off the coast of southern France, this wreck was dated to about the middle of the first century B.C. and was carrying nearly four hundred tons of cargo when it sank. Its length is estimated at 40 m and its beam at 9 m. In other words, this ship was nearly three times as long as

the Kyrenia ship, and its deep hold could carry almost twenty times as much cargo. That required a much stronger hull, which was achieved in several ways.

The 35-by-40 cm keel had double rabbets, since this hull was double-planked (Figs. 3–49a and 3–49b). The inner, or main, planking was 6 cm thick; outer planks averaged 4 cm in thickness. Later we will consider a hull with single planks 10 cm thick, but double-planked hulls such as this must have offered certain economic and structural advantages. First of all, there was less overall wastage of timber in using the thinner planks, and they were certainly easier to fit around bow and stern curvatures. Since the outer planks absorbed most of the physical and shipworm

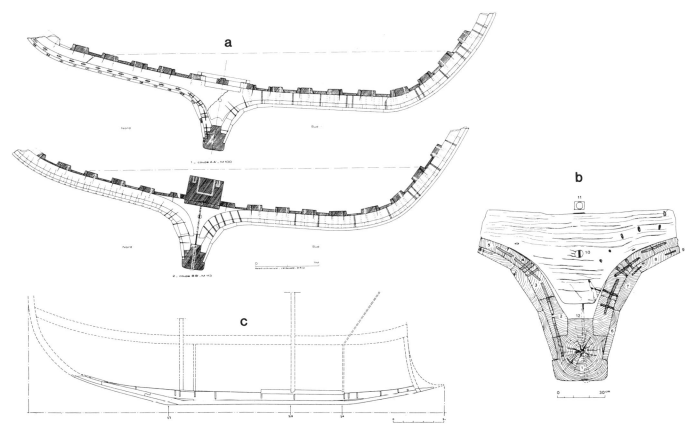

FIG. 3–49,a–c. Madrague de Giens hull details: (a) cross-sections of the hull, showing floor timber and half-frame arrangements; (b) keel area details in section; (c) sheer view of the hull (dashed lines are reconstructions). (Pomey: [a] 1978, pl. 36; [b] 1978, fig. 10; [c] 1982, fig. 8; all courtesy Centre Camille Jullian [CNRS])

damage, the inner lining would have required less frequent replacement. That is probably the reason for using thicknesses of 6 cm and 4 cm, rather than 5 cm, in both layers; the 4-cm-thick planks were still quite strong, and they were cheaper and easier to replace when necessary. The

extra layer of thick caulking material that separated the two skins undoubtedly improved the vessel's watertight integrity. The movement and subsequent distortion of tenons within mortises due to strains on the hull was probably less of a problem with double planking than with the double

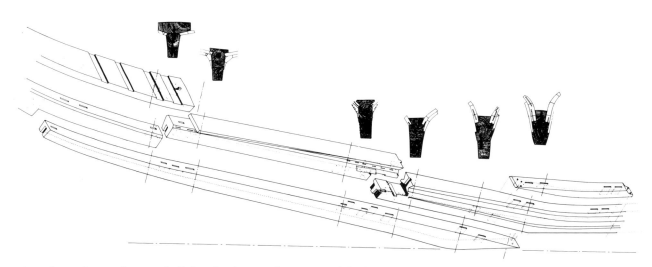

FIG. 3–49d. Madrague de Giens hull details: the complex joinery of the keel where it angles upward toward the stern. (Pomey, 1982, fig. 3; courtesy Centre Camille Jullian [CNRS])

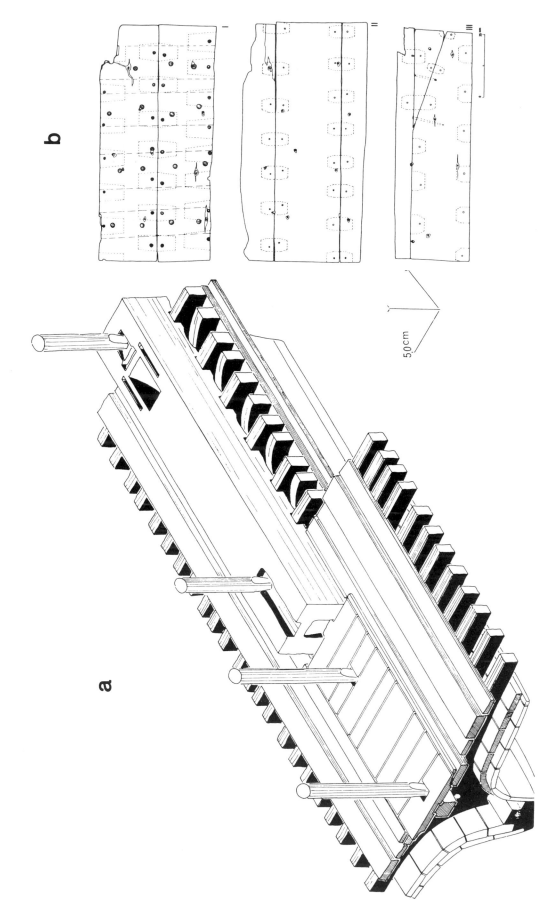

Fig. 3–50. (a) Madrague de Giens construction details in the area of the mast step; (b) planking details showing (1) outer planks, (2) inner planks, and (3) scarf details. (Pomey, 1978: pl. 40, fig. 11; courtesy Centre Camille Jullian [CNRS])

5,0 cm

rows of mortises required in extremely thick planks of single-layered hulls. Lastly, the laminating effect of a double skin should have produced a stronger hull, although the last two statements would have to be qualified with experiments to become fact. Higher labor costs would have been the major disadvantage of double planking. However, the fact that several large, double-planked hulls of this period have been found indicates that the Madrague de Giens form of construction must have been commonplace.

Mortises were 5.5–5.7 cm wide, 6 cm deep, and 0.7 cm thick in the exterior planking, and 8–8.5 cm wide, 10–12 cm deep, and 1.2–1.5 cm thick in the interior strakes. They were locked with tapered pegs and spaced about 15 cm between centers on the average (Fig. 3–50b). The framing system consisted of floor timbers alternating with paired half-frames. Frames were only about 2 cm larger on the molded sides than the Kyrenia frames and had approximately the same spacing. Every other ceiling strake, however, was quite heavy and contributed appreciably to the longitudinal strength of the hull. Frames were joined to planking with straight nails and treenails. Planking scarfs were diagonal.

Elm was used for the keel, ceiling, futtocks of floor timbers, half-frames, and interior (main) planking. Exterior planking was of fir, most futtocks were of walnut, and the mast step was shaped from a block of oak. Unlike many ancient Mediterranean ships, this one was built of a lot of hardwoods. Only the thin outer layer of planks employed a softwood. Michel Rival recently published a book on Roman ship carpentry wherein he describes the properties of various Mediterranean shipbuilding woods as well as the tools and techniques used to fabricate classical Mediterranean hulls.[27] Chapter 3 deals exclusively with the construction of the Madrague de Giens ship and introduces information and processes not discussed previously. This book is helpful to anyone interested in Roman shipbuilding.

Thus the solution to the additional strength requirements of this large hull was also concentrated primarily in the laminated, rigidly fastened outer shell of planking, although the ceiling stringers must have provided appreciable backing strength. Except for harder timber, however, framing system strength was not comparably increased over that of the Kyrenia ship, nor had a proper full-length keelson been installed to provide additional spinal support. It appears that shipwrights in the first century B.C. still considered the planking shell a primary source of hull strength, albeit to a slightly lesser extent than did the Kyrenia builder.

THE KINNERET BOAT

The Kinneret boat was excavated from the shore of Lake Kinneret (the Sea of Galilee), Israel, in 1986.[28] Tentatively dated sometime between the first century B.C. and the beginning of the second century A.D., this hull was preserved extensively (Fig. 3–51). It was removed intact

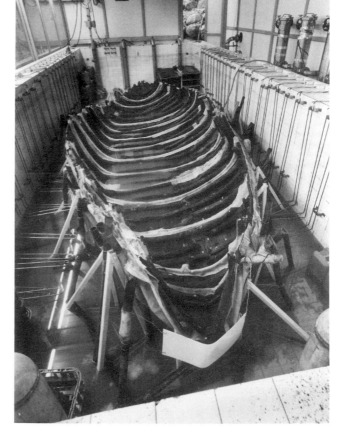

FIG. 3–51. The Kinneret boat shortly after it was lowered into its preservation tank at Kibbutz Ginosar. (photo by D. Syon; courtesy Israel Antiquities Authority)

and transported to a conservation facility, where it underwent treatment in a bath of polyethylene glycol.

The Kinneret boat was about 9 m long and had a beam of 2.5 m. Amidships it had a flat bottom, a rather hard turn of the bilge for an edge-joined vessel, and nearly straight sides (Fig. 3–52). Its maximum breadth occurred well aft of amidships, resulting in a full stern and a fine bow. The keel, which was rockered throughout, was rectangular in cross section and had no planking rabbet; the two sections were joined in a hook scarf forward of amidships.

The garboards entered the keel almost horizontally at amidships and were attached to it with mortise-and-tenon joints. Since the joints were nearly horizontal along most of the keel's length, tenon pegs were driven into the top keel surface rather than into its sides as on earlier vessels (Fig. 3–53).

Planking was installed in a rather curious pattern, one that is now believed to represent a shortage of broad timber or the use of secondhand materials (Fig. 3–54). Mortises were 5–6 cm wide, 5–7 cm deep, and 0.5 cm thick. They were locked with tapered pegs, 1–1.3 cm maximum diameter, driven from the inside of the hull.

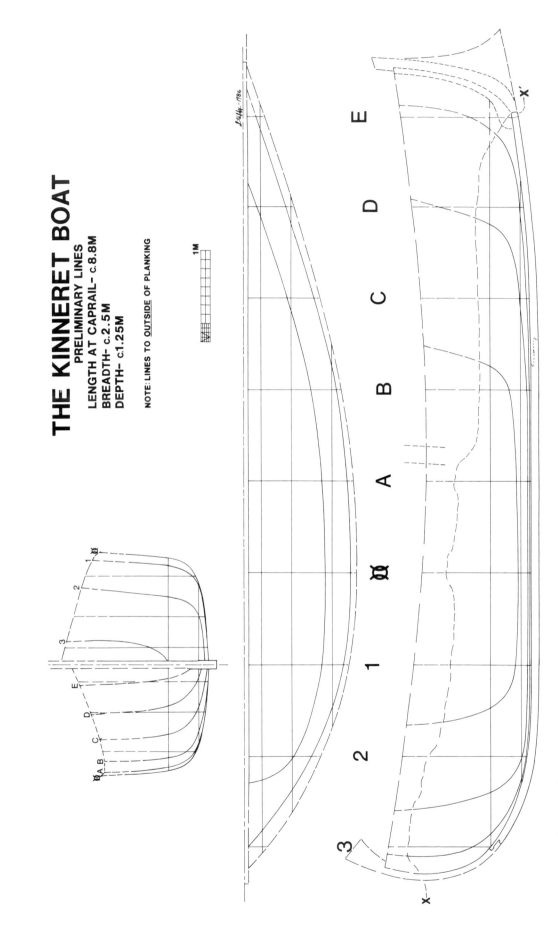

THE KINNERET BOAT
PRELIMINARY LINES
LENGTH AT CAPRAIL– c.8.8M
BREADTH– c.2.5M
DEPTH– c.1.25M

NOTE: LINES TO OUTSIDE OF PLANKING

1M

FIG. 3–52. The lines of the Kinneret boat, showing two possible stem configurations.

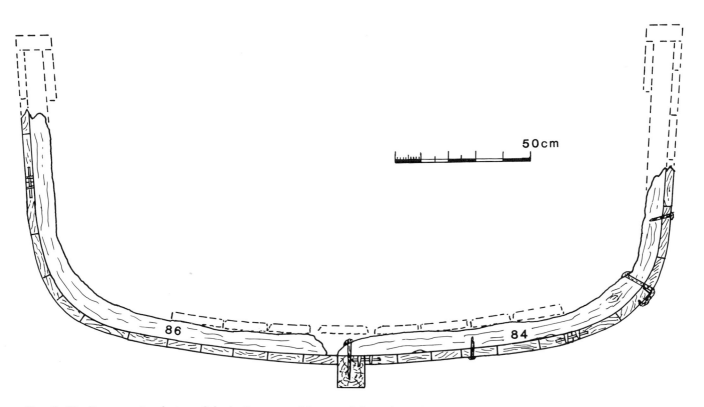

Fig. 3-53. Cross-sectional view of the hull near amidships, with hypothetical topside construction shown in dashed lines. Planking widths are approximate.

Joint spacing averaged 12 cm between centers throughout the hull (Fig. 3–55).

Frames were especially crude, with nondescript cross sections and wandering orientations (Fig. 3–54). On the average, though, they were sided 6 cm and molded 7 cm. Room and space was about 25 cm, the frames being arranged in the standard alternation of floor timbers and paired half-frames. Straight iron nails with 0.5-cm square shafts and 1.5-cm-diameter heads fastened frames to planks; they were driven straight into pilot holes without the surrounding treenails reported before.

One of the keel pieces and most of the planking were fashioned from cedar, the frames and tenons were mostly oak, and there were scattered examples of other varieties, such as hawthorne, sidder, rosebud, and jujube. Pitch covered the entire hull to prevent seepage and rot. While the quality of materials left something to be desired, the standard of workmanship was on a par with Mediterranean expertise.

This was an open boat, although small bow and stern decks were probably installed to simplify steering, store nets, and provide shelter for the crew. There were clues for a mast step just forward of amidships. Such a vessel could be sailed when the wind was favorable and rowed at other times, being used for fishing, transport, or whatever other assignment was found for it.

THE HERCULANEUM BOAT

Another boat of similar dimensions was uncovered at Herculaneum, near Naples, Italy. This one had been turned upside down, a victim of the eruption of Mount Vesuvius in A.D. 79, and now is completely carbonized.[29] In spite of its charred condition and the fact that it has not been possible to examine the hull's interior at the time this is being written, a number of details could still be determined. Figure 3–56 illustrates the in situ cross-sectional shape near amidships (now distorted). This was a lighter, more graceful, and better built boat than the one from Lake Kinneret, and more effort and expense had been invested in its aesthetics.

The keel, sided 7.2 cm and molded 6 cm, was rectangular in cross section with chamfered upper corners to seat the garboards. Planking was originally about 2 cm thick and contained mortises averaging 5.2 cm wide, 5.1 cm deep, and 0.5 cm thick. The pegged joints had average center-to-center spacings of 13 cm. No scarfs were found within the preserved after two-thirds of the hull, all planks extending either the full length of the hull or to points where they were terminated to compensate for smaller hull areas in the ends of the boat. Figure 3–56 also illustrates the complex, two-piece wale that surrounded the vessel.

The few exposed frame ends were 5 cm square. Patterns of bronze nails and treenails on the outside of the

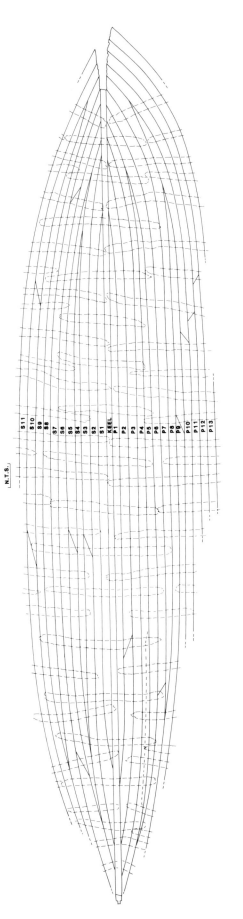

S11
S10
S9
S8
S7
S6
S5
S4
S3
S2
S1
KEEL
P1
P2
P3
P4
P5
P6
P7
P8
P9
P10
P11
P12
P13

N.T.S.

FIG. 3–54. Schematic planking and framing plan of the Kinneret boat.

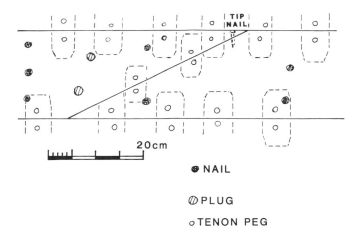

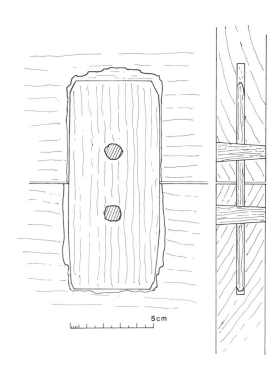

FIG. 3–55a. Mortise-and-tenon joint details of the Kinneret boat.

FIG. 3–55b. Mortise-and-tenon joint details of the Kinneret boat.

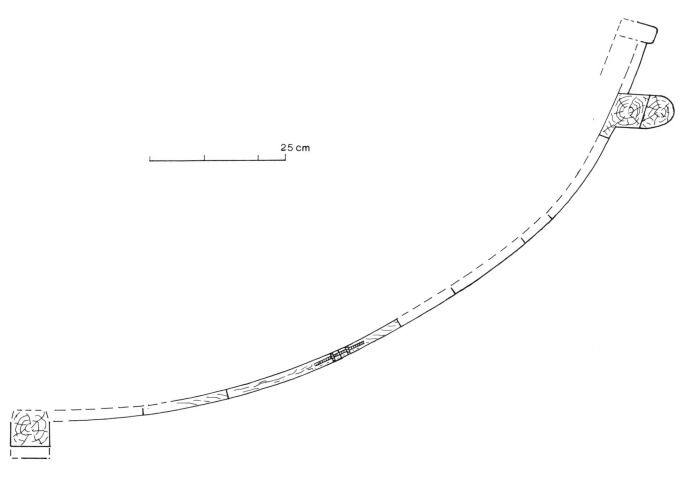

FIG. 3–56. A cross-sectional drawing of the Herculaneum boat made during excavation.

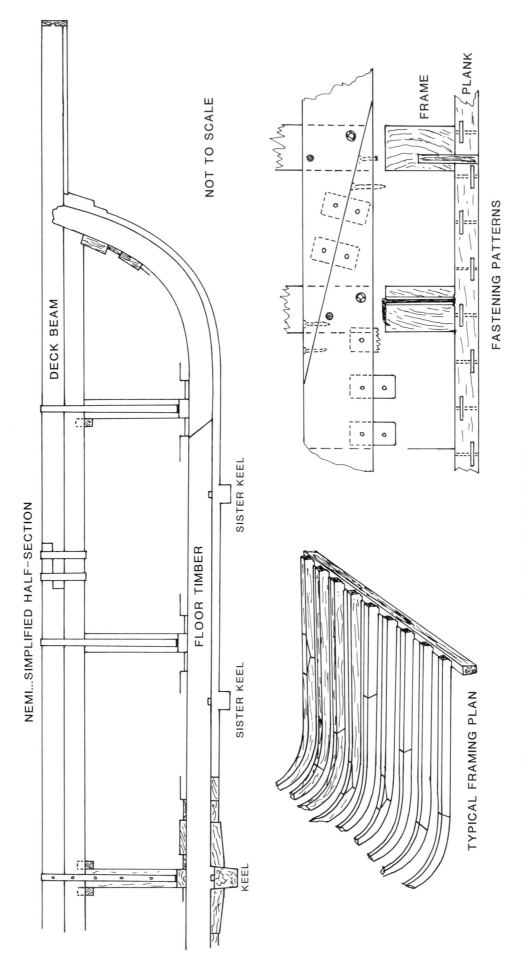

NEMI...SIMPLIFIED HALF-SECTION

DECK BEAM

FLOOR TIMBER

SISTER KEEL

SISTER KEEL

KEEL

NOT TO SCALE

FRAME

PLANK

FASTENING PATTERNS

TYPICAL FRAMING PLAN

Fig. 3–57. Construction details of the Nemi vessels. (after Ucelli, figs. 153, 155, 159, 184, 185)

hull indicated that this boat also had a system of floor timbers alternating with paired half-frames. Room and space appeared to average 24 cm. Nothing is known at present about the possibility of a sailing rig, although there are tholepins for six oars in a recessed area in the center of the hull.

THE NEMI VESSELS

A few decades before the Herculaneum boat was destroyed, magnificently appointed barges floated on Lake Nemi, north of Rome.[30] The fact that such gigantic vessels were placed on such a small lake, presumably serving as expressions of imperial grandeur, prevents us from considering them as examples of large Roman maritime or military vessels. However, their great size and complex design required exceptional expertise on the part of the people who built them, and in this light they become examples of good shipwrightery in the first half of the first century A.D.

The barges had lengths of 73 m and 71.3 m, the latter having a beam of 24 m. Figure 3–57 shows details of one of these vessels. Main keels were sided 30 cm and molded 40 cm, but the broad, flat bottoms required four smaller sister keels as well. The installation of the sister keels was actually part of the planking process. A single layer of pine planking, 10 cm thick, was pierced with mortises 10 cm wide, 10 cm deep, and spaced about 10 cm apart in staggered rows. All joints were pegged with oak. Diagonal planking scarfs were joined with mortise-and-tenon joints, and their tips were nailed. Planks and frames were secured to each other by means of clenched copper nails driven through oaken treenails. Floor timbers, sided 20 cm and molded 30 cm, were scarfed to futtocks to provide

continuous frames spaced about 50 cm apart. The Nemi hulls were sheathed in lead to the gunwales.

It has been suggested that the Nemi barges indicate changes in classical shipbuilding traditions, citing the single layer of heavy planking and the continuous frames as examples. Undoubtedly, shipbuilding traditions were improving throughout history as technology provided new methods and better materials. Interpreting those changes by comparing the Nemi barges to seagoing ships, however, is a bit like comparing improved species of apples by looking at oranges. What the Nemi vessels do indicate is the superb ability of Roman designers to produce new structures to suit specific requirements. Here the idea was to construct large and lavish vessels that would mostly remain stationary in a relatively calm freshwater lake. They did an excellent job without overbuilding.

Single layers of planking on large hulls do not necessarily indicate progress. Indeed, they coexisted with double-planked ships, as indicated by the wrecks at Antikythera and Caesarea.[31] Both of these large vessels had single layers of planking approximately equal to the combined thicknesses of the planks in the Madrague de Giens ship, and all three ships sank in the same century (Fig. 3–58). The Antikythera remains were so degraded when recorded that their value was limited to gleaning some knowledge about the frequency and form of edge joinery. The Caesarea ship was very large and had joints spaced on an average of 14 cm between centers in the 9-cm-thick plank illustrated. In this sample, mortises were about 9 cm wide and 9.5 cm deep, and their tenons fit them tightly. Note that the joints were staggered only slightly in the edge of the plank and that the tenon pegs

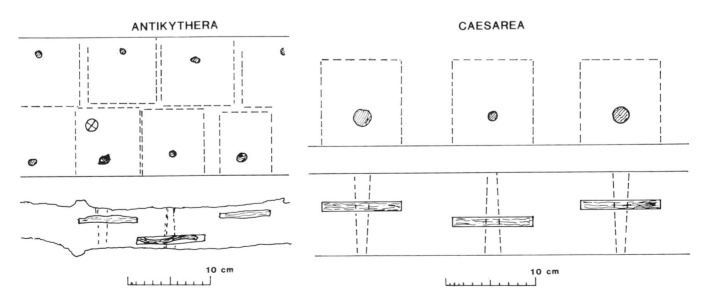

FIG. 3–58. Inner surface and edge details of planking from the Antikythera and Caesarea ships. The Antikythera plank's dimensions are now diminished due to collapse. (after Throckmorton, "The Antikythera Ship," figs. 8, 9, and information supplied by M. A. Fitzgerald)

were driven from the side of the plank closest to the joint. Single- and double-planking systems must have had their respective advantages and advocates, although much more must be learned about Greco-Roman construction before intelligent comparisons can be made.

Nor did the continuous frames signify general shipbuilding progress; alternating floors and paired half-frames would be used in Mediterranean ships for centuries to come. But the alternating framing systems mentioned previously were best suited for hulls that were subjected to the strains of constant rolling and whose depths were closer to their half-breadths. At Nemi, the demand was different, although if one looks closely, there was a form of alternating framing that was ideally suited for the wide bottoms and comparatively low sides. One type of frame was scarfed directly over the turn of the bilge (we will see this scarf again on eighteenth-century warships), while an alternating type was butted closer to the keel (see Fig. 3–57).

Why use lead sheathing on a freshwater lake? Lead sheathing, with its additional protective underlayment, would have lengthened the life of these vessels appreciably by protecting the wood against rot and whatever freshwater life might have attacked it. To date, the Kyrenia ship is the earliest hull to be found with a complete covering of lead; the Nemi barges are the latest.

WRECK 2 OF L'ANSE DES LAURONS

Space does not permit further lengthy discourse on vessels of the Roman Republican period lasting to the end of the pre-Christian era or any discussion of those from the Roman Imperial period of the next three centuries, although the reader would benefit greatly by examining reports of some of these later Roman excavations. One warrants brief mention here.

The well-preserved Laurons vessel, which was dated by coins to the end of the second century, was excavated in shallow water off the coast of southern France.[32] Figures 3–59 and 3–60 illustrate details of this small trader, whose length was about 15 m and beam about 5 m. The 16-by-20-cm keel was chamfered to receive a 4.5-cm-thick garboard. The garboard quickly thinned to 2.5 cm, the average thickness of the bottom planks. Side planking further thinned to 1.8 cm. Pegged mortise-and-tenon joints were spaced every 10 to 12 cm. Stem and sternpost were rabbeted to receive the ends of the planks.

The flat bottom, gently rounded bilge, and sloping sides of this hull presented a roomy, graceful appearance. This was an extremely well preserved wreck, complete with cambered deck beams (and a couple of large overdeck beams); 4-cm-thick, edge-joined deck planking laid in arcs opposing that of the hull sides; large hatches; removable bulwarks; and even part of the rigging. Although thin skinned, the Laurons vessel had a strong framing system, a moderately thick ceiling (3 cm), and topside construction that supplied considerable longitudinal and lateral integrity.

Northwestern European Vessels

Before ending this chapter, it is necessary to examine briefly what had transpired in northwestern Europe since the time of the Ferriby boats. Here, too, are many centuries without archaeological representation of watercraft. A few examples, all from the Roman period, follow.

COUNTY HALL

The County Hall wreck was excavated along the Thames River in London in 1910. The 12-m-long remains, which suffered from a lack of modern conservation techniques, were dated by coins and pottery to the third century A.D.[33] Constructed entirely of oak and estimated to be between 18 and 22 m long, this merchant vessel was built in the Mediterranean fashion. The keel was sided 21.5 cm and molded 16.5 cm; there was no garboard rabbet (Fig. 3–61). Two limber stringers provided longitudinal strength in lieu of a keelson. This vessel did not have the common alternating framing plan; instead, heavy floor timbers (sided 11.5 cm and molded 16.5 cm) were scarfed to futtocks on alternating sides of the vessel. Room and space was 53 cm. The garboards were 7.5 cm thick, and all other strakes were 5 cm thick. Planking scarfs were in the form of very long S-scarfs. Frames were secured to planks by means of 3.8-cm-diameter oaken treenails. Planking edges were joined by pegged mortise-and-tenon joints spaced about 15 cm apart; mortises were 12.5 cm wide and 6.25 cm deep.

BLACKFRIARS

The County Hall vessel was probably built by Mediterranean shipwrights, or at least by builders following methods initiated by the Roman occupation of Britain. A more likely candidate for direct descent from the Ferriby boats is a wreck excavated in 1963 near Blackfriars Bridge, London. This craft sank in the second century A.D. with a cargo of building stone.[34] Thought to be a sailing barge about 18 m long and 7 m in the beam, this heavy vessel was also built entirely of oak and had no keel. Instead, two central planks, 7.5 cm thick and 66 cm wide, stiffened the exterior centerline; four other planks, tapering from 7.5 cm to 5 cm in thickness on either side of the central planks, completed the bottom (Figs. 3–62a and 3–62b). The sides joined the bottom in an angular fashion, although the

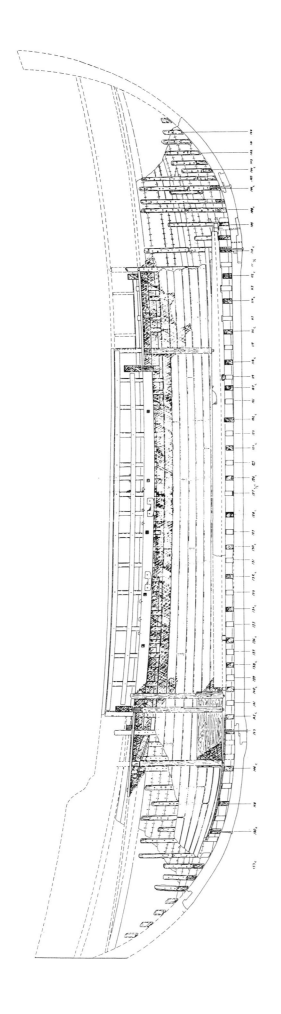
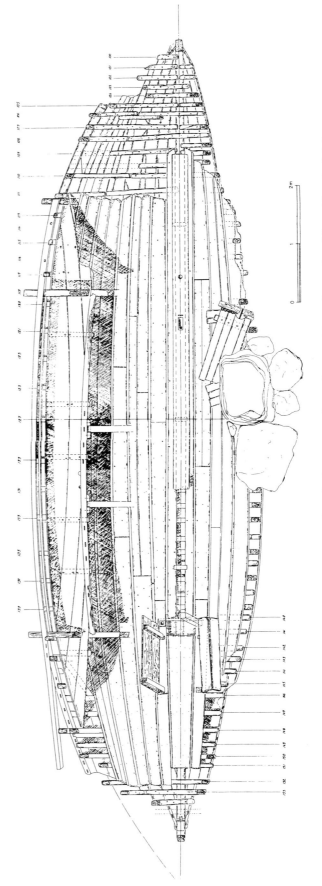

Fig. 3–59. Side and top structural views of the Laurons vessel. (Gassend et al., figs. 19, 21; drawn by Jean-Marie Gassend and Jean-Merc Joulain)

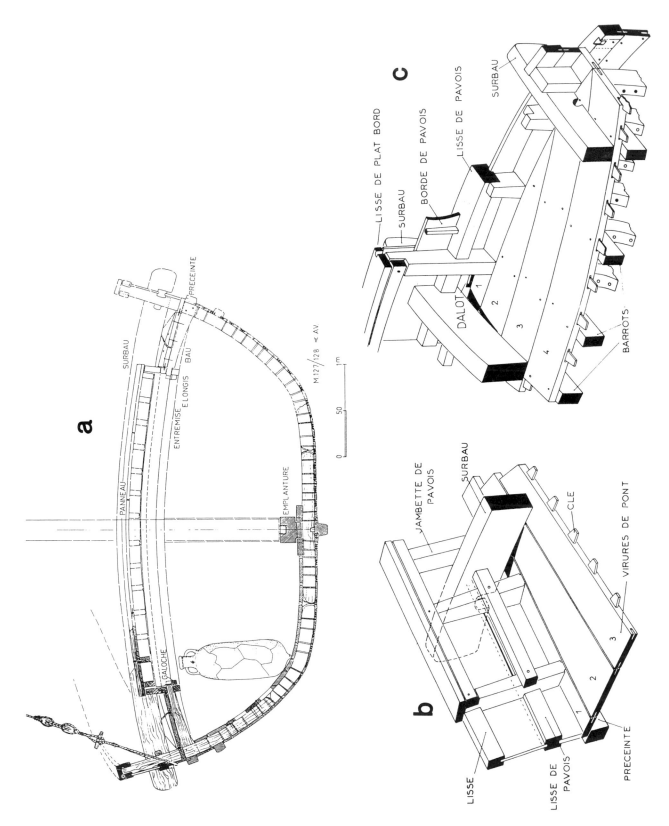

FIG. 3–60. Construction details of wreck 2 of l'anse des Laurons: (a) section at amidships, (b) and (c) deck and bulwark details. (Gassend et al.; fig. 17c, drawn by Jean-Marie Gassend and Jean-Merc Joulain; and figs. 10, 6, drawn by Jean-Marie Gassend)

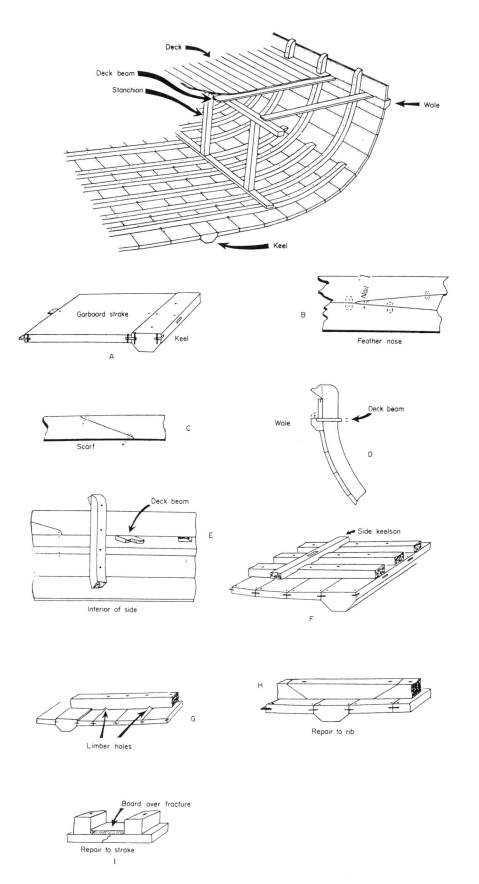

FIG. 3–61. The County Hall vessel; a sketch of the partially reconstructed hull and various structural details. Not to scale. (courtesy Peter Marsden, *IJNA* 3.1, figs. 4, 6)

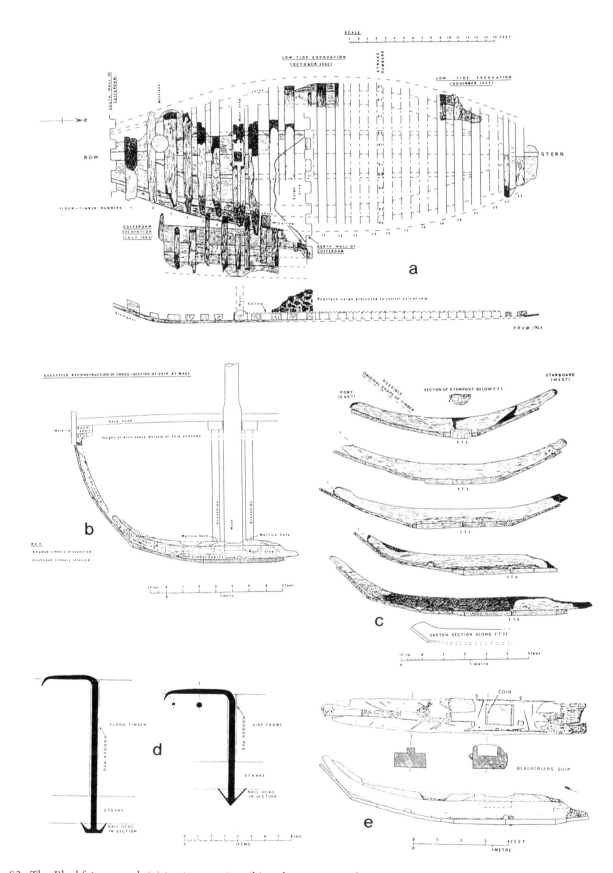

FIG. 3–62. The Blackfriars vessel: (a) *in situ* remains; (b) author's suggested reconstruction of the hull's cross-sectional shape at the mast; (c) sectional lower hull shapes at various timbers; (d) two types of nails, driven through treenails and double-clenched; (e) a broad floor timber that doubled as a mast step; a Roman coin was found in the step. (courtesy Peter Marsden, *Blackfriars*, figs. 3, 4, 5, 6, 7)

frames inside maintained a curvature that left a gap between planks and frames at this chine (Fig. 3–62c). Heavy floor timbers, sided 30 cm and molded 21.5 cm, were spaced on 20–25-cm centers. Planking was fastened to frames by means of mushroom-headed iron nails driven through oaken treenails, then clenched downward over the inner frame surfaces in herringbone fashion (Fig. 3–62d). One of these floor timbers was mortised as a mast step (Fig. 3–62e). Ceiling was nailed to the tops of the frames with iron nails. The wreck may represent an example of Celtic shipbuilding; certainly it fits Julius Caesar's description of the ships of the Veneti as being flat bottomed with heavy frames and lacking edge joinery, but fastened with large iron nails.[35]

THE MAINZ BOATS

Another Romano-British vessel with a round bottom and keel was excavated in London, but better examples of such vessels can be found at Mainz, Germany, where the remains of nine wrecks in various states of preservation were excavated recently from the banks of the Rhine River.[36] Most of these vessels date to the fourth century, and some of them appear to follow a form of construction that is similar to but more sophisticated than the Blackfriars vessel. Specific details of these craft are yet to be published, but certainly they will reveal a northern tradition and perhaps one that cannot be connected to Mediterranean influence.

In Retrospect

Some scholars believe that classical Mediterranean ships were constructed plank by plank without any form of predetermination of hull shapes, the ultimate design evolving as construction progressed. Others see complete predetermination of hull shapes, comparing construction techniques with those of latter-day sailing vessels and sometimes analyzing them as if they were modern vessels. I think the truth lies somewhere between. The Kyrenia builder did not determine frame shapes before the shapes of the planking shell evolved, nor were molds or control frames used; at least, that could not have been the case unless he were a clumsy craftsman, which was certainly not the case. The differences between port and starboard body shapes, the lateral shaping of planks, outwardly driven, tapered pegs beneath frames, and other factors all indicate that the planking shell was the initial standing structure, at least to a point above the level of the wales. Even so, one could hardly argue that this hull was constructed without any form of predetermination. The Kyrenia ship must have been a descendant of centuries of similarly constructed vessels, and so the form and methodology were already fixed in the mind of the trained ship carpenter. There was more to it than that, however. Present evidence suggests that there were not many varieties of hull types. In addition, each shipwright may have tended to specialize, or at least excel, in one specific hull form. The Kyrenia shipwright, when asked to build a vessel large enough to hold four hundred Rhodian amphoras, probably knew that required a hull of about 15 meters length, 5 meters breadth, and a bottom and sheer shaped just as it evolved. He would have known what design and dimensions were required to fit the anticipated trade routes, available materials, and period technology. That, in itself, is a form of predetermination.

Let's consider period technology for a moment. Eighteenth-century frigates were built somewhat like many large modern buildings, which have strong frameworks of steel enclosed by a skin of bricks or blocks. The Kyrenia ship was more like a large building I saw in progress last week, which had no framework at all but was composed of concrete cubicles joined together to form a strong shell, each contributing to the total strength of the structure. Strong, carefully joined planks provided a large share of the Kyrenia hull's strength, but like the new building, that strength was finally achieved by arranging the planks in such a way that the shell required a minimum of internal support. That meant a compound bottom and gently rounded bilge to the Kyrenia carpenter. And just as those concrete cubicles had to be made to predetermined dimensions so that the shape of the completed building turned out as specified, so planking widths and edge angles had to be determined with accuracy if the proper hull shapes were to be achieved. Once installed, planking rigidity must have been controlled by some means of bracing or clamping until the structure was sufficiently rigid. After the shell had reached an advanced stage of construction, however, it was by itself amazingly strong. The Kyrenia replica's unframed shell held firm as workmen walked around inside to apply preservatives or fit frames.

The Kyrenia ship is only the beginning of our story, of course. This was a period of startling progress and innovation. Iconographic and archaeological evidence both indicate a greater variety of designs as time progresses, and archaeology additionally reveals a comparable variety of materials and methods. Bottoms became flatter and hulls fuller, permitting greater hold volumes with less draft, an innovation brought about by the development of stronger internal structures. Double planking added a new dimension to the construction of large ships, while the wedding of frames to keels provided the extra strengths needed to carry larger cargoes. Keels became more rectangular, and mortises were made wider in proportion to their depths. Planking thicknesses also seem to have diminished for comparable sizes of vessels as time progressed—at least if the limited archaeological evidence can be taken seriously—and that was undoubtedly due to the stronger internal and topside construction. We also can presume that the methods of construction became more sophisticated. Perhaps in the later years of the classical period, Mediterranean shipbuilders were learning to project a few frame shapes, or more likely they were developing more accurate ways to control planking shapes, but it is almost certain that sophistication in design was accompanied by an equally sophisticated methodology. The most outstanding fact, however, is that at the end of the third century, planks were still edge-joined with frequently spaced, rigidly locked tenons. Roman shipwrights were still putting a lot of faith in the integrity of the outer shell of planking.

Not so with northern builders. Frames may have preceded planks on some of the Mainz boats and perhaps on parts of the Blackfriars vessel as well. Whatever the sequence of construction, the outer shell of planking, especially the side planking, was little more than a watertight skin stretched over heavy oaken frames. One of the great challenges facing ancient ship scholars is to discover the methods used to project and control early hull shapes of both regions.

4

MEDIEVAL VESSELS

Early in the eleventh century, in the same part of the world where the Kyrenia ship was built, a master shipwright supervised the launching of a little freighter. At first glance, it resembled the Kyrenia ship—it was about the same length, it was built of pine, and its ends curved upward sharply in caïque fashion. Closer examination, however, revealed some striking differences. The hull was much fuller, with a flat bottom and sharp bilges. There was an apron, a heavy keelson, and an inner sternpost, and some of the ceiling planks ran transversely across the hold. But the most important departures could have been apparent only if one had witnessed the construction process. Some of the frames were erected before any of the planking was installed, and there were no mortise-and-tenon joints in any of the planking edges.

We know this because some years later, about A.D. 1025, the little merchantman sank with a primary cargo of glass cullet in a remote cove now known as Serçe Limani (Sparrow Harbor) on the southern coast of Turkey. The wreck was excavated in 1977–79 by the Institute of

Nautical Archaeology under the direction of Dr. George F. Bass, and its cargo and artifacts provided a marvelous study of medieval trade and shipboard life in the eastern Mediterranean.[1] But the hull remains of that wreck are most important for our purposes, because this little vessel has proved to be a valuable vehicle in determining some of the ways in which Mediterranean shipwrights changed from classical forms of construction to the more modern processes of erecting frames first and then fastening the planking to them without the aid of edge joinery.

Only 20 percent of the original Serçe Limani hull survived, but even that amount of preservation was deemed important enough to raise it, preserve it in polyethylene glycol, and reassemble the fragments in the medieval castle at Bodrum, Turkey, for further study and for the benefit of interested visitors.[2] Parts of the recording and reconstruction processes are discussed in later chapters. The results of our discoveries will be presented below, but first we must evaluate briefly what went on before the time of our glass carrier.

The Yassi Ada Vessels

There is an island just off the Aegean coast of Turkey called Yassi Ada (Flat Island), a bleak little rock that seems to have no other purpose than to get in the way of passing ships. At its western tip is a long, submerged reef that spelled doom to a number of vessels that passed too close. We are interested in only two of them. The first, which sank there in the fourth century A.D., had the same alternating floor and half-frame pattern commonly found in the framing patterns of earlier vessels discussed in the previous chapter.[3] Its 4.2-cm-thick planks were joined into strakes by means of S-scarfs that reached lengths as great as 2.3 m. Nothing more will be said about this little

merchantman except to take note of its edge joinery. Mortise-and-tenon joints were smaller, more loosely fitted, and more widely spaced than those of comparably sized vessels discussed in the last chapter. Mortises were, with few exceptions, 5–5.5 cm deep, 7–9 cm wide at the seams and much more narrow at their bottoms, and 0.7 cm thick (Fig. 4–1). Tenons were smaller than the mortises, normally about 8.5 cm long and 4.5 cm wide at the seams, although thicknesses were approximately the same as that of the mortises. Pegs had a maximum diameter of 1.1 cm at inner planking surfaces and tapered to external diameters of 0.7–0.9 cm. Spacing was greater than that of the earlier

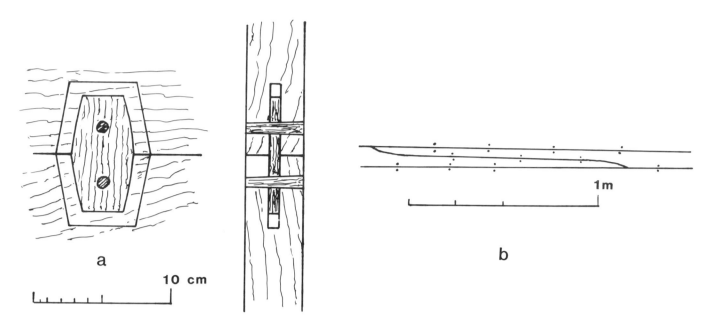

FIG. 4–1. Details of the fourth-century Yassi Ada vessel: (a) side and cross-sectional views of a typical mortise-and-tenon joint and (b) scarf and joint-spacing details. (after van Doorninck, *IJNA* 5.2, figs. 6, 1)

ships, too; in heavy concentrations of scarfs, where planking was relatively weak, joints were spaced 15 to 20 cm between centers, elsewhere as much as 32 cm.

THE SEVENTH-CENTURY YASSI ADA VESSEL

About A.D. 625, a 20-m-long Byzantine wine carrier hit the same reef and settled next to the fourth-century vessel. This wreck, excavated in 1961–64 under the direction of Professor Bass, deserves closer scrutiny; by the time this ship was built, nearly a millennium after the Kyrenia ship was launched, hull construction had changed radically.[4] The vessel's lines are reproduced in Figure 4–2; a construction section can be seen in Figure 4–3.

The Yassi Ada Byzantine hull was so sparsely preserved that the exact construction sequence remains in doubt. However, experimentation with a series of models and years of research have prompted us to suggest the following method of hull fabrication. A keel of cypress, sided 22 cm and molded 35.5 cm, was joined to stem and stern posts with short scarfs at the ends of the hold. Garboards of pine, 4.2 cm thick, were essentially held in the keel rabbet with nails; mortise-and-tenon joints were spaced no closer than 2.25 m between centers here. Pine bottom planking, 3.5 cm thick, was edge-joined with small and widely spaced mortise-and-tenon joints. Mortises were only 3.5 cm deep, 0.5 cm thick, and 5 cm wide at the seams, tapering appreciably toward their inner ends. Tenons, made of white oak, were about as long as the combined mortise depths but only 3 cm wide at the seams. They were not pegged (Fig. 4–4). Center-to-center spacing of joints was 35–50 cm in the stern area and as much as 90 cm in the middle of the hull. These joints served only

to align the planks until the planks could be secured to frames; joint placement apparently varied according to the tensions produced by longitudinal planking curvatures.

The first five or six bottom strakes were shaped, fitted, and aligned with mortise-and-tenon joints. Probably at this time the first floor timbers were installed, their arms extending not much farther than the planking just erected (Fig. 4–5a). All frames were made of elm and were, on the average, 14 cm square. Planking then continued to the turn of the bilge, about the tenth strake, when the longer-armed floor timbers were inserted (Fig. 4–5b). Next the turn of the bilge and the lower sides were planked up to, and including, the sixteenth strake, which was the approximate light-load waterline. In addition to the alignment provided by the mortise-and-tenon joints, each belt of planking probably had to be braced or cleated to maintain its shape until the frames were fitted permanently. Planking was simply nailed to the frames with iron nails that did not extend through the frames (Fig. 4–6a). There were no treenails or clenched nails below the wales.

Perhaps some of the half-frames were fitted as the bilge was being planked; certainly all half-frames and most of the futtocks were installed after the sixteenth strake was in place (Fig. 4–5c). Mortises were not cut into the upper edge of strake 16, nor was strake 17 fitted to it immediately. Instead, the next step was to shape and fit the lowest wale to its desired sweep and curvature. The wales were really half-logs, roughly 20 cm in diameter and made from cypress, their edges cut flat to fit against adjoining strakes. They were at first fastened to standing frames at wide intervals by driving iron nails outward through the frames

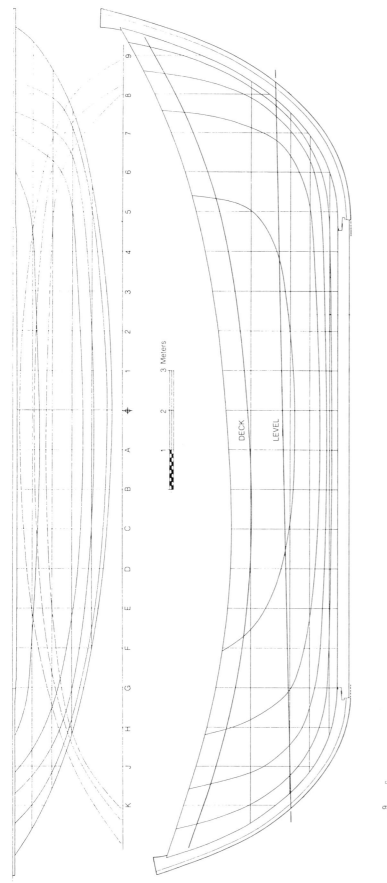

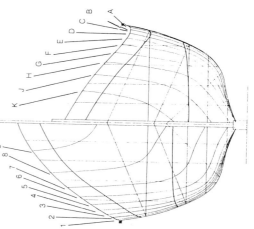

FIG. 4–2. The lines of the seventh-century Yassi Ada merchantman. The reconstruction is largely hypothetical, based on a 10 percent hull survival. (tracing and details by Susan Womer Katzev)

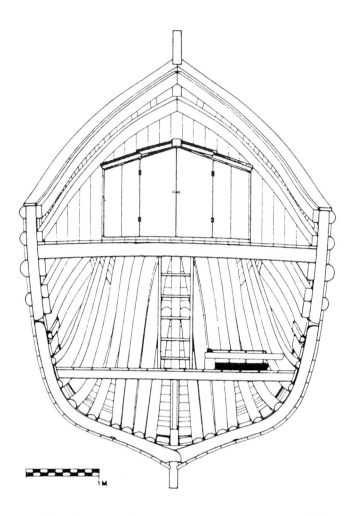

FIG. 4–3. A cross-section of the seventh-century Yassi Ada hull at the after end of the hold. (tracing and details by Susan Womer Katzev)

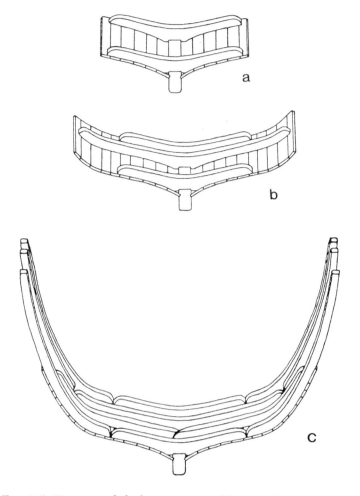

FIG. 4–5. Framing and planking sequence of the seventh-century Yassi Ada hull's assembly. (courtesy F. H. van Doorinck, *IJNA* 5.2, fig. 13)

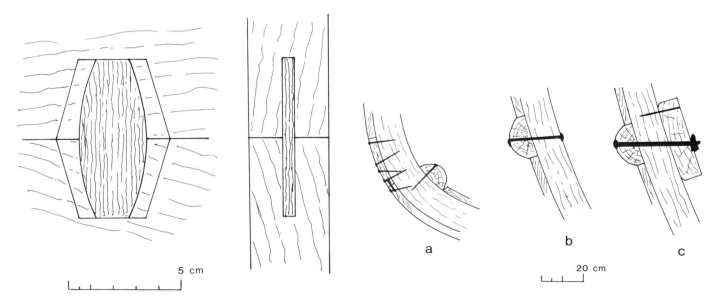

5 cm

FIG. 4–4. A typical mortise-and-tenon joint from the seventh-century Yassi Ada vessel—side and sectional views.

20 cm

FIG. 4–6. Typical fastening patterns of the Yassi Ada hull: (a) plank-to-frame; (b) initial attachment of wales by means of a clenched nail; (c) forelock bolting of frame and wales.

and wales and clenching the nail ends over the outer surfaces of the wales (Fig. 4–6b). After the first two wales were erected, all remaining futtocks and top timbers were fitted. Along with previously unfastened half-frames and futtocks, they were nailed to the wales with straight nails that did not pass completely through the wales. Later the wales were backed with clamps and both were bolted to every fourth or fifth frame with forelock bolts (Fig. 4–6c), so that virtually every frame was bolted to a wale. Each of the four wales was installed in succession. Then the spaces between them and between the lower wale and strake

sixteen were closed with 3.5 cm thick planks. There were no mortise-and-tenon joints above the 15-16 seam; here the planks and wales were fastened directly to standing frames.

At some intermediate stage, perhaps as soon as the floor timbers were in place, a keelson and some of the ceiling timbers were fitted and fastened (Figs. 4–3 and 4–7). The ceiling was mostly composed of rough half-logs made from cypress. The deck beams, especially the through-beams, must have been erected after the second wale was in place. The rest of the construction sequence is completely hypothetical.

Transitions in Construction

Now it is time to ponder what has been said so far about Mediterranean vessels. From the limited evidence available to us, it would seem that most of the strength of Bronze Age watercraft was vested in their shells of outer planking. Planking was thick, sometimes carved to shape, and its seams were reinforced with mortise-and-tenon joints that were locked with pegs, at least by the late Bronze Age. Frames and other internal structures were

relatively weak and undeveloped. Papyriform shapes of funerary vessels and contemporary illustrations suggest that keels were not utilized by the ancient Egyptians. That does not necessarily indicate, however, that other societies had not used keels quite early. The fourteenth-century B.C. Ulu Burun wreck appears to have a keel or thick central plank, but whether it served a true spinal function is as yet unknown. Indeed, even the fourth-

FIG. 4–7. An interior view of the author's reconstruction model of the seventh-century Yassi Ada vessel. (photo by Bobbe Clinton Baker)

century B.C. Kyrenia ship's keel did not serve that purpose fully, since it was not connected directly to the
framing system. That keel merely served as the keystone
of the inverted arch of planking (it even looked like a keystone in cross-section), and obviously its major role was to
connect the two hull sides. The Kyrenia ship's backbone
strength came from the rockered, chock-reinforced
trough above the keel, but the fact that the vessel split
along a line between the bottom of the chocks and the
top of the keel after it sank indicates this was still the
weakest area of the hull.

The Kyrenia ship's framework, with its strong bonding
of clenched nails, added a lot of strength, but the rest of the
internal structure contributed next to nothing. The planking shell was still the primary structure, and its major features were its strong system of edge joinery (Fig. 4–8a) and
the expeditious use of hull shapes for added strength. This
was a much more efficient planking shell than that of the
Bronze Age vessels, because it was lighter, stronger, and
better fastened.

A few centuries later, the first-century B.C. Madrague
de Giens freighter's double layer of planking revealed that
comparatively sophisticated methods were available to
build very large and strong seagoing ships. I believe that in
this century and the next, the expertise in building strong
shells and efficient systems of edge joinery reached its
peak. Two and a half centuries of progress were also evident in the form of a strong keel that was partially connected to the framing system, as well as an elongated mast
step and heavy ceiling that surely contributed additional
longitudinal support.

Throughout the remainder of the Roman period there
were improvements in design and structure, and hulls
probably became increasingly structurally efficient. But
much of this added efficiency was vested in innovations
and additions to the overall structure, not to the systems
of edge joinery. If the fourth-century Yassi Ada vessel is

representative of Mediterranean shipbuilding at that time,
then the strength of mortise-and-tenon joint systems was
being replaced with better framing, keelsons, ceiling, and
deck structures (Fig. 4–8b). By the beginning of the
seventh century, mortise-and-tenon joints no longer contributed measurable integrity to the hull structure. The
major sources of strength were provided by the backbone,
internal, and topside construction (Fig. 4–8c).

The progression just described may not represent the
exact sequence of structural transition for all of the Mediterranean area, although there are good parallels for all
periods; wrecks such as St. Gervais and Pantano Longarini
seem to support the idea that the use of mortise-and-tenon
joints declined in the early Byzantine period.[5] But in spite
of all the excavations now published for the classical and
early medieval periods in the Mediterranean, we still do
not know exactly how shipbuilders arrived at designs for
large hulls, such as the Athlit warship or the Madrague de
Giens merchantman, nor do we understand precisely how
they controlled hull shapes during construction. We can
be sure, however, that mortise-and-tenon joints played a
major role in this transition. If we are to understand the
workings of Greek and Roman shipbuilders, we must consider those joints more carefully. Certainly they made a
major contribution to overall hull strength in the earlier
periods when internal structures were weaker, and they
played a lesser role in the later periods as other hull components were improved. Whether or not some ancient
builders erected a few frames before planks is still an
unproven issue, but it is not such an important issue as
some scholars would lead us to believe. Most important is
the implication that ancient and early medieval Mediterranean builders could not build ships without placing
tenons or lashings in planking edges. From that, one infers
that they at least partially (I would prefer to say primarily)
relied on planks, rather than frames, to acquire and maintain the shapes of their hulls. The issue, then, is not so
much when shipwrights learned to predetermine frame
shapes as it is when they learned to predetermine them so
that frames alone could control hull shapes.

To answer that question we should first ask another.
Why was it necessary to change from shell-first to frame-
first forms of construction—what was wrong with the system as it existed in any period? For that answer we must
first recall a statement I made in an earlier chapter: a ship
was merely a conveyance, a means of getting someone or
something to a desired destination. Completed vessels, not
construction techniques, were the goal. Shipbuilders of all
periods were obliged to build their vessels as quickly and
cheaply as possible so that those vessels could be used to
fulfill their intended assignments. Quickly and cheaply,
however, meant different things in different periods.
Bronze Age and early Iron Age builders did not comprehend efficient internal hull structures, and so they invested a lot of time in sculpting planks and fashioning edge
joinery. But what they did was neither primitive nor

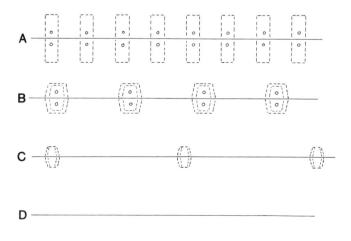

FIG. 4–8. Transitions in mortise-and-tenon joinery: (a) the
Kyrenia ship; (b) the fourth-century Yassi Ada vessel; (c) the
seventh-century Yassi Ada ship; (d) the Serçe Limani vessel.

inefficient. They were very much in step with their time, using the best tools, materials, and technology available to them.

Of all the shipwrecks with which I was associated, the Kyrenia ship impressed me most. What impressed me was its sophistication, which reflects the fact that its builders—people of the fourth century B.C.—knew quite a bit about such things as hull resistance, stability, and structural integrity. It is inaccurate to say that the Kyrenia builders could not predetermine hull shapes—they could and they did. Granted, they did not determine them geometrically in the modern sense, and it does not appear that they even considered cross-sectional shapes directly. It seems more likely that they thought of their hull in terms of longitudinal shapes; they were aware that by carefully controlling the longitudinal shapes of the planks they would arrive at the desired transverse curvatures. They were masters at shaping those planks and at wedding them with just the right system of mortise-and-tenon joinery to produce a strong, efficient outer hull structure. It is true that the resulting hull was labor intensive and rather wasteful of materials, but that also was a sign of the times. Labor does not seem to have been the dominating factor that it was in the later periods, and their frugality concerning materials probably surfaced in a form we have yet to recognize. The point to remember is that the ships of the Greeks and Romans were built so well that they were vitally important to the peoples' commerce, protection, and military expansion, and thus the ships were very much attuned to their times.

Probably there never was an ancient or early medieval shipwright who wished he could shape frames geometrically so that he could set them up before the planks and eliminate mortise-and-tenon joints. That was never a goal; rather, it was a natural result of millennia of shipbuilding progress wherein each generation progressed steadily by building vessels that best utilized the technology, materials, and other controlling parameters of the period. The demise of edge joinery and the introduction

of standing frames were fruits of that progression. And they did not evolve suddenly in the medieval period; they were in the making since the first human pushed away from shore.

Thus the seventh-century Yassi Ada ship is yet another example of that steady transition from logs and thick planks to modern steel freighters. But seventh-century Byzantium presented quite a different set of demands on its shipbuilders than did Greece and Rome. Technology had progressed, but more importantly economics and politics had changed so radically as to require a different shipbuilding philosophy. Shipowners were often independent businessmen with limited assets operating under what amounted to a free enterprise system.[6] The decline of slavery had changed the labor market, too, so that time-consuming processes, such as cutting deep and frequent edge joints and meticulous shaping of planks, became even less desirable. These owners needed floating cargo containers that required even less labor and more efficient use of materials than in the past. The Yassi Ada builders at least partially solved those problems with straight nailing, a strong internal structure, the use of half-logs for wales and ceiling to save time and timber, and a system of construction that relied on an almost simultaneous installation of planks and frames. Weak and widely spaced joints played a lesser role in hull shaping and contributed little or no structural strength. And after they had rounded the bilge, these shipwrights had already solved the problem of nailing planks directly to standing frames in this less complex part of the hull.

That brings us back to the Serçe Limani vessel, which had no edge joinery at all (Fig. 4–8d). It does not mean that these builders had solved the problem completely, however. They only took it one step further, so that mortise-and-tenon joints were no longer needed. But planks, or perhaps battens or ribbands used in their place, were still employed to project some of the hull shapes, as they would for several more centuries and even, in some parts of the world, to the present day.

The Serçe Limani Vessel[7]

The millennium of progress between the launchings of the Kyrenia and Serçe Limani merchantmen was evident in an initial view of the shipyard. There were still piles of pine logs—the vessel would be made entirely of pine with the exception of an elm keel—but more of the logs were straight, and there were dozens of large knees (trunks with large branches still attached). A smith was forging nails and bolts from iron instead of copper. There were more and larger saws and a smaller variety of adzes, the little mortising chisels were gone completely, and most importantly, there were now relatively sophisticated measuring devices. Let's begin with them.

Units of measurement, too prevalent to be coincidental, were detected during the study of these hull remains. They were evident in the scantlings of nearly all timbers and in the proportions of the hull, so much so that in later phases of research the metric system was abandoned and work was done exclusively with our newly developed scales. A 16-cm increment, perhaps representing a handspan or an inaccurate proportion of the Byzantine foot, was called a *unit* for our purposes. On our scale it was halved several times, as we assume the shipwright had done on his measuring stick or ell, and multiplied by four to produce a convenient larger increment, 64 cm,

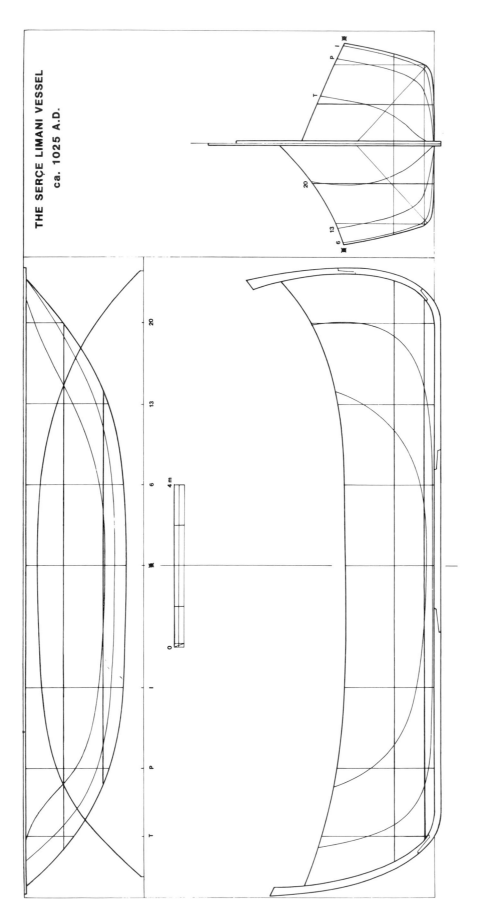

THE SERÇE LIMANI VESSEL
ca. 1025 A.D.

Fig. 4–9. Preliminary lines of the Serçe Limani vessel. (drawing by Claire Peachey)

which we called a *quaternary,* or *quat* for brevity. Thus the keel was molded 1 unit and sided ¾ unit; these were also the average frame dimensions. The keelson had twice the cross-sectional area of the keel. Planks were ¼ unit thick where they were not dubbed, and the main wale was cut about 1 unit thick and broad before being trimmed. Our reconstruction indicates that the ship was about 24 quats (15.36 m) long overall, had a molded beam of 8 quats (5.12 m), and had a breadth of floor of 5 quats (3.2 m), while its hold was 2 ½ quats (1.6 m) deep at amidships.

The lines of the Serçe Limani vessel are shown in Figure 4–9; a sectional view of the construction can be seen in Figure 4–10. First the keel was laid. It was composed of three pieces of elm, two of which curved upward at their ends to meet the scarfs of the posts (Fig. 4–11). Then a two-piece sternpost, and probably the inner sternpost, apron, and stem (for which only nailing patterns and other indirect evidence survived), were attached. There was no false keel.

Next the exact center of the keel was located and marked, and 2 units forward of this point another mark

was made. These were to be the locations of the only standing full frames, which are designated as ⊗ and A. If the shipwright had built several of these hulls before, he might have started shaping the frames with the use of an ell or even from memory. At some point, however, these frame shapes were predetermined by a very simple form of logic that I reconstruct as follows. The bottom had no lateral curvature within the limits of the hold, and the lowest meter or so of the sides was also straight, so that both bottom and lower sides could be represented by straight lines. The bottom had very little deadrise in the midships area, while except in the bow and stern, the sides made a constant angle of about 72° with the horizontal plane; this angle was easily determined by connecting the ends of a base of 1 unit and a side of 3 units.

To arrive at the frame shapes, then, our builder needed only to draw two straight lines that were joined at a constant angle to the horizontal plane. The resultant hard chine was softened by connecting the two sides with an arc (see Fig. 4–12). It was never a true arc, however, and although these curves are difficult to interpret because of subsequent dubbing for seating the planks, it

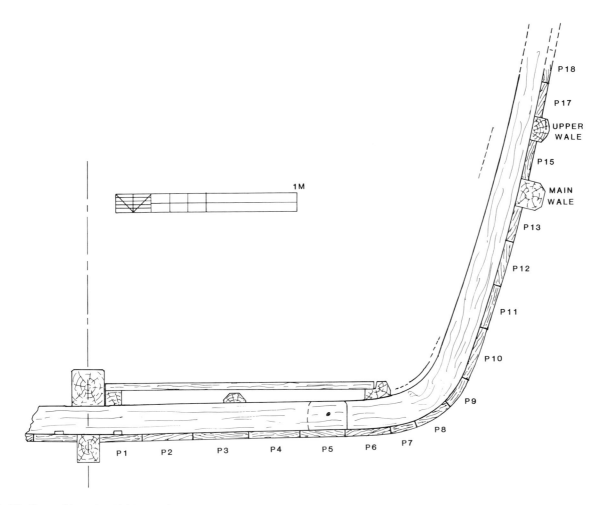

FIG. 4–10. Serçe Limani midship section.

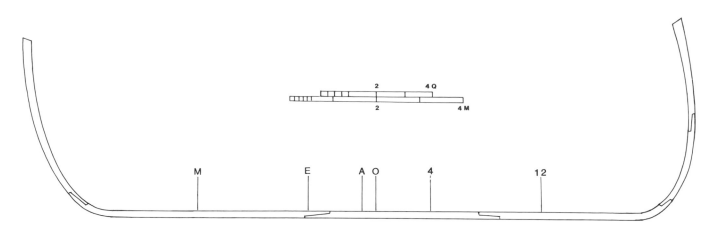

FIG. 4–11. The keel and posts, with predetermined frame locations.

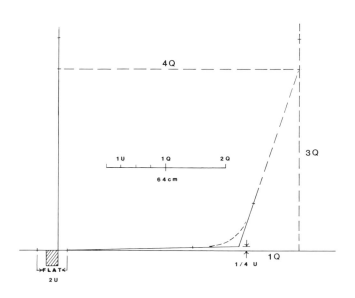

FIG. 4–12. Midship frame projection.

appears that the angle was simply rounded between points located about 2 units on either side of the intersection of the side and bottom lines. The midship frames (there was a pair of them, ⊗ and A) were given a floor length of 3 quats (1.92 m) from the side of the keel (all dimensions seem to have been taken from the sides of the keel, rather than from its centerline) and a deadrise of only ¼ unit (4 cm) at their ends (Fig. 4–12). Note that there was a 32-cm-wide bottom flat over the keel, the deadrise beginning one unit on either side of the keel centerline; it was at the ends of these central flats that the limber holes were cut. The sides angled upward as shown, but they only had to be projected for a distance of a meter or so for reasons to be described later.

After the shape of the midship frames had been determined, it was time to make the standing frames. Twelve nearly identical logs, each at least 5 quats (3.2 m) long with branches angling away at 70° or so, were selected for the ten standing frames and cut as in Figure 4–13. After midship floor timbers ⊗ and A were sawn roughly to shape,

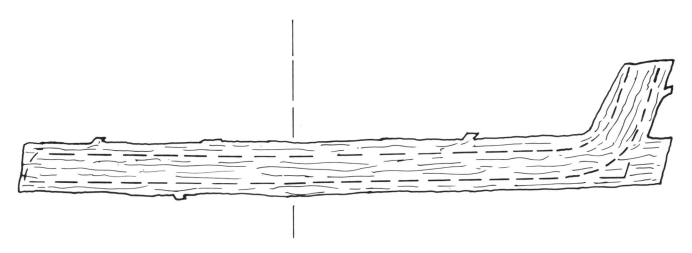

FIG. 4–13. Method of shaping a floor timber from a log.

their upward-angled arms were cut off about 1 quat above the baseline, and futtocks were scarfed and nailed to them. Next, logs that were shaped similarly to the floor timbers were cut, scarfed, and nailed to the long arms of floor timbers ⊗ and A as opposite futtocks (Fig. 4–14). The camber and height of the sides amidships have been projected from existing construction further aft, since the upper sides were not preserved amidships. If our projections are accurate, then these futtocks extended upward about 3½ quats (2.24 m), and the frame was 8 quats (5.12 m) wide at the top.

A cross-spawl was probably added to maintain the upper frame shape, surfaces and edges were trimmed and beveled, limber holes were cut, and the two frames were leveled and nailed to the keel with iron nails having 1-cm-square shafts and 2.5-cm-diameter heads. Floor timber ⊗ was mounted with its long arm to port and floor timber A with its long arm to starboard. Approximately 2 quats aft of frame ⊗ and two quats forward of frame A another pair of floor timbers, 4 and E, were nailed to the keel with their longest arms in the same alternate directions as ⊗ and A. Both these floor timbers were similar to the midship floors, but they had an additional deadrise of 2 cm at the bilge and a narrowing of 2 cm throughout. Between frames ⊗ and 4 another floor timber, frame 2, was installed with its long arm to port; between A and E, frame C was nailed to the keel with its long arm to starboard. Floor timbers 3, 1, B, and D were then nailed to the keel with their long arms in opposite directions to their neighbors (Fig. 4–15).

Now there were two full frames and eight floor timbers fastened rigidly to the keel, and careful examination of the hull remains indicated this was all the standing framework that was in place before planking began. The ten standing frames spanned only the central 2.7 m of the hull. However, although the evidence is limited to only a few nails, tool marks, and surface impressions, I suspect our builder determined at least one more pair of hull shapes before or during the planking process. Their locations and shapes are shown in Figures 4–11 and 4–16 and are located 4 quats aft of frame 4 and a similar distance forward of frame E, about half the distance between the standing frames and the posts. Toward the bow, frame M rises and narrows 1 unit more than frame E; toward the stern, where the hull diminishes more rapidly, frame 12 has an increased deadrise of 1½ units and a narrowing of 2 units. It is doubtful that frames M and 12 were installed initially. Rather, I believe there was a platform or braced cleat erected at some time during construction to support bottom planking, as shown in Figure 4–15. Nail head impressions on inner planking surfaces beneath frames attest to the fact that outer cleats were employed in a number of locations to hold the strakes firm until all the frames were in place.

Next the bottom was planked with five broad strakes. The planks were merely nailed to the floor timbers at first, treenails being added either later in the construction sequence or, more likely, during an overhaul when some of the planking was replaced. Like his predecessors, our shipwright still had trouble planking the turn of the bilge and postponed it until at least some of the side strakes were in place. The installation of strake 10, the lowest side strake, followed the planking of the bottom, and then framing and side planking progressed

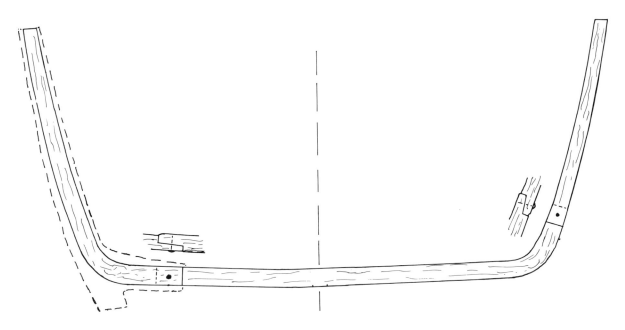

FIG. 4–14. Full midship frame assembly on the Serçe Limani vessel.

FIG. 4–15. The ten standing frames of the Serçe Limani reconstruction model. (model and photo by Frederick M. Hocker)

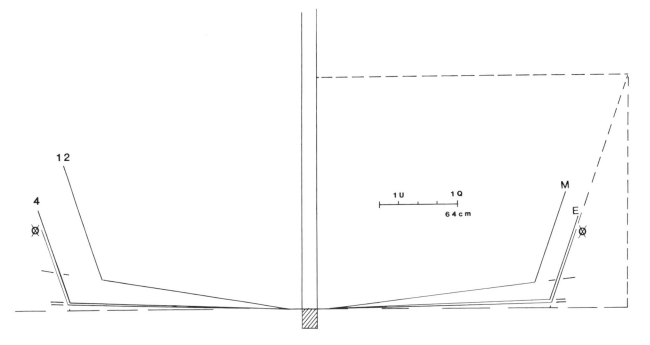

FIG. 4–16. Projections of six predetermined stations.

almost simultaneously. It seems logical that all the frames were in place before the wales and upper side planks were added. At some point after side planking began, the open area between the bottom and sides was covered with an odd configuration of strakes, at least three of which did not run the full length of the hull. When planking was completed, the external skin was covered with a liberal coating of a mixture of pitch and grass; it was even forced into open seams.

After all the floor timbers were in place, the keelson was bolted between the frames and through the keel at irregular intervals with 2-cm-diameter forelock bolts similar to those used on the seventh-century Yassi Ada vessel. Then stringers were added to the floor of the hold, on which removable transverse ceiling was placed. The purpose of this type of ceiling has yet to be determined. Next came the side ceiling, clamps, and deck beams; beyond that, there was not even fragmentary survival.

The Serçe Limani vessel was steered with a pair of quarter rudders and propelled by two lateen sails that must have closely resembled those in Figure 4–17.[8] It was probably a common type of seagoing vessel referred to in the Cairo Geniza—a collection of documents written in Judaeo-Arabic and dating primarily between the eleventh and thirteenth centuries—as a *qarib;* in Greek it was known as a *karabos.* [9] Such vessels often sailed in convoys, sometimes in company with larger ships. They occasionally served as consorts, or "maidservants," offloading freight and delivering it to shallow water ports where the big ships could not navigate. In most cases, however, they operated as independent freighters and were said to be capable of making long voyages and carrying heavy loads.[10]

Thus, four hundred years after the Yassi Ada Byzantine vessel was laid down, there was no edge-joined planking in at least one type of vessel; probably that was the case for all but a few local types. Planking below the waterline was now merely a watertight skin; it added little to the strength of the hull. More importantly, transverse hull shapes were controlled by frames rather than planks. There was a recognizable system of mensuration, and at least an elementary form of geometric projection was used

to derive some of those shapes. But this method did not begin in the eleventh century; it was too sophisticated for that. Probably these simple body shapes and rising and narrowing lines originated a few centuries before. Indeed, had the later Yassi Ada hull survived more extensively, we may have seen signs of its origins in that construction.

One of the advantages of predetermining frame shapes and erecting them before the planks was greater design flexibility. The hard bilge would have been difficult, if not impossible, to accomplish by the shell-first method unless the planking were much thicker and the fullness at the ends of the hold compromised. In other words, the Serçe Limani builder was able to produce a hold that was almost boxlike and, therefore, had a much greater cargo capacity than the similarly sized Kyrenia hull. Probably, too, it was built faster and at a lower cost.

The Cairo Geniza mentions numerous types of eleventh-century vessels, ranging from small river craft to very large ships. The largest ships were known in Arabic as *qunbārs,* which must have been similar to the Byzantine *kombarion* and the Venetian *gombaria.* [11] No known archaeological evidence exists for these big freight and passenger carriers, nor does the contemporary literature provide structural details for them, but it is safe to assume that their builders would have used somewhat different design methods and construction techniques than those employed by the Serçe Limani shipwright. It is unfortunate that so few medieval wrecks have been excavated in the Mediterranean, because the developments in design and construction in this period must have been extremely interesting. Contemporary iconography and literature provide tantalizing generalities about vessels that obviously represented constant improvements in design and construction. Galleys, round ships, and numerous types of small craft haunt us with obscure hints of structural uniqueness and complexity, an ever-changing parade of technological progress. For the moment, however, our curiosity about details can be only partially satisfied by the limited information from a couple of Venetian wrecks in the Po Delta and some interesting archival information, all from late in the period. Beyond that, we can only hope for an abundance of forthcoming archaeological discoveries.

The Po Delta Wrecks

THE FIRST CONTARINA SHIP

In 1898, while digging a canal at Rovigo, Italy, workmen uncovered the remains of two extensively preserved vessels. Marco Bonino has provided us with some interesting observations on these vessels and relates them to contemporary illustrations and documents.[12] We will consider only the oldest and best preserved hull, which has been dated to about 1300. Few objects were found in association with the remains. The bottom of the hull was well preserved, while the starboard side survived to just

above the turn of the bilge and the port side nearly to the top of the hull. Half of the stem and sternpost remained, and the keelson, two mast steps, and bottom stringers were still in place, although the upperworks were missing. The original hull was destroyed, but a model was made and is now on display in the Museo Storico Navale of Venice. A publication of 1900 describes hull details and other information about the discoveries.[13]

The first Contarina wreck was a two-masted, lateen-rigged *nave* with an overall length of about 21 m, a keel

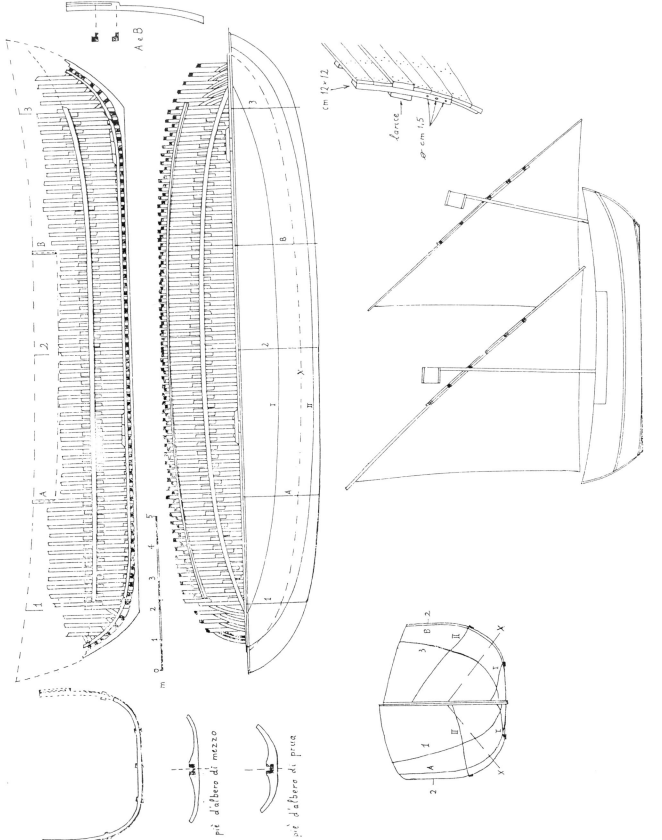

FIG. 4-17. Structural arrangement and details of the first Contarina ship. (courtesy M. Bonino, *IJNA* 7.1, fig. 4)

16.5 m long, and a maximum breadth of 5.2 m (Fig. 4–17). It was built entirely of oak except for the stringers, which were of larch. Three frames were said to have been assembled first and set on the keel to act as control frames, one at amidships and one at each end of the keel, upon which ribbands were bent to determine the rest of the frame shapes. All frames were made compositely of five pieces—a floor timber, two futtocks, and two top timbers. These timbers overlapped each other for 50 cm or more and were fastened to each other with three 1.5-cm bolts at each overlap. All frames are said to have been fastened to the keel with iron nails, which were driven from the top of the keelson through frames and keel, and then clenched over the bottom surface of the keel. However, it seems certain that the control frames were fastened separately to the keel before the keelson was installed.

The frame overlaps were all aligned, and they were reinforced externally by wales and bilge keels and internally by clamps and footwales. At the ends of the hull, forward and aft of the control frames, the floor timbers were canted to simplify frame fitting and planking; the futtocks remained vertical here.

The construction and bracing of the mast steps is interesting. They were made of four pieces of timber mounted on top of the keelson; each was braced laterally by being seated in three oversized floor timbers specially notched to receive and support the assemblies.

The flat part of the floor was about 2.1 m wide at amidships, which was the approximate distance between bilge keels. Thus the bottom flat was much broader than that of the Serçe Limani hull, and the bilge had a gentler

rounding. In fact, the entire structure showed a greater sophistication that was undoubtedly the result of three additional centuries of shipbuilding progress.

THE LOGONOVO BOAT

An extensively preserved boat was uncovered during excavations for a building foundation near Ferrara, Italy, in 1958. It is dated to the early part of the fifteenth century, and its missing parts (beams, decks, upper stringers, and part of the stern did not survive) have been restored by a boatbuilder. The vessel is now on display in the Museo Archeologico Nazionale in Ferrara. This two-masted, lateen-rigged *barca* had an overall length of about 10 m, a keel length of 8.65 m, and a maximum breadth of 2.55 m. Like the Contarina wreck, it was built entirely of oak except for the stringers, which were fashioned from larch.

There was no keel; there was simply a central plank on which the posts were notched and fastened. Nor was a proper keelson found, although there was a heavy central timber forward that housed the foremast step and curved upward into the bow. Bonino has reconstructed a similar arrangement for the stern (Fig. 4–18). Frame assembly is similar to that of the Contarina vessel, except that the overlaps were joined with two 1.5-cm treenails instead of bolts. Footwales reinforced the junctions of floor heads and futtocks (see section drawing, Fig. 4–18), but elsewhere the overlaps were not stiffened with stringers as on the Contarina ship. Planks were fastened to the frames with iron nails and were covered with pitch externally. The floor flat was 1.08 m wide, and the bilge was even harder than that of the Serçe Limani hull.

Medieval and Renaissance Documents [14]

In lieu of sound archaeological evidence at present, one must rely on documentary sources, particularly the Timbotta manuscript (written by a Venetian merchant in 1444, it includes sections on shipbuilding and other nautical subjects) and the *Fabrica di galere* of the fifteenth century (a Venetian document most valuable for its hull and rigging proportions), to understand how vessels such as the Contarina ship were conceived. Until the late medieval period, the precise roles of Mediterranean shipwrights, carpenters, and laborers in the construction of vessels are unclear. From about A.D. 1200, at least in the larger yards of Genoa, Venice, and Naples, we get a clearer picture. For instance, the master shipwright, the person in charge of one or several construction projects, seems to have acquired a high degree of management skills as well as an appreciably sophisticated expertise in construction. In addition to the construction duties cited below, the master shipwright also directed the tasks of the various guildsmen and common laborers, such as woodcutters in the forests, sawyers, carpenters, and caulkers.

Either directly or indirectly, he controlled purchases for timber and metals and set the rate of production.

One of the first steps in building a vessel was the determination of its hull dimensions. These were based on the proportions of a basic measurement, which was usually the beam of the vessel. Following is a set of typical proportions from the *Fabrica di galere*. [15]

> keel = 2.45 times the beam
> overall length = 3.6 times the beam
> depth in hold = 0.28 times the beam

These and others are then expanded to dimensions for a *nave quadra* (which had a square-rigged mainmast and a lateen-rigged mizzen) as below and in Figure 4–19. All dimensions are given in Venetian feet (1 Venetian ft = 34.8 cm).

> beam—26½ length of stem—32½
> overall length—95 length of sternpost—20⅔
> keel length—65 depth in hold—7½

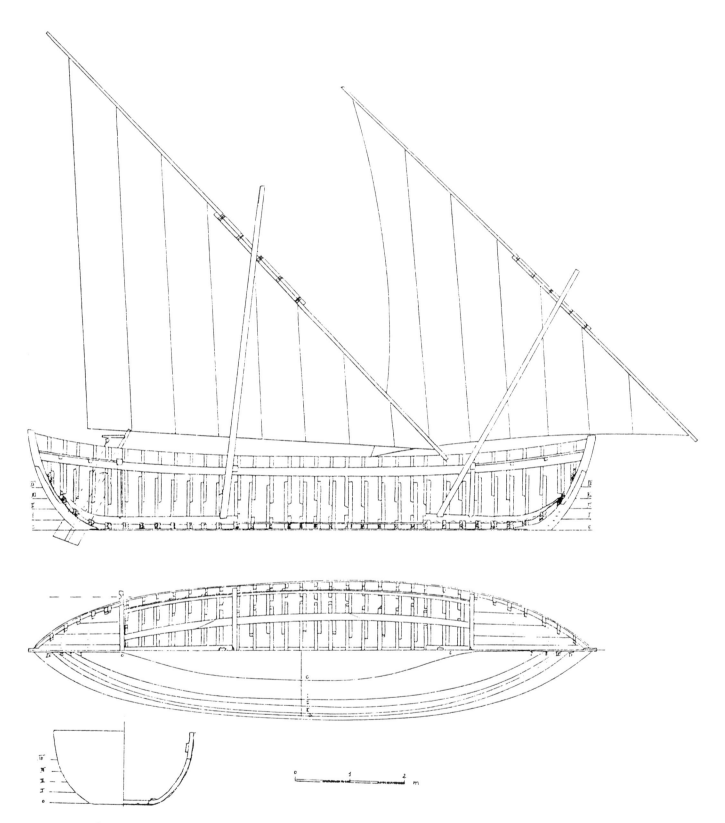

FIG. 4–18. The Logonova boat. (courtesy M. Bonino, *IJNA* 7.1, fig. 5)

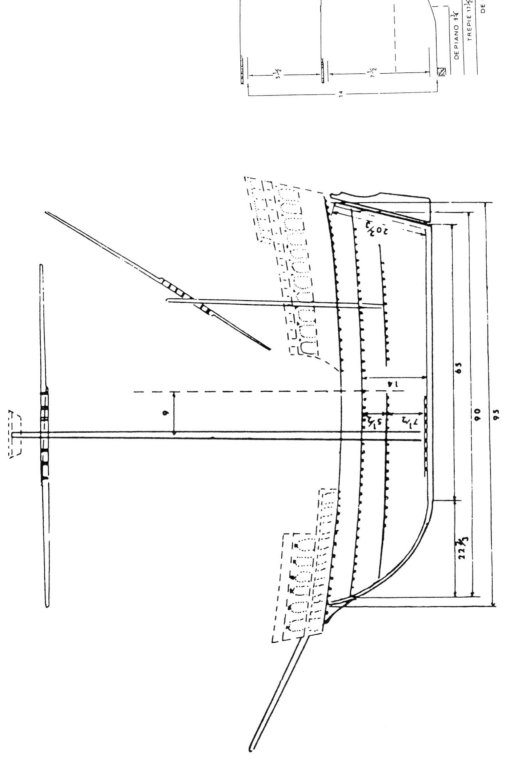

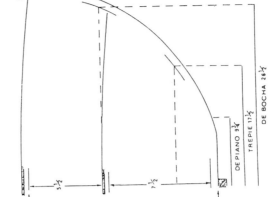

Fig. 4–19. Proportions of a Venetian ship with a keel of 13 paces. (courtesy S. Bellabarba, *MM* 74.2, figs. 1, 4)

rake of stem—22²⁄₃   height of second deck—5½
rake of sternpost—5   width of floor—9¾
width at three feet above keel—17½

Such proportions varied for galleys, round ships, cogs, and
other types, and they were different in different locations
and periods. Undoubtedly they began as very simple ratios
and became more complex as shipbuilding reached higher
degrees of specialization and sophistication.

After suitable quantities and types of timber were
brought to the yard, preparations were made to lay the
keel. Frederic C. Lane cites a Venetian method by which
piles were sunk three feet into the ground at seven-foot
intervals, projecting about two feet above ground.[16] These
formed the platform upon which the keel was laid. The
keel was given a slight sheer, perhaps to counteract anticipated hogging of the hull. This sheer was determined by
stretching a long cord, whose ends were slightly above the
desired horizontal baseline, and letting it sag to the baseline at its center.

After the keel was fashioned and its ends were
shaped to receive the posts, the next step was to produce
the stem and sternpost. In the later periods, when stern-
mounted rudders were used, straight sternposts were
scarfed to heels at the ends of keels or stepped directly
into the tops of keels at the desired angle of rake. But
curved sternposts were made in a similar fashion to
stems; one method from the Timbotta manuscript is
shown in Figure 4–20a.[17] Here the base of a triangle was
drawn from the keel scarf to a point where it intersected
a vertical line coinciding with the point where the deck
met the stem (or sternpost). The outer curve of the post
was then derived from offsets taken from the hy-
potenuse of the triangle. An even simpler method might
have been used by many shipwrights, especially for
smaller craft, as indicated in a drawing in the Timbotta
manuscript (Fig. 4–20b). Here the curve of the post was
probably derived from a batten bent to a suitable curvature between the two controlling points.

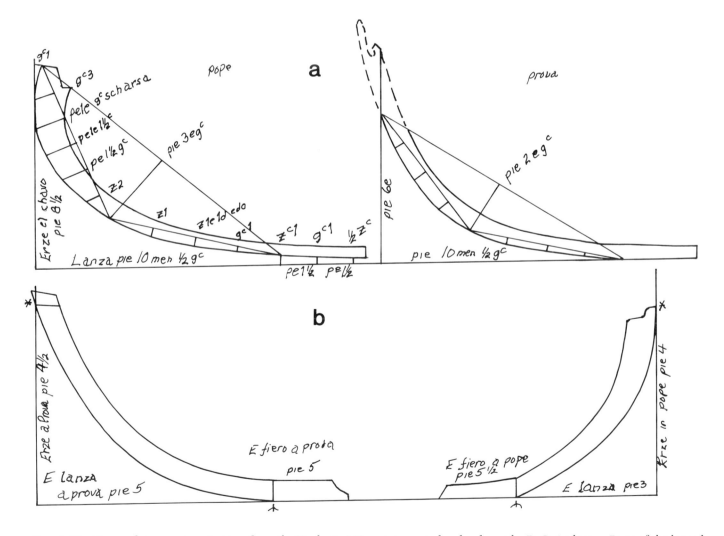

FIG. 4–20. Stem and sternpost projections from the Timbotta MS, as interpreted and redrawn by R. C. Anderson. Parts of the legend
have been omitted here for clarity; see the article cited for additional details. (a) stem (right) and sternpost of a *galia sottil;* (b) less
sophisticated projections for the posts of small craft. (after Anderson, figs. 1, 3)

With the keel and posts securely braced on the stocks, the shipwright next determined the location of the midship frame on the top of the keel. This was not necessarily located in the middle of the hull or the keel, but might have been afore or abaft the center, depending on the design of the vessel. When the location of the master frame was established, positions were determined for all other frames that were to be erected before the installation of planking.

Now it was time to project the shape of the midship, or master, frame. Its curvature was determined by a series of proportional lines representing frame widths at intervals ½ ft or 1 ft above the floor, as in Figure 4–21. These fifteenth-century methods were simplified and refined by the following century. For simpler ships and boats, battens may have been used to derive frame curvatures from much more elementary parameters, or standard molds in the builder's possession may have been used directly or altered to suit the vessel in question.

Similar proportions would have been used to determine the shapes of the forwardmost and aftermost full frames, called *tailframes* (see Fig. 4–17). After the amount of elevation of the floors, called the *rising*, and the total decrease in width of the frames, called the *narrowing*, between the midship frame and the tailframes were established, the shipwright had to decide how many standing frames to erect between these limits and what their dimensions would be. Undoubtedly there were common proportions for determining the shapes of three, or perhaps even five, standing frames. However, it is highly unlikely that such proportions could be determined accurately, or at

least executed successfully, for the construction of every fifth frame in a galley that had eighty to one hundred frames on the keel or for similarly complex hulls. This would have required longitudinal proportions as well, so that the amount of narrowing and rising of each frame could be determined. Those proportions were derived by a variety of ingenious methods, two of which are described below.

Two diagrams in the Timbotta manuscript, which were also illustrated and finally described nearly 150 years later by Bartolomeo Crescentio, reveal methods of determining the progressive shapes of a number of standing frames.[18] Crescentio was describing the framing of galleys at Naples, referring first to the *mezzaluna* (half-moon) (Fig. 4–22, top) and then to a Neopolitan two-stave method, which he seemed to consider superior to the *mezzaluna*.[19] He also explained the purpose of a triangle that was similar to one found in the Timbotta manuscript (Fig. 4–22, bottom). Both were used to mold the shapes of frames at designated intervals between the midship frame and one of the tailframes, that is, they described the rising of the floors and narrowing of the sides as they progressed from amidships toward the tailframes.

Crescentio refers to a galley having forty-five frames between the master frame and each of the tailframes, which were included in the count. Every fifth frame shape was to be predetermined, which meant that there would be nine standing frames in each half of the hull. For the *mezzaluna*, a vertical line AB represented the desired amount of narrowing or rising between the master frame and one of the tailframes. Arcs were scribed from

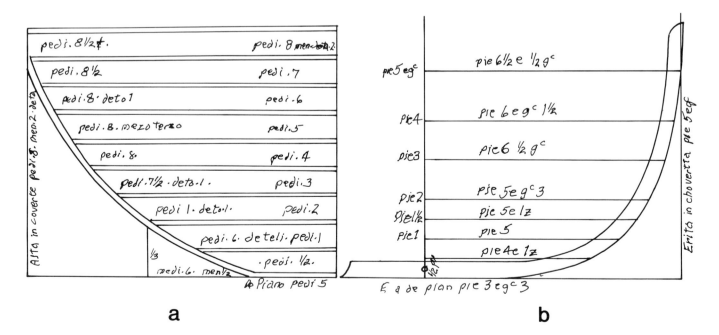

a   b

FIG. 4–21. Method of determining frame shapes: (a) midship frame of a Flemish galley from a diagram in the *Fabrica di galere* (c. 1410); (b) midship frame of a *galia sottil* from a diagram in the Timbotta MS (ca. 1445). ([a] after Lane, fig. 15; [b] after Anderson, fig. 1)

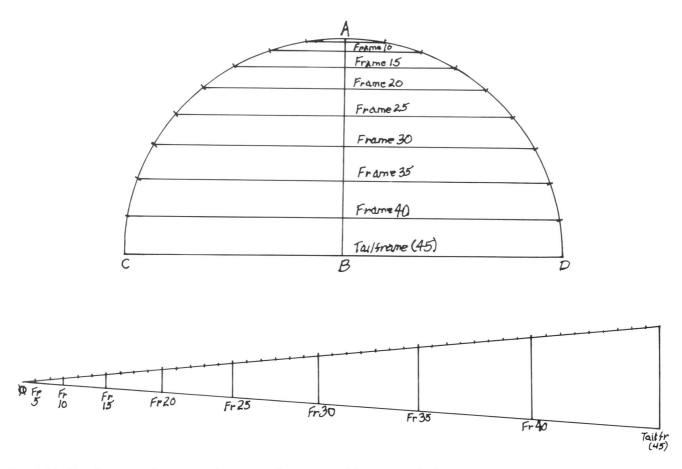

FIG. 4–22. Two devices used to project the rising and narrowing of frames in Italy during the Renaissance: the *mezzaluna* (top) and the incremental triangle (bottom). These illustrations are simplified and highlighted versions of those found in Anderson, fig. 7.

A to the base, forming the semicircle CAD. Each arc was then divided into the number of frames to be projected—in this case into nine parts—and corresponding points on each arc were joined by horizontal lines. Thus the distance from A to each line intersecting AB was the narrowing or rising increment for each successive projected frame, with the baseline representing the tailframe.

The triangle (actually, a series of triangles sharing a common vertex) shown in Figure 4–22 produced similar, perhaps more reliable, results. From a base representing the amount of narrowing or rising between the midship frame and one of the tailframes, two sides of identical length were projected to form an isosceles triangle. The lengths of the legs are arbitrary, although the longer they are the more accurate and convenient the results. If there are to be nine standing frames as before, then one or both legs are divided into forty-five equal increments. A line is next drawn parallel to the original base for each standing frame at the increment corresponding to the geometric progression 1, 3, 6, 10, 15, 21, 28, and 36.[20] The vertex, 0, is the midship frame, the main base is the tailframe, and

the lengths of the intermediate baselines represent the amount of rising or narrowing at that particular frame.

Rising and narrowing values were not necessarily equal for given frame sequences, nor can we be certain that bottom and side proportions were determined by the same methods. In addition, there must have been a variety of ways in which these diminishing increments could be transferred to the shapes of finished timbers. Lane mentions a "model midship frame," or midship pattern, whereon all narrowing values could be marked and the single pattern used to derive all frame shapes.[21] Perhaps it was similar to a pre–sixteenth century method described by John Sarsfield that is still used in Bahia, Brazil, for the construction of wooden boats.[22] Rising and narrowing increments are determined by a form of *mezzaluna*, as described above, and the resulting scales are marked on a common pattern. Then individual frame shapes are derived for one side of the hull, and the pattern is reversed to acquire the full frame shape.

Frame projections for the big *naves* and galleys were not quite so elementary, however. There must have been proportions for increased frame heights in forward and aftward directions (perhaps quite complicated ones where sheer was extreme) and other variations in basic frame design. The larger frames must have comprised several futtocks, which further complicated the transfer of curvatures. In any case, the shapes thus derived were marked on the timbers for cutting and assembling into frames, and intermediate frame shapes were determined after planks, or at least ribbands, were in place. But the frame shapes in the areas between the tailframes and the posts could not be determined reliably by such methods. Here ribbands were probably installed first, and the frames, which were Y- or V-shaped or canted as in the Contarina vessel, were formed with their guidance.

Exactly how the mold lofts for projecting frame shapes and the staging areas used for assembling and bevelling the

timbers were arranged remains a mystery. Nor are the contemporary manuscripts cited above specific about the myriad small details we should know about Mediterranean hull construction in the late medieval period. Until well-preserved archaeological examples surface for perusal, we will have to rely on the information supplied by the early sixteenth-century examples described in the next chapter. Certainly the ships of the late medieval period could not have been too much different in sequence and form of construction. It should be added here, however, that frame and spinal shapes were not the only recipients of mathematical control. Proportions were used throughout the hull, even for masting and rigging (Fig. 4–23). For example, the length of the lateen yard shown in the lower part of the illustration was one-quarter greater than the length of the

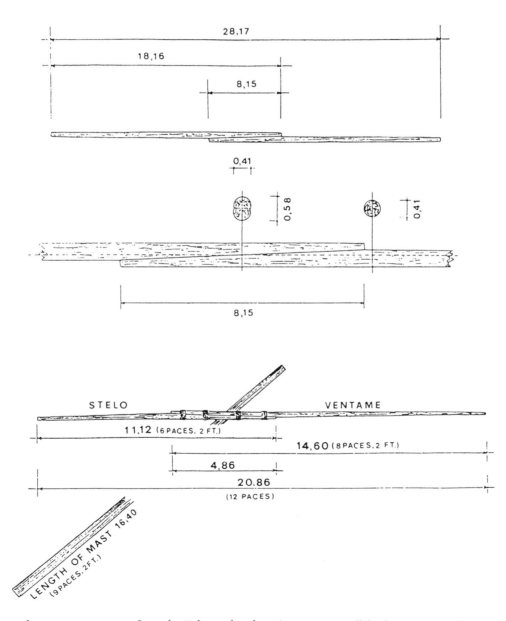

FIG. 4–23. Masting and rigging proportions from the *Fabrica di galere.* (courtesy S. Bellabarba, *MM* 74.3, figs. 5, 6)

mast above the deck. The overlapping portion was about one-fifth of the yard's total length, and the *ventame* was seven-tenths of the yard's length.[23]

The methods described above were probably the most demanding of the shipwright's skills and indicate that

formal naval architecture, however basic at this stage, was developing rapidly in the Mediterranean during the last half of the medieval period. That was not the case in north-western Europe, as the next paragraphs confirm.

Shipbuilding in Northwestern Europe

Caesar described the boats of the Veneti of Britanny as being built entirely of oak and fastened with iron. He stated, seemingly with a mixture of admiration and envy, that they were heavy, strong, and flat bottomed, being perfectly suited to the shallows and stormy seas of the area. They could not be damaged with rams, and they carried sails of skins or leather. Perhaps the first-century vessel excavated at Blackfriars Bridge in London (see Fig. 3–62) was an example of that kind of Celtic construction.[24]

Relatively little is known about Celtic boatbuilding, so the subject will not be pursued further here. Rather, our study begins with *clinker*, or lapstrake, construction. Two aspects of this form of hull planking assembly varied most noticeably from Mediterranean methods. Rather than being aligned, planking edges overlapped one another (usually the upper planks overlapped the ones just below them), and edge joinery was completely transverse (Fig. 4–24). Like their southern counterparts, clinker-built hulls were well adapted to the available timber supplies, existing technology, sea and riverine conditions, and controlling societal factors. Most notably, clinker construction was the product of cloven (split) oak, although fir, pine, and other wood types were sometimes used. Splitting produced rough planks that were very strong because they followed the run of the grain.[25]

Overlapping planks were being used before the time of Christ; this is evidenced by the Hjortspring boat, a 16-m-long vessel paddled by about twenty warriors. Excavated on the island of Als, Denmark, in 1922 and dated to the fourth century B.C., this canoe-like craft had two overlapping planks per side that were sewn together and attached to a broad, curved central plank. It was reinforced with ribs of hazel branches lashed to cleats that were carved from the planking stock (Fig. 4–25a).[26]

About A.D. 100, the 7.16-m-long Björke boat found near Stockholm, Sweden, reflected improvements in methodology. Single side planks overlapped an unexpanded dugout and were fastened to it with iron rivets. Cleats, which were a part of the dugout base, held lashings for the attachment of relatively heavy frames (Fig. 4–25b).[27]

At the beginning of the medieval period, Saxons were crossing the English Channel in clinker-built boats, some of which may have been similar to the Nydam oak boat found in 1873 in Schleswig and dated to A.D. 350–400 (Fig. 4–25c).[28] It has five lapped strakes per

side, each lap fastened with iron nails clenched over roves, and a heavy central plank instead of a keel. The Nydam oak boat (there was also a smaller Nydam boat built of fir) was reinforced with frames lashed to cleats carved from the planking stock. The cleats were about twice as thick as the planking.

The principal dimensions of the Nydam boat are controversial, but the Sutton Hoo vessel, excavated along the River Deben in England and dated to about 600, provided more reliable dimensions (Fig. 4–25d).[29] The Sutton Hoo vessel had rotted away and left a mere impression in the earth of a burial mound when excavated. Its length was approximately 27 m and its breadth about 5 m, attesting to the great sizes of some of these early galleys.

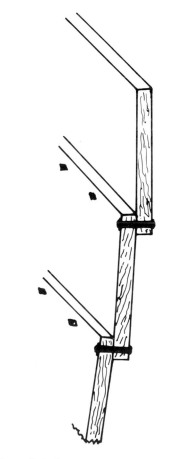

FIG. 4–24. Typical clinker construction.

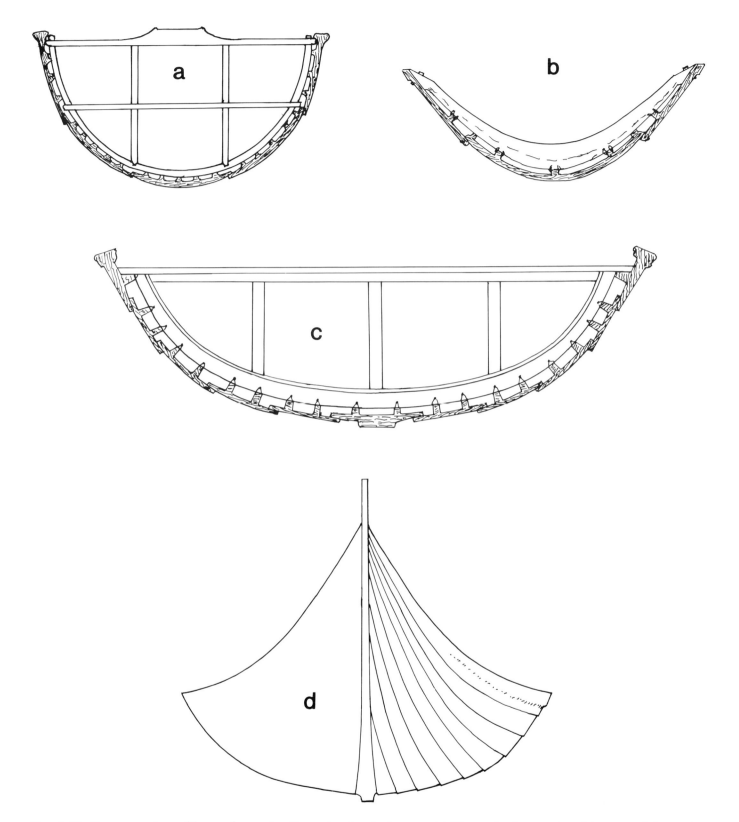

FIG. 4–25. Transverse views of four early vessels with overlapping plank seams: (a) Hjortspring boat section; (b) section of the Björke boat; (c) Nydam oak boat section; (d) median view of the Sutton Hoo vessel from forward, showing the run of the planks at right. The drawings are not to scale. (after [a] Rosenberg, vol. 3, part 1; [b] Greenhill, fig. 34; [c] Greenhill, fig. 119; [d] Bruce-Mitford, fig. 325)

But our serious analysis of clinker-built hulls must begin with the Vikings, for they got the most from these vessels. Caesar referred to sails on the ships of the Veneti, and Peter Marsden has reconstructed the Blackfriars vessel as a sailing barge; so far, however, there are no illustrative examples of sails on clinker-built craft before the time of the Gotland stone, which is dated to about 700 and shows a sail on a Viking ship. Let's investigate a few notable examples of Viking craft that could be either rowed or sailed or, in several cases, were predominantly built for wind propulsion.

THE GOKSTAD SHIP

In 1880, a burial mound was excavated on the Gokstad farms in the parish of Sandar, Norway, south of Oslo. Most important among the burial artifacts were three small boats and what has become known as the Gokstad ship. All were in relatively good condition and were extensively preserved; they have been reassembled and are on display in the Viking Ship Museum of the University Museum of National Antiquities near Oslo. The following details of the construction of the Gokstad ship are abstracted from Haakon Shetelig's chapter on the Viking vessels and the later interpretations and drawings by Werner Dammann.[30]

The Gokstad ship (Fig. 4–26) had an overall length of 23.24 m, a maximum beam of 5.2 m, and a height of 2.02 m from the bottom of the keel to the top of the gunwale. A seaworthy vessel, it could be propelled by sixteen pairs of oars or a single square sail. Its displacement is estimated at 20.2 tons. The hull was built entirely of oak. Unlike the broad central planks of the earlier clinker-built hulls mentioned above, the Gokstad ship's 17.37-m-long keel was a proper backbone. T-shaped in section, it was molded 37 cm amidships, increasing to 42 cm at its after end and 40 cm at the bow extremity. Its bottom surface was sided 13 cm at amidships, its upper surface 20 cm, and it was 10 cm wide just beneath the flanges (Fig. 4–27). Made of a single piece of oak, it was rockered so that the hull drew 30 cm more water amidships than at the ends.

At each end of the keel, the projecting wings diminished and were replaced by a rabbet, which continued up the sides of the posts. Transition pieces were connected to each end of the keel and the posts by short vertical diagonal scarfs, each of which was fastened with double rows of nails. These transition pieces were used to increase the keel curvature and decrease its thickness to that of the posts.

Stem and stern posts were not completely preserved (about 3 m of each survived), but it is assumed that each one was made from a single piece of oak. The greatest surviving molded dimension was 45 cm at the sternpost.

There were sixteen strakes of oak planking on each side, each strake overlapping the one below it. Except near the bow and stern, where there was not enough room to swing a hammer inside the hull, the planks were fastened to each other through the overlap by means of round-headed clinker nails (technically, rivets). By this method, a hole was bored through both planks and a nail was driven through it from outside the hull; a small square iron plate called a *rove* was then forced over the nail shaft, the point of the nail nipped off, and the end of the nail peened over the rove (Figs. 4–28c and 4–28d).[31] The clinker nails had shafts of 1 cm diameter and were spaced at intervals averaging about 18.5 cm (about one handspan). Each plank overlapped the one below it by a span (land) of 3.2 cm to 3.8 cm; planks had average overall widths of 24 cm amidships but narrowed toward the ends of the hull.

The ends of the planks were nailed into the rabbets of the posts. Planking scarfs were merely angular vertical overlaps fastened with nails driven in alternating directions and clenched over (Fig. 4–28f). Scarfs were placed in staggered locations to avoid areas of shell weakness, and their outer edges always pointed aft.

Although arguments have been presented in the past to support the use of molds or standing frames in this form of construction, the evidence seems to indicate that the extant frames were not in place before the planking was assembled and that free-form building was most probable. A review of the literature supports the sequence displayed in the Viking Ship Museum at Rothskilde, Denmark; the sequence was determined by the examination of one of the Skuldelev vessels described later in this chapter.[32] The progression is no different than that suggested for classical Mediterranean hulls in the previous chapter: keel and posts, bottom planking, frames (floor timbers), crossbeams and side planking.

Thus, after the keel and posts were erected and securely braced, the nine strakes of the bottom were installed and attached to each other as described above. As in the fabrication of edge-joined Mediterranean vessels, this was a process that was wasteful of labor and material by modern standards. Except for the garboards, planks were split from oak logs in dimensions much greater than their final thickness, then cut down as illustrated in Figure 4–28d to form cleats for the attachment of frames. Strakes were 2.5–2.6 cm thick exclusive of the cleats, and there were nineteen cleats per strake, each aligned with those of neighboring strakes.

As planking progressed, *luting coves* cut near the bottom of each interior plank surface were filled with animal hair spun into cords and dipped in tar, so that the seams were watertight when riveted (Fig. 4–28 top). This form of luting will be discussed further in our study of cogs to follow. Joints and scarfs were caulked as well.

After the nine bottom planks were assembled, a 4.4-cm-thick strake, called a *meginhufr*, was added to the shell (Fig. 4–28, no. 10). This thick tenth strake served a purpose similar to that of the main wale of the Kyrenia ship, separating bottom from side near the waterline and longitudinally reinforcing the perimeter of the hull.

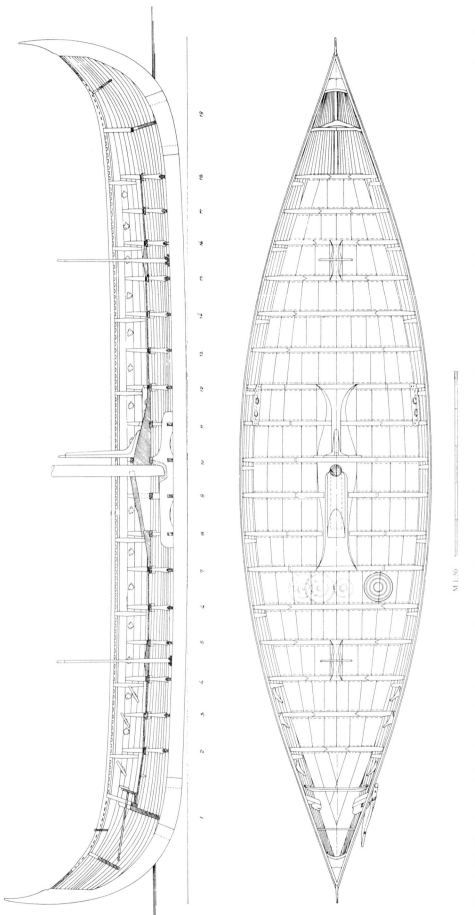

M 1:50

Fɪɢ. 4–26. The Gokstad ship; longitudinal section and top view. (Dammann, Plan II; reconstruction by W. Dammann and drawing by W. Seiss; courtesy Arbeitskreis historischer Schiffbau e.V., Rübezahlweg 21, 5790 Brilon-Gudenhagen)

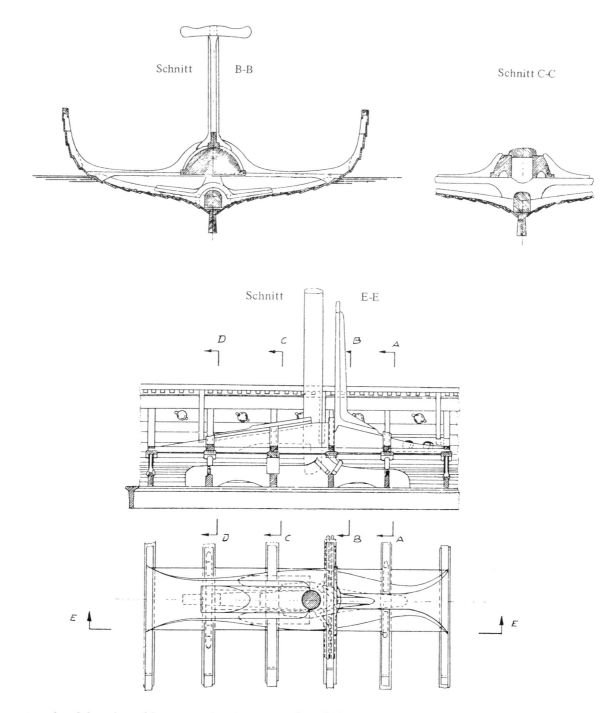

Schnitt B-B

Schnitt C-C

Schnitt E-E

FIG. 4–27. Gokstad ship: the midship section (B-B), a section through the crone (C-C), and two views of the mast supporting timbers (crone and fish—E-E). (Dammann, Plan III; reconstruction by W. Dammann and drawing by W. Seiss; courtesy Arbeitskreis historischer Schiffbau e.V.)

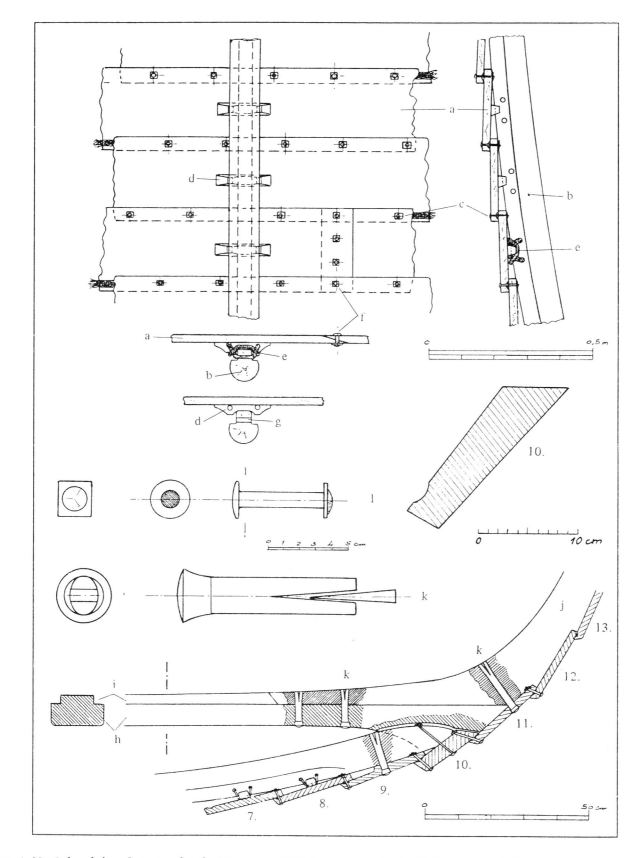

FIG. 4–28. Gokstad ship: fastening details. (Dammann, Tafel 3; reconstruction by W. Dammann and drawing by W. Seiss; courtesy Arbeitskreis historischer Schiffbau e.V.)

Once the *meginhufrs* were installed on each side, the nineteen frames were made and inserted. Each cleat was shaped to seat a frame upon it, so that the upper edge of the plank rested against the frame, as did its cleat, while the lower edge rested against the strake below it (Figs. 4–28b and 4–28d). Holes were drilled through the cleats, one on each side of the frames, and through the frames on each side of the cleats (Figs. 4–28d and 4–28g). Then the frames were lashed to the cleats through these holes with withy made from spruce roots (Figs. 4–28b and 4–28e). The garboards were riveted to the wings of the keel and to the second strakes, but they were not lashed to the frames. The frames were not attached to the keel at all; only at their upper ends were they treenailed to strake 9 and fastened with iron to the *meginhufrs*. Frames were spaced about a meter apart and were made from U-shaped, naturally curved stock.

Except in the ends of the hull, the naturally curved frames terminated at the eleventh strake, which was approximately at the waterline. Two frames in each end, one over the transition piece and another high in the end, were formed from tree crotches into solid pieces resembling bulkheads; they were notched to fit the lands of the planks and nailed to the lands.

The next step was probably the installation of the *crone*, which is a Scandinavian term for the heavy block of oak that supported the heel of the mast (Figs. 4–26 and 4–27). Although sometimes referred to as a keelson, such blocks were hardly long enough to perform a full internal backbone function but did stiffen the hull internally in the area of the mast. The crone of the Gokstad ship was 3.75 m long, 40 cm high, and 60 cm wide. It rested on the top of the keel and four frames (nos. 8 to 11 from the stern), but was not fastened to the keel; it was attached to frame 10 with two knees nailed on each side and to frames 8 and 11 with single knees on each side. A vertical arm, carved from the same block, rose just abaft the tenth frame and just forward of the mast location to partially support the mast partner above and brace the heel of the mast. The mast step mortise was cut about halfway into the crone, its after end cut square and the forward end rounded to facilitate removal of the mast.

Next, a deck beam was secured to the top of each frame. The mast partner, called a *fish* in modern terminology because of its fishtail-shaped ends but known to the Vikings as a *klofi* (fork), rested on the deck beams and supported the mast at deck level. This was the largest piece of timber in the ship; it extended over six beams and was 5 m long, 1 m wide, and 41.3 cm thick. It tapered sharply downward from its center to form fishtail-shaped ends, which were mortised into the beams. The four intermediate beams fitted into notches cut into the underside of the partner. Additional support was provided by the strong, partition-like shape of the beam over the ninth frame, sometimes referred to as a *snelle* (see detail in Fig. 4–27, section E-E). The hole in the partner was aligned at its

forward end with the step in the crone, but was elongated aftward to the eighth frame beam to facilitate the lowering of the mast. When the mast was stepped, the elongation was closed with a carefully made oaken plug. The mast diameter was 30 cm here.

Four strakes of planking were added above the *meginhufr*. Strakes 11, 12, and 13 were 2.6 cm thick, and strake 14 was made 3.2 cm thick to withstand the leverage of the oars, for it was in this row of planks that sixteen oar ports were cut in each side of the hull. The ports could be closed on the inside by means of lids pivoted on nails. There were no cleats on these strakes, but they were additionally stiffened by being riveted to knees that were nailed to the upper surfaces of each end of each beam.

The two uppermost strakes were quite thin—1.6 cm—but they were stiffened by the installation of futtocks, or side frames, that were also nailed to strakes 12, 13, and 14. A rectangular gunwale, 11 cm wide and 8 cm high, was placed inside the upper edge of strake 16; it reinforced the upper edge of the hull.

The frame over the after transition piece, which was solidly constructed from a tree crotch so that it gave the appearance of a bulkhead, supported a rudder on the starboard side only (Figs. 4–29f and 4–29a). Next to the gunwale was a heavy oak pad, 10 cm thick, that extended downward over two strakes. It was reinforced with a heavy internal backing piece. The pad supported the rudder post, which was kept in place by means of a rope or band of withy. Below it was a heavy oaken block called a *wart*, or boss; this was secured by nails driven through the planking and frame (Fig. 4–29h). A hole was drilled through the rudder, wart, planking, and frame, through which a thick withy was passed. The withy had a knot at its outboard end and was fastened inboard through holes in the frame. It held the rudder securely to the wart but was elastic enough to permit the rudder to turn on its axis or to be raised or lowered. The rudder (Fig. 4–30) was made from a single piece of oak and was 3.3 m long with a central blade width of 42 cm; it extended 50 cm below the line of the keel under normal steering conditions. The rudder post extended 50 cm above the gunwale and had a vertical slot cut into it to house the outboard end of the tiller. The tiller (Fig. 4–29e) was about 1 m long and was the only member on the vessel to be decorated with carvings.

Loose deck planks rested in ledges cut into the upper edges of the beams. A shield support-strip and posts used to store shipped oars completed the hull structure.

The Gokstad ship dates to about A.D. 850. Brøgger and Shetelig did not believe this sort of vessel was used for faraway raiding expeditions or overseas trading, but rather for offshore work closer to home port or in local waters.

THE OSEBERG SHIP[33]

A somewhat smaller vessel, definitely intended for service in sheltered waters, was excavated in 1905 from a burial mound on the Oseberg farm near Tønsberg, Norway. This

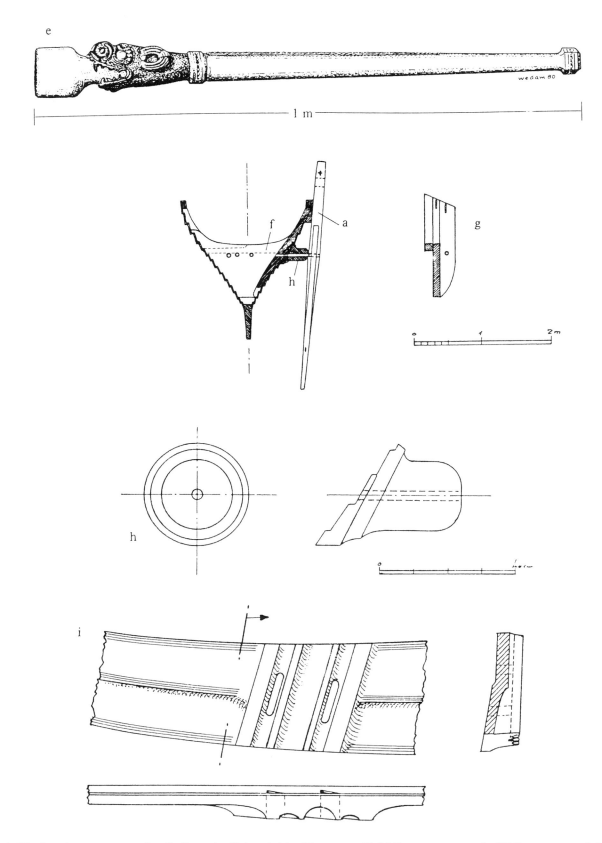

FIG. 4–29. Steering component details from the Gokstad ship. (Dammann, Tafel 7; reconstruction by W. Dammann and drawing by W. Seiss; courtesy Arbeitskreis historischer Schiffbau e.V.)

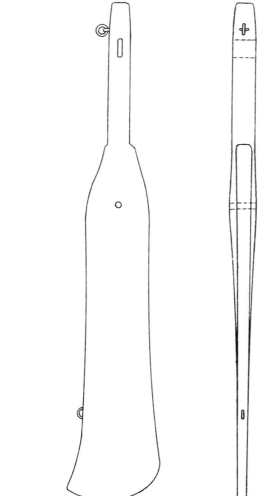

grave of a wealthy woman included sledges, a cart, beds, and other lavishly decorated items, all placed within a clinker-built hull that was decorated with equally magnificent elaborate carvings. The vessel survived extensively and is now reassembled and displayed in the same ship museum as the Gokstad vessel, which it predates by about 50 years.

The Oseberg ship is 21.44 m long overall, has a maximum beam of 5.1 m, and a keel-to-gunwale height of 85 cm (Fig. 4–31). It drew 75 cm of water and was square-rigged for wind propulsion or could be rowed with thirty oars. Built entirely of oak, it apparently was not as strong as the Gokstad vessel; strakes were narrower and more scarfs were used in the construction. This keel was also T-shaped, and frames were lashed to cleats in the bottom planking.

The Oseberg ship's form and construction were different from that of the Gokstad vessel, as can be seen in the cross-sectional drawing of the hull. There were twelve strakes of planking, but the *meginhufr* was shaped like an inverted L. At this point, the steep deadrise of the bottom changed to a nearly vertical orientation for the two side planks.

The Oseberg vessel is strikingly graceful in appearance and is a tribute to the aesthetic expertise of its builders. But it does not appear to be as practical or serviceable a vessel as the Gokstad ship, and it was probably never so intended in its conception.

THE SKULDELEV SHIPS[34]

Between 1957 and 1962, the remains of five Viking vessels were excavated from Roskilde fjord in Denmark. All five dated to about A.D. 1000 and were sunk deliberately to obstruct a channel in the fjord as a deterrent to maritime raiders. Few wrecks have been the subject of such an intensive scientific program of conservation and reconstruction. Two of the vessels were warships, two were cargo vessels, and the fifth was a smaller craft of unknown function, perhaps a fishing boat. The remains of all five have been reassembled and are now displayed in the Viking Ship Museum in Roskilde, Denmark, about twenty-five miles west of Copenhagen. The museum is a beautiful structure overlooking the fjord where the vessels were found, and inside one can quickly acquire a substantial education in Viking maritime history through the ingenious arrangement of watercraft and displays. Here the exhausting study of this variety of hull types continues, and it will probably never end.

SMALL TRADING VESSEL (WRECK 3)

The best preserved of all the wrecks, this vessel was built primarily for sailing but its sides were pierced for seven oars, four on the port side and three to starboard. Since only four of the seven oar holes showed signs of wear, Crumlin-Pedersen assumed that it was crewed by no more than five or six sailors. Wreck 3 had an overall length of 13.8 m, a beam of 3.4 m, and a depth from the top of the gunwale to the bottom of the keel of 1.3 m (Fig. 4–32). The hull was relatively short, wide, and high with a beam:length ratio of 1:4.1 and a hold about 4 m long with a volume of 350 cubic feet (a 3.5 tonner by modern formula). There were small half-decks fore and aft, so the cargo in the open hold must have been protected by skins or other cover against the elements.

The construction shows remarkable improvements over the older Norwegian vessels discussed above. No longer were frames lashed to cleats; they were rigidly fastened to the planking with treenails. Nor were the planks run into rabbets in the stem and sternpost; now they terminated at butts carved into elaborately shaped bow and stern pieces, which were substituted for standard stems and sternposts (see Fig. 4–34). Over each of the ten floor

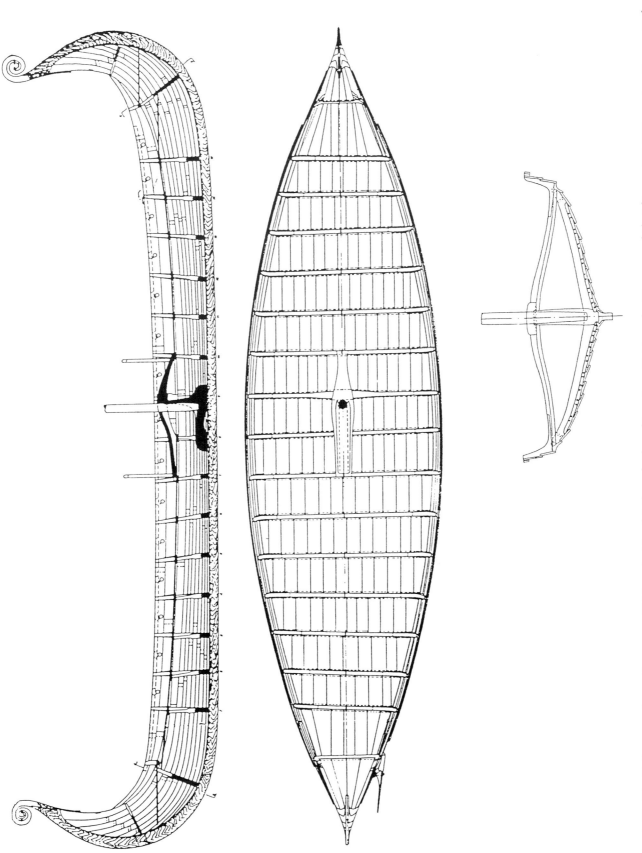

FIG. 4–31. The Oseberg vessel—section near amidships, planking details, and side and top views. Not to scale. (Brøgger and Shetelig, pp. 104, 105; courtesy Dreyers Forlag A/S)

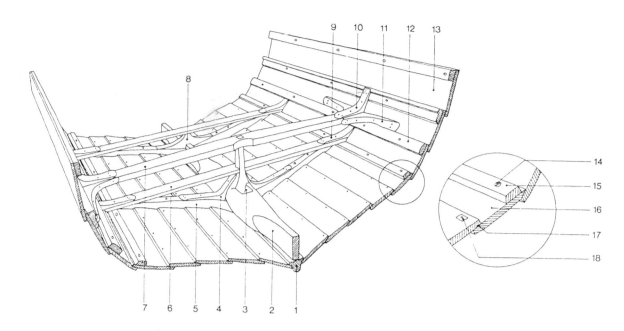

FIG. 4–32. Wreck 3, Skuldelev small trader—cross section and details. Identification of hull components is as follows: (1) keel; (2) keelson; (3) mast step; (4) keelson knee; (5) frame; (6) *bite;* (7) cross-beam; (8) *snelle;* (9) *bite* knee; (10) vertical beam knee; (11) horizontal beam knee; (12) beam shelf or shelf clamp; (13) gunwale plank; (14) treenail; (15) stringer; (16) plank (fifth strake); (17) land; (18) iron nail clenched over square rove. (Olsen and Crumlin-Pedersen, *Acta Archaeologica* 38, fig. 15)

timbers was a beam, also known as a *bite,* that was quite low in the hull. Standing knees were fastened to the upper surfaces of each end of each beam, and directly above the knees on the inside of the planking was a stringer that strengthened the area below the square oar holes and provided longitudinal stiffening to the upper hull. The four upper strakes were reinforced further with a stringer, or gunwale piece, nailed along the top edge of the hull. Both of these upper stringers were kneed to heavy, triangular wooden pieces in bow and stern, to which the four upper strakes were also fastened. The forward triangular bulkhead had a horn-shaped extension on top that served as a

bitt for holding anchor and mooring lines. Wreck 3 was built entirely of oak.

It should be noted that careful examination of the tool marks on wooden surfaces of this and the other four hulls revealed not a single saw mark. It appears that all timbers and planks were split, chopped, or smooth-hewn, but never sawn.

LARGE TRADING VESSEL (WRECK 1)

While longships may conjure visions of speed and adventure, the large trading vessel at Rothskilde is, in my opinion, the most magnificent of all extant Viking vessels. That

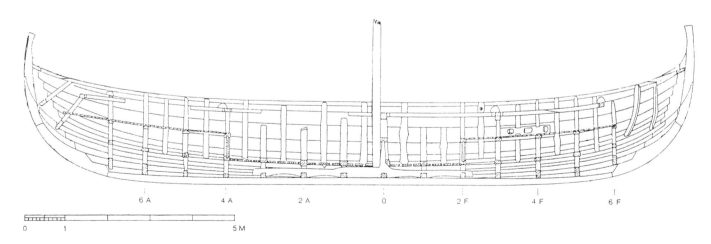

FIG. 4–33. Wreck 1, Skuldelev large trading vessel (sheer view). (Olsen and Crumlin-Pedersen, *Acta Archaeologica* 38, fig. 26)

magnificence is centered not in gracefulness—this was a rather tubby hull—but in good, practical shipwrightery and the expeditious use of materials.

This was definitely a deepwater cargo ship; it was a broad, deep, heavily built *knarr* about 16.5 m long, 4.5 m in the beam, and 2.1 m in depth. It was built somewhat like the smaller vessel, with heavy side stringers, carved stem and stern pieces, and half-decks in the ends with a depressed deck for cargo in the center of the hull (Figs. 4–33, 4–34, and 4–35). But all members were much heavier, and the framing system was more complex in that it combined floor timbers and separate side frames. Unlike most Viking vessels, this one had pine planking, although most of the rest of the hull was fashioned from oak.

The 12.1-m-long rabbeted keel was made from a single piece of oak and was preserved intact. Its upper surface was sided 12–14 cm in the central part of the hull, tapering to about 7 cm at its ends. The bottom surface was sided about 8 cm centrally and was 2 cm narrower at the ends. At amidships, the keel was molded 16 cm and it was 12 cm high where it joined the posts with vertical scarfs. There were no transition pieces between the keel and posts, but the stem and stern pieces into which the

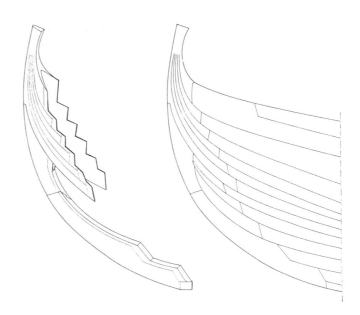

FIG. 4–34. Wreck 1: a reconstruction of the complex three-piece stern and (right) the way in which the planking joined it. (Olsen and Crumlin-Pedersen, *Acta Archaeologica* 38, fig. 19)

FIG. 4–35. The reassembled remains of the deep-sea trading vessel (Skuldelev 1) in the Viking Ship Museum, Roskilde, Denmark. (photo courtesy Viking Ship Museum, Roskilde, Denmark)

FIG. 4–36b. *Roar Ege,* a replica of the coastal trader (wreck 3) built at Roskilde in 1984–86, is a most attractive little vessel. (photo courtesy Viking Ship Museum, Roskilde, Denmark)

FIG. 4–36a. Replicas of the Skuldelev ships have contributed significantly to our understanding of Viking shipbuilding and seamanship; *Saga Siglar,* a replica of the deep-sea trader, sailed around the world in 1984–86. (photo courtesy Viking Ship Museum, Roskilde, Denmark)

plank ends were run were sculpted masterpieces of ship-wrightery (Fig. 4–34).

Garboards were nailed into the keel rabbet at intervals of 16 to 18 cm. Original pine planking (repairs had been made with oaken planks in a few locations) was overlapped for a distance of 3.5 to 4.5 cm and secured with iron rivets driven from outside the hull and peened over square roves. They were spaced 16 to 20 cm apart. These planks were not as long as the oaken planks found on most Viking vessels; the longest was about 6.4 m, and generally each strake was composed of four planks. There were twelve strakes on each side, scarfed together vertically so that the open edge outside always faced aft. The seven lowest strakes were slightly oval in section, being 2.8–3.4 cm thick at their centers and 1–2 cm thick at their edges. Upper strake dimensions varied.

There were fourteen frames in all with an average spacing of 92 cm, although the distance between them varied from 83 to 99 cm. They were sided 10–11 cm at the keel, 12–15 cm at the third strake, and 10–11 cm at their upper ends. At amidships they were molded 11–12 cm, but this height increased to nearly 30 cm at the bow and stern. All frames were of oak with the exception of one fashioned from pine. The frames fit closely to the curved top of the keel and to the first five strakes on each side. They were attached to all strakes, with the exception of the garboards, by one treenail per strake.

SMALL WARSHIP (WRECK 5)

Made mostly of oak, this vessel was slender and lightly built, and it must have been very fast. It was 17.4 m long, 2.6 m broad, and 1.1 m high at amidships; the beam:length ratio, then, was only 1:7. Each side had seven strakes, with the bottom strakes made from oak and the upper three side strakes made from ash (Fig. 4–37). There were sixteen frames of oak, each with a crossbeam above it to stiffen the hull laterally and to support a decking of loose planks. Narrow stationary thwarts were placed about 30 cm above the beams at twelve of the frames, indicating that the vessel was rowed by twenty-four men. A badly damaged mast step also survived. The ship was believed to have been very old when it was sunk, as there is evidence

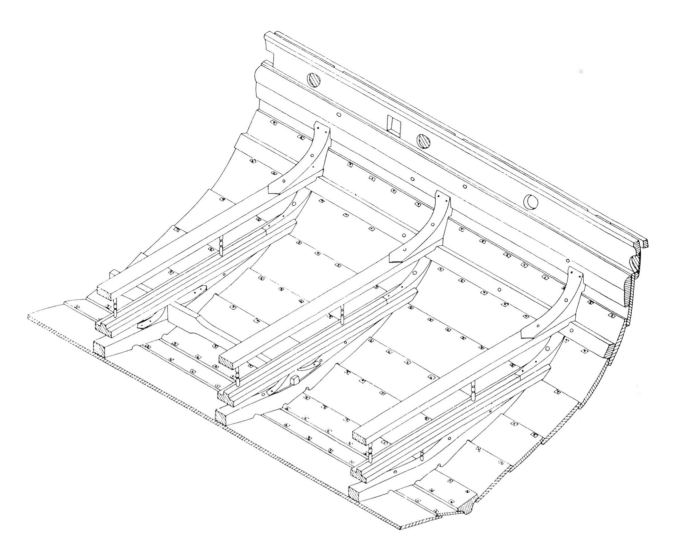

FIG. 4–37. Cross section of the small Skuldelev warship (wreck 5). (Olsen and Crumlin-Pedersen, *Acta Archaeologica* 38, fig. 54)

that it was repaired several times. The top three strakes had been used on a previous vessel; the extant planks, with lengths of 10 m to 14 m, were being used for the second time.

LONGSHIP (WRECK 2)

This poorly preserved warship was about 29 m long, 3.5–4 m broad, and is believed to have been propelled by forty to fifty oarsmen. It was built of oak, but so little survives that extensive construction details are unavailable. However, it should be noted that in spite of its length of nearly a hundred feet, the surviving planking was only 2–2.5 cm thick.

WRECK 6

The smallest of the five vessels, at 11.6 m length and 2.5 m beam, this also was planked in pine, although it did not otherwise resemble the knarr. Possibly it was an open boat that could have been sailed or rowed, depending on conditions.

OTHER CLINKER-BUILT CRAFT

It is tempting to continue discussing clinker-built vessels of the Viking era—Arby, Landby, the boats found inside the Gokstad ship, and the exceptionally thorough study of the heavily framed Graveney boat in England. Unfortunately, there is no space for it, but I refer you to the bibliography so that you might investigate them yourself.

Before leaving clinker construction, however, I would like to point out that it was employed in some very large hulls, as indicated briefly in the following English examples.

The Public Record Office in London contains documents, written in Latin, relating to the purchase of materials for the construction of eight galleys to be built for the Crown in various private yards in the last decade of the thirteenth century.[35] Especially informative are the records of payments for materials and labor for a galley built in Newcastle. These were large vessels with castles in each end and probably a fighting top on the mast; they shipped as many as 120 oars. While the accounts do not give construction details directly, the terms applied to certain hull components and to the tasks of various personnel (they even list a female painter's helper) leave little doubt that these were clinker-built hulls.

But the English built them even larger than that. At least two gigantic hulls were so constructed, the *Grace Dieu*, launched in 1418 by Henry V, and the *Great Galley* of Henry VIII built more than a century later, which was a four-master said to carry 207 guns and 120 oars. Relatively few details are known about the *Great Galley*, but the bones of the *Grace Dieu* (also listed variously as the *Gracedieu* and the *Grace de Dieu*) still survive.[36] It is listed as a two-masted carrack 125 ft (38.1 m) on the keel, 180 ft (54.9 m) overall, and 50 ft (15.24 m) in the beam. It was rated at fourteen hundred tons, making it the largest known northern European ship built up to that time. After being launched too late in 1418 to serve in the Hundred Years War, it was moved to a mooring in the Hamble River, where it was struck by lightning and partially destroyed twenty-one years later. Over the last century or so, the remains—also known as the Bursledon wreck—were intruded upon occasionally and some timbers were removed, but in 1933 the wreck still measured 135 ft by 37½ ft (41.15 m by 11.43 m).

The *Grace Dieu* was built with three layers of overlapping planking (Fig. 4–38). To allow for the overlap, the inner layer had about 4 in (10.16 cm) less width than the two outer layers.[37] Note that there were actually five layers of planking at the overlaps, and here the strake was about 8 in (20.3 cm) thick. Individual planks were said to be relatively short—most were 6 or 7 ft (1.83 to 2.13 m) long—and the individual layers were fastened to each other with small nails to form a composite plank. The overlaps were fastened with ⅝-in-square (1.6 cm) iron nails spaced about 8 in (20.3 cm) apart and riveted over 2-by-3-in (5.08-by-7.62-cm) iron roves. When launched, the ship was said to have been caulked with moss and pitch.[38]

Frames, sided 12 in (30.48 cm) and molded about 10 in (25.4 cm), were notched for the lands of the planks and must have had a room and space of about 16 in (40.6 cm). This assumption is made because that was the average distance between the 1¼ in (3.18 cm) treenails that joined them to the planking. Thus only 4 in (10.16 cm) of

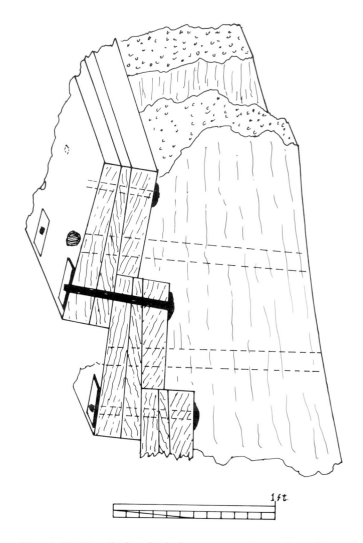

1 ft.

Fig. 4–38. Detail of triple clinker construction on *Grace Dieu*. (based on R. C. Anderson [figs. 4, 5], and information from the reports cited)

space existed between these timbers, whose futtocks were joined with diagonal scarfs.

Whether so large a vessel represented a practical form of clinker construction remains in doubt, but it does indicate that large, heavy hulls could be built by this method.

Cogs and Cog-like Vessels[39]

Ole Crumlin-Pedersen describes a cog as a double-ended craft with angular profile, flat bottom with flush strakes, and steep, lapstraked sides. That is, generally speaking, a very good definition—compact yet descriptive—although more recent discoveries in Denmark, the Netherlands, Poland, and Sweden have prompted Reinder Reinders to suggest a broader term of "cog-like vessels" in order to accommodate wrecks that do not fit Crumlin-Pedersen's description exactly.[40]

Cogs probably developed near the mouth of the Rhine in Frisia, expanding in size and technology as Frisian trade expanded and navigating the Baltic at least by the ninth century.[41] Early coins show cogs with broad, square sails, flat bottoms, steep ends, and several strakes of clinker-built sides. They were steered by side-mounted oars or rudders. During the thirteenth and fourteenth centuries, such craft apparently developed into the large, seaworthy cogs used by the Hanseatic traders. Eventually these vessels sported castles fore and aft and ranged as far as the Mediterranean in ever-expanding commercial, and sometimes aggressive, roles.

Here we will examine only three surviving versions of cog-like construction. Two of them were Zuyderzee vessels, and the other was a large, seagoing Hanseatic ship.

ZUYDERZEE VESSEL NZ43

The remains of a small cog-like vessel (Fig. 4–39) were discovered during irrigation work in lot NZ43 along the southern edge of the Zuyderzee polders in 1971. This extensively preserved wreck has been tentatively dated to between the thirteenth and sixteenth centuries, most probably to the late thirteenth or early fourteenth century. Aleydis Van de Moortel has conducted an extremely thorough and scientific analysis of the surviving timbers and has reconstructed them as follows.[42]

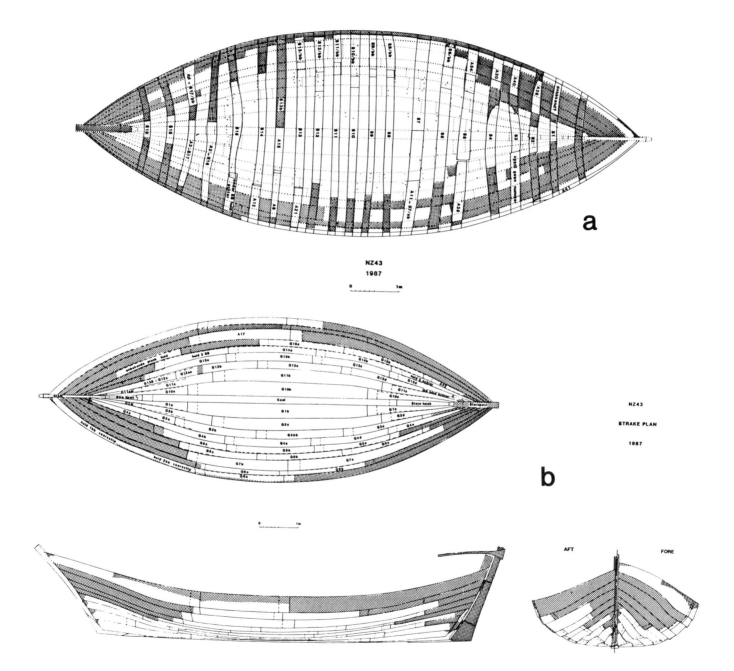

FIG. 4–39. The reconstructed NZ43 Zuyderzee vessel: (a) top view; (b) three views of the reconstructed planking. Shaded areas did not survive. (Van de Moortel, figs. 43, 62)

All hull members were made from oak. The keel was merely a thick plank, 6.5 m long; it was 18.5 cm wide and 7 cm thick amidships, tapering to slightly smaller dimensions at the ends. It was nailed to the hooks at either end (Figs. 4–39b and 4–40a). *Hook* is the term most cog scholars apply to these knees, which are used to change the horizontal orientation of the central plank to the vertical orientation of the posts; in later English shipbuilding terminology they are called *gripes* in the bow and *heels* in the stern. The central plank was reconstructed with a rocker of 14.5 cm over a length of 4.5 m, although it is uncertain if the entire rocker was initially formed this way or if this construction was a result of operational sagging. Stem and sternpost were then joined to the hooks by means of flat scarfs, each scarf being secured by one treenail.

The bottom of the vessel was assembled next, and possibly some or all of the side planking was in place before frames were inserted. There were three bottom strakes, two bilge strakes, and four side strakes of planking on each side of the hull (Figs. 4–39b and 4–41). Strakes consisted of three to five planks, so that there were an estimated forty planks on each side of the hull; each was connected to its neighbor by means of flat scarfs fastened with nails and sometimes treenails (Fig. 4–40b). Strakes varied in width amidships from 20 cm to nearly 40 cm, and nearly all of them narrowed appreciably toward the ends of the hull. Thicknesses averaged about 3 cm and were rather consistent throughout, thinning only at the extremities of

the hull. Garboard strakes were 37 cm wide, and second strakes were 35 cm wide to starboard and 32 cm to port. The next three strakes were considerably narrower, while the four side strakes alternated in width and thickness, the narrow ones being thicker than the broad ones. The sheer strake was the broadest of all, with a reconstructed width of 40 cm and thickness of 2.7 cm amidships. Because the bottom was so flat and the ends so sharp and peaked, some of the lower strakes twisted radically in this horizontal to vertical transition in the ends of the hull. Van de Moortel offers some interesting examples of notching, sculpting, and bevelling to accomplish these lateral twists.

Planking scarfs varied between 20 and 31 cm in length. In all cases, forwardmost planks were placed outboard of their after neighbors. The ends of the scarfs were not always flush with the adjoining planking surfaces, so that inner or outer scarf surfaces protruded as much as 2 cm (Figs. 4–40b and 4–40c). This feature was far more predominant on the outer hull surfaces, perhaps because the inner surfaces were trimmed more carefully to accommodate frames.

Until now I have avoided stating which planks were flush and which were lapstraked, largely because such designations would have been misleading. The bottom and bilge strakes, for instance, were flush along their edges and were not fastened to each other, while in the bow and stern these same strakes overlapped (Fig. 4–40c). The garboards were flush with the central plank in the middle

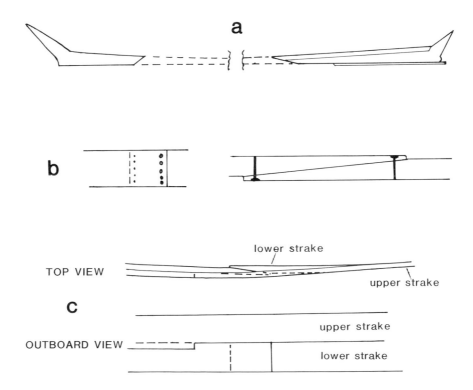

FIG. 4–40. Construction details of NZ43: (a) the hooks (stern hook to the right); (b) typical vertical planking scarf: top (right) and side views; nail clenching details are omitted; (c) the most common of several arrangements used to accomplish the transition from flush to overlapping edges in the lower strakes. Not to scale. (adapted from Van de Moortel, figs. 28, 44, 52)

port   starboard

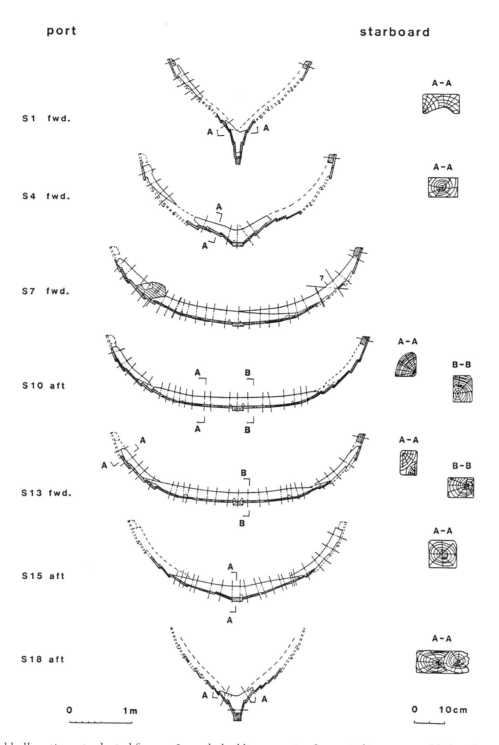

FIG. 4–41. Partial hull sections at selected frames. Long dashed lines crossing frames indicate treenail holes; short dashed lines represent reconstructed areas. (Van de Moortel, fig. 67)

of the hull and were not attached to it, while their ends were nailed to the rabbets of the hook. Side strakes overlapped throughout, the laps being fastened by nails driven from outside the hull and clenched over the inner strake. Small square holes, stopped with wooden plugs, were found throughout the flush planking and in a few lapped planks; they are believed to have been used during construction to attach cleats that would have held the planks in place until the frames were installed.

The seams were caulked with moss and covered with elliptically shaped laths that were fastened with iron clamps called *sintels*. The system was similar to that of the Bremen and Almere vessels described below (see Figs. 4–45 and 4–49). Flush seams were caulked from the outside, while overlapping seams were caulked inside, although eight overlapping planks were also caulked outside. Moss was found in some planking scarfs.

A sheer timber of varying dimensions (9 cm by 15 cm near amidships) ran along the frame heads and inside the sheerstrake to strengthen the hull longitudinally and to cover the tops of the frames. It was fastened primarily with closely spaced treenails whose diameters ranged from 3.5 to 5 cm.

Twenty full frames, and probably a pair of half-frames in the bow, reinforced the planking. They were notched at points of plank overlap (Fig. 4–41). Full frames consisted of floor timbers and futtocks joined together by flat scarfs and fastened with treenails, which usually penetrated the planking as well. Primarily, they were connected to the central plank, hooks, and planking by means of treenails, although iron nails also secured frames to planks in some instances. Most of these treenails were just under 2.5 cm in diameter, but larger ones were used in areas of potential stress. With the exception of the V-shaped floor timbers in the ends of the hull, which had molded dimensions as great as 35 cm, average molded dimensions of the floor timbers were 15 cm and average sided dimensions were 17.5 cm. Futtocks had slightly smaller molded surfaces, but their siding was somewhat greater. Average space between frames was 24.5 cm, although it varied greatly among individual pairs of frames (Fig. 4–39a).

The majority of the floor timbers had four watercourses cut into their plank faces, two at the limbers and two near the turn of the bilge. On the average, these triangular notches were 5 cm high and had a base width of 3 cm. Other floor timbers toward the ends had one or two holes, while the forwardmost three frames and the aftermost four were so far above the level of the bottom that they required no accommodations for the passage of bilgewater.

Three beams were found, one about 17 cm square near its center and the other two 10 cm high and 10 and 11 cm wide. All three decreased in size toward their ends. Their original locations and precise functions are speculative, but all are believed to have been deck beams. Also recorded were three knees, some ceiling planks, a low bulkhead forward, and some chocks or steps, which may have been used in conjunction with the mast or partners; since their functions are not completely understood, however, they will not be discussed further. There is some evidence to suggest that this vessel had a sternpost-mounted rudder.

Vessel NZ43 has a reconstructed overall length of 11.8 m, a maximum beam of 4.26 m, and a height from the sheer line to the bottom of the central plank amidships of 1.2 m (Fig. 4–42). Thus it is very beamy with respect to height and length, with a beam:length ratio of 1:2.8. Van de Moortel estimates total displacement at 17.8 metric tons, with a hull weight of around 8 tons and a cargo capacity of more than 9 tons. Fully loaded, this square-rigged vessel would have drawn nearly a meter of water. An elaborate analysis of hydrostatic properties, contemporary weights and measurements, and construction and operating costs are among the many fine investigations included in this study and are features that, unfortunately, we have no space to discuss here.

THE BREMEN HANSE COG[43]

The Bremen cog, discovered in the Weser River at Bremen, Germany, in 1962, was the first cog ever to be excavated. The initial discovery of any vessel type is always exciting, but this find was especially rewarding in that it was quite large and well preserved right up to the capstan on the aftercastle. The approximately fifty tons of timbers were disassembled and removed to the Deutsches Schiffahrtsmuseum in Bremerhaven, where the hull was reconstructed. It is presently being preserved in polyethylene glycol, a process that will require fifteen to twenty years to complete.

The hull is 23.23 m long, 7.04 m in the beam, and its sides are deep, extending 4.3 m above the line of the keel plank. It has been dated to 1380 by dendrochronology.

A midship section and construction details are illustrated in Figure 4–43, and a sheer view of the structure is shown in Figure 4–44. The construction sequence and arrangement of timbers are not greatly different from those of the Zuyderzee vessel previously described, but they are larger and more complex, and topside construction is considerably more elaborate. All timbers were made from oak. Keel plank and end hooks were assembled, and the long, straight posts attached to the upper scarfs of the hooks. Both posts were made from two pieces and were forked at their lower ends, fitting over matching projections on the hooks (Fig. 4–45a).

Next came the planking, which was much larger than that of the Zuyderzee vessel. The Bremen cog's strakes were made up of only three or four planks each, so that the starboard side contained only forty-three planks, three more than the estimated number for little NZ43. They were joined by means of flat scarfs as above. There were only twelve strakes on each side, too, even though this hull had three times the height of NZ43. The three bottom strakes on each side were laid with their edges flush. Garboards were about 40 cm broad and 5 cm thick amidships, the others only slightly smaller, and widths did not decrease much in the ends of the hull. The fourth strake was transitional in that it was flush amidships and overlapped the third strake in the ends. The fifth strake completed this transition in the middle of the hull. All overlaps were secured by means of closely spaced, double-clenched nails that were driven through pre-drilled holes from the outside of the hull.

Caulking was driven into the seams of the flush planking from the outside and into the groove formed by beveled upper surfaces of the lapped strake and the inner

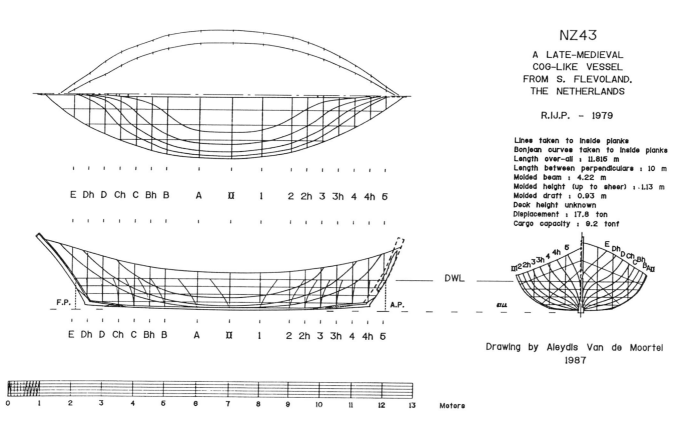

NZ43

A LATE-MEDIEVAL
COG-LIKE VESSEL
FROM S. FLEVOLAND,
THE NETHERLANDS

R.IJ.P. — 1979

Lines taken to inside planks
Bonjean curves taken to inside planks
Length over-all : 11.815 m
Length between perpendiculars : 10 m
Molded beam : 4.22 m
Molded height (up to sheer) : 1.13 m
Molded draft : 0.93 m
Deck height unknown
Displacement : 17.8 ton
Cargo capacity : 9.2 tonf

Drawing by Aleydis Van de Moortel
1987

FIG. 4–42. The lines of NZ43. (Van de Moortel, fig. 20)

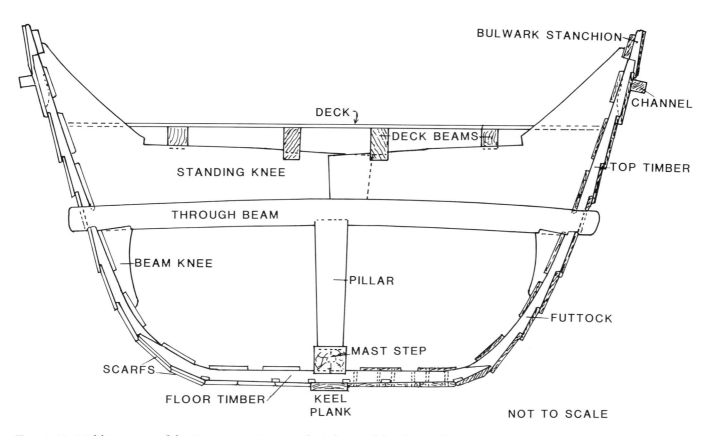

FIG. 4–43. Midship section of the Bremen cog. Not to scale. (after Kiedel and Schnall, pp. 40, 41; original drawing by R. Schultze and reconstruction by W. Lahn)

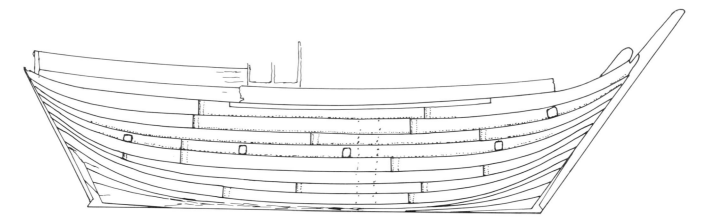

FIG. 4–44. A simplified starboard view of the Bremen cog. Not to scale. (after Kiedel and Schnall, frontispiece and ill. 11)

surface of its adjoining plank (Fig. 4–45b). Caulking was composed of moss, animal hair, and tar, and it was probably driven into the seams with caulking irons before being sealed with split willow laths secured by means of elliptical iron clamps.

Werner Lahn suggests that the twenty-seven floor timbers were installed after the first five strakes of planking were in place on each side of the hull. Floor timbers were treenailed to the keel and the planks. Each plank was fastened to each frame with two 3-cm-square treenails; the first was driven through plank and frame, and the second was installed later in the construction process, since it passed through the adjacent ceiling plank as well.

A timber that weighed 600 kg and was 11.4 m long, perhaps long enough to be called a keelson, was notched to fit over the floor timbers along the centerline of the keel. Made from a single log of oak, it contained the mast step and was treenailed to the floor timbers but not to the keel plank. The keelson was braced laterally in the area of the mast step.

After the eighth strakes were in place and secured, four of the five through-beams and perhaps some of the futtocks were installed. The through-beams, more than 20 cm on a side and weighing about 450 kg each, were notched on their sides to receive the ends of the ninth strakes and rounded at their ends to deter end damage and perhaps to present a more pleasing appearance. After the tenth strake was in place, all remaining futtocks could have been installed as well as the final through-beam in the bow. This beam, just above deck level, was called the *bitt beam* because the two inboard anchor cable bitts were stepped into them.

The eleventh and twelfth strakes were about 60 cm wide. A washboard overlapped this uppermost strake, but its overlap was merely nailed, rather than clenched, since its purpose was protective rather than structural. Thick, bulkhead-like members with upward-angling arms rested atop each of the four lower through-beams. These supported both the sides of the ship and its longitudinal deck beams.

The Bremen cog had an aftercastle, a windlass below the quarterdeck, and a large capstan in the middle of the aftercastle. It was steered by means of a rudder mounted on the sternpost and probably would have been

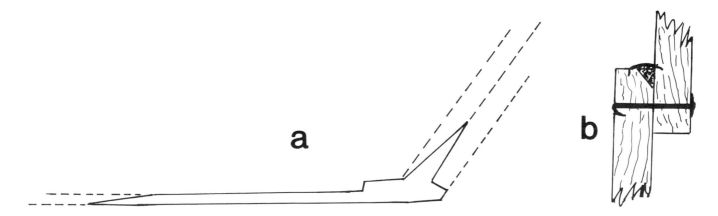

FIG. 4–45. Construction details of the Bremen cog; (a) arrangement of hooks; (b) caulking details at overlapping seams. Not to scale. (after [a] Ellmers, fig. 1.8; [b] Lahn, ill. 56)

propelled by one large squaresail, although it is believed the vessel sank before being completed and rigged. Hull weight is estimated at sixty tons and cargo capacity at about eighty tons.

ALMERE WIJK 13[44]

Remains of a fifteenth-century cog were discovered at a trenching project in 1968 near Almere, the Netherlands. The wreck was flattened but well preserved except for a two-meter gap cut through the stern by trenching machinery. Dated by coins to between 1422 and 1433, the timbers revealed wear and repairs that suggest a somewhat earlier date for the vessel's construction.

Frederick M. Hocker's reconstruction (Figs. 4–46, 4–47, and 4–48) shows a hull with an overall length of 15.95 m (which does not include the missing rudder), a maximum breadth of 4.2 m, and a depth of 1.93 m from the bottom of the keel plank to the top of the caprail at its lowest point. He estimates the full-load displacement to have been about 39.5 tons, of which 15 tons are the estimated weight of the vessel. The lines indicate a relatively wide bottom flat, a hard bilge, nearly vertical sides, and a full, shallow midsection. The stem and sternpost have the extreme rakes typical of cogs. Except for pine ceiling planks in the bottom of the hold, all timbers and planking were made from oak.

The keel plank was 9.94 m long, 32 cm wide amidships, and 6.5 cm thick. Double-clenched iron nails were used to fasten it to the scarfs that joined it to the hooks at either end. The forward hook was 2.11 m long and 0.68 m high; the after hook had a length of 1.44 m and a height of 0.53 m (Fig. 4–47). The posts were scarfed to the upper ends of the hooks, the scarfs being secured by means of wedged treenails. The stem was 3.4 m long and was molded 31 cm at the hook and 14 cm at its upper end; it was sided 18 cm on its lower after face (13.5 cm at the top of the after surface) and 11 cm on its inner face. A false stem protected the stem and upper planking ends. While the sternpost did not survive, it could be reconstructed from planking and hook details.

Each side of the hull was composed of eight strakes of planking, seven of them 4.5 cm thick and the sheerstrake 5.3–5.7 cm thick originally. The lowest three strakes were set with their edges flush amidships, becoming lapstrake in the ends of the hull. All other planks overlapped the ones below them. Laps were fastened with double-clenched iron nails (Fig. 4–49) spaced at intervals of 15 to 18 cm. Planking widths varied considerably; at amidships they were 30–34 cm wide over the turn of the bilge and 40–50 cm wide elsewhere except for the sheerstrake, which exceeded 55 cm in width. Garboards and bilge strakes were composed of two planks, all other strakes of three planks. Planking scarfs were flat and clench-nailed together.

Like the other cogs, this one was caulked with moss, lath, and sintels, except that these seams were caulked both inside and out (Fig. 4–49). Hocker estimates that more than six thousand sintels were used to hold the laths in place.

Thirty frames stiffened the hull; twenty-two of these were heavy floor timbers that were treenailed to the keel plank (Fig. 4–48). Each was sided 15–21 cm and molded 13 cm at the keel plank and had one arm longer than the other, with the longest arm usually reaching strake 6. These floor timbers were alternated so that long arms of adjacent timbers were on opposite sides of the hull. Three additional floor timbers were seated across each post but were not fastened to the posts. All floor timbers except the forwardmost and aftermost ones were accompanied by futtocks on each side; futtocks varied in size but were smaller in section than the floor timbers. Two pairs of half-frames, one pair over each hook, completed the framing plan.

Outer frame faces followed the planking surfaces closely, being flat over the flush planks and joggled over the lapped seams. Treenails, 2.3–2.7 cm in diameter, joined planks to frames in a pattern utilizing two treenails per plank per frame except along the bilge strakes, where only one treenail attached planks to each frame.

A heavy inwale protected the futtock heads, and a caprail topped each side. The lone mast step, 1.77 m long, sided 34 cm, and molded 23 cm at the mast heel, was notched over four floor timbers and treenailed to them.

The ceiling was 3 cm thick and was nailed to the frames. Bottom ceiling was fashioned from pine, while that on the sides of the hold was made of oak. The uppermost ceiling plank, 4.5 cm thick, acted as a shelf clamp by supporting the deck beams.

Survival of deck remains was so limited as to be virtually useless, although Hocker was still able to reconstruct much of the deck and supporting structure through other evidence. The hull was strengthened afore and abaft the hatch by heavy beams that had standing knees and intermediate timbers treenailed to them, in effect producing double beams (Figs. 4–48 and 4–49). The forwardmost of these beams was located just aft of the mast and served as its partner. The locations of several other beams have similarly been established. Gangways, at least 9 m long, 7.5 cm thick, and 28 cm wide, provided some longitudinal support along the widest areas of the hull. They were notched over the frames and were treenailed to them, strake 7, and the beams upon which they rested.

Hocker believes that the Almere vessel was not intended for open waters and provides evidence to suggest that it was originally intended as a vessel that could navigate the numerous canals of the Netherlands. He also provides convincing evidence for a typical cog construction sequence—the erection and temporary fastening of flush bottom strakes before the installation of floor timbers.

Hocker argues for recognition of a third classification of hull construction in addition to the previously recognized major forms in which the planking shell is the

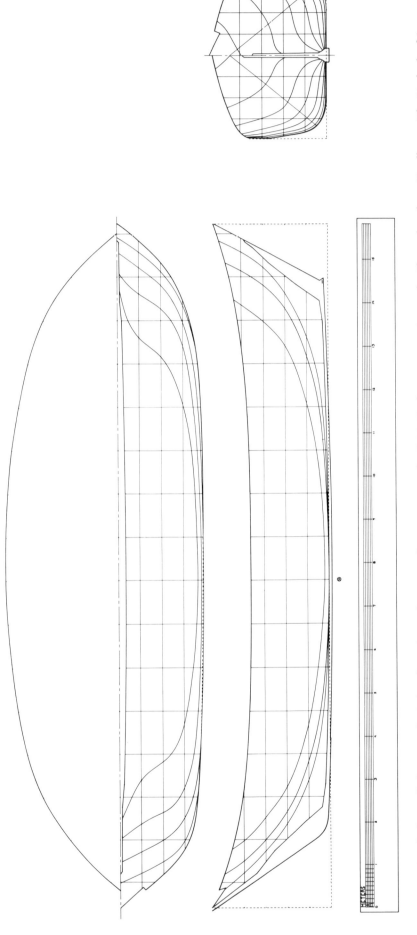

Fig. 4–46. The lines of Almere Wijk 13. (Hocker, Plan I; drawing and reconstruction by F. M. Hocker; courtesy Centre for Shiparchaeology, Ketelhaven, The Netherlands)

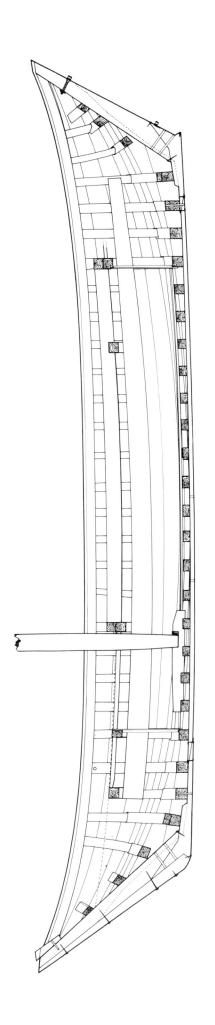

Fɪɢ. 4–47. A longitudinal construction plan of Almere Wijk 13. (Hocker, Plan II; drawing and reconstruction by F. M. Hocker; courtesy Centre for Shiparchaeolgy, Ketelhaven, The Netherlands)

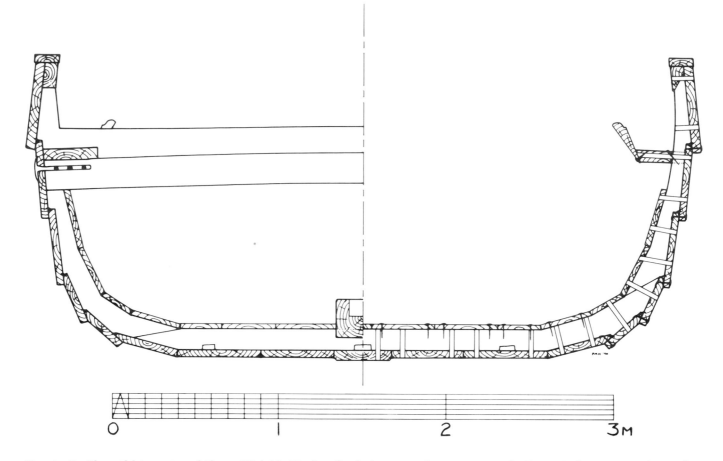

FIG. 4–48. The midship section of Almere Wijk 13. (Hocker, fig. 3; drawing and reconstruction by F. M. Hocker; courtesy Centre for Shiparchaeology, Ketelhaven, The Netherlands)

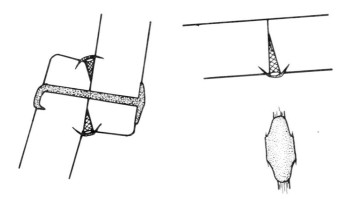

FIG. 4–49. Almere Wijk 13: fastening and caulking details. (Hocker, fig. 12; drawing and reconstruction by F. M. Hocker; courtesy Centre for Shiparchaeology, Ketelhaven, The Netherlands)

primary structure (shell-built) or in which the internal framing is preponderant (skeletal-built).[45] This third classification he calls *"bottom-built* construction, in which the bottom of the vessel is the primary component." It applies to a very large group of primarily inland and coastal craft whose hulls are mostly flat- or nearly flat-bottomed and were constructed by methods combining both shell and skeletal procedures. For the most part, these vessels fall into categories not unlike the cogs and cog-like hulls previously described, where heavy bottom planks were temporarily fastened together and those fastenings were later eliminated in lieu of frame attachment and subsequent erection of the sides.

The Far East

Shipbuilding in the Far East differed appreciably from that of the above areas during the medieval period, and three archaeological examples have provided some new and interesting information concerning Chinese construction. The first example dates to the Song Dynasty; the latest of the coins found on the wreck was struck in 1272, and archaeologists believe the ship sank shortly thereafter.[46] The vessel was discovered during canal dredging at Houzhou, in the People's Republic of China. In 1973 it was excavated, dismantled, and transported about 10 km to Quanzhou, Fujian Province, where it has been reconstructed and is now displayed in a museum.[47]

The surviving portion of the Quanzhou hull measures 24 m long by 9.15 m broad. A keel, twelve bulkheads, part of the transom, and the hull sides to just above the turn of the bilge are preserved. The sides include sixteen strakes of starboard planking and fourteen strakes on the port side. Original hull dimensions are estimated to be about 34 m long and 10 m wide, while its displacement is believed to have been about 375 tons (Fig. 4–50a).

The keel was made from three pieces of pine joined by complex scarfs—a horizontal central section and upward-sloping end pieces. The hull is double planked in cedar to the beginning of the turn of the bilge and triple planked above that point; it is laid in a combination of flush and overlapping edges (Figs. 4–50b and 4–50c). Inner planking

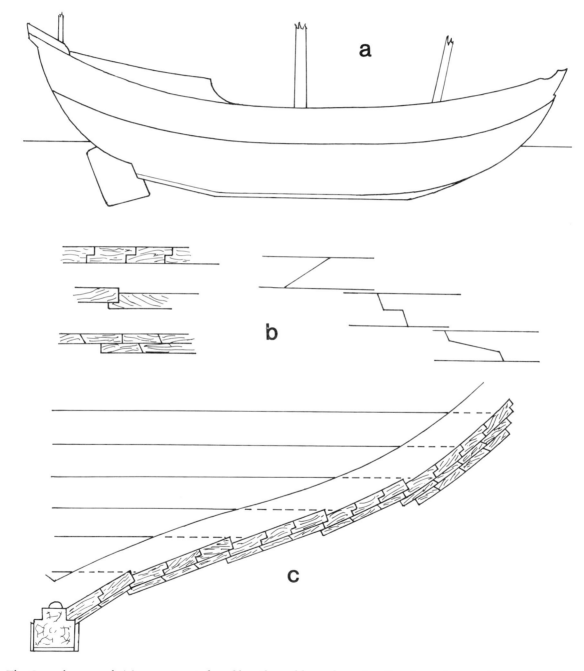

FIG. 4–50. The Quanzhou vessel: (a) reconstructed profile—the rudder and construction above the waterline are hypothetical; (b) planking seam (left) and scarf joins; (c) a composite, partial section of the hull, showing bulkhead planks and their backing frames, hull planking, and the fit of the garboard to the keel. These sketches are schematic only—not to scale. (after [a] *Wen Wu* 10, fig.4; [b] Green, fig. 4 and Li Guo-Qing, fig. 4; [c] *Wen Wu*, fig. 1)

is 8 cm thick. The lower edge of the garboard is set into a rabbet in the upper edge of the keel, while its upper edge is rabbeted to form a flush seam with the second strake. The upper edge of the second strake forms an offset rabbeted seam with the third strake. Above this point a sequence of two flush seams and one offset seam is repeated as far as the bilge, where a triple layer of planking begins.[48] Iron nails were driven diagonally from the outside of the plank through the rabbeted seams.

Outer planking is 5 cm thick. A plank is fitted against the side of the keel, perhaps to protect it and to form a rabbet with which to seat the outer garboard. The outer planks have flush, angled seams except where the inner planking offsets; in these cases they are overlapped as in clinker-built hulls. Outer planks are nailed to the inner planks. At the fourth offset of the inner planks, just below the turn of the bilge, a third layer of outer planking commences; its edges are apparently flush, resulting in a planking thickness at least to the waterline of 18 cm. The builder used t'ung putty and *chu-nam*, a mixture of putty, jute fibers, and shredded bamboo, to pay the planking seams and fill crevices on the exterior of the hull.[49]

Twelve massive bulkheads, made from planks 10–12 cm thick, were distributed more or less evenly throughout the hull (Fig. 4–50c). They must have contributed considerable lateral strength, but certainly they reduced volume and free movement in the hold. Bulkhead planking seams also were rabbeted and nailed diagonally. Inner planking was nailed to the edges of the bulkheads, and each bulkhead plank was attached to the outer planks by means of angled iron straps.[50]

A different system of construction was found in the Shinan wreck excavated in South Korea starting in 1976. The Shinan wreck is dated by a cargo tag to 1323 and is

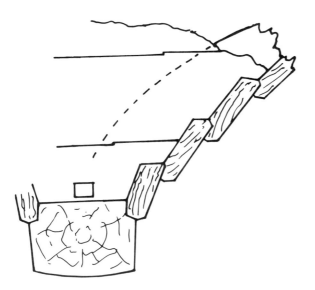

FIG. 4–51. A cross section of the lower part of the Shinan vessel, showing the arrangement of hull planking and bulkhead planks and frames. Not to scale. (after Green and Kim, figs. 1, 5)

believed to be of South Chinese origin.[51] Its extensively preserved remains are being conserved. The hull section in Figure 4–51 reveals a rabbeted form of clinker construction and notched bulkhead planks backed by frames.

The Wando vessel is of Korean origin and is believed to date to around the last half of the eleventh century. Discovered in southwestern Korea in 1984, the hull's original overall length probably did not exceed 9 m. There was no keel; five thick bottom planks were connected to the sides with a pair of curious, L-shaped timbers to form a hard chine. The bottom planks have flush edges; side strakes are rabbeted to each other (Fig. 4–52b). The planking is joined laterally by means of long mortise-and-tenon joints. Notice, in Figure 4–52a, the single pegs of the outer bottom plank tenons and the very long, unpegged joints in the three central bottom planks.

All three hulls display structural features that deviate considerably from previously published literary and pictorial sources. Consequently, even these brief reports, which I hope will be followed by more elaborate and detailed documentation, expand and challenge our present comprehension of Far Eastern shipbuilding and seafaring.

We have examined but a few of the many hull types that must have been plying the waters of the world before the time of Columbus, and even these have been investigated far too sparsely. But the stage is set, and at least the basic methods and most important traditions of construction have been introduced.

In the Mediterranean and surrounding waters, mortise-and-tenon joints and strong shells of planks gradually lost their dominance to stronger internal construction, and eventually the joints disappeared entirely. Frames began to stand on keels before planking was applied, and the methods by which their shapes were derived became increasingly sophisticated. New hull forms appeared, and by the end of the period, naval architecture as we know it today was beginning to emerge at Venice and Genoa and elsewhere.

In northwestern Europe, a completely different form of construction was evolving. Dominant shells of overlapping planks slowly gave way to bottom-based forms of construction. Here, too, new and stronger hull forms evolved, although clinker construction never completely disappeared. Nor were standing frames and their accompanying geometric projections apparent—not yet.

And in the Far East, bulkheads and overlapping, multilayered planking systems provide interesting clues, but we still know nothing about transitions in construction or the methods by which they built those fabled great ships of the Orient.

We must leave the medieval period now and go on to following centuries when seagoing ships went everywhere and influenced the very fabric of most coastal empires. It is time to examine the final centuries of wooden shipbuilding technology.

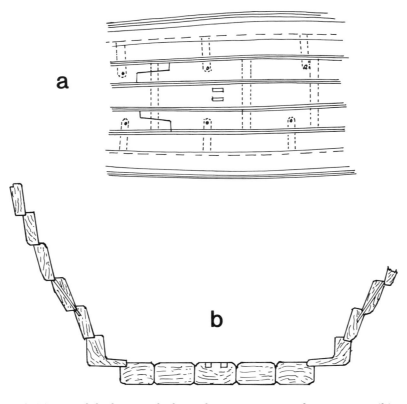

FIG. 4–52. The Wando vessel: (a) part of the bottom planking, showing mortise-and-tenon joints; (b) midship section. Not to scale. (after Green and Kim, fig. 14)

5

THE AGE OF GLOBAL SEAFARING

Contemporary documents indicate that Venice and Genoa continued to improve their techniques in the first half of the sixteenth century. For instance, the Venetians had a method for determining the midship section of a ship using breadth measurements at six prescribed locations based on the depth of the hull (Fig. 5–1), an improvement over the methods used a century before.[1] An even more complex procedure is illustrated in *Fragments of Ancient English Shipwrightery*, a late sixteenth-century document to be cited and described below. This shows a Venetian body section that was derived by striking four arcs whose centers were predetermined by mathematical projection. Both methods are dated to about 1550. Apparently such systems of body design were also being employed farther east at the same time, since *Fragments* shows a Greek body section derived from four arcs. Both illustrations are similar to the three-arc projections described for Figure 5–19.[2]

Sixteenth-Century Iberian Ships

To the west, Iberian shipbuilding had also reached an extensive and relatively sophisticated stage. Maritime activity there grew rapidly after the early fourteenth century, perhaps in part because Spain and Portugal were located along the burgeoning trade route between the Mediterranean and northwestern Europe and because the two countries had an abundance of timber, iron, and other shipbuilding materials. Not only were there numerous shipbuilding centers along the Iberian coasts, but later in the century Spain also established shipyards in such distant locations as Havana, Panama, and Mexico.

Recently published was a list of more than one hundred Iberian vessels known to have been lost in the New World between 1492 and 1520—caravels, pinnaces, *naos*, *bergaintins*, *chinchorros*, and others listed simply as ships or "unknown."[3] In two cases, entire fleets of about twenty seagoing craft failed to return from Caribbean waters. Although the ratio of losses to successful voyages is unknown, this list, limited to little more than twenty-five years and probably far from complete, indicates how much Iberian traffic must have engaged in New World voyaging early in the sixteenth century. Considering all the other Portuguese and Spanish maritime ventures during this period, it seems obvious that Iberian shipbuilding must have attained a sophisticated level in order to meet the demands placed upon it.

One of the earliest known Portuguese texts dealing primarily with shipbuilding was the handwritten document *Livro da Fábrica das Naus* by Fernando de Oliveira.[4] Probably written shortly after 1550, it provides information on ship design and rigging, hull proportions, the conversion of timber, as well as other topics. Oliveira produced various rising and narrowing scales and illustrated a *graminho* that was similar to the Venetian *mezzaluna* discussed in the previous chapter (see Fig. 4–22).

The earliest known text on shipbuilding in the Spanish language was *Instrucción Náutica para navegar*, published in Mexico City in 1587 by a lawyer named Diego García de Palacio.[5] Only the last part of the manuscript deals with shipbuilding and rigging subjects; its value centers predominantly in its lists of proportions of deepwater vessels and their rigging.[6]

An excellent modern source on Iberian shipbuilding, seafaring, and maritime logistics is Roger Smith's *Vanguard of Empire: Ships of Exploration in the Age of Columbus.*[7] Smith lists a broad variety of source material for this period.

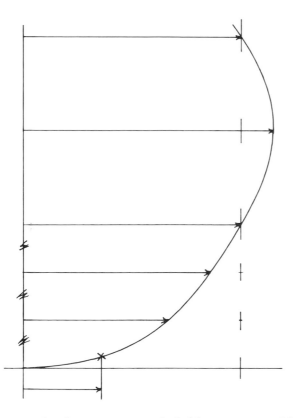

FIG. 5–1. Theodoro's Venetian method of determining a midship section, c. 1550. (after Lane, *MM* 20, fig. 7)

FIG. 5–2. A sectional model of a sixteenth-century ship representative of the Molasses Reef wreck. Note especially the bands of solid framing, the filling pieces, and the various ceiling components. (Oertling, "Molasses Reef," fig. 4; model and photo by Thomas J. Oertling)

We are also fortunate to have at least limited primary information from the sparse remains of two ships that sank in the New World.

THE MOLASSES REEF WRECK

Early in the sixteenth century, a vessel of probable Spanish origin struck Molasses Reef in the Turks and Caicos Islands, which lie directly north of Hispaniola. This wreck is believed to be the oldest yet discovered in the New World.[8] Based on the wreck distribution and the reconstructed arrangement of *bombardetas* on deck, the heavily armed Molasses Reef vessel is estimated to have been about 20 m long on deck with a breadth of at least 7.5 m. Ballasted with thirty-five tons of stone, it was most likely a *nao* or *caravela* and at the time would have been considered a medium-sized vessel. The hull remains have been carefully analyzed by Thomas J. Oertling, from whose final report the following details have been taken.[9]

Oertling estimates that only 2 percent of the hull survived between the keel and the turn of the bilge, yet preservation of the remains was such that he was able to develop a reconstruction whose features were included in the model illustrated in Figure 5–2. With the exception of one sample, all wood was white oak. The keel did not survive. There were twenty-four frames or frame positions identifiable on the inner planking surfaces; all of them were first futtocks and fragments of floor timbers

with sided and molded dimensions that averaged about 16 cm. Room and space averaged 32.5 cm (Fig. 5–3).

The spaces between the lower ends of the futtocks were filled by overlapping outer ends of floor timbers, so that there was a solid band of timber about 75 cm wide as seen beneath the stringers (or *sleepers* in early English texts) in Figures 5–2 and 5–4. Floor timbers were joined to futtocks with two lateral treenails and two iron nails driven from opposite directions, in addition to being securely locked with dovetail joints on the sides of the timbers (Fig. 5–5). In this case the fixed dovetail tenons were cut from the sides of the floor timbers and the mortises were cut from the futtocks. Similar methods of attachment for the frames of several other vessels will be discussed later in this chapter; in all these other ships, however, the tenons were on the futtocks and their widest parts were at the bottoms of the frames. Alternate nailing directions and arrangement of the side joinery indicates that these frames were assembled before installation. Oertling has established the existence of at least eleven consecutive frames so assembled. In addition, he has determined the location of the midship frame, even though it did not survive, because the futtocks were placed forward of the floor timbers on one side of the missing master frame and aft of the floor timbers on the other.

Planks of plain-sawn oak were butt-joined into strakes and had an average thickness of 4.5 cm. Generally they were fastened with two iron nails having 1-cm-square shafts, one near each seam along the frame centerline, and two 2.8-cm-diameter treenails driven on opposite sides of the centerline (see Fig. 5–3, strake 4 at frame C). At some locations there were additional fastenings with round-shafted nails of 1.3 cm diameter, which is probably an indication of further nailing during an

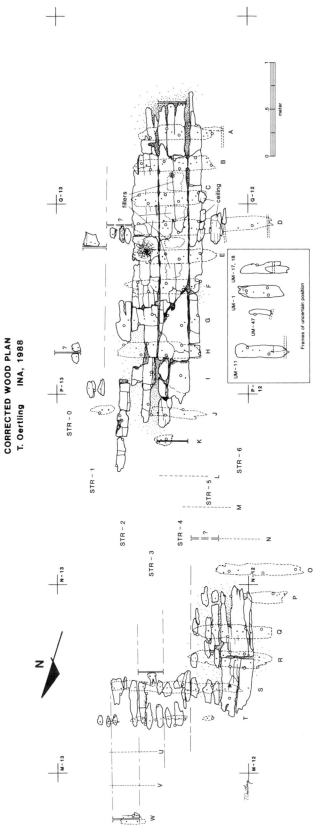

THE MOLASSES REEF WRECK
CORRECTED WOOD PLAN
T. Oertling   INA, 1988

Fɪɢ. 5–3. A revised wood plan of the Molasses Reef wreck, with all fragments placed in their original relative positions. (Oertling, "Molasses Reef," fig. 3)

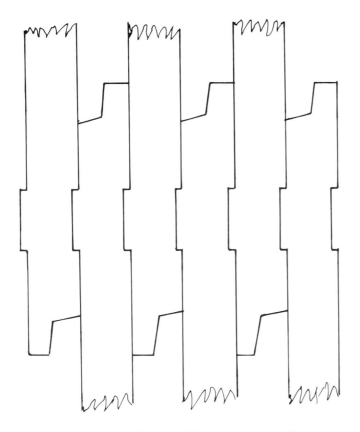

FIG. 5–4. A schematic diagram of the overlapping of floor timbers and futtocks on the sixteenth-century Iberian vessels discussed here. The shapes of the heads and heels of frames and the locations of their dovetail joints may vary from ship to ship.

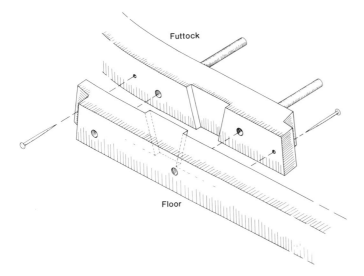

FIG. 5–5. The method of joining floor timber heads to futtock heels on the Molasses Reef wreck. (Oertling, "Molasses Reef," fig. 5)

overhaul. The ends of the planks at butt joins were secured with three square nails and two treenails. Nail heads were recessed and the cavity was filled with caulking; traces of a fibrous material were also wrapped around nail heads.

At the floor heads were *filling pieces*, short boards that closed the spaces between the futtocks and probably were intended to prevent debris and ballast from obstructing the bilges (Fig. 5–2). Their ends rested against the ceiling and outer planking, while each edge abutted the sides of the futtocks.

Nearly twenty-five hundred fastenings were recorded for this wreck, the majority of them being in the form of disassociated concretions. There were forelock bolts, headed and unheaded drift bolts, and nails and tacks of a variety of head and shank configurations. Three nearly complete rudder gudgeons and the fragment of a fourth survived to provide important information about the shape and size of the stern. Rigging artifacts included eyebolts, chain, hooks, sweating hooks, and bronze and iron coaks. A 273-kg anchor was found atop the ballast mound, as well as a gigantic cat-hook (44 cm tall and 33 cm across the throat) that was probably used to fish such an anchor.

THE HIGHBORN CAY WRECK

Another early sixteenth-century wreck was found at Highborn Cay in the Exuma Islands of the Bahamas.[10] Although hull remains were sparse (Fig. 5–6), their distribution was such that they supplied important information about hull dimensions and structural details. The sternpost and after end of the keel had disappeared, but their locations could be confirmed by the abrupt termination of a trough the keel had gouged into the hardpan seabed. In the bow, keel and stem were joined in a 30-cm-long vertical scarf, providing a reconstructed length of 12.6 m for the keel. The keel was sided 15–16.5 cm, and keel and stem were molded 21 cm at the scarf. It was made from white oak, as were all the other major timbers.

Room and space of the frames averaged 40 cm over the keel, except between the frames immediately forward and aft of the midship frame, where center-to-center spacing was 30 cm. Thus there were probably thirty or thirty-one square frames in the hull. The midship frame was located directly beneath the mainmast step. Its 2.35-m-long floor timber was sided 16.5 cm and molded 17.6 cm; the two adjacent floor timbers had the same dimensions. Forward of this point, floor timbers were sided, on the average, 14 cm and molded 24 cm. After floor timbers were poorly preserved.

Floor timbers and futtocks were cut down for nailing at their ends and were joined as in the Molasses Reef wreck (Fig. 5–7), except here the wide ends of the dovetails were at the bottoms of the frames. The midship frame (marked "master couple" on the site plan) had first futtocks attached to both its forward and after sides (Fig. 5–6); the other floor timbers had single futtocks arranged as at

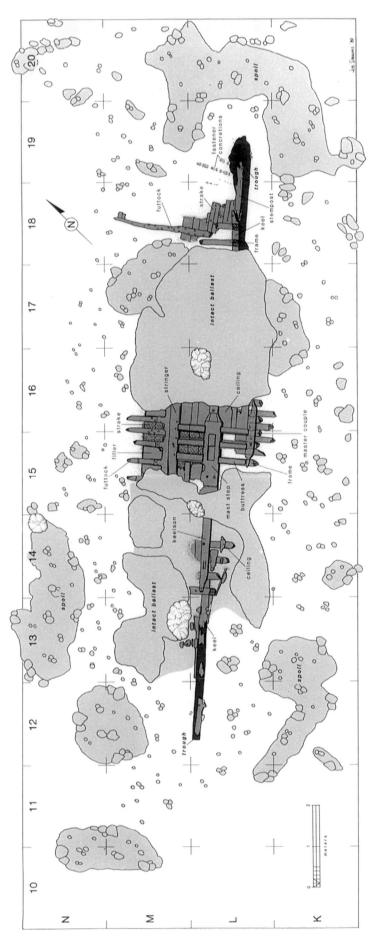

Fig. 5–6. A partial site plan of Highborn Cay wreck. (Oertling, "Highborn Cay," fig. 3; drawing by J. J. Simmons)

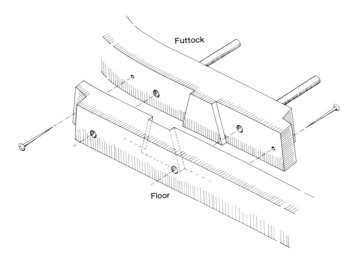

FIG. 5–7. The method of joining floor timbers and futtocks on the Highborn Cay wreck. (Oertling, "Highborn Cay," fig. 7)

Molasses Reef. At amidships, the floor was flat athwartships between the dovetail fastenings.

Planking was 6 cm thick and survived in widths up to 25 cm. It was nailed and treenailed to the frames.

The keelson—sided 16–21 cm, molded 17 cm, and preserved over a length of more than 8 m—had its lower surface notched for each frame. Keel and keelson were bolted together at four known locations, with three of the bolts passing through frames and the fourth passing between them. Over a length of about 2.25 m at the location of the mainmast heel, the keelson swelled to a width of 40 cm and a height of 25 cm to form the mast step. The mortise for the heel of the mast was 65 cm long, 17 cm wide, and 15 cm deep. Three pairs of unfastened buttresses were notched into the stringers and butted against the step to reinforce the step laterally. Two semicircular cuts were made into the side of the step for the pumps.

Three strakes of ceiling, 3 cm thick, were laid on each side of the keelson, outboard of which were placed thick stringers and a fourth ceiling strake. As on the Molasses Reef wreck, filling pieces angled downward from the ceiling to the outer planking to seal the space between the futtocks.

The Highborn Cay ship carried at least three anchors, the largest of which was estimated to weigh 270–300 kg and the other two about 180 kg. The vessel was heavily ballasted.

Using contemporary documentation, Oertling has calculated that the vessel was about 19 m long and 5–5.7 m in breadth. These calculations come close to García de Palacio's dimensions for a ship of 150 tons.

THE CATTEWATER AND RYE A WRECKS

The remains of these two sparsely preserved vessels were found in English waters. Although their nationality and the origin of their construction remains unknown, they

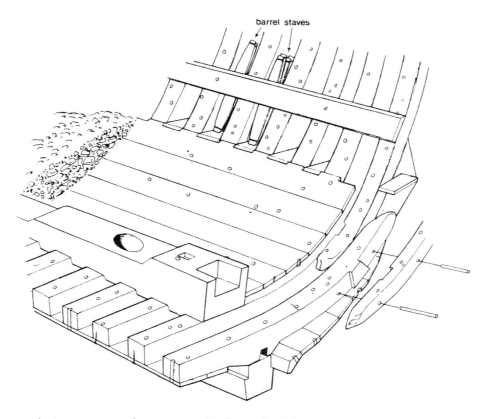

FIG. 5–8. The Cattewater ship's structure at the mast step. (Redknap, fig. 54)

have been placed here in order to compare them with the two vessels just discussed and the Red Bay galleon that follows.

The major timbers of the Cattewater vessel, which is believed to have sunk in the first half of the sixteenth century, were of oak.[11] The keel was sided and molded about 30 cm. Sawn planking was 6–7 cm thick and was both nailed and treenailed to the frames. Floor timbers were 20 cm square, and their ends were fastened to futtocks with treenails and dovetail joints (Fig. 5–8); their overlapping ends formed a continuous belt of timber as on the two previous vessels. The floor timbers were nailed to the keel with single offset nails and were spaced on 37 cm centers. The keelson, sided 30 cm and molded 27 cm, swelled at the mainmast to a sided dimension of 54 cm and a molded height of 40 cm. The mortise was 33 cm wide and 15 cm deep.

The poorly preserved remains of a wreck with features similar to those above were found at Rye, Sussex.[12] Details of the mast step and keelson are shown in Figure 5–9.

VILLEFRANCHE 1 AND YASSI ADA

Not all early sixteenth-century vessels had their frames and futtocks aligned with dovetail joints. The extensively preserved Villefranche 1 wreck—presently being excavated off the coast of southern France—has interlocked, or knuckled, timber connections at the wrongheads, although the belt of solid timbering—a midship frame with futtocks attached to both sides of its floor timber—and other features are similar to the Spanish wrecks just discussed (Fig.

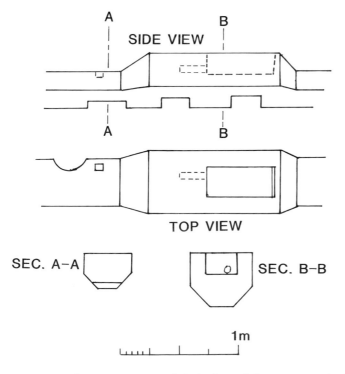

FIG. 5–9. The mast step area of the keelson of the Rye A vessel. (after Lovegrove, fig. 1)

5–10). The Villefranche wreck is believed to date to the early part of the century, possibly between 1510 and 1520, and is most likely of Genoese origin.[13] Its overall length is estimated at approximately 44 m. Surviving material includes the rudder, capstan, rigging, and part of the battery.

That troublesome reef off Yassi Ada in the Turkish Aegean, cited for two wrecks in the previous chapter, also spelled doom for a vessel dating to the early sixteenth century. Probably Islamic in origin, this round-sterned vessel also had knuckled timbers in its bottom. Details are shown in Figure 5–11.[14]

THE SAN ESTEBAN

The *San Esteban* was one of three *naos* wrecked in a storm at Padre Island, along the southern coast of Texas, in 1554. Only a 5-m-long section of the vessel's lower stern survived; it was excavated and preserved in polyethylene glycol.[15]

It has been reconstructed graphically (Fig. 5–12) and in model form (Fig. 5–13). The keel was sided 31 cm and molded 27 cm except at its heel, where it curved upward to support the stern knee and was scarfed to the sternpost with a vertical flat scarf (Fig. 5–14a). Planking rabbets were cut to within 15 cm from the bottom of the keel. The short surviving piece of sternpost was also rabbeted and had approximately the same dimensions as the keel.

In addition to reinforcing the junction between keel and sternpost, the knee acted as a deadwood for nailing the planks and supporting the frames. This grown curvature was bolted to the keel and sternpost with forelock bolts and contained five pairs of 5-cm-wide notches along its upper sides into which the stern frames were set. While none of the frames survived, fastening evidence atop the keel and knee indicated a room and space of approximately 43 cm for the floor timbers. Apparently, a bolt connecting the keel and keelson transfixed every fourth frame, while the other frames were nailed to the keel.

The planking was 10 cm thick, although hooding ends were shaved down to the 5-cm thickness of the rabbets. Caulking samples indicate both oakum and hair were used. Caulking was parceled in place by means of resin-soaked cloth overlaid with lead strips (Fig. 5–14b), the lead strips being fastened with tacks. A similar method of overlaying seams with lead strips was noted in the brief examination of a sixteenth-century Portuguese wreck in the Seychelles, although in this case bent strips of lead were additionally inserted into the seams.[16] Whether this condition existed throughout the hull or was merely an oddity found only in the small area that was examined remains unknown.

THE RED BAY WHALER

Terrestrial excavations of an elaborate sixteenth-century Basque whaling station on the north shore of the Strait of Belle Isle in Red Bay, Labrador, were extended in 1978 to include nearby underwater sites. To date, three galleons

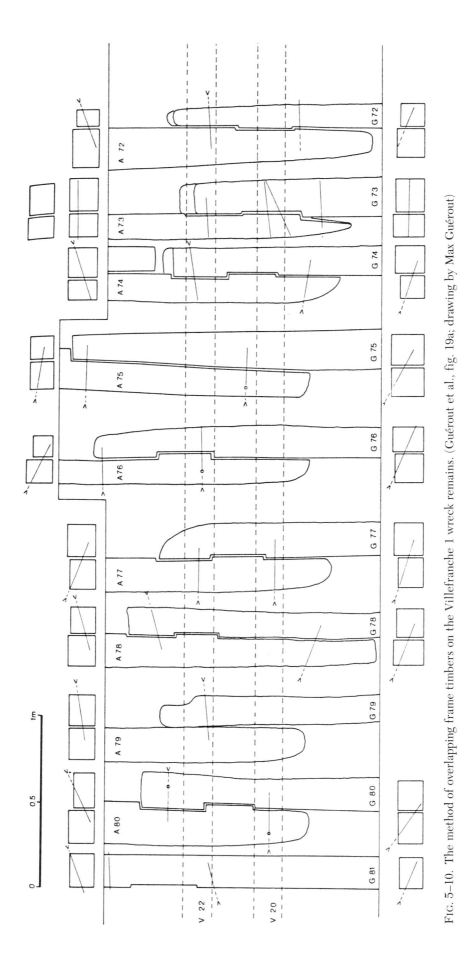

Fɪɢ. 5–10. The method of overlapping frame timbers on the Villefranche 1 wreck remains. (Guérout et al., fig. 19a; drawing by Max Guérout)

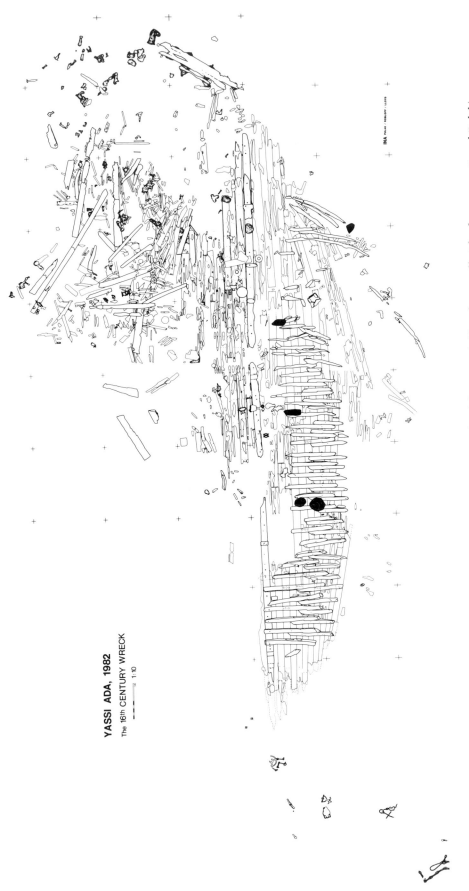

YASSI ADA, 1982

The 16th CENTURY WRECK

1:10

FIG. 5–11a. The sixteenth-century Yassi Ada wreck: wreck plan. (INA drawing by Cemal Pulak, Jay Rosloff, and Manuella Lloyd; courtesy Cemal Pulak)

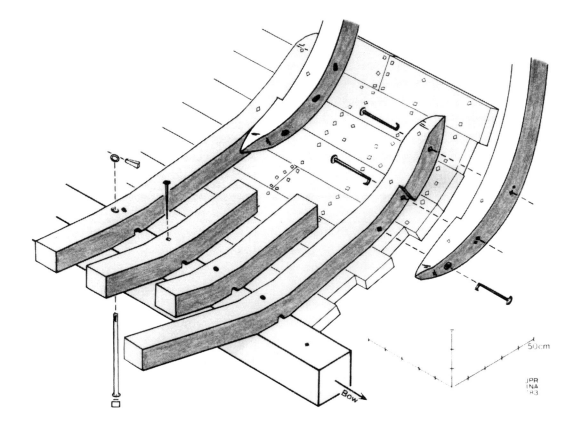

FIG. 5–11b. The sixteenth-century Yassi Ada wreck: framing and fastening details. (drawing by Jay Rosloff; courtesy Cemal Pulak)

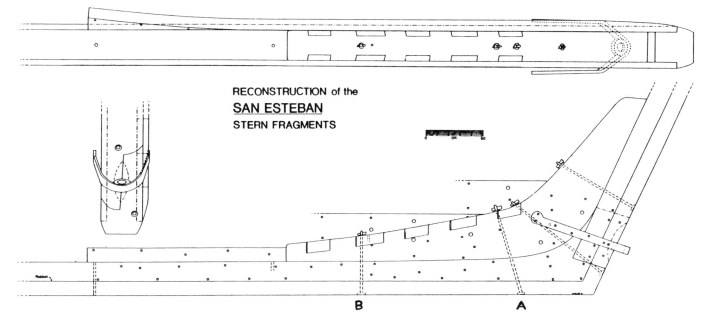

FIG. 5–12. A reconstruction of the remains of the *San Esteban*. (Rosloff and Arnold, fig. 1)

FIG. 5–13. A model of the *San Esteban* remains as viewed from aft. (Rosloff and Arnold, fig. 3B; model and photo by Jay P. Rosloff)

FIG. 5–14a. The *San Esteban's* vertical sternpost scarf and knee. (Rosloff and Arnold, fig. 4B; model and photo by Jay P. Rosloff)

have been found as well as a number of boats and other remains of this remarkable industry.[17] The most thoroughly examined galleon was extensively preserved and is believed to be the *San Juan,* a Basque whaler that sank in Red Bay with a cargo of 900–1,000 barrels of whale oil in 1565.

Although research on this vessel is far from complete, and detailed hull drawings and scantling lists have yet to be published, eight years of field work and research have produced some important information. The ship was a galleon with three masts and three full decks, and it had a cargo capacity of about 250 tons, a length of 22 m on the weather deck, and a beam of 7.5 m. Preliminary lines show a hull with a fine entry, extreme rake of the posts, and an estimated draft of 3–3.5 m. The vessel had a square tuck stern—a flat transom with diagonal planking (Fig. 5–15). Fore and stern castles were made of softwood, the keel of beech, and the rest of the hull structure of white oak.

The keel (Fig. 5–16), made from a single piece of beech whose length was slightly less than twice the beam (14.75 m), was a fascinating piece of ship carpentry.[18] Unlike the rectangular keels of the other two galleons at Red Bay and the vessels just illustrated, this keel was essentially a combination timber carved to include the run of the garboards. It was T-shaped amidships, similar to keels on Viking ships, and U-shaped at the ends, its wings dictating the direction of the lower plank edges in lieu of rabbets. These wings stopped well short of the ends of the hull, where they were replaced by rabbets to seat the

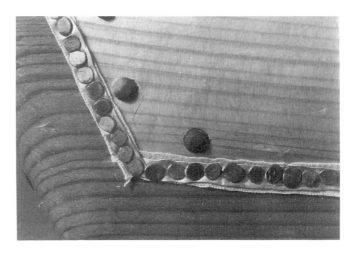

FIG. 5–14b. The parcelling of the *San Esteban's* seams. (Rosloff and Arnold, fig. 8; model and photo by Jay P. Rosloff)

FIG. 5–15. A reconstruction model of the sixteenth-century Red Bay galleon. (model by Marcel Gingras; photo courtesy Canadian Parks Service)

more complex end runs of separate garboards. Vertical flat scarfs joined the keel to the stem and to the heel, and a stern knee connected the after end of the keel to the lower end of the sternpost using a method similar to the one discussed in the previous chapter for the Bremen cog, where it was called a "hook" (Fig. 5–17, top).

Framing was similar to that of the Highborn Cay wreck. The midship floor timber was attached to a pair of futtocks on each side with treenails, nails, and dovetail joints (Fig. 5–17, bottom). All other floor timbers were attached similarly to single futtocks, the futtocks being placed on the side of the floor timber away from the midship frame. As on the vessels described above, there was a belt of solid timbering longitudinally where these overlaps occurred.

Only fourteen frames were assembled in this manner and thus had been preerected. The rest of the framing system must have been added as planking progressed, since none of the other floor timbers were fastened directly to their futtocks. Instead, they were held in place by the planking, wales, clamps, and other longitudinal members. Floor timbers were 20–22 cm square and were spaced 25–30 cm between centers.

The keelson was notched over the floor timbers and swelled and was buttressed at the mast step. A single semicircular cut was made to receive the base of a bilge pump.

Planking was fastened to each frame with at least one treenail and two nails; fastenings were recessed into triangular cavities filled with pitch.

These shipwrecks just discussed illustrate vividly the value of archaeological excavations. Many of those construction details could not be gleaned from documentary sources; even the poorly preserved examples added new information or confirmed what appears to be standardization of many of the structural features. The similarities of some of those features is striking. Whether the English wrecks were built in Iberian yards or certain English yards were following the same practices remains to be seen.[19]

Combining the information from the wrecks with contemporary documentation brings about a rather clear, if still sparse, picture of design and construction. Probably the form of these hulls was derived from projections similar to those illustrated in Oliveira's *Livro da Fábrica* or in the English manuscripts discussed later in this chapter. An aftward raking sternpost with a flat transom stern, gently rounded stem, and fairly heavy keel formed the backbone. With the exception of the Mediterranean wrecks, standing frames had flat floors amidships, full bodies, and probably some tumblehome. Frames were fairly heavy and closely spaced. Futtocks overlapped floor timbers for a half meter or more, producing a solid belt of timber at the turn of the bilge. The frames in the middle of the hull were dovetail-fastened and rigidly treenailed and nailed, which indicates they were pre-assembled. Midship frames had first futtocks attached to both sides of their floor timbers; fore and aft, futtocks were joined to the sides of the floor timbers that faced away from the master frame. Closer to the ends of the Red Bay hull, and probably the other hulls as well, frame timbers were left unconnected to each other. Their integrity was maintained solely by attachment to the planking and ceiling as was done on ancient vessels.

The dovetail joints on the standing frames are curious and bear some consideration. They required a lot of extra work and timber and, in light of the other fastenings, do not at first appear to have been necessary. But they did add some security to the joint and must have made frame assembly easier and more accurate. Their appearance on all of the above wrecks found outside of the Mediterranean indicates that, at least in the minds of their builders, their functional importance must have outweighed the additional labor and timber costs.

Extra timber and labor were also required to fashion mast steps from keelsons, and yet they are so similar to each other that this too must have been standard procedure. Horizontal keel scarfs may have been a rarity on oceangoing ships in this period; all the keel scarfs on the wrecks above were vertical in orientation. They were simple flat scarfs and most, if not all, were caulked. Oak was the standard raw material. Iron nails and treenails were used in combination as plank fastenings in most cases, bolting was done primarily with forelock bolts (although the Molasses Reef wreck also had drift bolts in some places), and limbers were kept clear with filler pieces. Even the later Red Bay galleon adhered to most of these

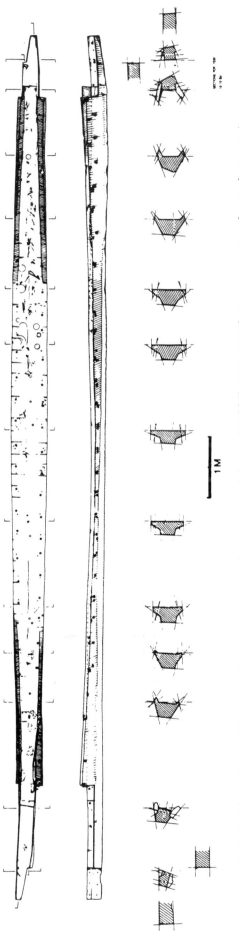

FIG. 5-16. The keel of the Red Bay galleon. Note the great variations of cross-sectional shapes. (Waddell, *IJNA* 15.2, fig 2; courtesy Canadian Parks Service)

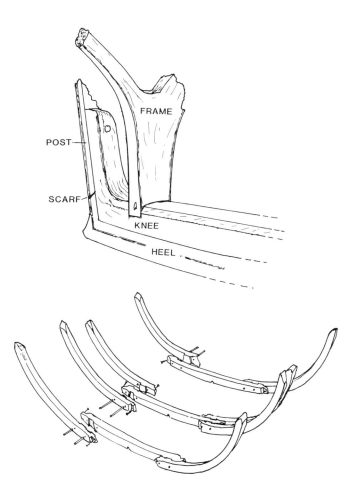

FIG. 5–17. Red Bay ship details: (top) heel connection of keel and sternpost; a Y-shaped frame has been mortised into the top of the stern knee, which rides atop the keel and heel; (bottom) the framing system amidships, where the master couple is formed with a floor timber (center) and a pair of first futtocks on each side. (after Grenier, figs. 10, 12)

construction processes, although its keel/garboard construction might indicate a departure from more southerly practices.

These widely scattered excavations have provided us with a wealth of new information. Future projects will fill in the gaps. Now let's return to northwestern Europe to see what happened there in the sixteenth century.

THE *SOVEREIGN* AND THE *MARY ROSE*

Northwestern European builders apparently did not adapt to the newer skeletal methods of construction as early as their southern counterparts, although at least some of them must have been adopting these changes in the fifteenth and early sixteenth centuries. The eight-hundred-ton English warship *Sovereign* was built in 1488 and rebuilt in 1509; in 1912, the remains of a large warship, believed to have been the *Sovereign,* were found at Woolwich. There was convincing evidence that the ship originally had been clinker-built and was rebuilt with flush planking, since parts of the notches in the outer

frame surfaces had been adzed away and fillets inserted into whatever voids remained in order to permit alignment of the new planking edges.[20]

Immediately after the *Sovereign* was rebuilt, the keel of the *Mary Rose* was laid, and by 1511 it was in active duty. The *Mary Rose* was a four-masted carrack built predominantly of oak but with an elm keel of 32 m length. Initially rated at six hundred tons (seven hundred tons at the end of its career), it was refitted and partially rebuilt in 1536 and sank nine years later during a battle in the Solent. After a lengthy excavation, the wreck was brought to the surface in 1982, and it is presently on display, along with its thousands of artifacts, at the Portsmouth Naval Base.[21] Although construction plans and scantling lists are not yet published, at least we can ponder the wreck's significance. The *Mary Rose* is a most impressive ship, even when viewed through the chilly mist that temporarily stabilizes its timbers. First of all, it is a large ship with a full bow, a fine run into the sternpost below the waterline, and an elaborate transom stern above it. The hull was quite deep—13 m of that depth still survives—and construction was heavy throughout. Thick planks are secured to frames with wedged treenails, their butts and hooding ends of the planks additionally secured with bolts. There are three decks amidships. Riders—internal frames set atop the ceiling—and a strong system of hanging and standing knees gave the hull the additional stiffening it required for the heavy battery of ninety-one guns. The keelson swells to form a mainmast step as in the wrecks discussed previously.

One feature has been published that is worth particular mention. At the starboard quarter of the main deck level, examination of frames and flush planking revealed that the frames had been cut originally for lapped strakes of planking. Part of the angles, or notches, for seating the original planks were cut away as in the wreck at Woolwich, but complete removal of these notches would have weakened the frames too much. Consequently, the carpenters merely cut away part of the frame surfaces and inserted wedge-shaped blocks to fill the voids between frames and planks.[22] This curious feature raises some interesting questions. If indeed the Woolwich ship was the *Sovereign* and all of the *Mary Rose* frames are found to be so configured, then the *Mary Rose* was begun as a clinker-built vessel at about the same time the *Sovereign* was converted to flush planking. Does this mean that the English naval constructors in the early sixteenth century were unable or unwilling to build flush-planked hulls initially on preerected frames several centuries after Mediterranean builders were commonly performing this task? Were smooth skins possible only by replanking existing clinker hulls, or were these simply reworked frames acquired from the breakup of another vessel? A much more extensive examination of the *Mary Rose* frames will be necessary to answer those questions, if indeed they can be answered at all with the evidence from this single find. One thing is certain, however. Even if this vessel were clinker-built originally, it must have required considerably more complex methods of planning and fabrication than the Viking ships and cogs discussed previously.

The coexistence of clinker construction and frame-first flush planking is to be found not only in England but also on the coast of France. For example, at Bordeaux the growing wine trade in the mid–fifteenth century prompted the construction of additional clinker-built merchantmen, yet documents dating to the late fifteenth century indicate a change to flush-planked vessels.

Perhaps the most striking examples of such a transition are two large English warships: the *Great Galley*, clinker-built in 1515 and rebuilt as a flush-planked hull in 1523, and possibly the *Mary Rose*. How such initial construction and rebuilding were accomplished is still largely a mystery, but it does indicate that clinker construction was no longer considered favorable for large vessels of war in England.[23] Indeed, a State Paper of 1545 considers "clenchers both feeble, olde and out of faschion."[24]

All of this leads to an interesting comparison between the evolution of shipbuilding in the Mediterranean and Atlantic coast of France, England, and much of the rest of northwestern Europe. In the Mediterranean, the change to frame-first construction of flush-planked hulls was the result of a steady progression that resulted in a change of the role of outer planking from structurally dominant to secondary. In the northwest, on the other hand, the chronological lag in shell-first development resulted in a situation whereby frame-first construction did not arise as a continuation of earlier techniques but as a substitution for it. Because the latter method was already in place in the Mediterranean and available in the northwest, it competed with the existing methods but, at least in some parts of northwestern Europe, never eliminated them completely.[25]

Henry VIII apparently understood the need for better shipwrightery and from the early years of his reign made profound contributions toward improving shipbuilding technology and expanding his naval fleet. He set up new dockyards at Deptford and Woolwich and expanded naval facilities at Portsmouth. Shipwrights were imported from Mediterranean countries, primarily from Italy, and he encouraged his own shipwrights to improve the state of their craft, rewarding the best of them with life pensions.[26]

Years later, Elizabeth I built on her father's legacy, greatly expanding and improving a neglected naval fleet and encouraging the construction of private vessels. In 1572 she made Mathew Baker her master shipwright, the first person to hold such a title. Master shipwrights were the chief technical administrators of the dockyards. They were responsible for the design and all phases of construction of government ships, including the selection, felling, and transportation of timber, and even the payroll and security of the dockyards. An intelligent and highly respected scholar and craftsman, Baker surely is one of two authors of the document we are about to investigate.

FRAGMENTS OF ANCIENT ENGLISH SHIPWRIGHTERY
MS 2820 in the Pepysian Library of Magdalene College, Cambridge University, is usually referred to as *Fragments of Ancient English Shipwrightery*. 'Fragments' is a good description for this little journal; it is a curious collection of ship draughts and short descriptive texts, sometimes illogically arranged or mixed with irrelevant little renderings on mathematics, navigation, and other subjects. But it is important to the history of naval architecture because the drawings, scales, and relevant textual material clearly illustrate the upper limits of English shipwrightery in the late sixteenth and early seventeenth centuries. Scholars have dated the document to 1586, although apparently it was started by Baker about the time he became master shipwright, and probably it was completed by his colleague, John Wells, about 1630.[27] It is the oldest surviving English-language text on ship design.

The forms of large English seagoing ships were, with the exception of topside construction, somewhat similar to each other. In fact, they were not much different from the Spanish wrecks just discussed. Figures 5–18, 5–19, and 5–20, the latter two of which are adaptations of illustrations in *Fragments* that have been altered to suit our purposes, show these forms. A straight keel, usually with a skeg at its after end, was scarfed to a gently sweeping stem whose curvature was derived from one or more arcs struck from predetermined centers. Arcs of circles played a predominant role in the drafting of hull shapes in this period. The sternpost had a considerable aftward rake. A pair of fashion pieces, which were actually the aftermost frames, and a specified number of lateral transoms were fixed to its upper half to form the familiar "transom stern." Proportions continued to play an important role in this period; the combined rake of the sternpost and radius of the stem sometimes were equal to a certain fraction of the overall length, perhaps one-third, or they were a proportion of keel length or maximum breadth.[28] Most sixteenth- and seventeenth-century ships had a full bow and relatively narrow stern, the maximum breadth being located forward of the center of the hull. The rising and narrowing lines for the floors on either side of the midship frame (Figs. 5–18 and 5–19), as well as the two lines indicating maximum breadth, were projected either as arcs of very large circles or from mathematical proportions. These lines controlled the body shapes fore and aft of the midship bend.[29] Figure 5–20 shows the projections used to derive the locations of the centers for the arcs forming the midship body section. For a more detailed description of a similar method of body projection, see Deane's Doctrine later in this chapter, after the discussion of the *Dartmouth*.

These projections, drawn to some convenient scale on parchment or wood, produced offsets from which

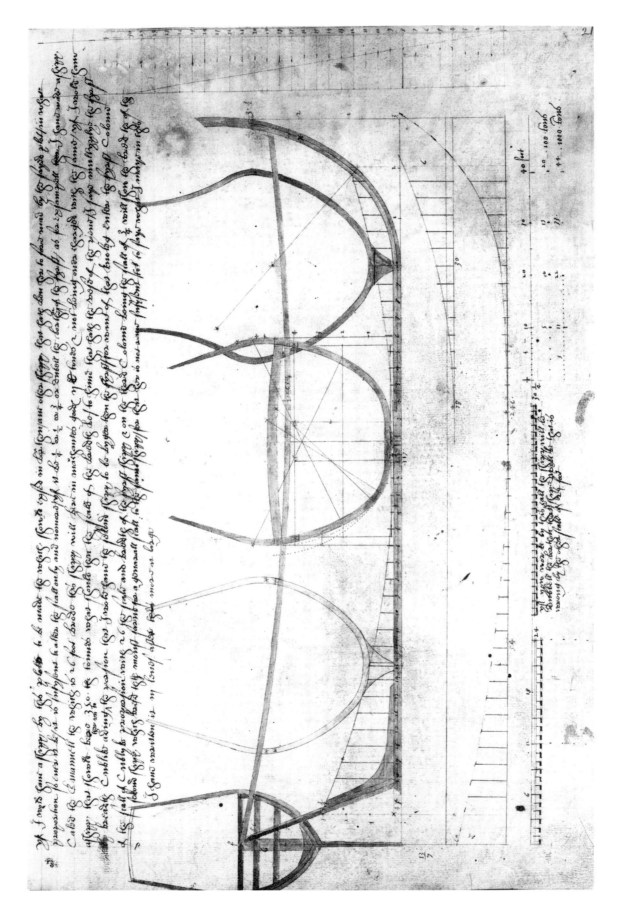

5–18. Rising and narrowing lines and body projections are shown in a drawing of the type found in *Fragments of Ancient English Shipwrightery.* (courtesy The Master and Fellows, Magdalene College, Cambridge)

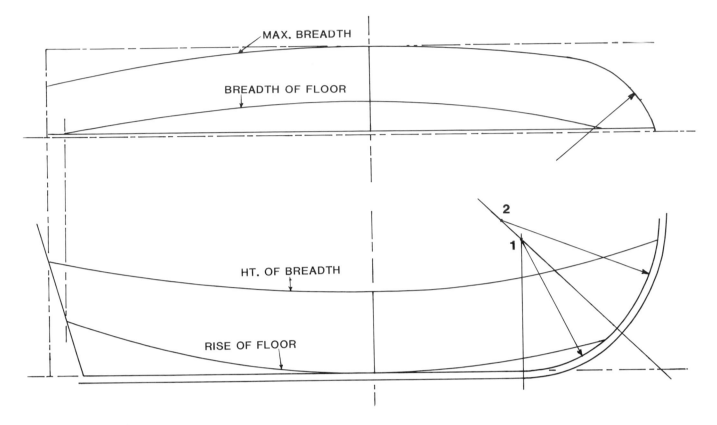

FIG. 5–19. Rising and narrowing lines. (after fig. 5–18 and W. A. Baker, fig. 4)

the molds could be made. As far as can be determined, these molds were used directly without the benefit of fairing on mold lofts as was done in later years. Mathew Baker's references to both older and improved Venetian projections indicate that similar design methods were employed in the Mediterranean at the time.[30]

The above descriptions are only a sampling of the contents of *Fragments*. Baker appears to have been improving upon Venetian systems he had observed from about 1550 on; similar methods may have been used by the larger, more progressive private shipyards, but lesser degrees of sophistication could be expected in the smaller yards and for smaller seagoing vessels. After all, these were rather complex projections at the time and were perhaps beyond the grasp of illiterate or innumerate shipwrights. The use of common molds and a series of battens to acquire shapes would have been one solution, but certainly there must have been many innovative variations of the methods of design discussed to this point.

TONNAGE

The most important principal dimension of this period's ships was tonnage. Tonnage in sixteenth-century merchant vessels related, directly or indirectly, to the amount of burden they could carry. It was a volume measurement, based on the size of the hold or other principal hull dimensions; displacement tonnage, the weight of a vessel and all it carried, was a later concept.

In earlier periods, holds were measured by various means to determine how many amphoras or casks could be stowed. By the late fourteenth or early fifteenth centuries in England, standards were developed based on the Bordeaux wine cask, or *tun,* which weighed 2,240 lbs (1,016 kg) when full and occupied about 57 cu ft (1.6 cu m) of hold space. *Tun* eventually became *ton* and its weight became known as the *long ton,* but as wine gradually relinquished major cargo status, its volume was no longer an acceptable indicator of cargo capacity.[31]

Although they varied in size, seagoing hulls in this period were somewhat similar in hull form. Probably late in the medieval period it was recognized that hull dimensions could be formulated to produce standard tonnage ratings that were fairly accurate indicators of carrying capacity, at least as far as port charges and taxation were concerned. For example, a fifteenth-century Venetian formula from a shipwright's notes was

$$\frac{\text{keel} \times \text{breadth} \times \text{depth}}{6},$$

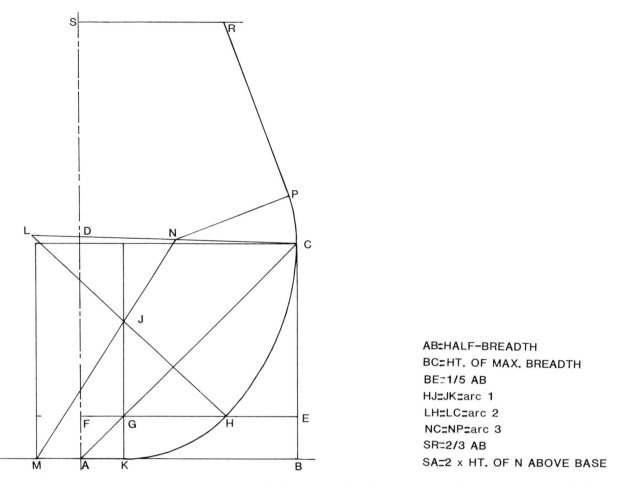

AB=HALF-BREADTH
BC=HT. OF MAX. BREADTH
BE=1/5 AB
HJ=JK=arc 1
LH=LC=arc 2
NC=NP=arc 3
SR=2/3 AB
SA=2 x HT. OF N ABOVE BASE

FIG. 5-20. One method of projecting a midship section in the late sixteenth and early seventeenth centuries in England. (after W. A. Baker, fig. 4, and R. Barker, fig. 3)

where the keel length was measured in Venetian paces, breadth and depth in Venetian feet, and the resulting capacity in *botte,* a standard cask of the period.[32]

Mathew Baker must have used his mathematical dexterity to produce more accurate formulas for tonnage. He cites one such formula as

$$\frac{K \times B \times D}{K + B + D},$$

where K is keel length, B is maximum breadth, and D is depth of hold. However, it has been determined that most of his examples in *Fragments* are worked to the rule of

$$\frac{K \times B \times D}{100},$$

a rule that was adopted by 1582 and remained a standard in England, although with occasional criticism and local modification, until 1694.[33]

Seventeenth-Century Shipbuilding

The notebook of Mathew Baker probably represented the upper limits of shipwrightery; less sophisticated processes must have been commonplace. In fact, one did not even need a proper shipyard in which to construct a seagoing vessel. I am amazed at the ways in which stranded explorers and colonists constructed new vessels in the most isolated locations and under all manner of duress,

yet from the time of Columbus historical records abound with such feats. A typical example is that of the survivors of the *Sea Venture.* This vessel, one of a fleet of seven ships and two pinnaces bound for the new Jamestown colony in Virginia, was wrecked on a Bermuda reef by a hurricane in the summer of 1609.[34] Bermuda was uninhabited then. After a longboat was dispatched to search

FIG. 5–21. Midship section, showing the construction of large Elizabethan vessel of the late sixteenth century. Note that the ladder actually describes radii of the section's arcs. (courtesy the Master and Fellows, Magdalene College, Cambridge)

for help but was not heard from again, the passengers built two pinnaces—the 40-ft (12.2 m) *Deliverance* and the smaller *Patience*—with cedar from the island and materials from the wreck. The vessels were ready to sail by the following spring, and the colonists arrived in Virginia by May of 1610. Since few of the 150 survivors could have been experienced shipwrights or ship

carpenters and since tools and equipment must have been extremely limited, their feat indicates how innovative and capable they were.

THE *SEA VENTURE*

Fortunately, at least part of *Sea Venture*'s bottom still survives on that reef off St. George's Island and has been

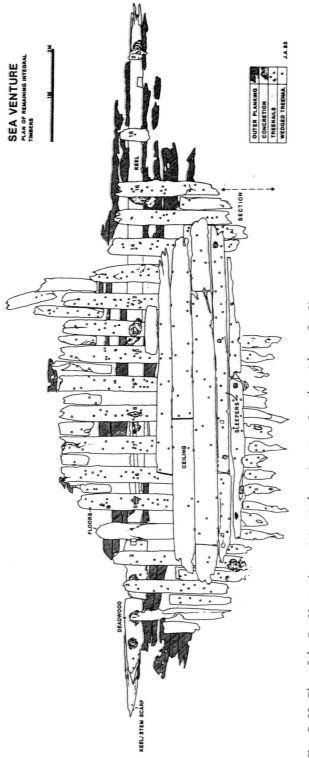

Fig. 5-22. Plan of the *Sea Venture*'s surviving timbers. (courtesy Jonathan Adams, fig. 2)

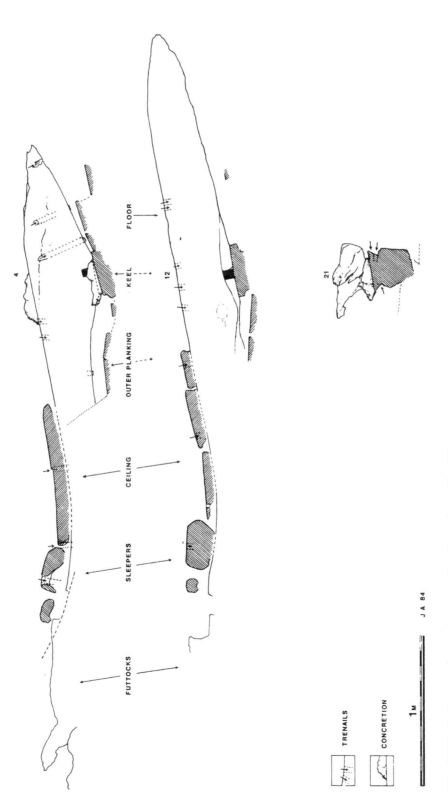

SEA VENTURE sections 4, 12, & 21

FLOOR

KEEL

OUTER PLANKING

CEILING

SLEEPERS

FUTTOCKS

4

12

21

TRENAILS

CONCRETION

1 M

J A 84

FIG. 5–23. *Sea Venture* details. (courtesy Jonathan Adams, Fig. 10)

the subject of archaeological study (Fig. 5–22).[35] Artifacts included one gun and a good representation of the possessions carried by those early colonists. This had been a large ship, probably a galleon. One account lists it as being "of 300 tunnes." Keel remains substantiate that magnitude. Fifty-two ft (15.5 m) of keel survived intact, while secondary evidence (keel bolts and worm casts) indicates it was as much as 72 ft (23 m) long. Adding the rakes of the posts to that figure suggests a deck length of about 100 ft (30 m).

The keel was keystone-shaped in section (Fig. 5–23) and was sided and molded about 13.5 in (34.1 cm) at amidships.[36] It was rabbeted for the garboards and had vertical scarfs caulked with animal hair and pitch. Eighteen surviving frames were erected on 2-ft (61 cm) centers, and every third one was bolted to the keel with iron in the central part of the hull (at the forward deadwood, every floor timber was bolted). Floor timbers were 1 ft (30 cm) square; their heads overlapped the heels of the first futtocks, leaving a solid belt of timber as in the earlier Spanish wrecks just discussed. Here, however, the futtocks do not appear to be directly attached to the floor timbers; frame timbers were united solely through their attachment to planking, ceiling, and the sleepers.[37]

The keelson did not survive. Planking was about 2.5 in (6.4 cm) thick; seams were said to be caulked with two strands of oakum. Most fastenings were treenails, and most of these were not wedged.[38]

LITERARY SOURCES FOR THE EARLY PART OF THE CENTURY

As might be expected, surviving contemporary literary sources are much more abundant for the seventeenth century than for the sixteenth century. A copy (the original has been lost) of a manuscript written about 1620 by an unknown author can be found in the library of the British Admiralty as part of a collection of naval documents dating between 1565 and 1695.[39]

The first part of the treatise describes the various timbers of a hull, the parts of a ship, and various hull proportions. This is followed by some very specific instructions for drawing the hull, making the molds for frames, and bevelling the frames so that they followed the rising and narrowing lines. Much of it is very similar to *Fragments of Ancient English Shipwrightery* cited earlier. It gives an especially interesting description of whole molding as it was practiced then. Whole molding can be a confusing topic because it took on various forms in different periods and regions. In its earliest form, the same basic body shape could be used for the entire hull, moving the mold inward and upward as required and resulting in a series of body shapes that were more or less parallel to each other. By the seventeenth century, the method was changing to accommodate demands for fuller ends and heavier batteries. While the arcs of body sections were still struck from the same radii, the rising and narrowing

values changed so that sides and bottoms were not necessarily parallel to each other.

The original version of whole molding survived, perhaps to this century, as a simple means of projecting smaller hulls. In this method, two standard molds are shifted to form the body shapes following predetermined rising and narrowing lines as in Figure 5–24.[40]

THE *VASA*

One of the most extensively preserved seventeenth-century shipwrecks, and certainly the largest, dates to 1628. Although Swedish by nationality, the *Vasa's* master shipwright and probably several other leading shipwrights involved in its construction were Dutch.[41]

The Netherlands had become a major shipbuilding center by this time. This was due to innovative developments in design, such as the *herringbuss* and the *fluit*, as well as the rapid development of trade and improvements in construction techniques. Dutch ships generally were more lightly constructed and thus could be built at far lower prices than those of most other competing countries. The result was a large, highly skilled force of shipwrights and artisans whose services were sought by other nations. Between 1600 and 1605, King Karl IX of Sweden engaged Henrik Hybertsson, who would later become master shipwright of the *Vasa's* construction; Henrik Jacobsson, also Dutch, was a leading shipwright for the *Vasa* project and a major witness at the Court of Enquiry following its capsizing.

The *Vasa* was launched at the Royal Dockyard in Stockholm harbor in 1627 and sank on its maiden voyage on August 10, 1628. The lavishly decorated hull was 50 m (165 ft) long from stem to sternpost with a maximum beam of about 12 m (38 ft, 4 in); displacement was about fourteen hundred tons, and draft was 4.6 m (15 ft, 5 in); the two gundecks carried sixty-four guns, most of which were twenty-four-pounders. In the stern it was

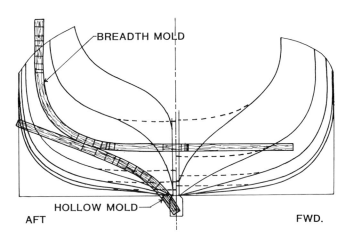

FIG. 5–24. A system of whole molding for small boats. (after Baker, fig. 5, and Chapelle, p.12)

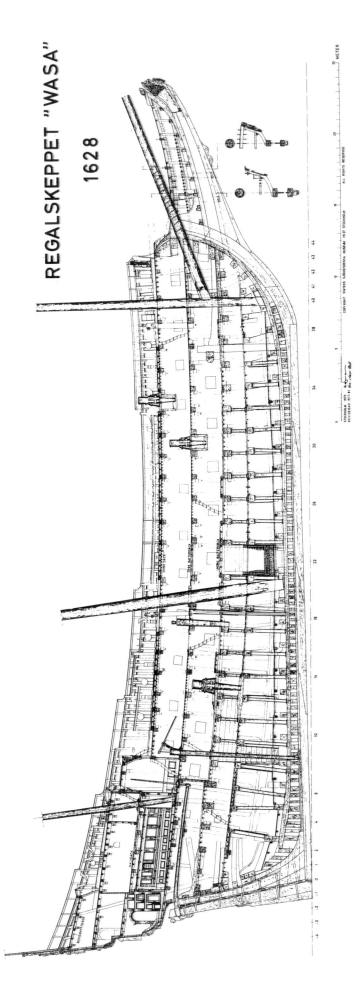

REGALSKEPPET "WASA"

1628

Fɪɢ. 5–25. A longitudinal section of the *Vasa*. (courtesy Statens Sjöhistoriska Museum)

18 m (59 ft) high—its whipstaff-operated rudder was itself 9.1 m (30 ft) high—and it is said to have been able to spread 1,100 sq m (12,378 sq ft) of sail.[42]

Much has been written about the *Vasa*'s history and its salvage, conservation, artifacts, and other features. Unfortunately, an extensive technical account of the ship's structural details is yet to be produced, although lines and limited construction drawings are available.[43] A brief examination of Figures 5–25, 5–26, and 5–27 will reveal its highlights. First of all, this is a very impressive oaken structure when viewed in its present restored state. Figure 5–26 shows a midsection that differs from the English sections discussed previously and following, in that the floors have only slight deadrise throughout and the bilge is much sharper. The hold is floored separately above the ceiling, and the ship has an orlop deck, two gundecks, and an upper or weather deck.

There is a heavy keel, rabbeted well down its sides for garboards, but there is no central deadwood. The keelson is shallow and rather small; in addition to the mainmast step, it holds a series of stanchions that support the weight of the lower gundeck. Above the ceiling and keelson, riders span the floor, while other riders alternately span the bilge and sides to the lower gundeck or the sides from above the bilge to the upper gundeck. The massive gundeck beams are backed by equally massive hanging knees, and there are standing knees above the deck as well. Large shelf clamps help support the deck beams; outside, thick wales are distributed above and below the gunports. The four lower wales in the area of the waterline, like the wales

SEKTION SPANT 22

SECTION FRAME 22

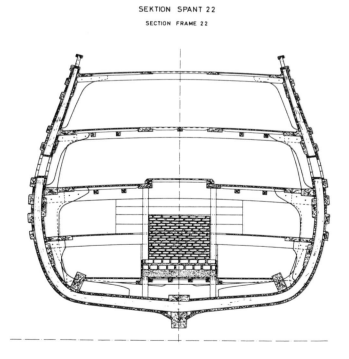

FIG. 5–26. A cross section of the *Vasa*'s hull at frame 22, just forward of the mainmast. (courtesy Statens Sjöhistoriska Museum)

above the gunports, are all separated from each other by belts of planking.

THE LELYSTAD *BUERTSCHIP*

Now let's look at the other side of the coin—still a form of Dutch construction, but one that was used to ferry people and produce around the Zuyderzee. The *buertschip* sank about 1620, probably within the same decade as the *Vasa*'s sinking, and was excavated near Lelystad when the Zuyderzee was drained in that area. It is preserved extensively (Fig. 5–28). Figures 5–29 and 5–30 illustrate the predominant features of this inland craft.[44]

Built almost entirely of oak, the hull has a wide, flat bottom, a hard bilge or chine, and gently curving sides that terminate in a slight tumblehome amidships. The bow is extremely full, the stern finer. The hull has an overall length of 18.25 m, including the rudder (16.25 m between perpendiculars), a maximum beam of 5.5 m, and a height amidships of 2.41 m. Draft marks carved in the stem and sternpost reveal that the hull originally drew 5 Amsterdam feet (1.42 m) of water, resulting in a displacement of 78 metric tons. Later in the life of the vessel the draft was increased to 6 feet and a displacement of 90 tons. Hocker estimates hull weight at 30 tons.

The keel had a length of 15.85 m and was sided 34 cm and molded 20 cm amidships. Rabbeted over most of its length, its after end was shaped into a skeg to protect the heel of the rudder. A stem made of three timbers rose 4.15 m above the keel. It was sided 25 cm over its inner surface, tapering to a 15 cm wide forward face, and had a maximum molded dimension of 61 cm. The four-piece sternpost rose 3.7 m above the keel and had maximum sided and molded dimensions of 24 cm and 41 cm. A rudder hung from the sternpost on three sets of iron pintles and gudgeons. Such a broad form of rudder could not have been carried by the *Vasa*; heavy seas (had it ever reached them) would have played havoc with such a broad, flat expanse. But here it was needed to navigate around tight harbors, lee shores, and shoals, often at relatively low speeds.

There were eight strakes of 5-cm-thick planking below the wales on each side of the hull: five on the bottom, a single bilge strake, and two side strakes. Three planks were joined together by means of nibbed scarfs to form each strake except the garboards, which were composed of only two planks each. Planks were fastened to frames with wedged treenails having a diameter of 3 cm. The strakes were broad; a maximum width of 52 cm was recorded for one of the bottom strakes, while the strake below the lowest wale had a maximum width of 65 cm and was more than 50 cm wide over most of its length.

Topsides comprised three wales separated by narrow planks. The lowest wale was 10 cm thick, the upper two were 8 cm thick, and the spacer planks had a thickness of 5 cm.

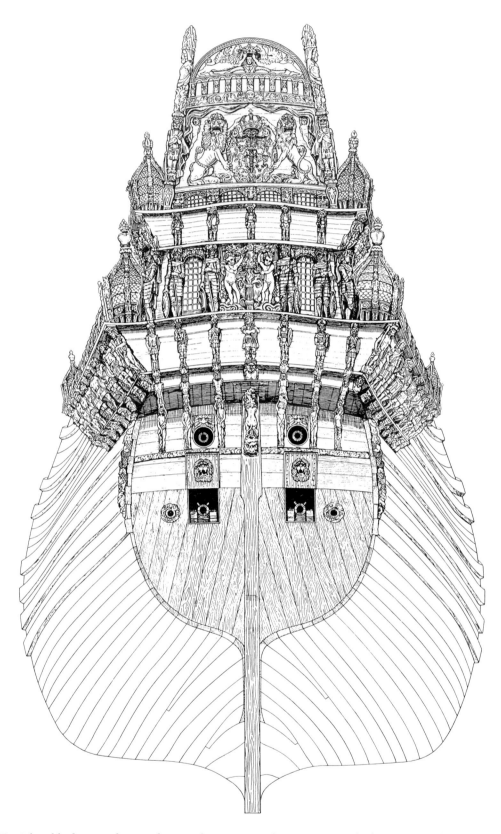

FIG. 5–27. The *Vasa*'s lavishly decorated stern, showing the transom and an interesting planking pattern. (courtesy Statens Sjöhistoriska Museum)

FIG. 5–28. The *buertschip* during excavation. (photo courtesy Rijksdienst voor de IJsselmeerpolders)

FIG. 5–29. A side view of the excavated *buertschip*. (photo by Frederick M. Hocker)

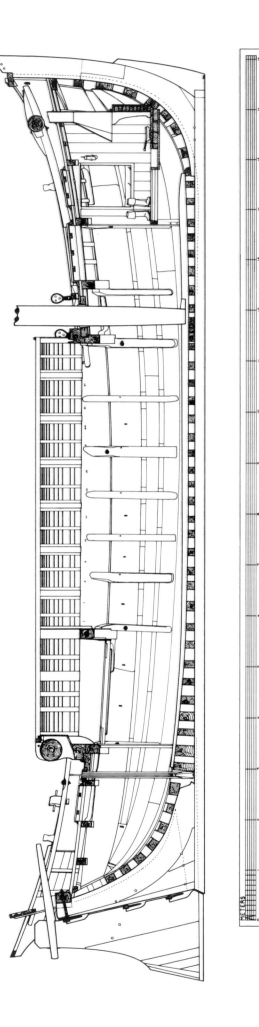
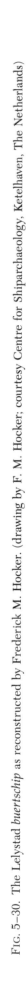

Fig. 5–30. The Lelystad *buertschip* as reconstructed by Frederick M. Hocker. (drawing by F. M. Hocker; courtesy Centre for Shiparchaeology, Ketelhaven, The Netherlands)

There were forty-nine frames in the hull, each made up of a floor timber and a pair of futtocks. A few extra futtocks and top timbers backing wales and bulwarks were scattered about the sides. Thirty-four of the floor timbers were notched over the keel and treenailed to it; those over the posts were left unfastened. Floor timbers were sided between 11 and 20 cm, most of them between 15 and 18 cm. They were molded about 14 cm over most of the bottom. Most futtocks were sided between 12 and 16 cm and molded 15 cm at strake 6 and about 6 cm at their heads.

The original keelson was made from a single, 12-m-long oak timber. It was sided 70 cm and molded 12 cm at amidships with diminishing dimensions both fore and aft. It lay directly atop the floor timbers and was fastened to each with three or four treenails. The keel and keelson were laid flatwise to reduce draft and increase hold space.

The single mast was stepped into a mortise, 50 cm long, 25 cm wide, and 7 cm deep, cut directly into the top of the keelson. Ceiling was 5 cm thick; a single clamp supporting the beams was only slightly thicker.

The illustrations best describe the large central hatch and its covering. The small passenger cabin was covered with a clinkered roof nailed to fixed rafters. Directly forward of this, the hatch was covered with seven removable clinker panels. The crew lived in the forepeak, where a tiled hearth with smoke hood and chimney was located.

The Lelystad *buertschip* was a spacious cargo box to which was attached limited shelter for crew and passengers and end structures necessary for navigation. It must have been an extremely practical craft. Hocker refers to this hull as another example of bottom-based construction. The bottom planking was laid before framing commenced, and it was stabilized temporarily by clamps, cleats nailed across seams, and probably various other forms of interim support. After a few floor timbers were installed on the bottom strakes, strakes 6 and 7 were erected, followed by the rest of the frames, planks, and wales. The keelson and bottom ceiling could be installed after all the floor timbers were in place.

THE *DARTMOUTH*

The HMS *Dartmouth* was built in Portsmouth in 1655 under the supervision of master shipwright John Tippets. A fifth-rate ship of the line, its principal dimensions were as follows:

Length of keel—80 ft (24.4 m)
Breadth—25 ft (7.6 m)
Depth in hold—10 ft (3.05 m)
Draft of water—12 ft (3.66 m)
Tons burden—266
Battery—16 9-pounders; 16 6-pounders; 4 3-pounders

The ship was overhauled extensively in 1678, and a detailed listing of the work done during that refit at Rotherhithe survives, parts of which are quoted below. In 1690,

after a long and varied career, it sank in the Sound of Mull, Scotland. Discovered in 1973, the remains were excavated over several seasons thereafter.[45]

The keel was 13 in (33 cm) square and made from elm. Although a false keel did not survive, refit records list one with a thickness of 8 in (20 cm) (Fig. 5–31b). The keel was bolted through the deadwood at 2-ft (61 cm) intervals with 1-in (2.5 cm) collared iron bolts, staggered so as to prevent splitting. The garboard rabbets were found to be caulked with oakum, tar, and resin. A vertical scarf, 4 ft, 3 in (1.3 m) long, was tabled with interlocking surfaces and fastened laterally with eight iron bolts (Fig. 5–31a). Capping pieces above and below helped protect the joint,

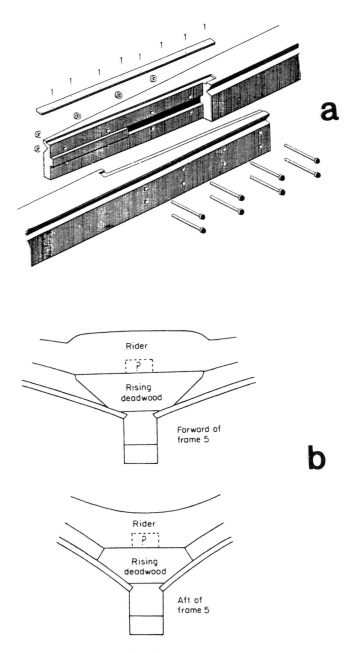

FIG. 5–31. *Dartmouth* keel details: (a) a reconstruction of the tabled keel scarf; (b) keel sections. (Colin Martin, figs. 16, 17)

which was caulked with resin on the tables, oakum at the butts, and hair and tar along the capping pieces.

This and other archaeological evidence reported in this chapter and the last, as well as contemporary records, indicate what seems to be a predominance of vertical keel and post scarfs in the centuries following the early medieval period. This was a complex scarf, but certainly a commonplace one for the period and not nearly as elaborate as those on later warships. According to the refit records of 1678, the entire keel was replaced, apparently with three pieces of elm that were each about 30 ft (9 m) long. Further examination of the nature of the deadwoods and frames will indicate what a momentous task this must have been.

The frames are curious, and their discovery indicates the value of archaeology to the historical record. Before the *Dartmouth* excavation was published, many of us thought that all large English ships of the period were framed with overlapping futtocks as revealed by the *Sea Venture* and Deane's *Doctrine* to follow. The *Dartmouth* told a different story. Frames were of oak spaced on approximate 1-ft (30.5 cm) centers throughout the surviving hull; they were sided 10 in (25 cm) and molded 8 in (20 cm) on the average. However, although construction in the area of the keel did not survive at the midship bend, only a few feet aft of that location frames were arranged as shown in Figure 5–32. Floor timbers did not span the keel; in fact, they could not properly be called floor timbers. Instead, these lowest timbers ended just short of the deadwoods and were attached to its under surface by means of angled chocks. Treenails fastened the chocks, deadwood, and garboards together. Second futtocks were similarly fastened to the lowest timbers (should we call them half-floor timbers?) with chocks and treenails, so there was a continuous line of futtocks making up a single frame on either side of the keel. The joints were staggered on adjacent frames, as if the frames were intended to be doubled, but adjacent frames were not fastened to each other and seldom abutted.

The deadwood was made from elm and must have required huge logs. Although it survived only in a partial state over a length of about 15 ft (4.6 m), it could be reconstructed reliably to widths of at least 4 ft (1.22 m). This was a curious form of construction, and one that could never have been gleaned in such detailed fashion from contemporary records. Obviously, such frames could not have been assembled completely and erected on the keel before planking began. Indeed, such an arrangement hardly could have been accomplished unless there were an almost simultaneous assembly of frames and planks as the structure rose, with the frames preceding the planks by no more than the length of a futtock if these hull remains represent original construction. At first glance it appears that rotten floor timbers were cut out and replaced by larger deadwood and chocks during the refit, or that what survives is the result of the re-keeling process in 1678, a process that included

the lower three strakes on each side. However, since the refit records do not indicate replacement of frames, efforts to solve this mystery continue.[46]

The *Dartmouth*'s elm planks were 2.5–3 in (6.3–7.6 cm) thick. They were fastened to the frames predominantly with oaken treenails 1.5 in (3.8 cm) in diameter, although iron also was used at scattered locations (Fig. 5–33). Most treenails went through the ceiling as well. Treenail heads had sawn cuts in various patterns, into which oakum was driven to better secure and protect the fastening. The planking was sheathed with ½-in (1.3-cm) fir over a matting of hair and tar about ⅛ in (3.2 mm) thick. The surviving ceiling was made from elm, 2.5 in (6.3 cm) thick, and plank ends were scarfed with flat, horizontal scarfs rather than butt joins. One stringer, also of elm and 4.5 in (11 cm) thick, was placed at the wrongheads. There probably were riders above the ceiling as well as a keelson, but neither survived. An oaken lodging knee and several lead scuppers were among the other hull remnants.

DEANE'S *DOCTRINE*

The last half of the seventeenth century abounds with contemporary documentation in the form of naval lists and orders, diaries, commentaries, and several books. A few of them are listed in the bibliography. Among the more interesting are Bushnell's *Compleat Shipwright* and two Dutch books by Cornelius van Yk and Nicolaes Witsen. Witsen's elaborate work, first published in 1671, is well illustrated and addresses a wide variety of hull forms and sizes, although he spends a lot of space on historical shipbuilding. From a modern perspective, this includes many ridiculous statements and illustrations on ancient craft. Van Yk, on the other hand, limits his historical analysis to a single chapter, much of it on the construction of the ark, which must have been a timely subject. Strangely enough, van Yk seems to have had a fascination for English shipbuilding methods, and his text is perhaps as much a source for English techniques as it is for Dutch construction methods.

Another important contemporary source of information is ship models; numerous good models dating to the last half of the century survive.[47]

One of the most valuable manuscripts from this period is known as Deane's *Doctrine of Naval Architecture* which is housed in the Pepysian Library at Magdelene College, Cambridge, under the listing MS 2501. It has recently been edited and published, along with some interesting commentary, by Brian Lavery.[48] Much of what follows has been condensed from his work.

Sir Anthony Deane became master shipwright of Harwich Dockyard in 1664 and Portsmouth Dockyard in 1668. He was made a member of the Navy Board in 1672 and was knighted a year later. In addition to his private shipbuilding enterprises, he constructed twenty-five of the ninety-four naval vessels built during the decade he was active as a government shipwright, far more than any of his peers. Among these were three first-rate ships of

SECTIONS THROUGH FRAMES

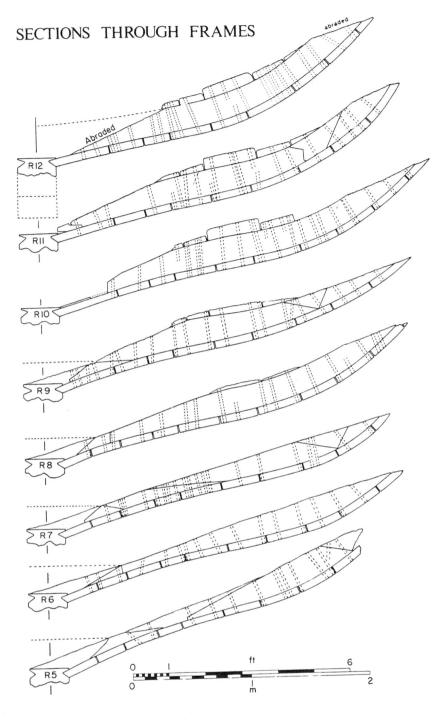

FIG. 5–32. *Dartmouth:* surviving construction at various frame locations. (Colin Martin, fig. 18)

one hundred guns, although his best work, and probably his interests, lay in the production of smaller and experimental craft. Deane was described as being arrogant, but he apparently had a brilliant scientific mind and was probably the best of the English shipwrights of his time.

In 1670 he wrote his so-called *Doctrine,* which he says was done at the insistence of his patron, Samuel Pepys. A large part of it deals with arithmetic and geometry, including the making of scales, the measurement of timber, and a system for determining the displacement

tonnage and therefore the draft of a vessel. There is also a section on rigging, including numerous tables and descriptions. But our study centers on the part about hull design, which begins with a warning to select a large enough paper, board, or plate to ensure sufficient space to include the complete drawing at the scale selected. Predominant among the designer's tools in the period were adjustable battens and bows for drawing long arcs and diminishing lines, straight edges, pen and lead holders, dividers with interchangeable lead and ink holders, and perhaps set

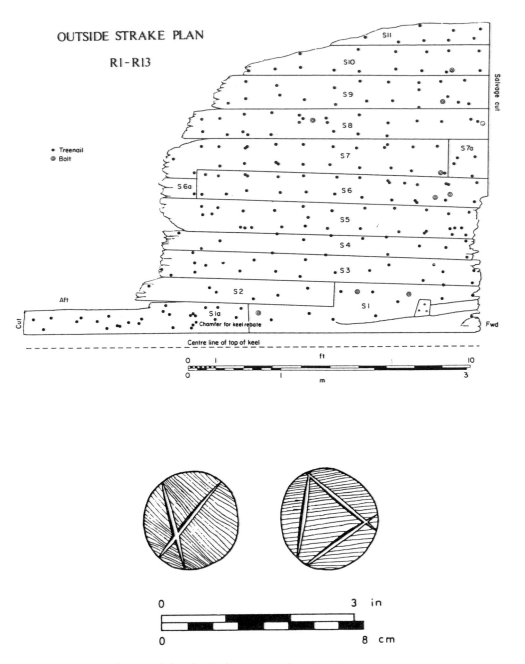

FIG. 5–33. *Dartmouth* planking and treenail details. (Colin Martin, figs. 21, 22)

squares. Deane advises that the draft be made first in lead, and when everything is in order, it then should be inked in its final form and the lead erased with crumbs of white bread.

The vessel used as an example in explaining the design process is a third-rate ship of the line with a keel length of 120 ft and a molded breadth of 36 ft, which he derives by taking 3/10 of the keel length. This, he says, is enough beam for a warship, although a merchantman's beam should be 1/3 of the keel length. The following descriptions are greatly abstracted, and the illustrations have been combined, or in some cases, only partially shown to save space. Please refer to the text cited to properly appreciate the many drawings

and fascinating commentary by which Deane accomplishes his instruction.

A baseline is drawn, upon which the scaled limits of the 120-ft-long keel are marked as A and B. Perpendiculars are drawn at these points, either with a set square or with a compass from arbitrary points fore and aft as shown in Figure 5–34. To the keel length forward is added the length for the sweep of the stem, BC, which is 3/4 of the breadth (27 ft). The same is done for the rake of the sternpost, AD. Deane mentions three ways to find the rake of the sternpost, but initially describes it as being 11/12 of 1/6 of the breadth, or 5½ ft. The arc of the stem is struck by placing one leg of the compass on the base of the keel at B,

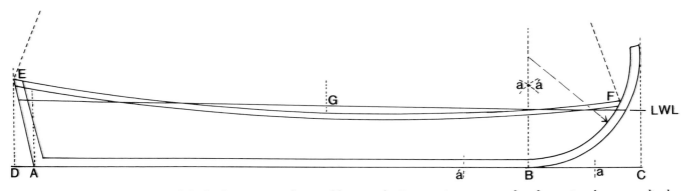

FIG. 5–34. Deane's projections of the keel, posts, waterline, and lower wale. Points a-á are arcs used to determine the perpendicular as described by Deane but not shown in this location. The original drawings illustrate what appear to be rabbets in the keel and posts, but they have been omitted here.

the other at a point on the perpendicular equal to the length of BC. The sternpost height to the point it meets the transom is determined by subtracting ½ ft from ⅔ of the breadth, in this case 23½ ft, which is marked on perpendicular D and from which point a diagonal line is drawn to the after end of the keel. Thus the distance between extremities of the posts is 152 ft.

The depth of the keel is given as 18 in—15 in for the keel and 3 in for the false keel—which he gets by allowing half an inch for every foot of hull breadth. This upper keel line is then drawn parallel to the baseline and outer stem curvature. The description for deriving the molded shape of the sternpost is both confusing and incomplete (part of it is based on proportions and part on that "which experience the work makes manifest"), but the resulting shape is as shown on Deane's drawings.

Next comes lengthy discourses on determining and drawing the full-load waterline EF, the sweep of the wales, location of decks and gunports, development of the

stern and forecastle, and the upper construction as seen on the sheer views. These will not be discussed here, but they are interesting and of value to anyone doing research in the period. Most of these features were derived from calculations (or experienced conclusions). For instance, the sweep of the lower wale was struck as the arc of a circle whose radius was 499⁸/₁₂ ft (arc EGF in Fig. 5–34).

The rising and narrowing lines of the floor and breadth (Fig. 5–35) were also mathematically derived sweeps, although what was produced in his drawings does not agree with his textual descriptions. They are reproduced here as they appear on the original drawings. These lines are an improvement over those shown in the documents discussed earlier. Altering the sweeps of these lines in the ends of the hull resulted in fuller or narrower hulls as desired. Although Deane does not explain such a procedure, or even indicate that hulls were altered, he appears to have been quite masterful at this design aspect.

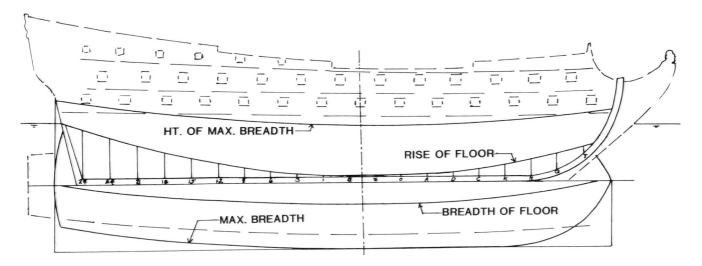

FIG. 5–35. Rising and narrowing lines (after Deane). Molded frame locations are shown on the keel. The complete hull outline is ghosted in dashed lines.

His next step is to derive the midship bend from five arcs, using the same third-rate ship with a 36-ft beam as an example. As in latter-day lines drawings, Deane projected his body stations in half-breadth form. He also mentions waterlines, but none are shown on his drawings. Early in the next century, both waterlines and buttock lines began to appear on hull drafts. One drawing (Fig. 5–36) is used here in place of the nine drawings he used to illustrate his description, which I have abbreviated as well. This, in abstraction, is what he did.

A rectangle representing the half-breadth (AB and EF) and the height of maximum breadth (AE and BF) is drawn with its sides extended to the full height of the frame (AD and BC). Next, mark off the half-breadth of the floor (which is ⅓ the half-breadth of the hull as seen on the breadth of floor line in the previous draft) on EF and AB (points G and H), and connect the two points with a straight line. The half-breadth of the floor, HB, is 6 ft in this case. At D, ⅔ of HB (4 ft) is subtracted from the half-breadth of the hull and connected with a line, DI, that indicates the tumblehome of the hull at the weather rail. A line representing the height of the floor at the midship station, ab, is drawn parallel to the baseline AB. Although this line is shown on Deane's drawing (I suspect it represents the height of the deadwood), he neither labels nor mentions it. Since the rise of floor line was separated from the top of the keel by this amount at midships, ab actually represents the minimum floor deadrise.

Now it is time to strike the arcs making up the body curvatures. Mark ¼ the breadth of the hull, HK, on GH and, putting one leg of the compass at K, strike the floor sweep HL. Subtract ⅞ of the floor sweep radius HK from EF, mark at M, and strike the arc EN. Now connect those two arcs with a sweep tangent to N and L and whose radius is 20/36 of the whole breadth and found to be at O. All but one foot, 17/18 of the half-breadth, is then subtracted from EF to locate P, the center of the arc ER, which begins the sweep of the tumblehome above the greatest breadth. That same radius is then extended in the opposite direction from R to find S, from which point the hollow sweep RI is drawn to complete the shape of the top timbers.

Deane illustrates and explains the similar projection of two more body stations, one forward and one aft of the midship bend. Figure 5–37 shows all of the projected frame shapes as can be seen on his completed ship's draft. Note the breadth and rising line projections. There are some obvious shortcomings in this split drawing when one compares it with later drafts that include keel and posts, a

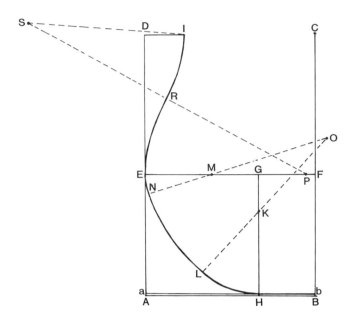

FIG. 5–36. A combined form of Deane's midship body projections.

common centerline, and the control provided by water and buttock lines. Nevertheless, the progress in ship design during the previous century or two is quite evident. From these half stations, Deane states, one can make the molds for the various frame timbers, which must be made long enough for a good scarf for every timber. Scarf, for the third-rate warship described here, probably meant flat scarf; frames were most likely arranged in a double row of timbers consisting of a central floor timber and three overlapping futtocks and a top timber on each side of the keel.[49] Lesser ships, however, may still have been framed in belts of overlapping futtocks as shown in Figure 5–38. Indeed, Deane's doctrine was probably too sophisticated for many shipwrights of the time to either comprehend or execute. While undoubtedly it represents the ultimate in period construction and may indicate what was being built in the dockyards and larger private yards, the design and construction of many merchant vessels and smaller craft must have taken on a far less complex form.

Deane goes on to describe and illustrate the rest of the hull's construction, and he lists timber sizes for all rated warships. There is also an interesting section on masting and rigging. Deane's work, as presented by Lavery, is an invaluable source for scholars of the period.

The Eighteenth Century and Beyond

By the beginning of the eighteenth century, ships flying a variety of colors were poking their bowsprits into the bays and rivers of the far corners of the world. Societies that had been isolated were now visited frequently by seafarers from faroff lands, their ideas and goods being exchanged with those of the visitors, and the traditions of both

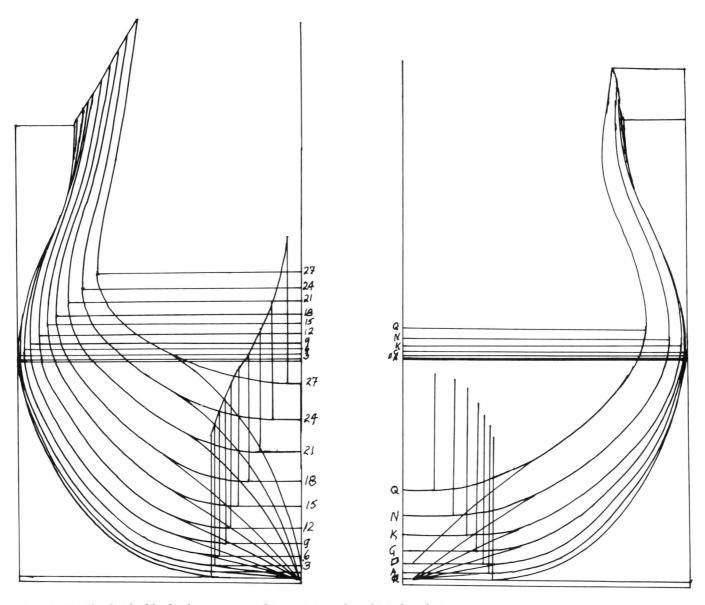

FIG. 5–37. The finished body plan, one part of Deane's "complete ship's draught."

became diffused as a result. The explosion of global travel resulted in an increasing variety of influences on ship and boat construction. These influences were so great and so numerous that many volumes would be required to document all the resulting vessel types and procedures used to design and build them.

Fortunately, there are numerous contemporary books on shipbuilding and naval architecture dating to the eighteenth century and later, many of them well written and illustrated. This book's bibliography lists the most important ones. In the United States, England, France, Holland, the Scandinavian countries, and elsewhere, there are extensive archives of plans, contracts, naval records, and other documentary sources, as well as collections of ship models, tools, and other subject matter of interest to the ship scholar. In fact, actual vessels from the end of the eighteenth century onward still survive to enlighten us.

Even though most of them have been rebuilt and in some cases altered from their original forms, they still provide a good general sense of the design and construction methods of their origins.

Also, there are many modern texts dealing with all manner of ship and boat design and construction, revealing the excellent research done in the last few decades on subjects ranging from early drafting and designing, timber acquisition, deck machinery, and scantling lists to the actual construction processes and analysis of designs. These, too, are noted in the bibliography.

Since our subject is so broad and our space so limited, little would be gained by rehashing what the bibliography's sources reveal. Instead, the rest of this chapter will concentrate on what cannot be found in contemporary documents and collections—the structural details that can be supplied only by archeology. We will consider a series of

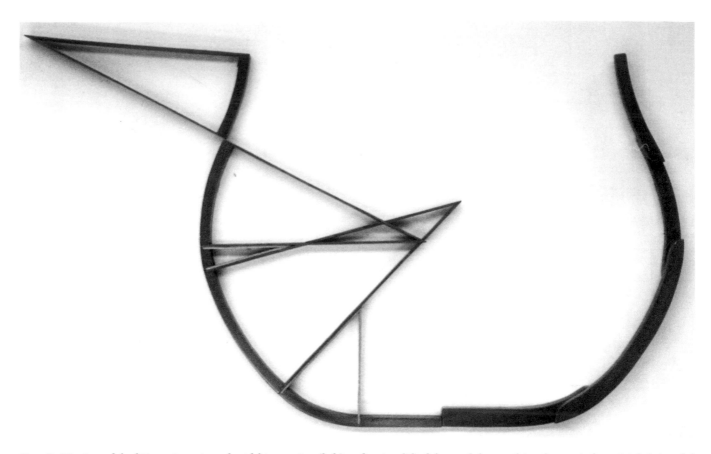

FIG. 5–38. A model of Deane's projected midship section (left) and a simplified form of the resulting frame timbers (right). (model by Frederick M. Hocker; photo by Ralph Pedersen)

excavated ships and boats that covers a broad spectrum of hull forms and details not usually found in the texts or better model collections. These are the vessels of the real world—not as the designer drew them or the model builder visualized them, but as they actually turned out.

THE BROWN'S FERRY VESSEL

During the summer of 1976, the remains of a hull that was largely intact to above the turn of the bilge were hoisted from the Black River at Brown's Ferry, South Carolina (Figs. 5–39 and 5–40).[50] Detached side planks and timbers provided further hull coverage, in some areas to the caprail. Artifacts, which were extremely limited, tentatively date the sinking to the mid–eighteenth century. No coins were found to pinpoint a date, and dendrochronological analysis was unsuccessful. The sole cargo consisted of approximately ten thousand bricks weighing about twenty-five tons. The hull has been preserved in polyethylene glycol and soon will be transferred to a museum.

The Brown's Ferry vessel had an overall length of about 50 ft (15.25 m) and a beam of about 14 ft (4.25 m), and it must have been nearly fully loaded when it sank. There was no keel. Instead, a flat bottom formed the base of the hull and was composed of three yellow pine planks, each having a thickness of 3–3.5 in (7.6–8.9 cm).

FIG. 5–39. Intact part of the Brown's Ferry vessel suspended from its lifting frame. (photo by Gordon Brown; courtesy South Carolina Institute of Archaeology and Anthropology)

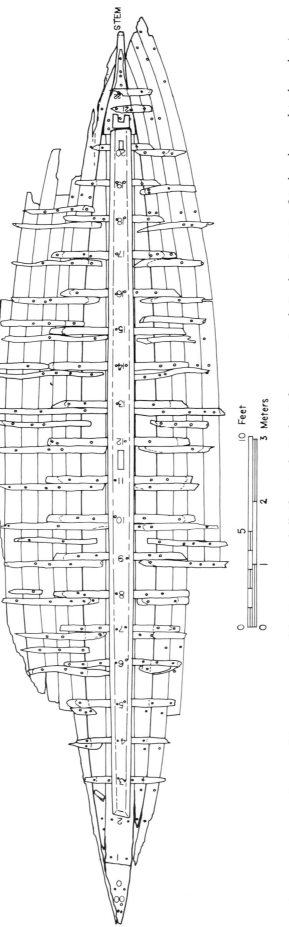

STEM

Feet
Meters

Fig. 5–40. An excavation drawing of the intact portion of the Brown's Ferry hull. (drawing by Darby Erd; courtesy South Carolina Institute of Archaeology and Anthropology)

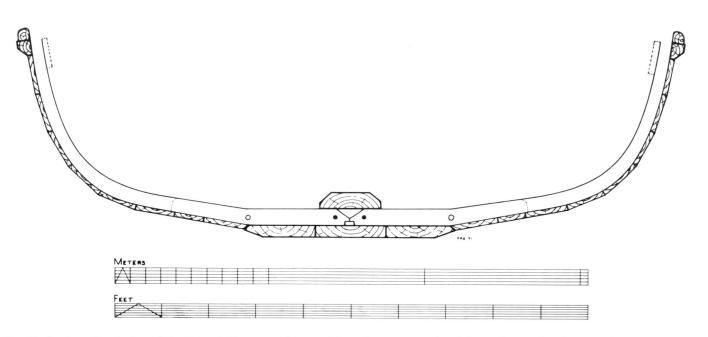

Fig. 5–41. A sectional view of the Brown's Ferry vessel at amidships. (reconstructed and drawn by Frederick M. Hocker; courtesy South Carolina Institute of Archaeology and Anthropology)

The central plank ran the full length of the hull, with the others shaped to the desired hull curvature (Figs. 5–41 and 5–42).

The stem was composed of three pieces of live oak—a false stem, the main piece, and an apron—that survived to a height of 4½ ft (1.4 m). Sided 4¼ in (10.8 cm) at the rabbet and tapering to half that thickness at the false post, its maximum molded dimension was 23½ in (59.7 cm) where it was scarfed to the central plank. It was assembled first with iron nails and then bolted with 1½-in-diameter (3.8 cm) forelock bolts as shown in Figure 5–42. The bolts were nearly identical to those found on the Yassi Ada Byzantine ship of a thousand years earlier. The apron was really a long knee, 5 in (12.7 cm) thick at its after end, where it was attached to the bottom plank with eleven 1⅛-in-diameter (2.9 cm) unwedged treenails. At its widest part on the bottom, the apron was molded 19¼ in (49 cm).

Except for the lower extremity of the inner post or knee, the sternpost did not survive. What did survive was similar to the apron of the stem, except that two iron bolts angled through this after fragment and probably attached either a deadwood or the main post to it. The stern was more narrow than the bow and has been reconstructed as in the lines drawing, Figure 5–43, where a transom stern has been projected for the missing area. A preliminary study, made more than a decade earlier, hypothesized a double-ended hull (Fig. 5–44).

Frames of live oak were spaced on approximate 2-ft (60 cm) centers. On the average, they were sided 5 in (12.6 cm) and molded 4½ in (11.5 cm). Twenty floor timbers were attached to the bottom planks at 6–8-in

(15–20 cm) intervals with 1⅛-in-diameter (2.9 cm) treenails. Each floor timber had chamfered upper, forward edges and central, rectangular limber holes that averaged 2½ in (5.7 cm) wide and 1 in (2.5 cm) high. At least two additional U-shaped floor timbers were located in each end of the hull, where they were nailed to the inner posts (Figs. 5–41 and 5–42).

Unlike most vessels previously recorded or described in contemporary documents, all futtocks overlapped the after sides of the floor timbers exclusively. Note in Figures 5–40 and 5–42 that most futtocks ended fairly close to the sides of the keelson. In the center of the hull these futtocks were gently sweeping timbers, but toward its ends where their curvatures compounded, their heels were club-footed. These heels were attached to the bottom planks with one to four treenails; a few were also fastened laterally to floor timbers. Intermediate futtocks were inserted after every third frame, such as those between frames 9 and 10 in Figure 5–40, and along with second futtocks as on frame 14, additionally strengthened the sides of the hull.

The keelson was laid flatwise to permit more hold space in this shallow hull. It was 36½ ft (11.2 m) long, sided 15¾ in (40 cm) near the mainmast step, 13 in (33 cm) in the bow, and 10 in (25.4 cm) in the stern, and was molded up to 4 in (10 cm) along its centerline. Made from cypress, its upper edges were chamfered broadly (Fig. 5–41). The keelson was fastened through each floor timber to the bottom planks with two treenails, 1⅛ in (3 cm) in diameter. Rectangular mortises were cut completely through the keelson for stepping the two masts. An auxiliary step, probably used to steady the heel of a

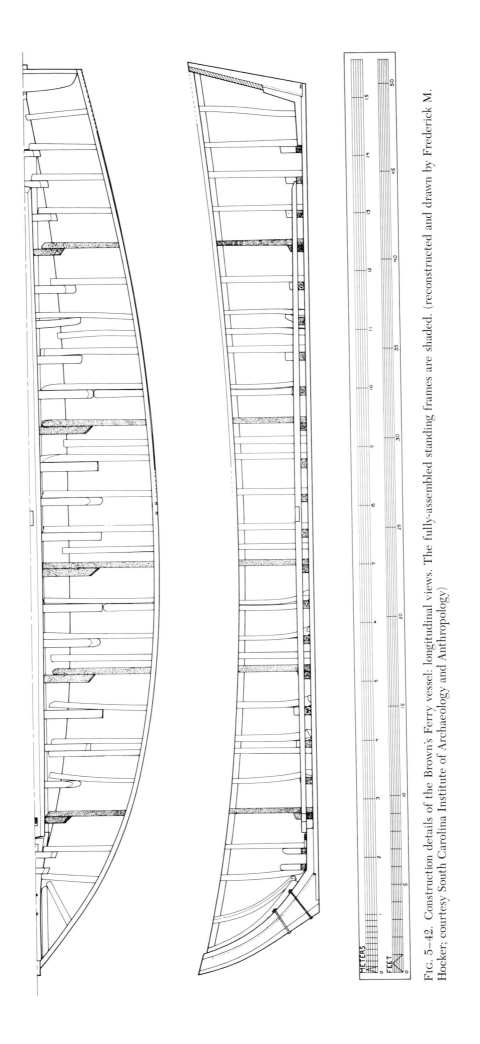

FIG. 5–42. Construction details of the Brown's Ferry vessel: longitudinal views. The fully-assembled standing frames are shaded. (reconstructed and drawn by Frederick M. Hocker; courtesy South Carolina Institute of Archaeology and Anthropology)

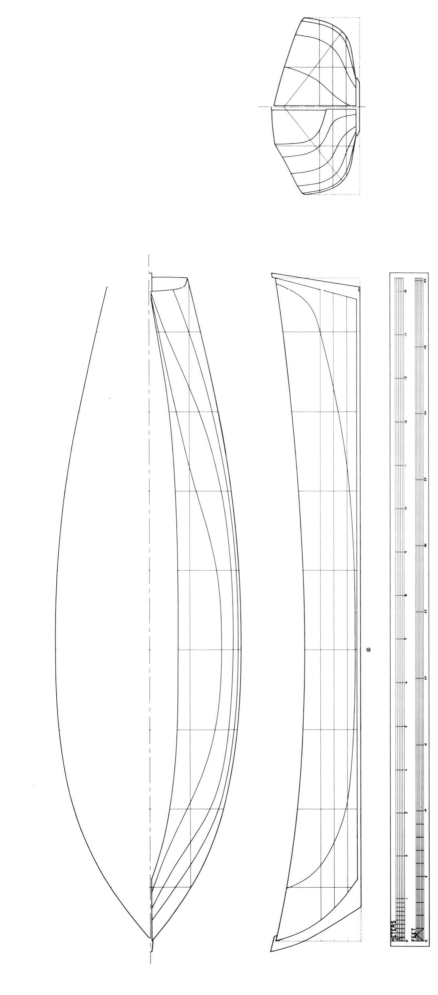

FIG. 5–43. Lines of the Brown's Ferry vessel. (reconstructed and drawn by Frederick M. Hocker; courtesy South Carolina Institute of Archaeology and Anthropology)

FIG. 5–44. The Brown's Ferry research model. (model and photo by J. Richard Steffy)

riding bitt, was cut out of the edge of a short board, which was nailed to the top of the apron just forward of the keelson.

Eight strakes of yellow pine planking, 1⅛–1¼ in (2.8–3.2 cm) thick, covered each side of the hull. Although the fastening pattern varied, most planks were attached to each frame with one treenail and one or two nails. These treenails had diameters of 1⅛ in (2.8 cm) in the frames and at least some of the treenails had square heads on their planking ends. A few were wedged with ½-in-square (1.3 cm) wedges driven into their centers. Seams were caulked with oakum and pitch, and traces of pitch or resin on both sides of the planks suggested the hull was coated completely, inside and out, at least to the waterline.

There was a single wale, made from cypress and originally about 3½ in (9 cm) thick, directly above the eighth strake on each side. The sides are topped with a caprail about 3 in (7.5 cm) square, of which only a short fragment survives.

No fastenings could be found on inner frame surfaces to indicate the presence of permanent ceiling, although plank fragments directly beneath the brick cargo suggested that boards may have been laid loosely in the hold for supporting cargo.

A lodging knee and waterway also were excavated, both almost certainly from the area of the foredeck. There was no other evidence for the existence of decks.

The broad, flat bottom, the lack of a keel, and the shallow hull design indicate the Brown's Ferry vessel was intended to operate in shallow waters. However, were that solely the case it might have been built more simply, perhaps in the form of a bateau. Those compound curves in the quarters suggest that this was probably a coaster, designed to navigate shallow rivers and harbors and cross bars, but also to beat along the coast, delivering its cargoes of bricks from upriver plantation kilns to rapidly growing coastal towns and cities. The excavated cargo probably represents a full or nearly full load for this vessel.

The model in Figure 5–44 shows my interpretation based on limited examination of the hull shortly after its excavation. The hold is open, and there are short decks in bow and stern. A log windlass and riding bit occupy the foredeck, and the broad rudder is operated with a simple tiller. I have reconstructed a sprit rig, based on artifactual evidence and the small size of the foremast step, but it might just as readily have been schooner-rigged.

No American or European parallels could be found for this vessel. It has been suggested that this form of construction may have descended from the *periagua,* a form of dugout developed by earlier Spanish settlers for carrying cargoes on inland waterways.[51] If so, it developed from a log-built rowing vessel into a rather complex planked sailing craft.

The final hull analysis by Frederick Hocker revealed that only five frames (numbers 4, 9, 13 [the midship frame], 16, and 20) were completely assembled and set up on the bottom. The rest of the side framing was shaped by means of ribbands or even planks fastened to the standing frames. And it is quite likely that those standing frames were shaped by means of standard molds, similar to the way William Baker described the method for whole molding smaller vessels (Fig. 5–24).

THE RONSON SHIP

The extensive remains of a large seagoing ship that was contemporary to the Brown's Ferry vessel were excavated from a construction site in lower Manhattan early in 1982.[52] Although the site was located more than a block from the East River, the ship had been placed there as a crib ship, a retired vessel filled with rubble and used as cribbing to reinforce a wharf or extension of the shoreline. Although its identity has not been determined, existing evidence suggests the Ronson ship was built in Virginia by a British shipwright between 1710 and 1720. It was probably no longer serviceable when placed in its final location, most likely between 1747 and 1755. It was fairly intact nearly to the weather deck, although deck beams had been cut and the decks collapsed under the enormous weight of the rubble poured into and on top of it. Site logistics limited the excavation to a two-month period, but much of the bow was salvaged for preservation and display.

The Ronson ship, as reconstructed, had a length of 82 ft (25 m) between perpendiculars, a keel length of approx-

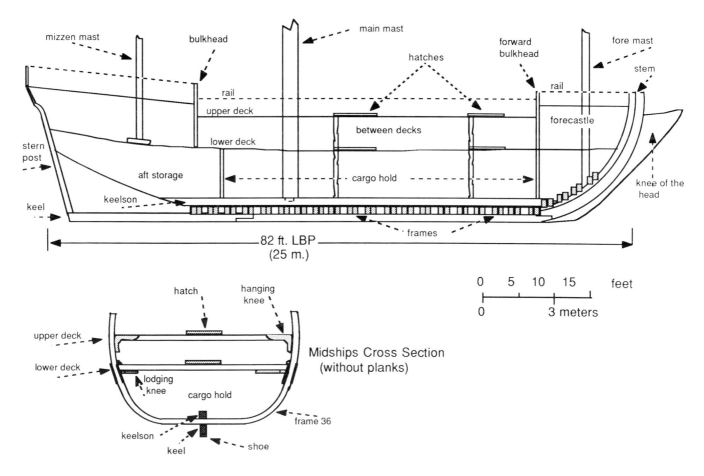

FIG. 5–45. The Ronson ship's reconstructed interior arrangement. (drawing by Warren Riess)

imately 68 ft (21 m), a maximum breadth of 27 ft (8.2 m), a depth of hold of 7½ ft (2.3 m), and a draft of about 11 ft (3.4 m). It was built almost entirely of oak with the exception of pine decking and was ship-rigged. It had an interior arrangement as in Figure 5–45, with a large head knee, full bow, flat floors, and square tuck stern.

In the hold area, square frames, sided 17 in (43 cm) and molded 8½ in (22 cm) on the average, were composed of seven futtocks and spaced at 2-ft (60 cm) intervals. One-ft-square (30 cm) deck beams were crowned slightly and dovetailed into clamps at the side. Lower deck beams were braced with lodging knees, and upper deck beams were reinforced with hanging knees. Decks were 1½ in (4 cm) thick and let into a slightly thicker nibbing strake; at the sides, a 6-in-wide (15 cm) and 4-in-thick (10 cm) waterway tapered inward to match the thickness of the decks. On the lower deck were two hatches. The after hatch, just forward of the mainmast, was 6 ft (1.8 m) long and 5 ft (1.5 m) wide; the forward hatch was 1 ft (30 cm) smaller all around. Aft of the hatch was a stanchion notched for use as a ladder.

But as is often the case, the bow of this ship was the most interesting from a structural point of view. The stem was made of two pieces of oak and was sided 11.6 in (29 cm) and molded 31.8 in (79.5 cm) just above the lower scarf (Figs. 5–45 and 5–46).[53] It tapered in thickness as it went forward and contained rabbets centrally in its sides for seating the hooding ends of the planks. A two-piece apron was fayed to it.

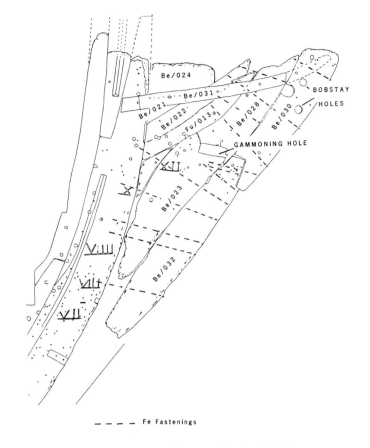

FIG. 5–46. The upper stem and knee of the head of the Ronson ship. (Rosloff, ill. 13)

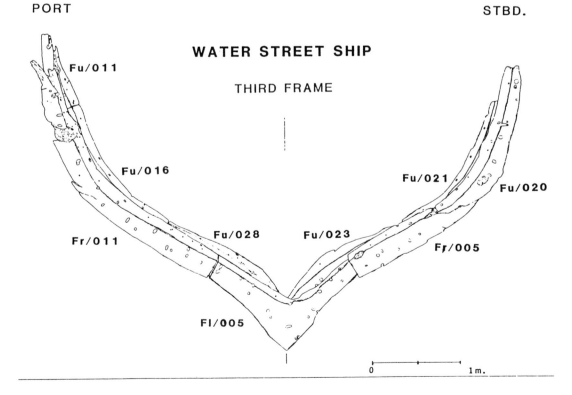

FIG. 5–47. The after side of the third frame from the Ronson ship's bow. (Rosloff, ill. 5)

There were no cant frames in this ship. The forward-most three frames were all square and set into steps or notches cut into the apron. Each of these square frames was made up of seven timbers as in the middle of the hull, and the floor timbers were made from tree crotches with alternating thick and thin arms (Fig. 5–47). Between the second and third frames a single row of timbers served as filling pieces, so that there was a nearly continuous wall of timber here. Forward of this was a solid row of hawse pieces whose heels abutted, but were not fastened to, the forward side of the first square frame (Fig. 5–48).

A belt of three wales, 4 in (10 cm) thick with a combined width of 31.2 in (78 cm), were not attached to the stem but were nailed and treenailed to the hawse pieces and bolted through lodging knees and deck clamps. Hull planking was 2 in (5 cm) thick; lower strakes ran into the stem rabbets, while those higher in the hull butted against the bottom edge of the lower strake of the main wale belt (Fig. 5–49). The hull was sheathed with planks

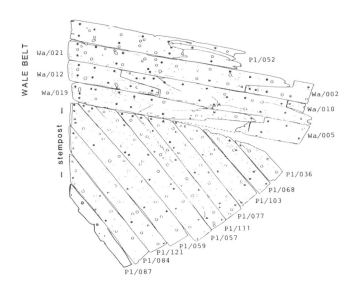

FIG. 5–49. The Ronson ship's portside wales and planks in the bow. (Rosloff, ill. 7)

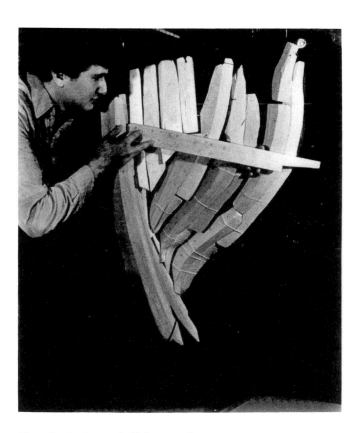

FIG. 5–48. Jay Rosloff fits a wale on a reconstruction model used to study the bow of the Ronson ship. Note the extreme outer face angles of the uncanted bow frames. (model and photo by Jay P. Rosloff)

more than half as thick as the hull planking; it overlaid a layer of felt or hair bonded with a mastic material and was fastened with square iron nails.

The arrangement of deck framing and foremast partners can be seen in Figure 5–50. There were four additional breast hooks below the deck hook shown here, the lower two of which were installed on top of the ceiling. Ledges were notched into the lodging knees. The head and bowsprit had been removed when the ship was buried, but the knee of the head survived. It was assembled from the several pieces shown in Figure 5–46. Note the cheek piece, the gammoning and bobstay holes, and the lading marks, which were incised into the starboard sides of the knee and stem. Both sides of the knee were sheathed in wood similar to the hull.

A capstan was located in the bow and survived in good condition (Fig. 5–51).

THE *BOSCAWEN*

Among the many interesting artifacts discovered by the Fort Ticonderoga King's Shipyard Excavation on the western shore of Lake Champlain, the most valuable has been the remains of the 115-ton British sloop *Boscawen*. Documents indicate that it was built there in 1759, shortly after the British drove the French from the area, and was fitted with sixteen cannon. A thorough study of the remains of this French and Indian War relic has determined that the hull was approximately 70 ft (21.2 m)

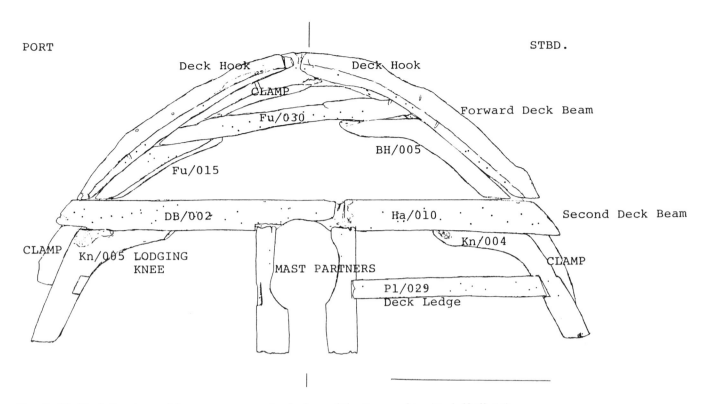

FIG. 5–50. Deck framing and foremast partners in the bow of the Ronson ship. (Rosloff, ill. 10)

long and 22 ft (6.6 m) in the beam.[54] Figure 5–52 shows the arrangement of the hull and rig. Of greatest interest here is the framing system, shown in Figure 5–53. Unevenly spaced floor timbers, twenty-six of them in all, were sided between 8½ and 10 in (21.3 and 25 cm); they were molded 1 ft (30 cm) over the keel and tapered to about 7 in (17.5 cm) at the ends of their 6-ft-long (1.8 m) arms. They were notched over the keel and draft-bolted to it. Limber holes were cut at the edges of these notches. But there was no continuity to the frames; second futtocks were unconnected to the floor timbers, and first futtocks overlapped the two without being fastened to them. Indeed, except for the spacing of the first futtocks, the system is reminiscent of the floor and half-frame arrangement of ancient Mediterranean vessels. Since the futtocks were nailed and treenailed only to the planking, the planking process must have begun as soon as the floor timbers were in place and proceeded in concert with the erection of each additional set of futtocks. Crisman believes there were four futtocks on each side, making a total of nine unattached timbers in each frame.

Also of interest is the fact that both outer planking and ceiling were of 2-in-thick (5 cm) white oak. The step for the single mast was notched underneath to fit over the keelson and was braced securely. It was a large block of oak—4 ft, 3 in (1.3 m) long, 18 in (45 cm) wide, and 16 in (40 cm) high at the keelson (Fig. 5–54). Perhaps some

of the structural oddities found here reflect the urgency to complete a warship quickly in order to answer the crisis at hand as well as its intended service in a relatively calm, freshwater environment.

THE CHARON

HMS *Charon* was built in Harwich, England, in 1778. A fifth-rate, forty-four-gun warship, it was 140 ft (42.4 m) long on the gundeck, nearly 38 ft (11.5 m) in the beam, and drew more than 16 ft (4.8 m) of water at full load. A beautiful ship-rigged vessel with a lavish figurehead of the Boatman of Hades and a well-decorated stern, it was rated at 880 tons and had a crew of three hundred. The battery consisted of twenty 18-pounders, twenty-two 9-pounders, and two 6-pounders. Built of English oak and elm and bolted with iron, the ship's construction included the latest technological advances, such as high-speed chain pumps and copper hull sheathing.

In October, 1781, the *Charon* was set afire by hot shot during the siege of Yorktown that, for all practical purposes, terminated the hostilities known as the American Revolution. Parting its mooring cables, the *Charon* drifted downstream, a raging inferno that floated ever higher as rigging and timbers were shed or consumed by flames. Eventually it grounded on Gloucester Point, across the York River from Yorktown, Virginia, and settled onto the shallow bottom.

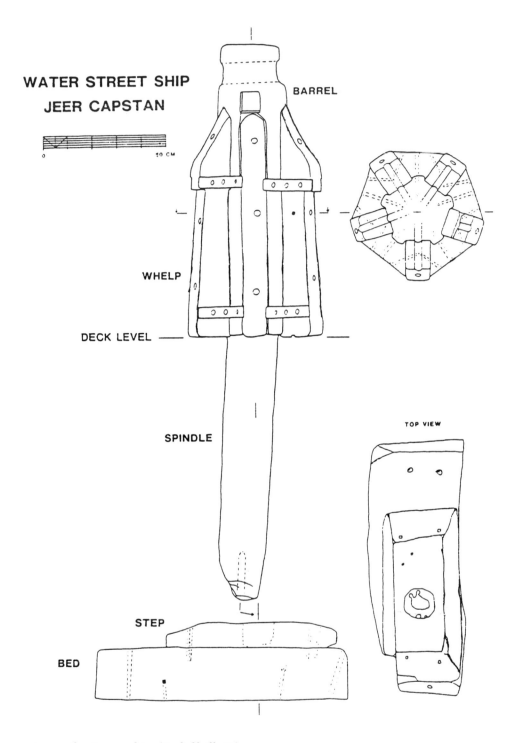

WATER STREET SHIP
JEER CAPSTAN

BARREL

WHELP

DECK LEVEL

SPINDLE

STEP

BED

TOP VIEW

FIG. 5–51. The jeer capstan on the Ronson ship. (Rosloff, ill. 15)

FIG. 5–52. Drawing of the *Boscawen* under sail. (drawing by Kevin J. Crisman)

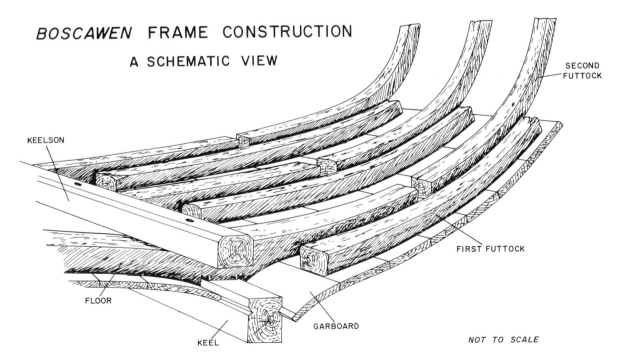

BOSCAWEN FRAME CONSTRUCTION
A SCHEMATIC VIEW

SECOND
FUTTOCK

KEELSON

FIRST FUTTOCK

FLOOR

GARBOARD

KEEL

NOT TO SCALE

FIG. 5–53. Oblique cross section of the *Boscawen* hull. Note the curious framing plan. (drawing by Kevin J. Crisman)

H. M. SLOOP *BOSCAWEN*

THE MAST STEP

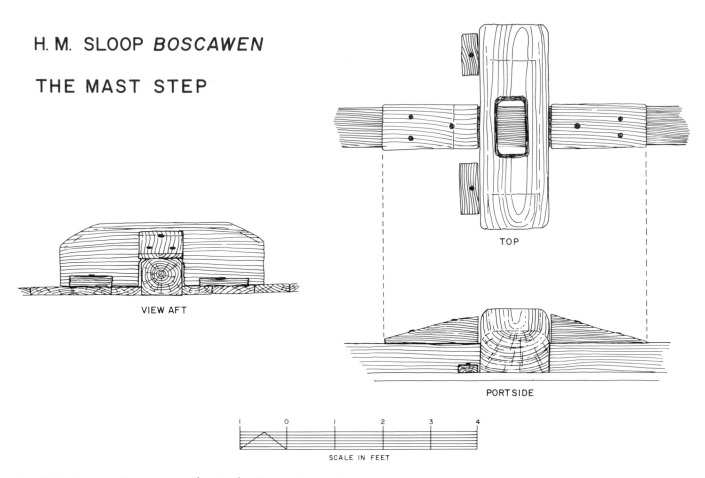

VIEW AFT

TOP

PORTSIDE

SCALE IN FEET

FIG. 5–54. *Boscawen's* mast step. (drawing by Kevin J. Crisman)

In 1980, an excavation was fielded to determine whether a wreck listed as GL136 was the remains of the *Charon* or one of some sixty other ships assigned to Cornwallis at the time.[55] Charred timbers and fused artifacts attested to the intensity of the conflagration, and perhaps less than 5 percent of this once proud ship survived, but our study was nevertheless rewarding.

Figure 5–55 is a photograph of a fine model of the *Charon* made in the 1930s and now in the Science Museum in London. The original drawings of the vessel, on file in the National Maritime Museum in Greenwich, are shown in Figure 5–56. Note the relatively flat floors in the body plan, the combination of small and large arcs forming its full body, and the tumblehome of its topsides. In a sense, this view is reminiscent of the body sections in Deane's *Doctrine* of a century earlier, although this hull is much more refined and the entire drawing reflects the progress made during the previous hundred years of English shipwrightery. Note also the extreme depth of the hull, and on the half-breadth plan, the flat ends of the sheer line that provided more room at the ends of the upper deck. In spite of this fullness, however, the model indicates how striking the ship's appearance must have been when immersed to the waterline and with canvas set.

The sheer view shows major bolting patterns in the deadwoods, the way in which transoms and breast hooks were situated, the shot lockers fore and aft of the mainmast, and the pumps between them. Enough of the shot locker bases survived to permit limited reconstructions, as did many of the other bottom features on the sheer draft. Partial survival of the lower parts of the starboard suction and chain pumps (port pumps were found in scattered fragments) was such that they permitted extensive reconstruction.[56]

Table 5–1 is a partial list of the features that permitted us to identify wreck GL136 as the remains of the *Charon*. It is included here as an indication of some of the dimensions, scantlings, and appointments of frigate-sized vessels of the period. The table also shows how closely the shipwright followed the draft. The column marked *Charon* lists contemporary information from several sources; those data followed with an asterisk were compiled directly from the builder's draft, and the rest were taken from scantling lists and specifications of fifth-rate vessels of the period. The column marked GL136 lists similar statistics resulting from the excavation of that wreck.

The *Charon* was among the earliest ships to be sheathed in copper. The British Admiralty had begun

FIG. 5–55. A modern model of the *Charon* in the Science Museum, London. (photo courtesy Trustees of the Science Museum, London: neg. no. 5578)

experimenting with bottom protection years before in attempts to solve the problems of fouling and worm infestation experienced by their far-ranging fleets. Wooden sheathing like that found on the Ronson ship had been commonplace, as were bottom coverings of closely spaced iron nails, lead or zinc sheathing, and various forms of encaustics. Experiments in copper began in 1761 by sheathing the thirty-three-gun frigate *Alarm* with that metal. In 1765 a second ship was covered, and by 1777 at least fourteen more are said to have been sheathed in copper. But the entire British naval fleet was not coppered until several years after the *Charon* was commissioned; merchant vessels would not be so

sheathed for another decade, and then only rarely at first. The earliest American vessel to be coppered was the frigate *Alliance* in 1781.

Usually underlaid with felt and pitch, copper sheets came in specific sizes and weights and were laid in specific patterns.[57]

THE COFFERDAM WRECK

During the Yorktown campaign, General Cornwallis scuttled a number of ships, most of them small British merchantmen, to form a defensive line along the beach at Yorktown. One of them, known simply as 44YO88, was surrounded by a cofferdam before being excavated.[58] This

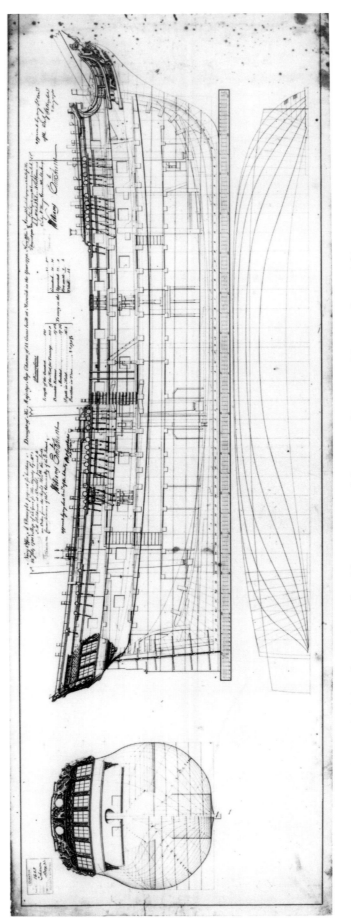

FIG. 5–56. The original builder's draft of the *Charon*. (reproduced by permission of the National Maritime Museum, Greenwich)

TABLE 5–1. Comparative data: HMS *Charon* and GL136

Dimensions, etc.	*Charon*	GL136
Length on gundeck	140' 0"*	130'+
KEEL, square afore and abaft	1' 3"*	1' 3"
FALSE KEEL, thick	0' 6"*	0' 6"
DEADWOOD, thick at amidships	0' 6"*	0' 6"
DEADWOOD, breadth	1' 7"*	1' 7.5"
APRON, thick at deadwood scarf	1' 0"*	1' 0"
APRON, breadth	1' 10"*	1' 10"
APRON SCARF, in length	c. 1' 6"*	c. 1' 6"
APRON SCARF, direction forward	up*	down
APRON SCARF, lips, thick	c. 0' 3"*	0' 2.75"
APRON SCARF, from mainstep	50' 2"*	50' 6"
KEELSON, square	1' 3"*	1' 3"
KEELSON, scored down on floors	0' 1"	0' 1"
KEELSON, number of pieces	5*	5
KEELSON scarfs, in length	5' 0"*†	5' 0"
KEELSON scarf lips, thick	0' 4.5"*	0' 4"–0' 5"
KEELSON, bolts at each scarf end	2	2
KEELSON, scarf bolts, in diameter	0' 0.75"	concreted
KEELSON, through bolts, diameter‡	0' 1.25"	0' 1.25"
ROOM AND SPACE	2' 4"*	2' 4"
FLOOR TIMBERS, midships, sided§	1' 2"	1' 1"–1' 2"
FLOOR TIMBERS, fore & aft, sided	1' 0"	1' 0"–1' 1"
FLOOR TIMBERS, midship length	c. 21'	c. 22'
FLOOR TIMBERS, molded at heads	1' 0"	1' 0"–1' 1"
PLANK OF BOTTOM, thick	0' 3"	0' 3"
TREENAILS, in plank, diameter	0' 1.5"	0' 1.5"
LIMBER BOARDS, thick	0' 3"	0' 3"
COMMON CEILING, thick	0' 3"	0' 3"
MAINMAST STEP, sided	2' 3"*	2'+ (eroded)
MAINMAST STEP, deep over keelson	0' 11"*	c. 0' 10"
PILLARS, under capstan in hold	3*	3
PILLARS, stepped on	keelson*	keelson
PILLARS, square at lower end	0' 9"*	0' 8.5"
CISTERN (WELL), located at	mainmast*	mainmast
CISTERN, fore and aft	7' 6"*	7' 6"
CISTERN, forward bulkhead to step	0' 10"*	0' 10"
CISTERN PLANK, thick	0' 3"*	0' 3"
PUMPS, main	chain*	chain
PUMPS, backup	suction*	suction
CHAIN PUMPS, casing width	1' 0"	1' 1"
SUCTION PUMPS, aft of main step	0' 10"*	0' 10"
SHOT LOCKERS, in number	2*	2
SHOT LOCKERS, fore and aft clear	2' 0"*	2' 0"
SHOT LOCKERS, planking thickness	0' 3"*	0' 3"
COPPER SHEATHING?	yes	yes

* compiled from builder's draft of the *Charon*
† midship keelson scarf length was not confirmed
‡ keelson bolted through every second floor timber
§ includes frames 5 through D in scantling lists, the midship area in GL136 (limits not determined)

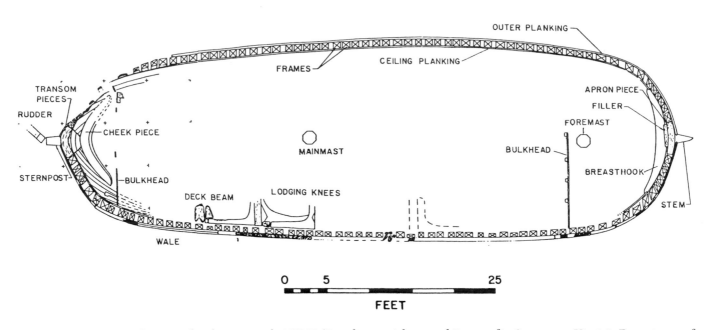

F<small>IG</small>. 5–57. Excavation drawing of Yorktown wreck 44Y088 (Broadwater, Adams, and Renner, fig. 3; courtesy Virginia Department of Historic Resources)

wreck is extensively preserved to a length of nearly 75 ft (23 m) and a breadth of nearly 24 ft (7.3 m). I include this vessel as an example that not all eighteenth-century seagoing ships had broad transom sterns. Figure 5–57 shows the overall hull plan as seen from above the excavation. Notice the canted frames at each end of the hull and the two mast locations. This was a brig of approximately 170 tons. It is believed to have been a collier from the east coast of England, probably similar to Captain James Cook's *Endeavor*.

Especially interesting in Figure 5–57 is the stern construction. Here the transoms were quite small, and the sides of the vessel had to be held together in the same fashion as those in the bow. Although such horizontal framing pieces do the same job as the breast hooks of the bow, in the stern they are known as *cheek pieces,* or sometimes as *stern crotches* or *crotch pieces.* Of course, the wales of this vessel had to run into the sternpost. They appeared to be very similar to the belt of wales on the bow of the Ronson ship. 44YO88 also was sheathed in wood in a similar manner.

Figures 5–58 and 5–59 show additional details of this interesting wreck.[59] Note that there are canted framing timbers in both ends of this hull, as well as transverse chocks to fill the voids over the posts.

THE PRIVATEER *DEFENCE*

One more participant in the Revolutionary War must be examined—the 170-ton privateer brig *Defence*. Built in Beverly, Massachusetts, and carrying a battery of sixteen 6-pounders, the *Defence* was scuttled in a reach of Penobscot Bay, near the modern-day village of Stockton Springs, Maine, on its first voyage while serving there with an ill-fated American expeditionary force during the summer of

1779.[60] Although the ship's construction is probably typical of American privateers and light warships during the period, a few details are worth mentioning. Just aft of the foremast in Figure 5–60, a brick hearth with a partitioned copper cauldron built into it was faced with pine boards. Note the manner in which the foremast was stepped in the keelson and its heel braced. But the most notable feature of the *Defence* was the curious bifurcated timber alongside and beyond the forward end of the keelson. Crudely made from the crotch of a large oak tree, the branches served as an extremely low breast hook and the trunk as a short apron, although only at its forward end did it make contact with the stem.

The *Defence* had a sharp deadrise in its bottom and is believed to have had fine lines throughout. It was probably typical of the beauty and sophistication that went into some of these smaller American vessels. They became even more refined and graceful a few decades later, when the Baltimore clippers and other fast types roamed the seas.

FRESHWATER WARSHIPS—*EAGLE* AND *JEFFERSON*

In 1814, a dramatic race was underway along the northern lakes between shipwrights of the warring nations, the United States and Great Britain, to produce superior fleets and thereby control the northern frontier. One of these vessels, the twenty-gun American brig *Eagle*, was an excellent example of the speed and capabilities of these marvelous shipbuilders. It was built on Lake Champlain by the highly respected Brown brothers, Adam and Noah, who had constructed many fine naval and private vessels. The *Eagle*'s 106-ft-long (32.1 m) keel was laid on July 23, and the completed hull was launched twenty days later on August 11. It was a major participant of a fleet under the

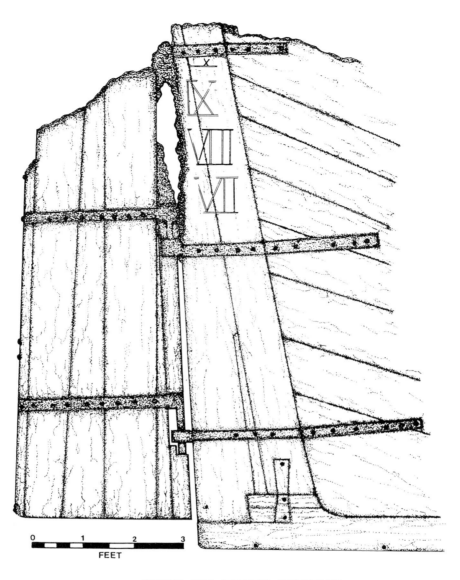

STERN AND RUDDER, EXTERIOR

FIG. 5–58. Sternpost and rudder details of the cofferdam wreck (44Y088) at Yorktown. (Morris, fig. 6)

command of Thomas Macdonough that, a month later, turned back the British land and sea invasion at Plattsburgh and greatly contributed to a quick end to the War of 1812.

After the war, the *Eagle* was placed in ordinary at the naval station at Whitehall. Sometime after the closing of the base in 1825, before salvagers could dismantle the ship completely, it sank to the bottom of the Poultney River. Rediscovered in 1981, it was excavated over three seasons and the remains documented and graphically reconstructed.[61]

The *Eagle's* lines are shown in Figure 5–61, and a midship section is shown in Figure 5–62a. Both illustrate a vessel designed for a specific body of water. The hull was shallow so that it could navigate rivers and shorelines of this relatively small area. Because it would always be close

to shore, it did not require a voluminous hold to store enough water, supplies, and ammunition to sustain vessel and crew for long periods. Compare the section with that of the *Peacock* in Figure 5–62b. A twenty-two-gun ship-rigged sloop-of-war, it was built by the Brown brothers in 1813 and was probably their finest. Both vessels are almost identical in length and breadth, but notice the greater depth and more complex construction of the oceangoing *Peacock*.

Stempost and keel were joined by a flat scarf that was secured by drift bolts and iron fish plates (Fig. 5–63a). Stopwaters discouraged seepage at either end of the scarf table. An apron was notched horizontally to seat three notched square frames. Forward of the scarf, wedge-shaped cuts were made into the sides of the apron to seat the heels of cant frames.

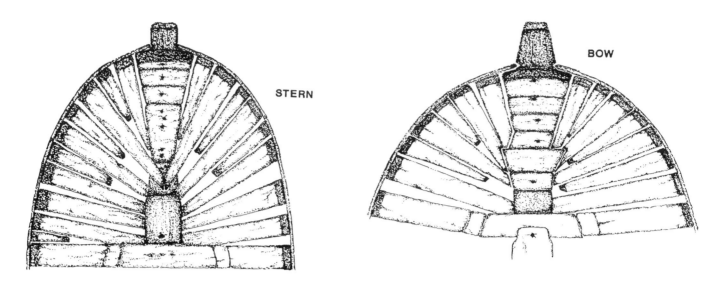

BOW AND STERN CANTS AND TRANSVERSE CHOCKS

Fɪɢ. 5–59. Bow and stern construction in the lower part of the bow and stern of Yorktown wreck 44Y088. (Morris, fig. 8)

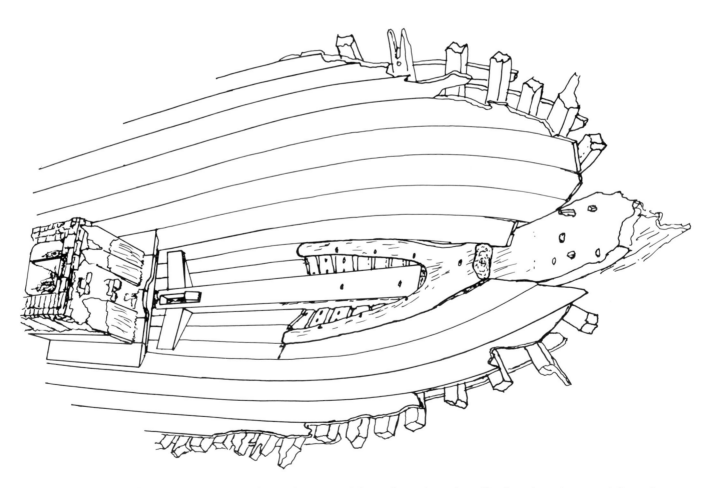

Fɪɢ. 5–60. An overhead view of the surviving forward portion of the *Defence*, from the galley hearth to the stem. (after a drawing by Peter Hentschell)

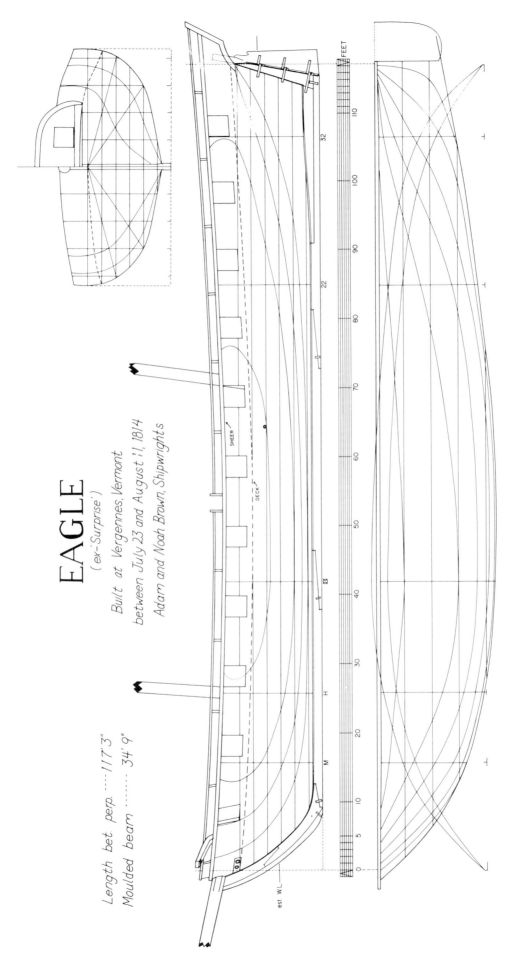

EAGLE

(ex-"Surprise")

Built at Vergennes, Vermont
between July 23 and August 11, 1814

Adam and Noah Brown, Shipwrights

Length bet perp ---- 117' 3"
Moulded beam ------- 34' 9"

FEET

FIG. 5-61. The lines of the *Eagle*. (reconstruction and drawing by Kevin J. Crisman)

THE US NAVY BRIG
EAGLE

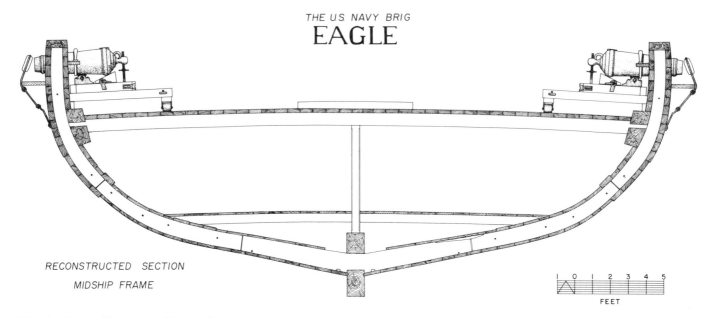

RECONSTRUCTED SECTION
MIDSHIP FRAME

FEET

FIG. 5–62a. Hull sections of the *Eagle*. (courtesy Kevin J. Crisman, *The Eagle*, fig. 64; drawing by Kevin J. Crisman)

THE U.S. NAVY SLOOP OF WAR
PEACOCK

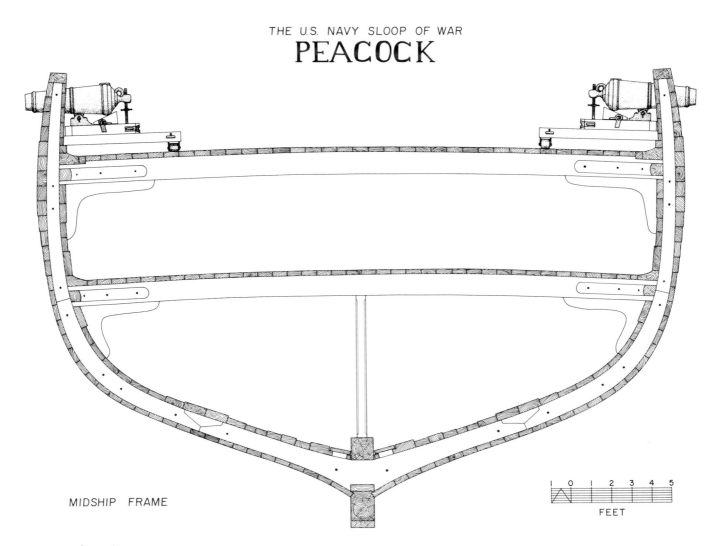

MIDSHIP FRAME

FEET

FIG. 5–62b. Hull sections of the *Peacock*. (courtesy Kevin J. Crisman, *The Eagle*, fig. 64; drawing by Kevin J. Crisman)

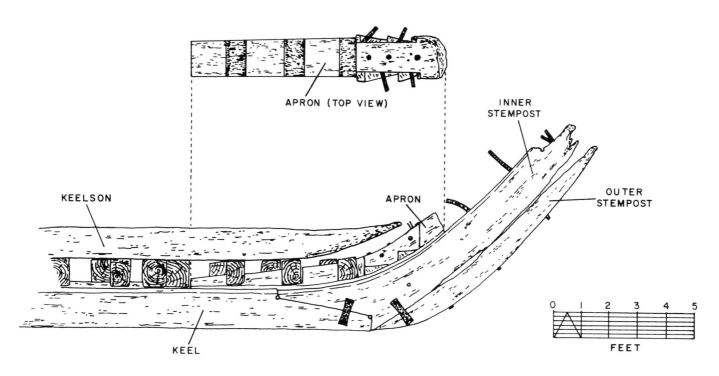

FIG. 5–63a. Surviving bow timbers of the *Eagle*. (courtesy Kevin J. Crisman, *The Eagle*, fig. 44)

There was a small skeg at the stern end of the keel and the keel was cut down 6 in (15 cm) to receive the lowest deadwood timber (Fig. 5–63b). Three more deadwoods were located above this timber, one of them a small, wedge-shaped piece. All were drift-bolted together and to the keel and sternpost. The garboard rabbet was scored into the lowest deadwood, while the sides of assembly above it were notched to receive the heels of half-frames. The sternpost probably was tenoned into the top of the keel; a pair of iron fishplates further secured the joint. Two rudder gudgeons were fastened to the post and the after ends of the deadwoods with riveted bolts.

Perhaps the most curious structural arrangement was the method of securing the deck beams (Fig. 5–64). There were no knees of any sort used here. Instead, the beams were locked in place by means of notches cut into the clamp and waterway. While such a procedure would not have been satisfactory for a seagoing ship, it probably was deemed sufficient for service on this body of water. Certainly it would have expedited the construction process,

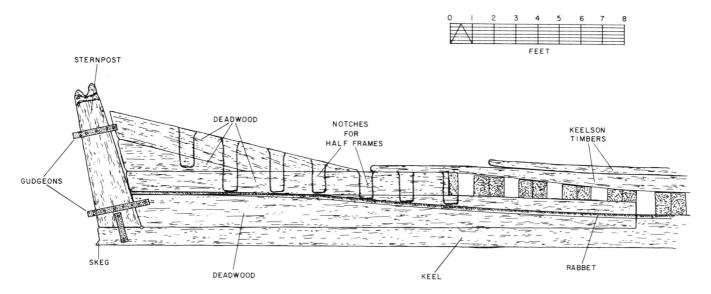

FIG. 5–63b. Surviving stern timbers of the *Eagle*. (courtesy Kevin J. Crisman, *The Eagle*, fig. 45)

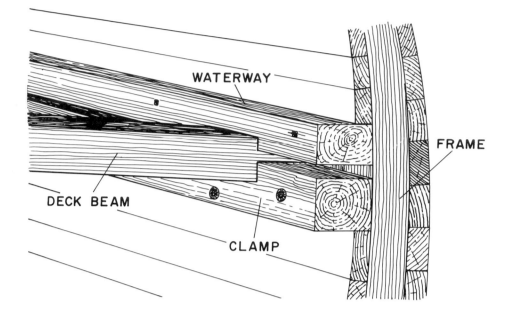

WATERWAY

FRAME

DECK BEAM

CLAMP

FIG. 5–64. The method of securing the *Eagle*'s deck beams. (courtesy Kevin J. Crisman, *The Eagle*, fig. 52)

THE U.S. NAVY BRIG
JEFFERSON

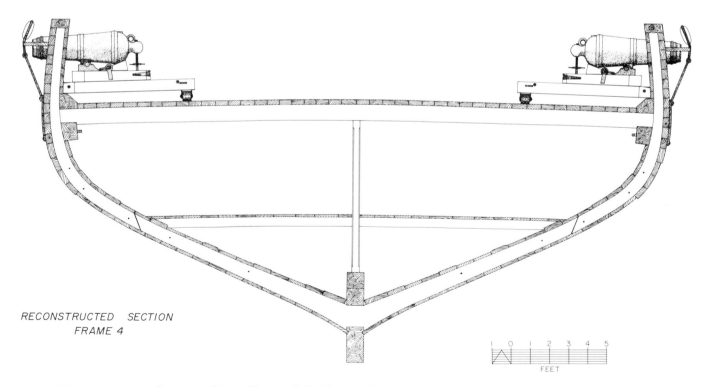

RECONSTRUCTED SECTION
FRAME 4

FEET

FIG. 5–65. A reconstructed section of the *Jefferson*'s hull. (drawing by Kevin J. Crisman)

and it was probably one of many time-saving features that permitted Adam Brown to launch the ship in twenty days.

The *Jefferson* was built in the same year at Sackets Harbor on Lake Ontario by Henry Eckford, another outstanding American shipwright. The vessel was found abandoned at the same location and also was recorded and reconstructed.[62] There are many similarities between these two twenty-gun brigs, although the *Jefferson* was slightly larger and deeper and had an exceptionally steep deadrise. Figures 5–65 and 5–66 illustrate design and construction features.

And that is all the excavated examples we will consider. We missed so many of them—the little clinker-built colonial boat at Lyons Creek, Maryland; that marvelous *Amsterdam* project in England; the numerous post-medieval wrecks in Scandinavia; and on and on. It would be interesting to spend several more pages on vessels such as

that at Browns Bay in Canada, which was somewhat larger than the Brown's Ferry vessel but featured a centerboard and double-clinker construction up to the eleventh strake (Fig. 5–67).[63] Nor have we touched on those interesting clipper ships in the Falklands, or those gigantic Downeasters that required so much backbone strength that their builders stacked keel and keelson timbers on top of each other to provide enough support (see glossary illustrations). But, as stated earlier in the chapter, it would require volumes to list all the vessel types and their construction features. The last century of wooden ship construction has, as yet, relatively few excavated examples. However, the period is well documented by contemporary sources, and worldwide there are museums, models, and even surviving vessels illustrating many of these types and the industry that fostered them. The bibliography lists many of these sources. It is time to go on to the business of recording and research.

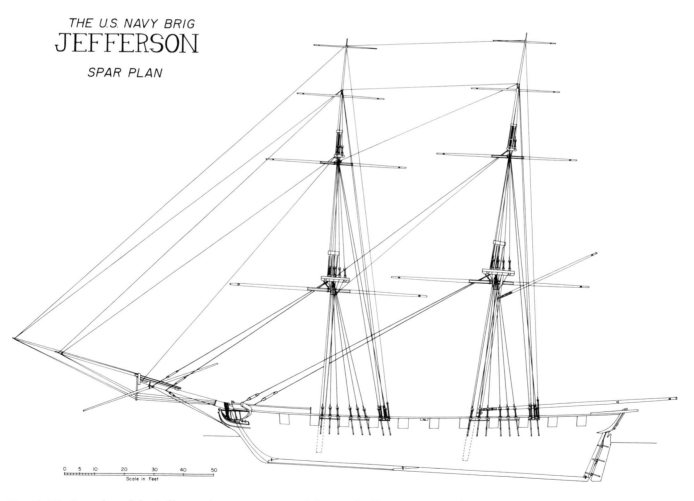

THE U.S. NAVY BRIG
JEFFERSON
SPAR PLAN

0   5   10   20   30   40   50
Scale in Feet

FIG. 5–66. Spar plan of the *Jefferson*. (reconstruction and drawing by Kevin J. Crisman)

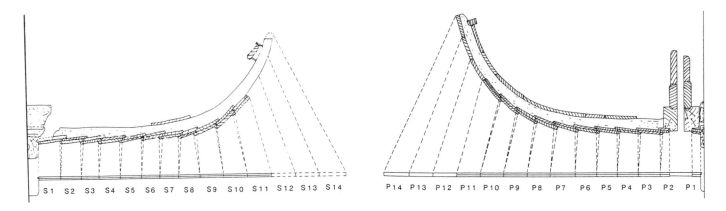

FIG. 5–67. A sectional view of the starboard (left) and port (right) planking plans of the Browns Bay vessel, showing the double clinker construction. (drawing by C. F. Amer and C. Piper; Amer, fig. 36)

PART   III

Research and Reconstruction

6

ABOUT SHIPWRECKS

I am writing this book on a computer. When this session is completed, I will remove the backup disk from its drive and place it in a storage file until there is time to write again. About sixty pages of text are stored in unrecognizable form on that little disk. If I want to see what has been written the past several days, I can only gain access to that disk by first typing a code word, in this case RESRECM. Those letters don't make any sense to you, but they are part of a system I have developed that permits me to recognize immediately what is on each of the dozens of disks in my storage files. Those disks contain a wealth of information—excavation catalogs, texts of articles and books, hull data for dozens of ships, correspondence, and so on. It has taken many years to accumulate all that information, yet it is unrecognizable and inaccessible unless one knows the proper access codes.

Shipwrecks are like that. Piles of rotted timbers and broken artifacts constitute a wealth of information, yet much of that knowledge will remain unrecognized unless one develops a proper method of access to it. In the case of shipwrecks, though, access is the mastery of a discipline rather than a code word. That discipline, which is essentially the means of access to the wealth of information stored in the remains of ships and boats and the orderly dissemination of the knowledge derived from them, will be examined in the remaining few chapters.

The previous chapters on shipbuilding history indicated the vast amount of information one might be looking for in a shipwreck. Hundreds, even thousands, of people may somehow have influenced the construction and operation of that vessel. Ships and boats were products of contemporary technology, social structure, economics, politics, and a host of other factors. Some of that information still survives in their remains, regardless of the state of preservation. The amount of knowledge gleaned from any wreck is limited largely by the ingenuity of those who analyze it.

Let's consider a single shipwreck—make it the ancient Kyrenia ship. Its potential owner had to consider possible trade routes and the types of cargoes to be carried. That, along with limiting economic and technological factors, determined the approximate size and type of vessel, its design, rig, construction features, and crew size. The proposed vessel was discussed with a shipbuilder, who set laborers to work cutting the necessary timber, shipwrights to construct the vessel, smiths to make the nails and hardware, ropemakers to spin the cordage, and sailmakers to fashion the sail. Even small ships built in small yards were the products of numerous people. Perhaps an offering was made, or a ceremony of some sort staged, at its launching. The crew was selected, and then the ship became a small empire of its own, a sort of satellite of the society it represented.

It called at many ports, was visited and taxed by numerous port officials, exchanged an interesting variety of cargoes handled by stevedores of various origins and tongues. In time, seams opened and planks rotted; repairs were made by other shipwrights using timber cut by other sawyers. Caulkers boiled pitch, mixed it with spun agave, and applied it to the planks. Metalworkers made great sheets of lead with which they covered the entire hull. New sails and new ropes were added from time to time, crew members were replaced, merchants were conveyed from one port to another, and there may have been new owners or home ports. And finally there were the pirates who are believed to have ended its career.

The old ship disappeared from the eyes of the earth in the fourth century B.C., but it is inaccurate to say that this was its demise. Phase one was over, certainly, but now it began the next step in a very long life. Before the time of its sinking, the Kyrenia ship was somehow touched by dozens, perhaps hundreds, of human beings, many of whom left their mark on the vessel. For the nautical archaeologist—

especially the reconstructor of ships—such a sinking represents the ultimate challenge. Here is a marvelous artifact, big and complex, whose very fabrication and operation symbolized everyday commerce and society. It is up to the excavators and researchers of such a shipwreck to glean as many of those marks from their find as possible. But that is not the next step; that is phase three. There is a discouraging phase two in the life of every sunken vessel, and it goes as follows.

When the Kyrenia ship sank beneath the surface of the Mediterranean, a subtraction process began. Perhaps it had already begun when pirates removed crew and valuables, but they could not do nearly as thorough a job as the sea. The process commenced in earnest as soon as the ship started to sink. The vessel's thirty-meter ride to the bottom must have left a trail of loose material, and all of it was probably lost forever. The ship settled gently in an upright position; a surprisingly large number of ships do. And then the slow, methodical processes of rotting and silting began.

Sunken wooden ships don't simply lie there and gently rot away. There are long periods of quiet disintegration, of course, but there are also times of violence, of lurching and breakage. Ships seldom die peacefully. In warm waters, shipworms combine forces with oxidation, erosion, and corrosion to speed up the disintegration process. They completely eliminate exposed areas of the hull, causing deck beams to fall or cargo to shift. Cargo and ballast press against the weakened hull sides. As supporting hull timbers lose their integrity, others bear the strain. When their weakened fastenings let go, planks or entire hull sections can be projected far from their original orientation. Mast partners eventually release their grip, and as the masts fall, their heels can move nearby timbers to new locations. Anchors crash through weakened decks to the hold beneath, smashing everything in their path. Rotted topside timbers fall and mix with bottom material, and in time they become indistinguishable from lower members. Ships come apart in combinations of fits and solitude. If they rotted away like old barns, dropping their pieces around them, our job would be easy. But residual buoyancy, currents, and the form of ship construction seldom treat us that generously.

Nature always sprinkles its cruelty with a little kindness, however. While the ship is being attacked by those various destructive forces, cargo weight is pushing bottom planks into the seabed and assuring their preservation. Waterborne silt settles over the wreck and smothers oxidation, insuring survival of whatever it covers. Eventually a point of surrender is reached where whatever has survived will deteriorate no further. However many days, months, or years it took to reduce the vessel to its final state of equilibrium are past; if left undisturbed, it will remain that way for millennia.

While the remains of most wooden vessels will never be detected, whether they perished in the fashion just described or in some terrestrial site, a very small fraction of the world's ships and boats will undergo a third phase. Some of them will be looted and abandoned, suffering yet another form of piracy. A select few will be properly excavated, recorded, and studied. For the Kyrenia ship, phase three included hull reassembly, replication, and continuing research. For the sparsely preserved *San Esteban*, it was something less. Yet each contributed new knowledge and warranted careful analysis.

Perhaps half of the hull has remained intact, perhaps less than 10 percent, but whatever the extent of survival, there remains a greater increment of original information. Where planks have disappeared completely, maybe a few nails remain to describe their thickness or width. There are patterns for hull dispersion on the seabed, however violent the dispersion may have been. It is up to the reconstructor to discover and evaluate those patterns. Even where nothing has survived it is often possible to learn what could have been simply by finding out what could not have been. As stated before, how much information one extracts is limited largely by one's own ingenuity. Do you like a good puzzle? Do you enjoy sorting clues, playing with logic, overcoming an especially difficult challenge? Then follow me; there is nothing—absolutely nothing—that matches the challenge of reconstructing a partially preserved shipwreck.

7

RECORDING

Imagine a partially excavated shipwreck, its clutter of broken cargo, ballast, timbers, and overburden appearing as if some giant hand had stirred it into a potpourri. The grid system overlying the wreck looks like the wall of a crowded gallery of abstract art, each square framing a similar, yet notably different, scene. If you are like me, your eyes tend to focus on the outer squares, where the rotted ends of frames and planking project from the silt with tantalizing brevity. What is beneath that debris, how much of the hull has survived, and what will they tell us?

Time and the efforts of others will provide answers to the first two questions; the magnitude of the answer to the last question will depend largely upon those who record and study the hull remains. At this stage the hull is a relative unknown, the extent and integrity of its preservation speculative. But that really shouldn't affect the preparations for the work at hand. The extent of hull survival is not the issue; what is important is how well that extant structure will be recorded, researched, and reconstructed.

Research and reconstruction are contributions; recording is a debt. Ideally, the same individual might be in charge of all phases of such a shipwreck interpretation, from the first day of excavation to the writing of the final reconstruction report. But that happens infrequently, and it really isn't necessary. The research and reconstruction of shipwrecks can be done in a variety of ways, at various locations, and by people not involved with the excavation. They must be done well, of course, but the results are contributions to an existing bank of knowledge.

Recording, on the other hand, is a restrictive procedure that must be accomplished while the site is open or while a particular timber awaits conservation. It is limited to those who are at the right place at the right time and therefore are the only ones available to perform this important phase of work. Once the site has been opened, once the sanctity of this public legacy has been entered, the select few who have intruded become indebted to the rest of us to tell precisely what they have observed.

Recording is the most important step in the whole process. The parameters of research and reconstruction are defined by the quantity and quality of the recorded information from which they are conceived. Some very scholarly shipwreck excavations were performed in the past by entire staffs whose training was limited to terrestrial archaeology and terrestrial structures. They were done well, because the recorders were extremely proficient in logging details of excavated material. But think how much more might have been learned from those same wrecks had they been recorded by equally proficient people knowledgeable in ship construction. A good shipwreck catalog can be restudied generations later, and it can perhaps be compared with later parallels to provide a more accurate or complete ship reconstruction. Good recording is the key to the success of the whole project, and the person who records the hull remains should be someone who knows enough to recognize the possibility of a scarf in the gap between two keel pieces with dissimilar heartwood and someone who knows the difference between a futtock and a lodging knee.

The Parameters of Recording

Since we have determined that excavation recorders should be able to recognize what they are looking at, it becomes necessary to define what is to be recorded. The obvious answer seems to be "everything in sight," but there are two problems with such a statement. In the first place, one must be aware of what is in sight. Secondly, it may be physically or economically impossible to record everything, such as the thousands of teredo holes or barnacles likely to be found on some hulls. And yet, teredo holes reveal plenty of information about the life and death of the ship, and barnacles can indicate floatation lines. It is a matter of knowing what to document, and how.

Archaeological methodology is beyond the scope of this book. As long as the hull remains' integrity is respected and recording is complete and accurate, excavation procedures need not be a technical concern of those interpreting the shipwreck. The content of the recorded material is a concern, however.

Obviously, the method of recording must be controlled and consistent. It should be planned so that nothing of importance is overlooked, the records are compatible with research and reconstruction techniques, and the excavation data can be reevaluated, even after the site has been abandoned. Each site has its own combination of features that affect recording, and no two sites are ever quite the same, which means a single "best" system of hull documentation cannot be recommended. The magnitude and goals of projects are equally different. A few examples follow.

THE *CHARON*

Much has already been said about this vessel, and we are now ready to discuss the recording phase of its excavation. Most frequently, the assignment is to record and reconstruct, but in this case it was to identify. The *Charon* had been set afire by hot shot from French and American shore batteries as it lay at anchor in the York River during the last days of the siege of Yorktown in 1781. There were reliable contemporary descriptions of the warship slipping its moorings and drifting downstream, a blazing spectacle that lit up the night sky. It drifted toward Gloucester Point, burned to the waterline, and sank from sight. Recent surveys of the York River located a number of wrecks, some of which were believed to be of late eighteenth-century origin. One, listed as GL136, was believed by some historians to be that of the *Charon*.[1] Our assignment was simply to determine whether or not GL136 was the remains of the *Charon*, so that it might be declared a historical site. If the vessel or its artifacts were to be raised and preserved, that would have to be done at a later date when funds and facilities were available.

The length of the excavation could not exceed six weeks, the time determined by staff and local operational constraints. The budget was extremely limited; exotic recording equipment was out of the question. The small staff was provided a barge with the necessary basic equipment and a small field laboratory and drafting area. The wreck lay at a depth of only 12 ft (3.7 m), but environmental problems were numerous. Stinging nettles were at a record concentration, while visibility varied from 18 inches to 0, with the latter occurring all too frequently. Tides and currents were quite strong.

Disposition of materials was hardly a factor here. It was a study assignment; any timbers raised for closer inspection had to be returned to their original locations, while all artifacts the state representatives thought necessary to remove would be forwarded to the laboratory in Williamsburg for further treatment and study.

Archival information was plentiful in this case. The British navy, the siege of Yorktown, and eighteenth-century shipbuilding all were well documented. Original drawings of the *Charon* (Fig. 5–56) and specifications of a similar 44-gun ship were still to be found in the Admiralty records in London.

The first step in preparing the recording procedure was to mentally reenact the demise of the *Charon*. Imagine a ship of 880 tons burning furiously as it floated downstream, its rigging, decorations, and topside gear dropping into the river as the flames severed their attachments. Apparently it maintained stability as it burned to the waterline, although the waterline must have steadily approached the keel as topside weight was consumed or fell overboard. Perhaps only the bottom of the hull survived. That was the key word—*bottom;* it was the first word recorded.

Now what would one expect to find in the bottom of a warship that was destroyed by fire? One could ponder all of the things that might still remain in such a shallow hold, but there was a better way. The builder's draft and extant Admiralty scantling lists for fifth-rate, 44-gun ships of the period would provide more accurate information. Our check list started taking shape as follows:

    Keel—length
        —sided
        —molded
        —no. of pieces
        —length of scarfs

and so on until there were several hundred blanks to fill in. All of the categories came from Admiralty scantling lists, and most of the first set of dimensions under each category came from the original builder's draft of the *Charon*.

Underwater, the timbers were carefully freed of overburden, starting with the highest surviving one (the keelson), and dimensions and shapes were recorded for each. Wherever reliable information could not be determined, we quickly went to the next set of timbers. All dimensions were entered in a second column of blanks labeled GL136 and compared with those from the draft of the *Charon*. A partial list of the resulting data is shown near the end of chapter 5.

Several items were included in the check list that did not appear on contemporary drawings or scantling lists. One was copper sheathing; the *Charon* was one of the early British warships to have copper sheathing on its bottom, an important feature of identification when compared with its size and location. There also was a list of topside timbers that might have survived total destruction and wound up in the hold. The fire was worse than we suspected; none of this material was found, while fused metal and glass attested to the extreme heat.

At the start of the final week of excavation, in spite of bad weather and equipment failure, we had compiled an impressive list of comparisons that left no doubt that GL136 was indeed what was left of the *Charon*.

This was an example of one type of small, single-season excavation in which severe limitations must be placed upon the goals of the work. Time and money were limited, murky water prevented site photography, details had to be acquired by touch or the use of makeshift devices, and there were no facilities for handling large quantities of timber or artifacts. In this case, the design and construction of the hull were already well documented and the cause of its destruction was known (or at least suspected). Essentially, recording was designed to take advantage of relatively large timbers and joinery in near-zero visibility. There were no attempts at recording tool marks or other fine details. The many precise sketches and details of the midship area that resulted were an extra benefit that was not planned, as well as a tribute to the ingenuity of the young archaeologists involved.

The *Charon* project was essentially a survey and is indicative of a form of excavation in which all recording ends with the last dive. There are few preserved materials to examine later, no bottom photographs to peruse in the laboratory, not even a detailed site plan. And of course there is no knowledge of the lower surfaces of the hull, which were pressed against the riverbed. Yet such projects are not uncommon, and they have contributed their share of information that might otherwise have gone undetected. The important thing to remember about recording such excavations is that the methodology and scope of the documentation must be kept within the practical limitations of prevailing administrative, operational, and environmental logistics. To attempt more might be to learn less.

THE SERÇE LIMANI VESSEL

The second example is that of the Serçe Limani vessel, which was described at length in chapter 4. The form of hull recording employed on this wreck can be used for the majority of excavations. It does not matter whether six or six thousand hull fragments have survived, whether the water is clear or murky, or whether the date is Bronze Age or Colonial American; one need only adjust the method of recording to suit those particular conditions. Here the vessel was a relative unknown, and the assignment was to learn as much as possible about the ship and the people associated with it.

Initial artifactual interpretation identified both Islamic and Byzantine origins and a date of about 1025. The wreck lay in approximately 30 m of water on a soft bottom with one large rock outcropping near the stern. Visibility was good. A site plan made during the first season of excavation is shown in Figure 7–1. It reveals a scattered material distribution, with areas of glass, ballast, amphoras, a stack of anchors and two separate anchors, and widely scattered artifacts. Portions of the hull project from around the perimeter of the main concentration of cargo, while fragmentary remains are widely scattered and disarranged. Years before, members of the group working on the site had excavated a seventh-century Byzantine shipwreck in the Turkish Aegean. That hull (see "The Seventh-Century Yassi Ada Vessel" in chapter 4) showed evidence that a transition from the ancient Mediterranean methods of edge-joined planking construction to more modern forms of skeletal construction was already in an advanced stage, and that perhaps true skeletal construction, with its accompanying geometric projections, was only a few centuries away. With the Serçe Limani vessel, we now had a shipwreck dating about four centuries later. One of the reasons this site had been selected for excavation, from among several candidates located by a previous survey, was its possible contribution to the history of shipbuilding.

It was decided that if as little as 20 percent of the hull survived, it would be advantageous to raise and preserve those remains. Furthermore, the hull fragments were to be reassembled, since that method yields far more information than graphic or laboratory methods. This would require greatly enlarged conservation facilities, climate-controlled space in which to reassemble the timbers and display them, and perpetual care. It was a big order, but inquiries proved that we could do it with the proper effort.

After the goals of hull excavation and recording were established, it became necessary to determine the recording procedure. First came the list of major objectives:

> Construction
> Design
> Technology
> Cargo and artifacts
> Economics
> People

These objectives influenced not only recording but also the direction of research and reconstruction. It is best to keep such lists small and general; the subcategories will come automatically as work progresses. For the Athlit ram project, naval logistics were substituted for cargo and artifacts. For the Dashur boats, one might substitute religion in that spot. In a sparsely preserved wreck, construction and design could be combined. But in all cases there should be major subject guidelines.

Let us look briefly at the meaning of these categories. In this case construction was the most important subject, thus it was listed first. At the start of the project, it was

FIG. 7–1. The eleventh-century Serçe Limani wreck plan, 1977 season. (courtesy Institute of Nautical Archaeology)

noted that the visible planking seams in this hull had no mortise-and-tenon joints. Since the seventh-century Yassi Ada vessel had them, the primary interest in this study was centered around that change in construction and what appeared to be a major transition from ancient to more modern fabrication methods. But that was only one special interest. The construction category encompasses every detail of the hull structure.

Design is a more subtle subject but is just as important. It includes the documentation of all hull shapes, the arrangement of the structure, and just about every other physical property of the hull that cannot be assigned to the construction category.

Technology encompasses the practical sciences and mechanics as seen in the metals, timber usage, structural arrangements, measurements, tool marks, surface coverings, repairs, and other applications found in the hull.

Cargo and artifacts, not a factor in some shipwreck studies (the *Charon,* for instance), possibly could contribute a lot of information about this ship. They often determine hold parameters, suggest trade routes, portray shipboard life, help define hull dispersion on the seabed, and provide countless other features that may assist in research and reconstruction. With the exception of hull-related artifacts, this material is recorded by others. It is included as a major category to serve as a reminder during the recording process, and as a valuable aid in later phases of work.

Economics deals with the timber trade, metallurgy, trade routes, shipbuilding and mercantile economics, labor applications, and other financially controlled features of the hull.

People—I have never done a reconstruction without this category. Years ago it was "social studies," but "people" is more accurate. People influenced the design, purchase, construction, operation, and perhaps the sinking of this ship. They left their marks everywhere, as they do on all ships if only one can find them. The shipwrights especially are in evidence through their tool marks and other surface impressions; so much so that on the larger projects one feels an acquaintanceship with some of them. Never omit this category. It is the most interesting, most challenging, and sometimes the most fruitful part of the work.

LABELING

One should adhere to established archaeological procedure where necessary and practical, of course, but it is sometimes impractical and usually cumbersome to label ship timbers in the same manner as artifacts. Standard designations for certain ship timbers have been around for a couple of centuries; since they are so practical, why not use them? One need only expand a traditional system used by shipwrights in building the frigates, clippers, and downeasters. In some cases, the distribution of hull remains is such that standard timber designations can be assigned at the beginning of the excavation and retained through the final publication. The way it was applied to the Serçe Limani wreck is described in the following.

In chapter 2 you learned that the widest part of the ship was given a ⊗ or similar designation; frames or stations forward of this midship bend were lettered consecutively, those aft of it were numbered in the same order. On vessels built after the medieval period, the midship frame can sometimes be recognized because it has a different form of construction than the other square frames. It might be a single line of scarfed timbers, or a floor timber with doubled first futtocks as on the Red Bay wreck. When the recording system for the Serçe Limani wreck was developed, the first season of excavation had just been completed, and the first site plan was available (Fig. 7–1). Based upon the location at which the visible planking and frames reached maximum breadth, indicating the fullest part of the extant hull, the selection of the midship frame was made as shown in Figure 7–2. The bow end of the wreck was evident from the location of the two concreted bower anchors (at the left of the drawing). Thus frames forward of ⊗ were labeled with consecutive capital letters, while those aft of that station were numbered consecutively. All frames were given an F prefix. No differentiation had to be made between floor timbers and complete frames on such a simple ship; in other words, both floor timbers and their frames were designated FD, F6, etc. On larger ships, where six or more futtocks were used in the assembly of a frame, it is advisable to give the floor timber a separate suffix of 0; thus the floor timber of F12 would be F12-0 on such complex frames.

Futtocks on the Serçe Limani wreck were given suffixes. A dash followed by an odd number indicated a port futtock, while even numbers identified starboard futtocks. Thus F5-1 was the port futtock of frame 5; its starboard futtock, if one had survived, would have been labeled F5-2. Larger frames should have their futtocks numbered successively, as F5-1, F5-3, and F5-5, if there were a port top timber (Fig. 7–3). There is nothing original about this system of labeling frames. Many shipwrights used similar methods to make certain that the various timbers they had shaped were used in the correct frame assemblies.[2] It is, in fact, a feature to anticipate when studying composite frames made in the last few centuries, since numbers or symbols were sometimes applied to timbers with paint, chisels, punches, labels, or other media of permanence.

What about individual fragments of the same frame? They were assigned the full frame designation followed by a slash and the special fragment number. For instance, if floor timber 5 broke into two pieces and its futtock into three, the largest pieces would assume the frame or futtock designation, while the fragments would be assigned fragment suffixes. The largest floor piece would be labeled F5 and the largest piece of futtock F5-1; the fragments would be F5/1, F5-1/1 and F5-1/2.

Keel pieces were given K prefixes followed by a capital letter in their order of excavation—KA, KB, etc. It is

not necessary to use a more sophisticated labeling system for single timbers or lines of timbers, such as keels and keelsons, except in cases of severe breakage or on the big freighters, where two or three 30-cm-square oak timbers were stacked atop each other to make a keel.

Outer hull planking was numbered sequentially from the keel outward and upward, preceded by a P prefix for port planking and S for starboard planking. Thus the port garboard was P1 and the fifth starboard strake S5. Fragments were numbered sequentially from the bow and were separated from the strake number by a slash; thus, S5/44.

Ceiling gets a C prefix; if there is transverse ceiling as on the Serçe Limani hull, it becomes TC. Where ceiling survives extensively on both sides of the keel, a P or S precedes the designation. Lodging knees are LN, hanging knees HN, and so on. There usually are so few keelson fragments that one can spell the word out or use SON. If wale preservation is extensive, use its sequence in the outer hull planking system; the wale just above port strake 16 would be labeled P17. Where wale preservation is sparse, they are listed simply as Wale 1, Wale 2, etc.

There remains the problem of what to do with all those unidentifiable or unlocatable fragments. Every excavation has them by the dozens, hundreds, or thousands. One practical system is that devised for the Serçe Limani project; it has to be digested, but saves time if you are dealing with many fragments of unknown origin. The master prefix is UM (for unidentified member), followed by the grid letter and number, and the number of the fragment in the sequence it was excavated.[3] Thus the fourteenth unlocatable fragment to be excavated from grid P3 becomes UMP3/14. We have tried in the past to refine this system by labeling frame fragments as UF and plank fragments as UP. In theory that works fine, but badly degraded pieces are sometimes impossible to recognize even by major category. Since degraded fragments make up a large percentage of UM's on most wrecks, I advise against it.

If all this is not clear, please refer to the partial fragment drawings in Figures 7–2 and 7–4, where it is illustrated. A word of caution, though. It is possible to make labeling systems too complex. Once all this information gets to the laboratory, research becomes difficult enough without having to deal with a labeling system of several dozen categories. In recording, as with all other forms of ship interpretation, keep the basics basic. And if hull preservation is such that midship frames and planking sequences cannot be determined, alter the above systems or number fragments sequentially and convert their designations later for publication.

The Serçe Limani wreck consisted of at least two thousand extant fragments representing less than one-third of the original hull. Consequently, the above system of fragment designation was necessary to maintain

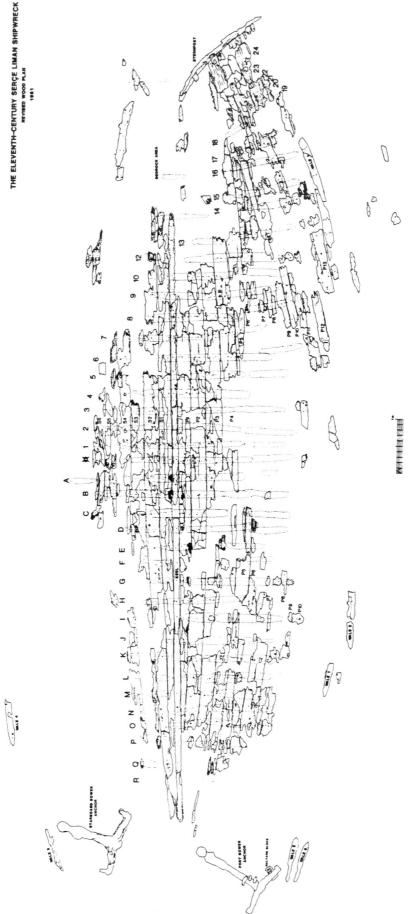

FIG. 7–2. The eleventh-century Serçe Limani hull remains *in-situ*. (courtesy Institute of Nautical Archaeology)

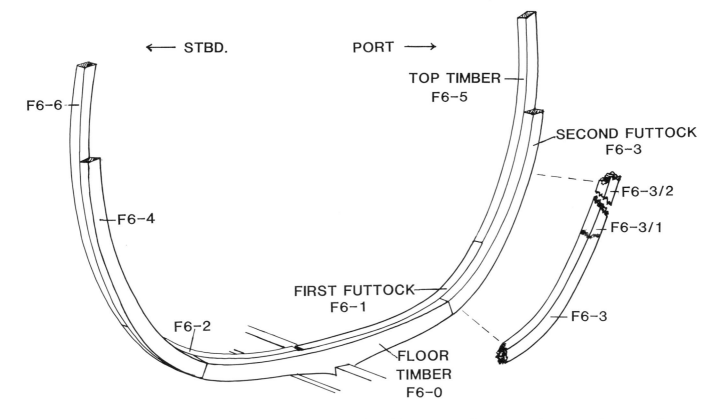

FIG. 7–3. A convenient method of labeling the sixth frame aft of amidships on a merchant brig with seven-timber square frames. Fragment designations of a broken futtock are illustrated at right.

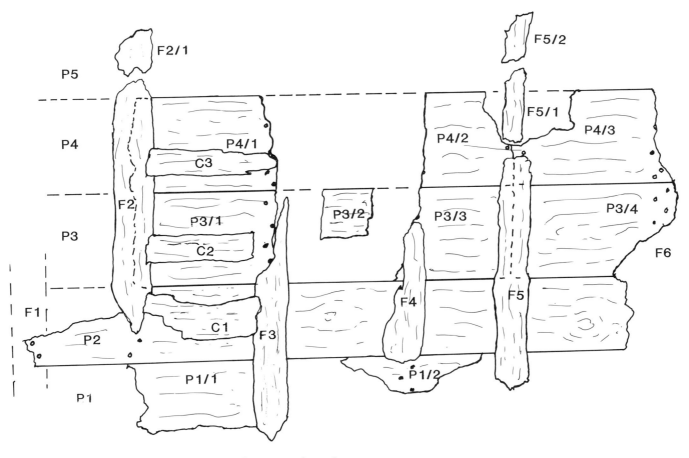

FIG. 7–4. Timber identification for a sparsely preserved wreck.

efficient recording, research, and publication. But what about wrecks that are sparsely preserved? One example can be found in the Athlit ram (Figs. 3–45 and 3–46), where only sixteen fragments of a warship bow survived. But a more common form of sparse hull survival is shown here in Figure 7–4, where only four frames, parts of six planks, and a few ceiling fragments were preserved. Thorough recording is just as important for this wreck as it was for the Serçe Limani vessel, although that degree of sophistication would be wasted effort in this case. Such a wreck will never be represented by an elaborate construction plan or lines drawing. It may not even be possible to relate this section to a keel or midship frame; therefore, any simple system that will segregate the various hull members will suffice. Since the direction of the bow was unknown, the frames were labeled from left to right, including the lines of nails where two were missing. But it would have been just as proper to have labeled them from right to left. Planks are tagged from bottom to top because ballast stones and a cluster of shot suggested that the keel was below P1.

No matter how sparse or complex your wreck, the following important rules should be kept in mind:

1. Keep the system as simple as possible to serve the demands of the conservation, research, and reconstruction processes that follow.
2. Design the system to serve ship reconstruction and ship terminology; segregate hull members from general tagging systems applied to other forms of artifacts.
3. Avoid confusion; for instance, use "N" for knee, because a keel is more commonly designated with a "K."

INTACT VESSELS

Extensively intact vessels may require different recording procedures than those which have broken up or flattened on the seabed. The *Vasa*, the Brown's Ferry vessel, and the Kinneret boat are underwater examples of this type. Terrestrial discoveries have been equally, if not more, impressive, both in numbers and extent of preservation. The Dashur boats, the Ronson ship, the Herculaneum boat, and some of the polders vessels found when the Zuyderzee was reclaimed in the Netherlands are but a few examples.

Hulls such as the Dashur boats (Fig. 3–9) and the *Vasa* (Fig. 5–25) were sufficiently well preserved and retained so much of their original shape that their lines could be taken off directly. There is a different approach here from that of the Serçe Limani vessel, where the site plan could only reveal flattened or dispersed hull remains and where individual fragment drawings were required in order to determine the design of the vessel. The locations of all or most of the timbers are already known, and as far as design and construction are concerned, the

function of research will be altered to determine the degree of distortion or loss suffered by the hull. Most of the timbers can be recorded either individually or as part of a predetermined assembly in the form of construction plans, section drawings, and the like. Suggestions for measuring intact vessels are discussed and illustrated later in this chapter.

COMPILING INFORMATION

If hull remains must be recorded entirely on the seabed, one surface of the hull will be largely inaccessible and therefore will remain a mystery. Fortunately, it is usually the outer hull surface that is pressed to the seabed, and that surface normally supplies less information than the inner hull structure. It is difficult—and pointless, really—to prescribe distinct methods of seabed recording. For the most part, it is straightforward archaeology. The important thing to remember is that the wreck will be available for measurements for a very limited time; once the site has been covered over, errors and omissions are difficult or impossible to correct. What you will be looking for is as much of the data listed on the following pages as is possible.

If timbers are to be brought to the surface and preserved, much of the recording can be done away from the confusion of the site. Excavation schedules and seabed environment will then place no restrictions on the work. Furthermore, one can study all surfaces, measure curvatures atop grid tables, and examine timbers individually from many angles. As soon as the member has undergone conservation treatment, it can be analyzed for hours without fear of further shrinkage or breakage. But even in such cases, some form of seabed recording is necessary. Each fragment must be related to the others on the site, and at least elementary descriptions of the timbers are necessary in case of damage during handling. Beyond those minimum requirements, the complexity of seabed hull recording is an archaeological matter, the answers to which depend upon depth, budget, seabed conditions, stability of the hull remains, and a host of other factors.

Regardless of the nature of the project, all the recorded hull information will ultimately have to be compiled into some orderly collection so that it can be conveniently utilized for research. I prefer to call this a *hull catalog*, and my catalogs usually consist of the following material.

1. Pertinent background information—information from previous excavations that have produced vessels of the same period or type. You will want to know what they determined and what questions were left unanswered. It is also valuable to know something about the general historical background of the period, especially in maritime history.

2. Pertinent excavation information—notes from the excavation logs, such as the sequence of removing individual fragments, and notes on breakage or other applicable data.

3. Relevant cargo and artifactual information.

4. Photomosaics, general site photography, site plans, and wreck drawings.

5. Hull lines, or tables of offsets of the hulls curvatures, if the vessel is intact or nearly so.

6. Drawings, photographs, and verbal descriptions of each hull member or fragment.

7. The results of laboratory analyses of the hull materials.

8. An account of the disposition of the timbers, whether they were reburied, moved to a conservation facility, or dealt with in some other fashion.

9. Pertinent conservation information, where applicable.

10. Post conservation recording, if applicable.

11. Reassembly recording, if applicable.

The heart of the catalog, of course, is its illustrative material and verbal descriptions of everything that cannot be made clear by photographs and drawings. They are discussed below.

Photography

Ideal shipwreck recording employs a liberal combination of photographs and drawings. The dark, wet surfaces of hull remains are usually poor photographic subjects, but photography is nevertheless an indispensable part of the catalog. I cannot overstress the importance of quality in this phase of the work—good equipment and experienced photographers are imperative, and conveniently located, well-equipped darkrooms are equally vital, especially on the larger projects. The methodology of photographing wrecks is a large and highly technical subject, one that is beyond the scope of this book. However, some comments about the subject material are in order.

Stereophotography or photomosaics of the entire wreck are important wherever visibility permits. They complement site drawings, provide an inventory of the hull remains, and often reveal details not available from drawings and logbooks. Sector photography is helpful, especially in areas where non-contiguous fragments are located. *In-situ* details (Fig. 7–5) are equally helpful in the reconstruction process.

FIG. 7–5. A photographic detail of the Kinneret boat's scarf. (photo courtesy Israel Antiquities Authority)

On wrecks that have broken up on the seabed, especially those in which large numbers of fragments overlay each other, it becomes difficult to determine the relationship of one fragment to another. In such cases the provenance and sequence of removal from the site become extremely important to the reconstructor. The problem can be greatly simplified by the use of "flyovers," general photographs of a sector taken at frequent intervals as the excavation progresses.

Individual fragment photographs, although not usually as revealing as drawings, are certainly important to the recording process and often helpful in reconstructions. Figure 7–6 illustrates such a photograph. This single end view of a keel fragment reveals erosion, teredo infestation, wood grain pattern and heartwood location, the original shape of the port side of the keel, the garboard rabbet with the port garboard seated, details of two mortise-and-tenon joints with an exceptionally good view of the peg hole in the starboard joint, a pair of square pegs in the lower keel sides, and a lead sheathing tack shaft. Timbers should be photographed on all surfaces where details or shapes warrant it.

Drawings

Drawings are the most vital part of the catalog; without them, ships could not be reconstructed. The more comprehensive one makes the graphic forms of recording, the less one is required to depend on verbal descriptions and, consequently, the more convenient research becomes. Hull drawings come in a variety of forms and, on the larger projects, can number in the thousands by the time recording is completed. To a certain extent, their form and content are a matter of personal preference, although it is necessary that form and content include all the necessary information when the catalog is completed. The more important forms of graphic recording, along with some of the methods that have worked well on my own projects, are discussed below.

WRECK PLANS

Wreck plans, graphic descriptions of the wreck *in-situ*, illustrate the distribution of hull timbers and related artifacts. Unlike photographic records, they can be produced in a precise scale, so that measurements may be taken directly from them. Whether they are derived from photogrammetry, triangulation, or one of the new electronic measuring programs linked to a computer, they should reveal framing plans, planking seams, visible scarfs and butts, scattered fragments, and other structural information as indicated in the various examples in this book. If the hull is to be dismantled, separate drawings of interior and exterior construction should be produced, such as the Kyrenia wreck plans shown in Figures 3–23 and 7–7. These drawings were produced from stereo-photogrammetric recording. Additional site information might be included in separate drawings of small finds, such as scatterings of planking nails, which could supply information about construction that did not survive. No matter how many wreck plans are produced, they should be made to the same scale; 1:10 is usually a convenient wreck plan scale, although 1:20 may be more practical for large vessels. Like all catalog and reconstruction drawings, wreck plans should be signed and dated to avoid confusion with subsequent recording.

TIMBER AND FRAGMENT DRAWINGS

Wreck plans can only supply general information about the hull's construction. Except for the most sparsely preserved wrecks, it would be virtually impossible to include every visible detail on a wreck drawing of manageable

FIG. 7–6. A photograph of the end of a keel fragment from the fourth-century B.C. Kyrenia ship reveals many important features. (courtesy Kyrenia Ship Project)

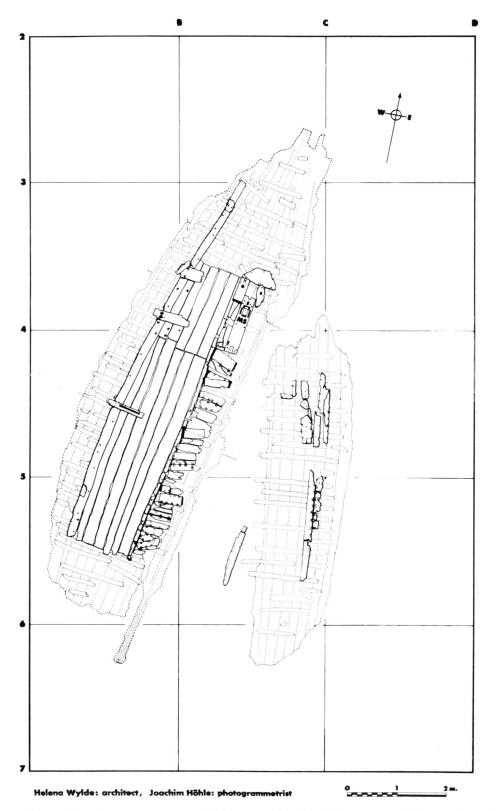

Helena Wylde: architect,   Joachim Höhle: photogrammetrist

FIG. 7–7. The Kyrenia ship's ceiling, beams, mast step, and other internal timbers before removal. (drawing by Helena Wylde Swiny and Joachim Höhle)

size. On those wrecks that remain on the bottom and are reburied, some excavators have gone to extreme lengths to record details on individual planks and timbers. Full scale drawings traced on heavy plastic placed against the various members, detailed sketches and measurements, combinations of detailed photographs and sketches, and actual casts of the various timbers are some of the methods of detailed recording done successfully *in-situ*. But such recording has the distinct disadvantage of limited access; certain surfaces and measurements are inaccessible. The following discussion deals with hull members that are removed from the site, either temporarily or permanently, for complete recording; *in-situ* recording will accomplish something less.

Depicting all the details of a wreck that has broken into several thousand fragments requires a great amount of effort and discipline. The wood must be kept in its original environmental state, and that usually means keeping it very wet. It must be handled with extreme care, and yet every surface must be scrutinized again and again. The work can be repetitive and boring, but it is an indispensable step in accumulating all the information the wreck has to offer.

As was the case for wreck plans, project logistics can be a determining factor in the production of fragment drawings. Most of my research has been done with drawings that were scaled down from full-size drawings. In most of these cases, the original drawings were produced on heavy, clear acetate that had been laid atop a sheet of glass supported at either end so that it just cleared the surface to be recorded. They were color-coded in waterproof inks—black for outlines, red for wooden fastenings, green for nails and bolts, blue for sheathing, and so on.[4] In recent years, many of our wood drawings have been reproduced directly in 1:10 scale on grid paper from timbers mounted on grid tables or overlaid with transparent grids, and the process has been very successful. For direct 1:10 reduction of fragment drawings, some European museums now use a reducing field pantograph. The initial cost of the pantograph is high, but the reduction is very accurate and the saving in labor is substantial.

Some project directors insist on full-size drawings as a matter of archaeological discipline, and that too is a matter of preference. From a reconstructor's point of view, however, a full-scale drawing of a 40-cm-square, 30-m-long keelson is about as useful as a full-scale drawing of a temple column. At some stage, full-size drawings will have to be reduced to a practical, workable scale because the hundreds of large drawings required to document an extensively preserved wreck are far too cumbersome to handle in the laboratory. The Kyrenia ship, the timbers of the Athlit ram, and a couple of boats were researched in 1:5 scale because of the close proximity of large numbers of details. For most vessels, however, 1:10 scale is far more convenient. In selecting working scales, it should be remembered that these small fragment drawings will be assembled into large planking and framing plans, and too large a scale could tax drafting and research facilities as well as deplete budgets for drafting paper and reductions for publication. Whatever scale you choose, keep it large enough for accuracy, small enough for convenience, and consistent for all phases of the work.

Eventually, rugged field-type computers with sophisticated transfer devices and limitless memory will become practical enough to draw the hundreds of hull fragments from a well-preserved wreck directly onto a graphics system at the excavation site or conservation lab. When such systems become economical and easy to manage, most hull recorders will abandon the above methods. But the basics will remain the same. Making wood drawings is a mechanical process not unlike the drawing of any other artifact. And like all other archaeological drawings, it is necessary to be as observant and precise as possible. You will constantly be reminded of what should be included in wood drawings as you read the section on compiling hull catalogs and the chapter on reconstruction that follow. Two examples are shown here. Figure 7–8 illustrates the inner surface of a section of planking from the Kyrenia ship that was drawn full-size on clear acetate. Notice that width dimensions are given at various intervals, even though the outline of the plank has been drawn as carefully as possible. This is done to insure

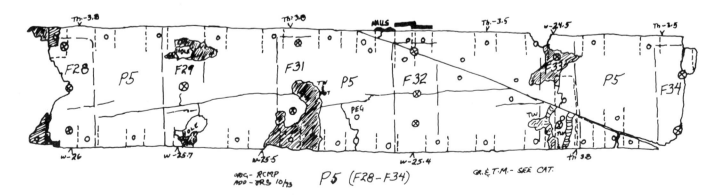

FIG. 7–8. A reduction of a full-size drawing of a Kyrenia ship planking fragment. (courtesy Kyrenia Ship Project)

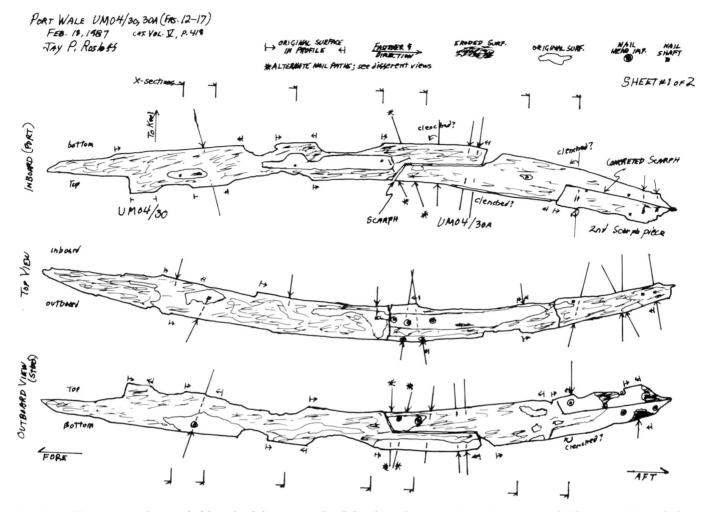

FIG. 7–9. Three views of an eroded length of the main wale of the eleventh-century Serçe Limani vessel. (drawn to 1:10 scale by Jay P. Rosloff)

against inaccuracy due to parallax, a disadvantage of this system of drawing. Parallax is the distortion or apparent displacement of an object as seen from two different points not on a straight line with the object; it can occur when one part of a curved piece of timber may nearly touch the glass surface while another area is perhaps 5 or 10 cm away.

Figure 7–9 shows an eroded section of main wale from the Serçe Limani medieval wreck. This drawing was produced directly at 1:10 scale on grid paper while the timber was supported on a grid ten times as large.

Note the extent to which the artist, who is an experienced ship reconstructor, has gone to clarify bolt directions and other details, a contribution that was greatly appreciated in the laboratory. Verbal notations on drawings such as this are usually a welcome addition, although in some cases they are mere repetitions of the verbal descriptions in the catalog. Still, I do not discourage verbal descriptions on drawings; it is far better that the reconstructor receive an overdose of information than a scarcity of it.

Measuring Intact or Partially Intact Hulls

Taking off the lines of an extensively preserved hull can be a mixed blessing. It is fortunate to have found a vessel so well preserved, but recording its hull shape is seldom easy. In the case of terrestrial finds, hulls that were locked in the earth must be strongly braced wherever supporting

overburden has been removed, and that bracing interferes constantly with attempts at measuring. Water sprays, projecting and broken surfaces, wales, discontinuous sheer lines, and widespread distortion are but a few of the annoyances encountered. If the vessel is found underwater, severe listing, encrustation, scattered cargo and ballast, and all the problems of the aquatic environment add to the difficulties. It seems a waste of time to attempt to specify distinct methodology for measuring hulls, since each project will vary so much from others that a specific set of rules will not apply in many instances. Additionally, there are a number of electronic measuring systems being perfected, some of which are so advanced and so easily managed that most intact hulls, especially those in deep or murky water, will probably be measured by such systems in the immediate future. Laser pulse systems (EDM) for terrestrial work and SHARPS (Sonic High Accuracy Ranging and Positioning System), which is already being used for underwater site mapping by the Institute of Nautical Archaeology and other groups, are examples of such programs.[5] The latter system measures the speed of acoustic

signals transmitted by a probe at the point of measurement to three transceivers placed in a triangular arrangement around the area being recorded. The signals are monitored by a remote computer, which can convert them into x-, y-, and z-coordinates; a computer-assisted drafting program, if in the system, can further convert the coordinates into lines drawings. Although problems remain with the system as currently implemented, anyone who has attempted to measure hull curvatures underwater will appreciate the fact that the future bears hope.

A less expensive method, combining manual tape measurements with computer programs to process the data, was used on the *Mary Rose, Amsterdam, Sea Venture,* and other projects. Known as the Direct Survey Method (DSM), it seems to work well on complex structures, even in limited visibility.[6]

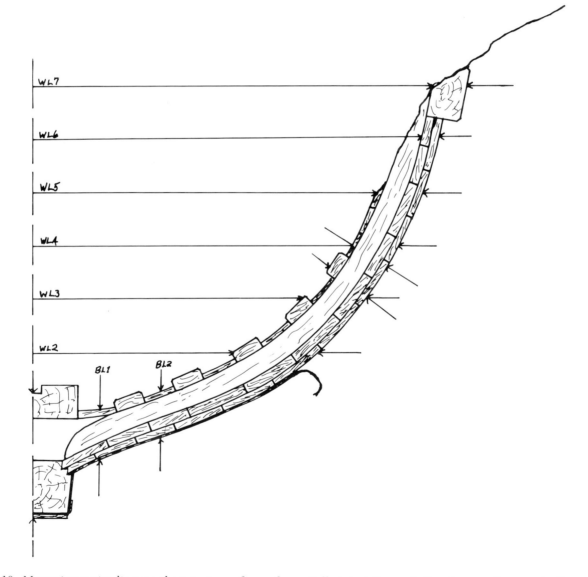

FIG. 7–10. Measuring station lines on the interior surfaces of a partially intact Roman hull, using equally spaced offsets. Note the variations in hull thickness caused by sheathed areas, alternate ceiling thickness, and broken frame patterns.

But regardless of whether you are measuring partially intact hulls electronically or by means of transits, tapes, levels, plumb bobs, contouring devices, and other aids, it is important to realize what is to be measured. That remains the same, regardless of methodology. The idea is to compile tables of coordinates that can be used to produce the three views of a lines drawing of the hull as found. Those lines, which will reflect all the distortion and destruction suffered by the hull, will be faired when research and reconstruction reveal their original contours. Ideally, the offsets should be taken from the inside of the hull planking, but ceiling planking and other internal construction usually interfere. Measuring to the inside of ceiling and adding the distance between ceiling and outer planking surfaces, if indeed those distances can be determined, is seldom very accurate due to the lack of direct access to the interior or exterior of the planking and due to problems posed by lower decks and compartments. Furthermore, ceiling often varies in thickness or does not fully cover the interior of a hull, making the process even more difficult. Figure 7–10 illustrates this problem when using equally spaced offsets; employing arbitrary reference lines or points alleviates the problem somewhat.

One method of deriving stem, stern, and sheer curvatures is shown in Figure 7–11. Keels of excavated vessels are seldom reliable baselines due to distortion; check them before measuring or use an alternate baseline. Determining external body shapes by means of horizontal and vertical coordinates can be seen in Figure 7–12; a triangulation method is shown in Figure 7–13. Table 7–1 contains a list of offsets taken from the station in Figure 7–12. Offsets can be measured with plumb bobs, tapes, rules, bars, ells, or specially fabricated devices, depending on site logistics and personal preference. In actual practice, stations can seldom be taken off at regular intervals because of shoring, other obstructions, or missing areas. Nor can one expect to work exclusively from vertical and horizontal reference lines, since intact or

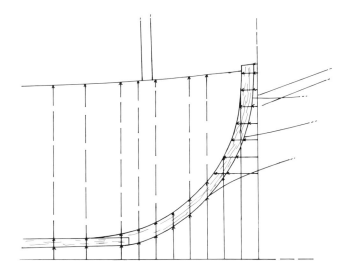

FIG. 7–11. Deriving stem, stern, and sheer curvatures of a seventeenth-century warship. Additional accuracy can be achieved by taking horizontal offsets of the upper stem.

partially intact hulls may have to be measured before removal from the seabed or site at various degrees of list. For instance, the Herculaneum boat was found upside down; the shape recorded in Figure 3–56 was made with plumb bobs dropped from a horizontal bar suspended over the keel. Those readers interested in further details on measuring intact hulls are referred to the U.S. National Park Service's Historic American Engineering Record publication *Guidelines For Recording Historic Ships* and *Boats: A Field Manual for Their Documentation*, a publication of the Museum Small Craft Association and the American Association for State and Local History.[7] Both volumes contain elaborate sections on measuring and drawing extant vessels; the first deals predominantly with historic vessels of all sizes, the second with small craft of any period or interest.

Catalogs

Now let's compile hull catalogs. If the ship remains on the seabed, acquiring this information is part of the excavation; if not, this phase of work can be done independently. Again the medieval Serçe Limani wreck will be used as an example. Those timbers were transported to our headquarters in Bodrum, about a hundred kilometers away, where better freshwater storage tanks and recording and conservation facilities were available. We now had a wreck plan of the wood, artifact and cargo distribution plans, an excavation log, an assortment of notes and sketches, and hundreds of informative bottom

photographs. Next it was time to start dealing with individual hull fragments.

Remember that priority list we prepared at the beginning of the project? It is time to glance at it again.

Construction
Design
Technology
Cargo and artifacts
Economics
People

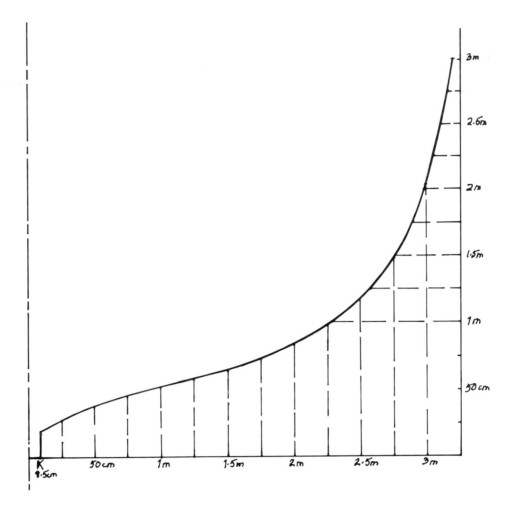

FIG. 7–12. Measuring body shapes with horizontal and vertical determinants. Coordinates derived from this station are shown in Table 7–1.

TABLE 7–1. Offsets—Station 4

Line Number	Buttock	Water
0.085/K	0.190	3.165
0.250	0.270	——
0.500	0.380	——
0.750	0.470	——
1.000	0.520	0.970
1.250	0.590	0.680
1.500	0.655	0.490
1.750	——	0.360
2.000	0.840	0.260
2.250	0.980	0.190
2.500	1.170	0.140
2.750	1.480	0.095
3.000	——	——
Caprail	3.050	0.060

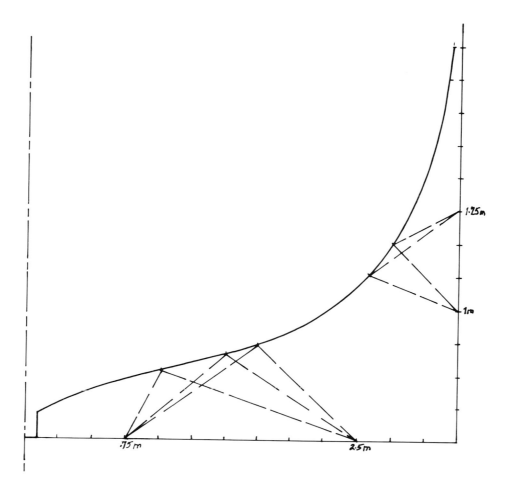

FIG. 7–13. A few examples of measuring the same body shapes by means of triangulation.

These are the subjects to be kept in mind as each fragment is documented. Every detail is important, of course, but things contributing to those major categories are of primary interest.

On wrecks as extensive or as fragmentary as this one, it is best to break the catalog into sections called catalogs or sub-catalogs. On the Serçe Limani project, it was most convenient to segregate the remains into the following separate catalogs:

Keel, Keelson, and Sternpost
Frames
Planking
Ceiling
Unclassified Members

The latter catalog included mostly UM labeled fragments that could not be associated with a particular strake or frame, as well as rigging artifacts and those members that could not be assigned to the other catalogs. The size of the catalog was only one reason for breaking hull data into sub-catalogs. Each of these categories also had a particular recording format, and that more or less determined the number of sub-catalogs to use.

Ideally, one writes a complete catalog as soon as the timbers can be examined; in reality, this is not always possible. In the case of the Serçe Limani hull remains, a preliminary catalog was begun for each of approximately two hundred larger or more important pieces as soon as they were delivered to the Bodrum storage tanks. Thus a preliminary reconstruction, which was required to determine hull parameters so that a museum could be designed and displays planned, could begin immediately. Such preliminary recording is usually advantageous, especially since one then becomes familiar enough with the timbers to do a better job of the rest of the documentation.

Upon completion of the preliminary study, full-size drawings of each fragment were made on sheets of clear plastic, along with notes and photographs of the same pieces. The wood was placed into tanks of polyethylene glycol shortly afterward, where it was treated for nearly three years.

Then the most important inspection began. After wood has been conserved one can stare at it for hours without hindrance. Gone are the constant interruptions to keep it wet, as well as the disadvantages of glare on the surfaces. It is much stronger in this preserved state, and it can be handled with comparative safety. Surface grime and concretion have been eliminated, exposing obscure tool marks and colorations. It was necessary to do the initial fragment recording as soon as possible after excavation, before the fragments entered the conservation process, since dimensions are only reliable in the waterlogged state. Planks and timbers can shrink as much as 10 percent in lateral dimension during treatment. Even where claims of minimal shrinkage are made for certain processes, the risk of stability in this unnatural environment cannot be taken for granted. On the Serçe Limani and similar projects, fragment lengths, widths, and thicknesses were measured before and after treatment to determine shrinkage rates and confirm approximate original dimensions. We also reconfirmed curvatures, found new fastenings or other details, and added them to the original catalog lists.

A final recording phase automatically took place during the hull reassembly in the museum, where the mechanics of fitting the fragments prompted us to notice things that were ignored before. During these various inspections, several people trained in ship interpretation looked at each fragment. That is important. No matter how observant you think you are, a second pair of eyes will usually notice something that yours overlooked.

Thus the catalog examples discussed below evolved from several inspections by several people, but always the new information was simply added to the original listings. Let us start with the catalog describing the principal timbers, which were in this case the keel, sternpost, and keelson. For purposes of brevity, some verbal descriptions have been condensed.

At the beginning of every sub-catalog there are partial site plans illustrating the pieces in question and a series of seabed photographs showing the subjects from various perspectives. Next comes a general statement, as shown below for the keel.

THE KEEL

Length of survival—11.25 m
General statement of condition—Was found in 8 major pieces, labeled from bow afterward as STEM, KF, KE, KB, KA, KD, KC, and KWW. It is in fair condition on its sides and upper surface, but the bottom surface is completely missing. No false keel survives. No garboard rabbets are in evidence. The entire keel appears to be rockered on the seabed, and its upper surfaces are noticeably sagged. Its forward extremity was labeled STEM, because it curves sharply upward into a short, eroded stump, although there is no scarf in the area; the forward section composed of KF and KE bends slightly to starboard. Near amidships, a short section is completely missing. A partially preserved scarf is located below frame 8. The aftermost end is badly damaged on all surfaces and sags slightly downward.

Then the individual fragment recording was compiled, as in the following example. Each list begins with 1:10 scale drawings and photographs of the subject.

Keel piece KD
1. *Drawings*—1:1, top, port, and starboard views (1/27/80); 1:10, same views (2/10/81; additions 10/7/84).
2. *Photos*—wood: closeup profile, 5/29A–33A; general profile, 5/27A and 28A; top views, 5/34A and 35A; closeup of top, 5/36A–40A. Suggested seabed shots: 167/6, 7, 13; 170/35; 156/18.
3. *Max. length remaining*—1.665 m.
4. *Description*—Condition, fair. Modern break at bolt forward, fits well on port side with KA, but break is open on starboard side. Broken portion of the lower part of a hook or flat scarf at after end, which photos indicate is overlaid by KC. Top surface is in fair condition; has some finished surface but many breaks along edges. Port side is in collapsed, rather poor condition; starboard side has some good finished surface, but entire lower edge is gone and upper edge is partially broken. The entire bottom surface has disappeared; the present surface is eroded and uneven. Teredo damage is minor. There is no evidence for a false keel.
5. *Sided (upper surface)*—11 cm at break; 10.2 cm at 40 cm from KD/KA break; no other reliable edges.
6. *Molded*—14.5 cm remaining at ends; 14.7 cm at 40 cm from forward break.
7. *Fastenings*—6 nail shafts in upper surface, all 9 mm square; 1 bolt shaft, 1.7 cm diameter; all fastenings of iron. See drawings for spacings, angles, and details.
8. *Frame impressions*—frames 4, 5, 6, and 7 centered at 23 cm, 48.4 cm, 89 cm, and 124 cm from forward break. Impressions are well defined. See top surface drawings for configurations.
9. *Rabbets or bevels*—none; preservation is good enough to indicate that there was no form of seating for the garboard, nor are there garboard nails in the side of this piece.
10. *Curvatures*—upper surface has a sag of 1.3 cm.
11. *Tool marks*—small adze marks just aft of F4 near starboard edge, size of blade indeterminable; possible chisel marks at forward end of scarf table; large saw marks both sides, angle of cut nearly vertical (see port side drawing for angles and spacing).
12. *Surface coverings*—pitch along starboard side is barely discernable except for a thin, beaded line 3.8 cm from upper edge, which is about 1 mm thick; pitch is similar to samples taken elsewhere

on hull surface; line is visible at broken intervals between F4 and F6; garboard location easily recognized by light brown area above this line. No other surface coverings.

13. *Other features*—end of scarf bevels 25 degrees (see drawing); scarf table is 16.5 cm long; cut is 7.7 cm deep at forward end of scarf, 8.7 cm below keel top at offset (slopes 1 cm in 16.5 cm); offset is 5 mm; see drawings for fastenings running through scarf. Scanned bottom surface and found no fastenings except exposed ends of frame nails and keelson bolt; false keel could not have been fastened to bottom surface.

14. *Wood identification*—elm (Ulmus), no further breakdown; USDA Madison 2/81.

15. *Wood characteristics*—heartwood at forward break is near bottom of keel, is about 8 cm in diameter (see cross-sectional sketch). This is a rather poor piece of timber for a keel—many knots, and grain does not run parallel to the line of the keel. Grain is not very regular or compact for elm. There was some structural collapse on the seabed, which increased slightly during treatment.

16. *Dimensional change after shrinkage*—sided shrinkage, 4 mm; molded shrinkage, 6 mm; length, indeterminable.

17. *Comments*—3 glass frags removed from upper surface during drawing; sent to glass lab.

That was the format for each of the eight keel pieces, the sternpost, and the keelson. The sternpost had an additional entry called "offsets," which was a table of coordinates describing its curvature.

At the end of this sub-catalog a few sentences were devoted to explaining recording problems and noting any unanswered questions that future examination might clarify. There was a list of people who did this recording and the dates of their involvement. Excavation and conservation records concerning these fragments were left to those disciplines.

Not all fragments must be recorded as extensively as was keel piece KD. This was an important part of a major timber, and it is certain to figure prominently in future research. Not all fragments supply information to all categories, nor are such elaborate descriptions necessary for each minor fragment. Often a group of fragments can be assembled and described as a unit, thereby saving catalog space. The idea is not to compile a mammoth volume of repetitive data, but rather to make a concise, accurate, and complete description of the hull remains that can be converted efficiently into a reconstruction of the vessel and part of the contemporary world that surrounded it. The listing for KD could not have been shorter, nor should it have been longer. This literary description, accompanied by the necessary drawings and photographs, was precisely what was needed to document the timber and fulfill the requirements of those research categories listed at the beginning of this section.

The first two entries are necessary references for researchers who use the photos and drawings in the course of their work, as well as for writers who will want to know what illustrations are available without spending long hours searching through photo and drawings files. Illustrate wherever possible. The ideal catalog would be one composed entirely of drawings and photographs, but practicality demands a sensible mixture of illustrations and words.

Entry 3 prevents confusion. Should a label become detached, one of the reduced scale drawings (a copy of which I always place at the head of the listing) and this surviving length will quickly identify the piece. In addition, breakage during handling is an undesirable possibility; this dimension calls attention to missing fragments. Entry 3 can also be used for determining percentages and ratios of hull survival.

The description (entry 4) should say only what might not be determined from the drawings. This is your assessment of the piece; write it exactly as if you were explaining it to someone. Nobody wins Pulitzer prizes for writing catalogs, so use language that will be clearly understood. And be consistent. Notice that throughout this portion of the catalog a specific sequence was used. My own recording sequences go from fore to aft, top to bottom, and port to starboard. Use any convenient sequence, but if you are consistent there is far less chance for confusion.

Now we get to the data section. Thus far only supporting information has been listed, but from here on the entries will supply direct clues toward reconstruction. Always use *sided* and *molded* for describing cross-sectional dimensions of rigid timbers; terms like *thick, wide,* and *high* are confusing and improper. The glossary defines their usage. Use the metric system; it is an international standard and is the most accurate system for reconstruction. But I disagree with those who argue that everything below a meter in length should be written as decimal parts of a meter (even though these same people express great distances in kilometers). If one is dealing with only one or two hundred dimensions, this is a manageable system, but we are listing measurements by the thousands on most projects. It is simply too awkward to deal with endless lists of dimensions such as 0.0045 m or 0.0027 m, and the risk of error is much greater. Throw away the zeros and use centimeters or millimeters wherever convenient; those increments are part of the beauty of the metric system.

A final comment on measurements. There is a research value in using the English system for ships that you are *certain* were built to the 12-inch foot. It is easier to recognize incremental relationships between timbers, thereby making research easier and often more fruitful. A

1½ inch treenail makes a lot more sense than one of 3.81 cm when working with hulls built to that standard. In such cases it is wise to publish the results in both systems, the reasons for which will be discussed in chapter 9.

In this computer age, the way in which measurements are recorded becomes even more important. The listing for KD shown above was the way the recording came in from the field, and it illustrates my subject perfectly, but it could have been recorded directly onto a computer data system. With such a system, one can call up all sorts of information in minutes that may take days if done manually. In some instances, it reveals information that might otherwise go undetected. Database systems may not be absolute necessities as yet—we did successful work without them for years—but they do add a new and profitable dimension to research. With field work and publication costs inflating as they are, it is likely that archaeological recording will be entirely data-oriented in the near future.

Back to the catalog. Things like fastening patterns and frame impressions on keel tops are often better illustrated than tabulated, at least during the initial recording process. Notice that there is an entry for curvature. Keels can become distorted on the seabed, or they may have sagged or hogged during the active life of the vessel, or the ship may have been built with a rockered keel. Never assume that a keel was straight; I have seen very few of those on shipwrecks.

Tool marks reveal something about the contents of the shipbuilder's tool box, his working habits, and his methods of fabrication. This is a most important entry; record it well. Samples of surface coverings should be taken after they are recorded. Recording a pitch is not enough; entry 12 should get a later addition stating whether it is a pine pitch, bitumen pitch, or something else. The same applies to the wood. Samples must be analyzed for all types of timbers, and a description of wood characteristics will be useful in later studies. By all means, record the heartwood locations of all major timbers, such as this keel piece. That is important in understanding the methods of timber fabrication, and in some cases, the timber trade in general. The last few entries supplied information for our study of economics and people, as well as making contributions to the investigation of design, technology, and construction.

Entry 16 is largely for the conservator's benefit, although it allows us to compare this process with others on similar types of wrecks. It also tells those in charge of reassembling the hull how much space they can expect between timber joints. The last category is simply a catch-all for anything that could not be said elsewhere.

FRAMES

Frames are the most important group of timbers to be recorded for most ships. They describe the curvature of the hull and are the primary indicators of a vessel's strength, design, and technological status. The form of catalog recording has been explained already, so we need only examine the finer points of documenting these fascinating timbers. Instead of a specific hull member, a composite form of catalog entry is presented.

The catalog begins with the usual wreck plans, photographs, and a general description of the surviving framing system. Then comes the individual frame or frame fragment listings.

Frame 12
1. *Drawings.*
2. *Photos.*
3. *Maximum length remaining*—in this case you may want to use some other method of identification because of similarity of surviving frame lengths.
4. *Description*—say it as you see it, avoiding superfluous language.
5. *Number of pieces*—this entry is not necessary for simple, single line frames, such as those on the Serçe Limani hull, but if you are recording a partial or complete frame of a colonial brig comprising a floor timber and six futtocks, here is where you describe its composition.
6. *Sided*—floor timbers should be measured at the keel centerline, at their heads, and at intermediate locations. Futtocks are measured at their heads, heels, and a central point. For composite frames, individual and assembled timber measurements are desirable. A word of caution: inner and outer faces of some frames are sided differently, in which case you must list two sets of dimensions.
7. *Molded*—the same as for sided dimensions, but be consistent. Usually it is most advantageous to measure after sides of frames located forward of the midship bend and forward surfaces of frames aft of the midship bend.
8. *Offsets*—there are several angles and curvatures to be recorded in this section. First is the lateral curvature of the frame, which should be recorded by drawings and/or tabulated offsets. The drawn curvature (always to scale) can be used for developing hull lines or sectional shapes; the table of offsets is handy for comparing body lines or for database systems. Curvatures of detached, well-preserved frames can be measured in the same way as the outer hull shape in Figure 7–12; a partially preserved frame would be done similarly, but on a more limited scale. Wherever possible make the floor baseline parallel to, or even with, the top surface of the keel. The vertical reference line should be perpendicular to the baseline. In the case of accessible frames that are measured *in situ,* the

planking next to the frame edge is measured and the baseline and vertical reference are placed inside the curvature. You need only take offsets for one edge, but consistency is important. Wherever possible, measure the greatest edge—after edges for those frames forward of the midship bend and forward edges for frames mounted aft of the midship bend.

Where frames do not touch the keel or have any form of horizontal reference—as in the ancient Kyrenia floor timber in Figure 3–31—or where frames have not survived at the keel, as in Figure 7–14, arbitrary baselines can be established as illustrated. Such baselines do not provide common reference lines with other frames. An arbitrary reference point or two is also recommended for such frames, as shown in Figure 7–14. While such points may seem meaningless at first, they often can be related to seams, fastenings, or other structural features during the course of reconstruction, which in turn may relate them to reference points on other frames. Such points have proved valuable in the past.

Make certain that true frame curvatures are recorded. Frames in ancient ships or local types like the Brown's Ferry vessel were made from grown curvatures, often with very little dressing of the sides and inner surfaces. Sometimes bark is still present, and the frames wander back and forth in the same erratic centerlines they had as tree branches (see the site drawing for the Brown's Ferry vessel, Fig. 5–40). Frames are best recorded flat on grid tables or other surfaces where grid squares have been drawn. The frame is blocked with polysterene plastic or other noninjurious material so that it is approximately perpendicular to the keel centerline as indicated on the wreck plan. Then the curvature offsets can be taken by using squares, levels, plumb bobs, pantographs, or whatever device will produce accurate readings.

The fore-and-aft angles of outer frame surfaces (planking faces) also must be taken at frequent intervals so that the longitudinal hull curvature can be confirmed or determined with lines drawings. With the frame still blocked up on the grid surface, place a square on the grid with its vertical face against the frame's great edge and measure the distance to its trailing edge as in Figure 7–15. The section of Serçe Limani frame illustrated is part of an asymmetrical floor timber that bends aftward as it approaches the turn of the bilge. Since frames on many excavated ships are asymmetrical or distorted, it is important that their true vertical or horizontal orientation be recorded if known. The dashed line in Figure 7–15 represents the horizontal orientation of the timber at the keel.

It is convenient to do all this recording simultaneously, measuring the sided dimensions and face angles at the same location. Face angles are measured every 50 cm or so in the midships area where there is little change, every 25 centimeters where face angles increase, and even more frequently in the ends of the ship where face angles are large and change constantly. Inner (ceiling) face angles need not be measured unless they differ radically from those of the planking face. It is not as complicated as it sounds; once you have done a few frames you will quickly become adept at it. One cannot record this section too thoroughly. Usually it supplies most of the information for design and construction drawings.

9. *Bevels and chamfers*—record the builder's method of preventing frame edges from breaking or of reducing surface contact with planking.
10. *Watercourses*—dimensions of limber holes, etc. Usually it is easy to see how they were located and cut; record that too.
11. *Fastenings*—most frames will have fastenings on at least two surfaces, many on all four. They will include planking, ceiling, keelson, and keel

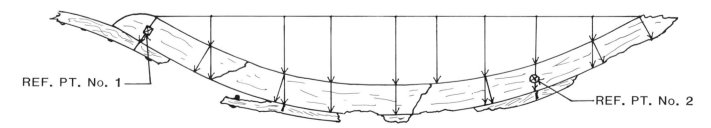

REF. PT. No. 1

REF. PT. No. 2

FIG. 7–14. Arbitrary reference lines and points for taking offsets from a partially preserved frame. The lines that run perpendicularly across the face of the frame determine molded dimensions.

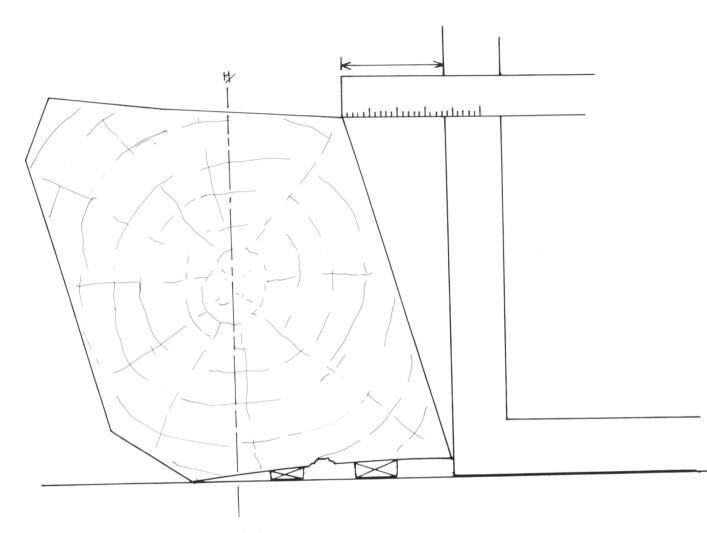

FIG. 7–15. One method of measuring the planking face angle of a frame location selected at random from the Serçe Limani hull. The dashed vertical line represents the horizontal axis of the frame.

fastenings, and perhaps lateral fastenings used to attach futtocks to each other. Also look for signs of attachment for mast steps, bulkheads, stanchions, shot lockers, pumps, etc. Fastenings may be of both wood and metal, sometimes with the two used in combination.

12. *Impressions*—look for indications of planking and ceiling seams, keel, keelson, and everything else listed above. Impressions indicate how well an adjacent member was seated, in addition to determining or acknowledging the spacing of attached timbers.

13. *Tool marks*—the same as for keels, but frames are often better protected and retain marks made by tools more readily. Look for awl marks used to locate limber holes, flats dubbed into outer surfaces to seat planking better, and indications of whether the frame was sawn or hewn.

14. *Surface coverings*—ancient frames may be covered with pitch, for instance.

15. *Wood identification.*

16. *Wood characteristics.*

17. *Dimensional change after treatment.*

18. *Comments.*

PLANKING

Planking catalogs can start in the same way the others did, with introductory statements, identification of drawings and photographs, surviving length, and a brief description of the fragment. Planking descriptions for fragmentary or extensively preserved hulls sometimes can be combined into sections or strakes. Catalogs can become unbearably cumbersome if plank fragments are recorded as extensively as major timbers. Usually there is no need for such elaborate descriptions.

5. *Thickness*—not all planks are of even thickness, especially in the case of ancient and clinker-built craft. In addition to measuring edge thicknesses, also check thicknesses in the centers of planks with calipers.

6. *Width* —planks are always thick and wide, never sided and molded.

7. *Fastenings* —don't forget nail head sizes, whether or not they were recessed, and treenail wedges.

8. *Mortise-and-tenon joints* —for ancient or Far Eastern hulls, you should note mortise dimensions (deep, wide, and thick), tenon sizes if they differ from those of the mortises, shapes of each where available, peg sizes inside and out or the amount of peg taper, peg distance from the seam, etc.

9. *Frame impressions* —omit this if made clear on the drawings.

10. *Edges* —for lapstrake hull forms you may want to include roving in this entry; also use for shuttered edges, extreme bevels in the case of some ancient ships, rabbeted edges, luting channels, caulking bevels, etc.

11. *Curvatures.*

12. *Tool marks.*

13. *Surface coverings* —look inside for dry rot protection; outside for pitches, paints, encaustics, and felt, hair, or vegetation used beneath sheathing.

14. *Sheathing* —it is best to keep this as a separate entry where hulls are sheathed in wood, copper, lead, zinc, or other materials. In the case of extensively preserved hulls, you may find it necessary to treat sheathing in a separate catalog section, where underlayments, pitches, tack patterns and other sheathing properties are combined.

15. *Wood identification* —usually can be done once for each strake or in a few selected strakes for the entire hull.

16. *Wood characteristics* —an introductory description of all the planking, plus abnormalities in individual strakes or fragments, will suffice.

Attempt to determine whether the strakes were hewn, split, or sawn.

17. *Dimensional changes.*

18. *Other features and comments* —look for graffiti, carpenters' marks, barnacle lines (which might help establish the original waterline or average ladening). Note the difference between inner and outer teredo patterns; teredo holes outside, where the hull had been pressed to the seabed, may be contemporaneous with its sailing career, while those which were initiated on the inside of the hull almost certainly occurred after the sinking.

CEILING

Ceiling catalogs, which usually include limber boards, stringers, thick stuff, footwales, clamps, and just about any other form of longitudinal internal timber except keelsons, are treated much like outer hull planking. Although some people seem to have a lesser regard for ceiling, I find it fascinating. Here is where the crew and stevedores left most of their graffiti and stowage marks. Ceiling planking, especially the common strakes, is often made from scrapped vessels that happened to be in or near the shipyard at construction time. The Kyrenia ship had secondhand limber boards cut from at least two smaller vessels. That sort of thing makes interesting research and reporting. Don't overlook it.

A lot of space has been devoted to the mechanics of recording, because of its importance. Good recording results from thoroughness and ingenuity. One must anticipate the unexpected and notice the obscure. Recording is not done because it is good archaeological discipline; its only function is to supply information to the historical record. Be aware of the potential of that information. Understand that what will follow will be based on what you have just done, and hampered by what you have overlooked.

8

RESEARCH AND RECONSTRUCTION

Research and reconstruction are practically synonymous in the interpretation of shipwrecks. With the exception of archival studies, it is often difficult to determine where research ends and reconstruction begins. Unlike some laboratory projects, where a series of investigations results in an end product, the end product of shipwreck research—reconstruction—evolves continuously as the research progresses. For the moment we will put research aside; it will keep cropping up as our study commences. It is reconstruction that must be analyzed before its methodology can be understood.

Reconstruction, according to the dictionaries, is to rebuild, reenact, reassemble, or restore. That, in a broad sense, is what we do. The problem begins when we connect the words ship or boat to reconstruction; to say we rebuild or reassemble ships and boats by whatever means is insufficient. One does not reconstruct the ruins of a temple without wondering whose temple it was, nor does one reassemble a broken statue without delving into the life behind the likeness. That is because temples and statues are inanimate objects that represent real events and lives. The real fascination is the animation behind the inanimate object, and the reconstruction of one spawns investigation of the other.

The same is true of ships and boats. Those rotten timbers we work with are what is left of an inanimate object (if indeed one dare call a ship inanimate), but they in turn can open a window to the world of which they were once a part. And that too is our target—their trees, their tools, their people, their world. Ship and boat reconstruction, in the archaeological sense, is the partial recreation of the remains of sunken or abandoned vessels and the people and processes that influenced them. The word *partial* is vital to the definition. There is no such thing as a complete reconstruction. Seldom, if ever, are complete shipwrecks discovered. It is never possible to determine everything that went on during their building and operating phases; even their crews and shipwrights could not

have been aware of everything that transpired. The purpose of this chapter is to assist researchers so that partial becomes a greater percentage of complete.

Now that we have permitted ourselves to go beyond the mere determination of the design of the vessel, our nearby horizons of research have been expanded almost to the point of limitlessness. People and processes cover a lot of territory. We can work on either side of the design problem, starting with the need for such a vessel and the way in which it was ordered and planned. We follow the forester into the woods to fell trees, the smith to the forge, the sawyer to the stage, the cordage maker to the walk, and on and on. But even after your research is considered as complete as it can be, a point I have never reached, the work is not finished. You have only reconstructed the ship and its surroundings; others, meanwhile, have been performing their own interpretations of cargoes, artifacts, seeds, bones, and a host of other shipboard material. It is when the ship or boat reconstruction is combined with all those other studies that the old wreck's world really unfolds.

There are three basic types of ship and boat reconstructions: *graphic, three-dimensional,* and *physical.*

Graphic reconstructions, most frequently used on sparsely preserved wrecks but by no means limited to them, are two-dimensional in scope. Research might include such things as archival information, computer data and graphic programs, tabular and mathematical analyses, drafting, and photography. Presentation is also in graphic form, usually as published reports composed of a combination of words, photographs, and drawings.

Three-dimensional reconstructions, when used for all but the most sparsely preserved wrecks, increase the research potential through the added dimension. The same research sources are used here as in graphic work, except that models, replicas, and experimental devices are added to solve problems and recognize details, which could not be readily accomplished with graphic forms of reconstruction. Presentation is similar to that of graphic reconstructions, although further use for research models can sometimes be found as museum exhibits or teaching aids.

Physical reconstructions are the deluxe method of reconstructing ships. They are time consuming, very expensive, and are normally limited to well-preserved or historically important vessels. This method is sometimes referred to as a reassembly, but such a designation is misleading because the work entails far more than merely reassembling hull fragments. This is reconstruction at is best—and its most complex. One is actually rebuilding the ship full size while studying the work of the original craftsmen each step of the way. Archival, graphic, and three-dimensional research go hand in hand with this method, all four being used simultaneously in most cases. Presentation is the reconstructed vessel itself, along with the usual models, articles, and other forms of dissemination.

Groundwork

Regardless of the extent of hull survival or the type of reconstruction, research begins the same way. First of all, a plan of action must be formulated so that one will know whether to start at the library or the drafting board. In a sense this was done when the research priorities were established at the beginning of the project. Now that plan must be elaborated and refined to accommodate all sorts of research. Gather what information is available already: site plans, photographs, drawings, sketches, and the hull catalog. Those are the raw materials, and they amount to an inventory of what has been seen or excavated. The next step is to convert those raw materials into a finished product—the reconstruction.

There must be many ways to reconstruct ships, but the ones described here work best for me. They need be altered only slightly to accommodate any type of project. Let's call back my favorite list of objectives.

    Construction
    Design
    Technology
    Cargo and artifacts
    Economics
    People

The object is to combine these avenues of research with the information at hand and wind up with a good reconstruction. Along the way we will recognize all sorts of new information that was not on the original list; this is one of the benefits of the system.

One part of that list can and should be dealt with at the beginning. It is important to be as familiar with your subject as possible, and that includes the cargo and artifacts it was carrying. An English cargo, and artifacts that indicate the crew and passengers were English, does not necessarily signify that the ship was built in England. Ships were captured, chartered, or purchased from numerous sources, so that the vessel itself could be American, French, Dutch, or one of a dozen other nationalities. But at least one would be prompted to investigate an English origin. Cargo and artifacts usually provide research clues in a more subtle manner, however. Distribution helps establish hull parameters, certain items may suggest the location of cabins or compartments, and tools and hardware provide parallels for technological studies. Discussions with specialists in the various supporting fields are always helpful; one of the more exciting aspects of reconstruction is exchanging ideas with them and watching the story unfold.

Thus the cargo and artifact category has essentially been turned into a raw material too, and that information is added to the catalogs and other source material. It remains a research objective as well, since part of the job will be to supply information about trade and seafaring if at all possible. Now for the other five.

Perhaps the best way to describe reconstruction methodology is to first break down the major subject. There are two general categories of ship and boat survival, which I like to designate as *capital* and *contributory*. Capital reconstructions are those resulting in hull lines or elaborate construction plans, making major contributions to shipbuilding or seafaring history, and incorporating extensive research procedures. The Cheops boat, the Kyrenia ship, the Skuldelev vessels, and the Madrague de Giens wreck are examples of capital reconstructions. Contributory reconstructions are those resulting from less extensively preserved wrecks, thereby supplying new information but lacking the potential to provide elaborate design or construction contributions. The Molasses Reef and Highborn Cay wrecks are examples of contributory projects.

This form of wreck segregation may at first seem clear cut. The Athlit ram obviously belongs to the contributory classification; it makes an important contribution to our understanding of classical warships, but its sixteen pieces of wood can never be expected to result in a major ship reconstruction. The *Mary Rose*, on the other hand, is clearly a capital reconstruction; a large enough part of the hull has survived to permit elaborate lines and construction plans, and a great research effort is underway to analyze the missing areas. But these are obvious examples at either end of the spectrum. Most wrecks lie somewhere in between, like the seventh-century Yassi Ada wreck with 10 percent hull survival.

It must not be assumed that capital reconstructions are always more important or provide more new information than contributory projects. If a sister ship to the Serçe Limani vessel were excavated and found to be in a similar state of preservation, its overall contribution to the historical record might be far less than that of the Athlit ram, which gave us a first limited look at the ramming structure of an ancient warship and changed so many of our theories. It does not matter that one vessel presented several tons of wood and the other only a few hundred pounds, nor do the number of drawings produced, the extent of research, or the size of the budget have any effect on the potential. The dominant factor here is that one wreck is a duplicate of another major project and may only confirm or compliment the original discovery; as such it is essentially a contributory project in spite of its size. The sixteen wood fragments of the Athlit ram, on the other hand, are so unique and have so much research value that the importance of this work borders on the realm of a capital project.

Contributory Reconstructions

For an example of a contributory reconstruction, I have created an imaginary wreck in order to better illustrate the potential of such sparsely preserved remains. We will call it the Albemarle wreck, since it was hypothetically excavated in that sound during the summer of 1975. No cargo was found, and artifacts were sparse and scattered—a couple of clay pipe stems, poorly preserved remains of what are believed to be cooking utensils, a wooden knife handle, and several dozen unrecognizable iron objects of various sizes. Nothing survived by which the wreck could be dated, although signs of earlier intrusion suggested that it might have been datable a few years before.

The hull remains were equally secretive, being limited to the few timbers and scatter of nail concretions shown on the site plan. Since planks were detached from frames, each timber was recorded thoroughly on all sides, then returned to its *in-situ* location and covered with overburden as found. Wood samples were taken from the various members, nail concretions were removed for analysis and casting, and a thick, mushy residue that had collected at the junctures of frame sides and inner planking surfaces was removed for analysis.

At this stage there was a site plan similar to that of the Molasses Reef wreck in Figure 5–3 and individual fragment drawings as described in chapter 7. The hull catalog, which in this case might be less than twenty pages long, describes three U-shaped floor timbers and five futtocks, all made from live oak to maximum dimensions of 12.7 cm (5 in) square. Two of the best-preserved futtocks are shaped to compound curvatures, and one of them has a clubbed heel. The floor timbers have limber holes cut amidships and are treenailed to what appear to be broad bottom planks; these plank fragments average 7.5 cm (3 in) in thickness and were sawn from yellow pine logs. Atop the floor timber of frame 2 is a fragment of another pine plank, which was made from cypress to a thickness of 10 cm (4 in) and a breadth of 30 cm (12 in).

Even though the bottom planking survived directly beneath what appears to be the center of the hull, there is no evidence for a keel. At the sharp turn of the floor timbers, there seems to have been a hard chine where the bottom and side planking were fitted together carefully. The side planking is made from quarter-sawn pine logs to a thickness of 2.5 cm (1 in) and a maximum surviving breadth of 30 cm (12 in). It is both nailed and treenailed to the frames; the oak treenails are 2.7 cm (1⅛ in) in diameter with square external heads, and the nails have iron shafts that are 8 mm (¼ in) square and heads with a diameter of 2.5 cm (1 in). Traces of pitch dot the outer planking surfaces, while the seams were caulked with a material analyzed as hemp and pitch.

That, in abstracted form, is about all the direct information that can be gleaned from the hull remains. Additional help may come from the fact that no cargo was in evidence, or that whoever intruded on the wreck before can be located and perhaps supply enlightening facts, but don't hold your breath waiting for such revelations. There is, however, another clue that might help us—the material that was collected where the frames touched the inner planking surfaces and inside the limber holes. Some people call that "bilge grunge," which is a marvelously definitive word for it. Never neglect the grunge. Few people who chose a life at sea were candidates for an award for neatness; they threw all manner of things into the bilges that, when carefully analyzed, can provide interesting sidelights into life at sea. In this case the grunge contained the remains of pecans, various kinds of seeds, fragments of rat bones, and two rather predominant items—tobacco stems and leaf veins, and a coarsely woven material resembling burlap.

Now what should be done about all this? Certainly it isn't the find of the century, but it may be far more important to the historical record than is immediately obvious. Twice in the past my research has been bolstered enormously because other people carefully published their findings of sparsely preserved wrecks, one of them with less wood than this. Again, research and reconstruction procedure is a personal matter that is shaped by one's preferences, abilities, and experience, so there will be no rigid set of rules defining the proper procedure for reconstructing this wreck. But I can tell you what course I would follow and you may profit from that.

In this case I would develop a list of questions about the most important or most curious features of the wreck. The list might look something like this:

1. Sequence of construction.
2. Probable shapes of extant timbers.
3. Are construction parallels published? What periods and nationalities?
4. Why the flat, keelless bottom?
5. Is interior plank a keelson?
6. Why the need for a hard chine?
7. Why no cargo or ballast in evidence?
8. What does grunge have to do with a possible cargo or shipboard life?
9. How do answers to 1 through 8 relate to hull form?
10. Reason for combination fastening.
11. Sequence of fastening.
12. What do wood types suggest about nationality or date?

Eventually the list, even for a wreck as sparsely preserved as this one, might include a hundred or more questions. But that is the unstructured, sporadic part of the job. A more disciplined study would soon be underway to determine the form of construction and probable hull shapes. This can be done graphically, with the best results coming from the flexibility of computer graphics, although I would prefer to build a little research model. For me, studying and handling a three-dimensional object made from original materials, even a scaled-down object, is much more fruitful than using anything produced on a drafting board or computer screen. In this case every member would be reproduced in 1:5 scale and assembled as logically as possible. One need not be an expert model builder to accomplish this task, nor must the model present a pleasing appearance. It is merely a research vehicle designed to produce answers more quickly, accurately and, one hopes, in greater numbers. That is how Thomas Oertling learned so much from the sparsely preserved Highborn Cay wreck (Fig. 5–2) and Jay Rosloff from the bow of the Ronson ship (Fig. 5–48).

If the model will be discarded at the end of the project, it can be made from any soft scrapwood. Mine are usually built from scrap pine; the pieces are held together with transparent tape and pins so that they can be shifted at will until the correct assembly is achieved (Fig. 8–1). It is important, however, that all mating surfaces are shaped accurately and all fastening locations are determined precisely.

From the model assembly comes a construction drawing and a statement of construction details as follows:

> The portion of the hull being studied probably lies midway between the midship bend and one of its ends. There was no keel. Three-inch thick bottom planks, made

FIG. 8–1. A reconstruction model of the type suggested for developing the hypothetical Albemarle wreck. This model is being used to begin the second phase of the Serçe Limani reconstruction. (photo by Jay P. Rosloff)

> of pine, were laid edge-to-edge and aligned with 1-inch treenails spaced at unknown intervals. Floor timbers then were treenailed to the bottom planks, the room-and-space being approximately two feet. Futtocks probably were assembled on their floor timbers before erection, since the treenail angles and close proximity of adjacent frames makes standing assembly improbable. One-inch thick side planking was erected next, the lowest strakes being faired and seated onto the outer edges of the bottom planks. A study of the adze marks on planking surfaces indicates that they were nailed first, then treenailed (because trimming adze marks surrounded, and stopped short of, nail heads; treenails were trimmed separately). Caulking was driven into conventional seam grooves, and outer planking surfaces were entirely coated with pine pitch. A 4- by 12-inch keelson was treenailed flatwise atop the floor timbers, the only internal timber for which fastenings were noted.

> The hull appears to be completely flat bottomed with no rocker or longitudinal curvature. There is a hard chine toward the end of the hull which gradually becomes less acute as it approaches amidships. The side contours follow a wineglass shape toward the end of the hull, gradually softening to a gentle rounding toward amidships.

Now we have a drawing and a verbal description that define, albeit partially, the original hull. The tobacco and burlap remains found in the bilges suggest that perhaps baled tobacco or tobacco and something else shipped in burlap (cotton?) was part of a cargo that disappeared after the vessel sank.

The next step is to search for parallels. In 1975 there were none, or at least none had been published. All of these materials could be found in other wrecks or contemporary builder's specifications, but never in the combination noted here. The hull design also had approximate parallels, the closest being the gundalow *Philadelphia* on display in the Smithsonian Institution, but even that one had less sophistication and clearly followed a different form of construction. Not until a couple of years later would a parallel be published, the Brown's Ferry vessel, and that one was well preserved and could be dated.

Not always does a Brown's Ferry vessel appear, however. The identification of such a hull type might well be the result of a half-dozen poorly preserved wrecks, each one contributing a little more until the entire form of construction can be understood. In such a way the Pantano Longarini and Yassi Ada Byzantine vessels were complimentary to each other, and several sparsely preserved Spanish wrecks each added more information about Iberian shipbuilding in the early sixteenth century (chap. 5). That is why all wreck remains, no matter how sparse, should be documented carefully and published.

Capital Reconstructions

Contributory projects, such as the hypothetical Albemarle wreck, are the backbone of nautical archaeology. They can be accomplished with relatively small budgets, limited time, and smaller staffs. They are excellent field training subjects, they keep the pages of scholarly journals filled with fresh information, and they provide the means for introducing or improving new equipment and processes. If we are to continue developing new talent in our profession, we must keep the ratio of contributory to capital projects high.

Capital projects, especially capital reconstructions, are usually enormous undertakings. If done properly, they require gigantic quantities of skill, time, money, facilities, and administration. Too often contributory efforts are applied to wrecks with capital potential, and the result is a loss of knowledge.

Consider some of the more popular capital reconstructions—The Royal Ship of Cheops, The Pittsburgh Dashur boat, the Kyrenia ship, the Marsala Punic wreck, the Madrague de Giens ship, the Kinneret boat, the Nemi barges, the Viking ships at Oslo and Roskilde, the Serçe Limani vessel, the Bremen cog, the *Mary Rose,* the Basque whaler *San Juan,* the *Vasa,* and the Brown's Ferry vessel, to name a few. The logistics involved in simply handling the recorded material for some of these vessels is staggering. Many of these hulls represent tons of timber, thousands of fragments and fastenings, and tens of thousands of dimensions. Computerization has eased the information storage problem for the later projects, but the mass of information is still there to confront the reconstructor. Proper arrangement and handling of recorded information is an important early step in the reconstruction process. It is, however, a purely mechanical process that can always be solved with a little ingenuity, so it will not be discussed further here.

Members of some of the above projects have published their research and reconstruction methodology, while others are in the process of publication. They are listed in the bibliography; space does not permit their repetition here. Let us, however, examine some highlights from a few of them.

Ideally, for those vessels that have been raised and preserved, one should complete all the recording first, compile a formal catalog, and then go through the reconstruction process step by step, ending with a completely reassembled vessel in a museum and a final publication describing it. It seldom, if ever, happens that way. Conservation schedules sometimes interfere with the orderly study or assembly of fragments. Restudy and reassembly are a foregone conclusion, especially for the undocumented periods; the genius has not yet been born who gets everything right on the first attempt. Nor is it possible to complete the hull catalogs before reconstruction begins. Previously unrecorded discoveries are commonplace as the treated hull fragments are assembled or analyzed. A line across a plank may have been recorded as an awl mark; during the reconstruction process it is determined to be the edge impression of a frame instead, and the catalog entry must be changed. Candidly stated, there is no single correct sequence for reconstructing well-preserved vessels.

Directors of many of the larger projects listed above assigned specific categories to specialists, and each of those specialists established their own research procedures. On several major projects, it was found advantageous to conduct preliminary reconstructions first, then conserve the timbers and proceed with a final reconstruction. This is what we did with the Kyrenia, Serçe Limani, Kinneret, and Brown's Ferry projects. Let's look briefly at the procedure for the Serçe Limani project; additional details can be found in the publications of that reconstruction, which are listed in the bibliography.

For vessels dated to undocumented (as far as ship construction is concerned) periods, a preliminary reconstruction program is a logical first step. It provides important information quickly, sets guidelines for future studies, and permits some reconstruction progress during the period when the timbers are in conservation. It began for the Serçe Limani hull, as it did for the hypothetical Albemarle wreck, with an evaluation of the catalogs, field notes, archival information, and other available material. From this came a list of important features about the ship. Although it quickly became a very long list, here are some of the more important entries:

1. Extremely simple lines—no compound curves in the frames, flat bottom, sharp bilge, flat sides, double-ended.
2. Small keel, no false keel, large keelson.
3. No garboard rabbet, no garboard attachment to keel except at ends.
4. Strange framing pattern; rather heavy, requiring laborious timber selection and shaping.
5. No edge fastenings in planks.
6. Combination plank/frame fastening system.
7. Transverse ceiling.
8. Heavy wales.
9. All softwood construction.
10. Light, curving sternpost.

And on and on. An artifact and cargo list was also made for features that might contribute information to our preliminary study.

The preliminary reconstruction was expected to accomplish a variety of specific goals:

1. Architects were about to design a new museum within the Castle of Saint Peter in Bodrum, Turkey, to house the hull, anchors, models and display, and some of the cargo and artifacts from the wreck. They needed dimensions and details so that they could design the galleries accurately. A preliminary reconstruction would supply principal hull dimensions, permit them to consider traffic flow patterns, and provide the necessary information for environmental requirements.
2. It was imperative to envision the extent and locations of existing hull remains so that complementary museum exhibits could be planned and funded.
3. Temporary supporting scaffolds, upon which the hull remains would be assembled, and final supporting systems to permanently cradle the hull had to be designed as soon as possible. The preliminary reconstruction had to provide the details for those designs.
4. Methods of fastening the fragments, on a temporary basis as well as a permanent one, could not be predetermined without more knowledge from a preliminary study.
5. Funding for the remainder of the project could not be acquired unless we could give intelligent estimates of the material and labor costs. Such knowledge could only come from a thorough understanding of what was involved, and the preliminary reconstruction had to supply that information.
6. It was obvious that years would pass before the conservation and reconstruction of this extremely fragmentary hull would be completed. Since eleventh-century hull design and construction were virtually undocumented for the Mediterranean, it would be desirable to publish a preliminary report outlining the most important features of the hull as soon as possible. This was the most important goal of the preliminary reconstruction.
7. A preliminary reconstruction would provide the staff experience and familiarity with the hull remains, probably making the final reconstruction more efficient and fruitful.

There were other reasons for, and benefits from, this preliminary work, but the point should be well made. In cases such as this, one cannot afford to charge blindly into mountains of recorded material and hull remains without some understanding of what lies ahead.

First an attempt was made to limit the preliminary reconstruction entirely to graphic methods. Using recorded keel, sternpost, and frame shapes and spacings, a lines drawing was made that was accurate enough to supply information to the architects but lacked the precision required for publication, support designs, and other details. In fact, when planking widths were marked on each of the body stations where planking survived and when attempts were made to develop a construction plan, we quickly learned of the ambiguity of these small surviving hull fragments and the problems their limited quantity would present. And so we turned to three-dimensional research for additional information.

A variety of models were produced for this work. A site diorama, several mold-and-batten models, and a series of fragment models were used to develop an improved set of hull lines and an elementary construction plan. More will be said about such models in the next few pages. The final fragment model was a miniature approximation of the reconstructed hull as it would look in the museum, and so little museum walls were placed around it to plan displays and other features. This model was also used to design the scaffolding for construction. Our lines and models were not precisely accurate, as we would confirm later, but at least they were close enough to fulfill the requirements of the preliminary reconstruction.

More than three years passed while the pine timbers of the Serçe Limani hull were being conserved in polyethylene glycol; it was during this period that the preliminary reconstruction was completed and the museum built. Once the wood was removed from the treatment tanks and cured sufficiently, each fragment underwent careful scrutiny and new information was added to the catalogs. In some cases, new drawings were made. Each fragment was also given an initial cleaning at this stage, and any cracks and breaks resulting from the treatment process were repaired.

Next the hull parameters were located and marked on the ship gallery floor. Construction scaffolds were erected and the fragments assembled in a sequence resulting from a study of the preliminary fragment model. As the hull remains were installed, all new discoveries (there were many) were noted and added to the existing hull data. Research and reconstruction occurred simultaneously now. Sometimes, when fragments would not fit, it was necessary to revert to the drafting board or model shop to determine where the error had been made. On other occasions, problems with the research and drafting could sometimes be answered by studying or altering the assembled fragments.

Hull studies will never be completed because there is so much to question and to learn on such a reconstruction. But the temporary scaffolding was eventually replaced with permanent steel supports and ghosting was added to make the original hull design comprehensible to lay visitors. A replica of the central starboard hull section was inserted where wood survival was extremely sparse, and it was in turn loaded with cargo and artifacts placed exactly as they were found on the seabed. A 1:10 scale, rigged model, now under construction, will show visitors what the vessel looked like just before it sank. Most of the fragments are now in their original places too, although the locations of some of them will never be determined. Most, if not all, shipwrecks have degraded wood fragments whose correct orientation can never be determined.

RESEARCH

By now you are realizing that each of these steps in the Serçe Limani reconstruction must have been a very complicated process. Can you imagine the logistics involved in the simultaneous reconstruction of five wrecks from a single site, as was done at the Viking Ship Museum in Roskilde, Denmark? How, exactly, does one start with a site plan and end up with a major publication on the structure of a ship? How does one turn a pile of rotten hull fragments into a reassembled hull standing proudly in a museum gallery? I can only refer you to the various project reports as far as logistics are concerned. My next project or your next project will be entirely different from the Serçe Limani project. The hull design, amount and type of hull survival, funding, personnel, administration, geographic location, and existing knowledge will never be identical to that effort. In other words, each new shipwreck requires a new design for

hull reconstruction, and that will be the case until the world is full of excavated parallels.

As for the methods of executing some of these steps, perhaps it would be advantageous to look at them briefly. Let's call back that list of research priorities for the last time.

Construction
Design
Technology
Cargo and artifacts
Economics
People

That list, or a similar one, covers the analysis of the wreck itself. If your capital reconstruction involves the raising and reassembling of hull remains, you may want to add another few categories, some of which might be methods of fragment fastening, supporting structures, complementary exhibits.

There must be hundreds of ways to produce a successful reconstruction, but for me it was always easier to concentrate on the first two items of that research list; the other four then automatically became evident. A word of warning about those last four items, however. Unless you have had excellent training in things like economic history and sociology, it is not likely that you will ever do a complete job of interpreting them. Those items are, in part, placed there to remind the reconstructor to document the research well enough so that experts in those fields can glean still more information from the wreck.

Back to construction and design. The two are practically synonymous as far as the reconstruction process is concerned; from here on we will treat them as a single subject. The idea is to investigate the wooden structure found on the seabed and to convert it into its original form, or one that is as complete as possible. It is usually best to begin by evaluating what is there. Note the areas of continuous preservation, what remains in the sparsely preserved sections, and what you are missing entirely. If the wreck has broken up and is scattered over the seabed, the task will require additional effort. Using scaled drawings of the various timbers, fastenings and impressions on planks can be aligned with matching frames. Frames can be fitted similarly to keel fragments. It is often a tedious job, something like trying to assemble a jigsaw puzzle with many missing and poorly fitting pieces. Eventually, however, enough of them can be joined to suggest the extent and nature of hull survival and provide a general sense of how everything fits together.

A logical next step is a preliminary set of lines. If your hull has largely maintained its shape, as the Kinneret boat did, you can immediately draw a set of lines from measurements taken directly from the hull. If the hull has broken up, it requires a lot of shifting of frame shapes and planking widths until you have reasonably satisfied the excavated evidence.

The advantages of preliminary lines drawings were explained earlier in this chapter, but they serve an additional purpose. By the time you arrive at three compatible views of the hull, you will have raised dozens of questions about its construction. Make note of them. They will provide direction for the research to follow.

Three-Dimensional Research

Your ship is a three-dimensional structure, so why not research it in three dimensions whenever possible? The next step, finding the proper locations for all your hull fragments and the shapes they produce in combination, is quite involved for wrecks that have been flattened or scattered on the seabed. In such cases the three-dimensional perspective is a necessity when attempting to fit the fragments together properly. It can be done with computers or research models. If you prefer working with computers, by all means do so. Eventually most of us may be reconstructing ships that way. But a bargain basement computer program won't do the job. Computers can't reconstruct ships—you must do that. A good graphics system—one that can produce isometrics and shift the various fragments around as required—is essential. You will need a sense of "feel" too, so the program should include a data system with wood and fastening properties in it and, ideally, the catalog database system.

Many of us either do not have access to such exotic equipment or we lack the funding or the expertise to alter the programs as required. For us the best research medium is models, and they can be more interesting and revealing than you might think. Below is a brief listing of various types of models that can be used to simplify ship reconstruction. Once you have made some of these assemblies, you will be able to design your own media to best suit your requirements. People working on computers may want to try some of these models on the screen.

MOLD-AND-BATTEN MODELS

One of the drawbacks of pure graphic reconstructions is their two-dimensional nature and the accompanying lack of physical control. It is quite easy to curve a pencil line in any direction when bridging a gap between two surviving hull areas, but experience and common sense are the only checks for such lines. In undocumented forms of construction, those virtues become questionable. Therein lies the value of the mold-and-batten model. By adding the third dimension, you also add the accompanying physical limitations.

Mold-and-batten models are probably the most helpful three-dimensional assemblies one can use in reconstructing ships and boats, especially for vessels that broke up after sinking. They are actually variations of eighteenth- and nineteenth-century builders' half-models known as hawk's nest, or bracket, models. They can be made quickly and easily from scrap material and have dozens of uses. One of their more important functions is to develop or check hull lines.

Except for the largest ships, these assemblies should be made in 1:10 scale. If you are going to add a lot of details later, such as planks with all the mortise-and-tenon joints or roves scribed on them, or if you are working on a small boat, you may prefer a larger scale. Too small a model usually makes the job more cumbersome and reduces the reliability of the sharper bends.

A typical mold-and-batten model of many uses is shown in Figure 8–2. Its first purpose was to help correct and expand a preliminary set of hull lines. The scale was 1:10. The molds were formed from ⅛-inch hardboard to the station shapes on the preliminary body plan (or the suspected hull shape at that location, based on surviving frame curvatures). They were cleated at the desired intervals to a sturdy backboard (see Fig. 2–12 for a slightly different version using full molds). Thin wooden battens, strips of straight-grained wood without knots or bad grain, were stretched over the outer surfaces of the molds to check the fairness, or accuracy, of the reconstructed hull shapes. They were attached to the molds with clamps in such a way that they could be shifted or removed at will. Figure 8–3 shows an early Serçe Limani development mold-and-batten model. In this case the battens on the port side represented diagonals in a three-dimensional version of the diagonals found on the body plans of lines drawings. Where the body shapes were too full, material was removed from the mold surface until the battens seated properly; where the shape was slack, material was added. After it was determined that the resulting lines satisfied the excavated evidence—timber curvatures, sums of planking widths, frame spacings, etc.—the corrections could be made on the preliminary draft or a new set of drawings produced.

In similar fashion, battens can be used to develop rising and narrowing lines, study planking arrangements as is being done with the starboard battens in Figure 8–3 or, in some areas, as buttock lines and waterlines. Don't be discouraged if everything has to be torn down and started over from time to time. On an extensively preserved ship there are hundreds, perhaps thousands, of points and dimensions to consider in developing the hull lines. Just as the shipwright had to rework and realign to make all the

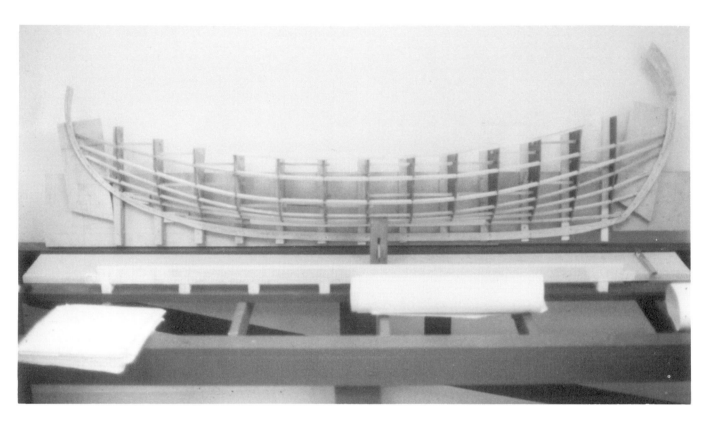

FIG. 8–2. A multi-purpose mold-and-batten model used for early Kyrenia ship research. (photo by J. Richard Steffy)

FIG. 8–3. An inverted Serçe Limani mold-and-batten model. Battens on the port side represent three diagonals used to check fairness of hull shapes; starboard battens are being used to assist in determining certain planking seam locations. (photo by J. Richard Steffy)

timbers fit well, so must one readjust research models in order to interpret the remains of that vessel.

Now for the shocker. Just because the lines are compatible with the excavated evidence, do not assume that the correct shape has resulted. What was just done merely proves the lines are workable and were *approximately* those of the original hull. You should want to do better than that; if you intend to reassemble the remains in a museum, you will have to do better than that. The fact is that there may be other arrangements of lines that would approximately fit the evidence. It has been determined that the surviving timbers will fit these curvatures, but will they do so and properly align themselves with all the fastenings, butts, and scarfs? And will the projected shapes beyond the areas of hull survival accept construction synonymous with that of the existing structure? That cannot be answered affirmatively without physical proof, which means additional work must be done with molds and battens.

Using the same set of molds (or a new set, or a set of full-body molds with the lines on one side and construction features on the other), place a series of battens over the mold edges so that one inside edge of each batten represents a planking seam. Use smaller battens for this task—⅛ inch square or less—and extend them beyond the areas of preservation, completing what appears to be a sensible run of planking (Fig. 8–4). Your logic for the unpreserved areas should be compatible with the construction that survived, and of course, must conform to the physical laws of displacement vessels and the characteristics of the timbers on the original hull. If a good job was done on the hull lines, the planking seams in the preserved areas should lay smoothly over the molds and arrive at the limits of preservation with the same widths and curvatures listed in the catalog. If not, corrections or

adjustments will have to be made to the mold shapes, and subsequently the hull lines, or it should be determined whether there were errors in the recording.

As soon as the seam locations are confirmed, mark them on the molds and cut notches for the battens so that they will be recessed with their outer surfaces flush with the mold edges. Next, cut planking shapes to fit between each seam in all of the preserved areas (the shapes of the sum of the fragments for each strake) from thin sheets of wood; thin cardboard is acceptable, but a better job can be done with wood about 0.5 mm thick. Make reductions of the wood drawings on heavy drafting film, indicating fastening and frame locations, scarfs or butts, and other pertinent information, and tape each to the proper model plank at the proper location (Fig. 8–5). Now you have a mirror image of the inner planking surfaces on the outside of the hull; fastenings and frame impressions also located outer frame faces. It may take a good deal of shifting of battens and fragments until you are satisfied with the results, but this method is a lot faster and safer than shifting original timbers around on a scaffold.

This is not a precise method of alignment, because it does not take advantage of planking edge angles and internal timber alignment, nor does it account for the repairs or unusual planking alignments sometimes found on hulls. When the original ship is finally assembled in the museum, adjustments will probably still have to be made. In addition, where rotten seams were cut out and replaced with new planks, or where unknown problems or unknown logic caused the shipwright to adopt some strange planking shape, the above method is not always reliable. It is, however, still more accurate than graphic reconstructions under the same difficulties.

Mold-and-batten models are not limited to the study of excavated vessels, however. An article by René Burlet

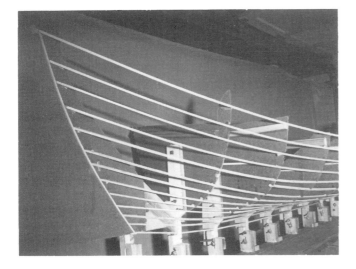

FIG. 8–4. Battens used as planking seams. (photo by David A. Steffy)

FIG. 8–5. A mold-and-batten model to which planking fragments will be taped. (photo by Sheila Matthews)

FIG. 8–6. A fragment model of the Serçe Limani vessel, utilizing about six hundred of the most definitive pieces. (photo by Cemal Pulak)

and Eric Rieth is a fascinating example of the use of models in developing textual information from Diego García de Palacio's publication, written in 1587, into three-dimensional form and consequently providing additional information about such vessels.[1]

FRAGMENT MODELS

If you are good at building models and appreciate the challenge, go one step farther and build a fragment model. This is a lot more work, and I do not guarantee that the results will be worth the extra effort, especially

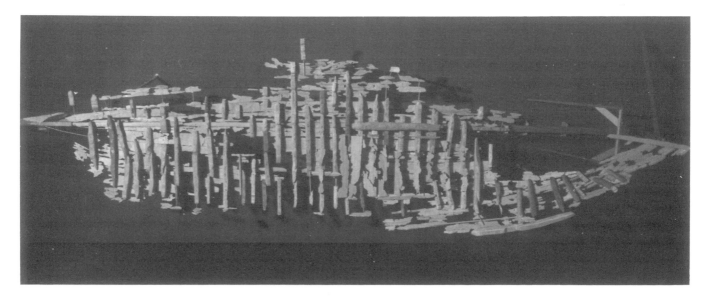

FIG. 8–7. A fragment model of the Serçe Limani vessel—top view. (photo by Cemal Pulak)

FIG. 8–8. A model of the Kyrenia ship's mast step. (photo by J. Richard Steffy)

for extremely fragmentary wrecks. Each fragment, or at least each fragment of appreciable size, must be duplicated precisely with all the fastenings and angles in their correct locations; they are then assembled much as the original fragments will be assembled if you have raised and preserved the hull (Figs. 8–6 and 8–7).

Such a model also lacks a certain amount of precision—because something is lost in scaling down the pieces, and it is impossible to precisely duplicate all the broken edges—but it has distinct advantages over the mold-and-batten model. The fragment model can be used for a dress rehearsal of the assembly of the original ship in the museum, or as a guide in planning auxiliary museum displays, construction scaffolding, permanent stanchions and supporting systems, ghosting, replicas, and other features of the final reconstruction and display.

OTHER RESEARCH MODELS

We built eighteen research models and replicas in reconstructing the Kyrenia ship, and quite a few for some of our other projects. Sometimes it is necessary to model a single timber or device to understand it better, such as mast steps (Fig. 8–8), pumps (Fig. 8–9), capstans (Fig. 8–10), or

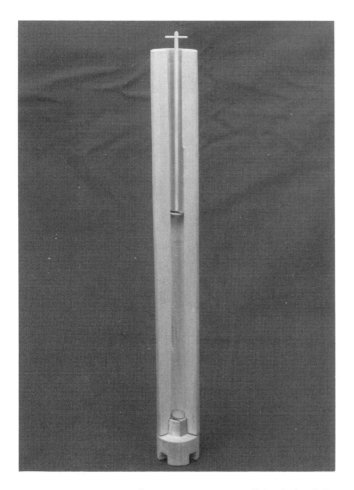

FIG. 8–9a. A 1:10 scale reconstruction model of the bilge pump on the Molasses Reef wreck. (model and photo by Thomas J. Oertling)

FIG. 8–9b. A close-up of the valve assemble of the Molasses Reef wreck model's bilge pump. (model and photo by Thomas J. Oertling)

FIG. 8–10. A model of the capstan found on the Ronson ship. (model and photo by Jay P. Rosloff)

mortise-and-tenon joints (Fig. 8–11). Research models can become elaborately detailed if the research problems are difficult, such as the models of the Kyrenia ship (Fig. 8–12), the Yassi Ada Byzantine ship (Fig. 8–13), and the Brown's Ferry vessel (Fig. 5–44); the latter two were begun to answer research problems, then embellished with tophamper and varnish and placed on display as temporary museum models. On the other hand, one of the most ingenious research models I have seen was made from cardboard and computer paper.[2]

FIG. 8–11. Replicating a row of mortises on a full-scale sectional model of the Kyrenia ship's keel. (courtesy Kyrenia Ship Project)

FIG. 8–12. A Kyrenia ship model under construction. (courtesy Kyrenia Ship Project)

Sometimes interdisciplinary studies are aided by sectional models, such as the model of the sloop-of-war *Peacock* in Figure 8–14. Sectional models are excellent for discussing the relationship between cargoes, artifacts, and hull timbers. Where hull or artifact dispersion seems contradictory, it may help to study the site in three dimensions with a site diorama (Fig. 8–15). The wood fragments must be approximately faithful in shape, but they certainly do not need to be as precise as fragment models. Dioramas can also be used to move miniature artifacts around for study by others, or they can be used for diver orientation. The diorama illustrated was made from scrap wood, sawdust, and plaster.

Dynamics, handling, and sailing tests can be made in model form if the extent of preservation warrants it. Tank testing—the use of models to test hydrostatic properties of hulls under controlled laboratory conditions—can be very expensive. If much of the underwater portion of the hull remains hypothetical, the value of such tests is questionable. Models for formal tests must be made to the

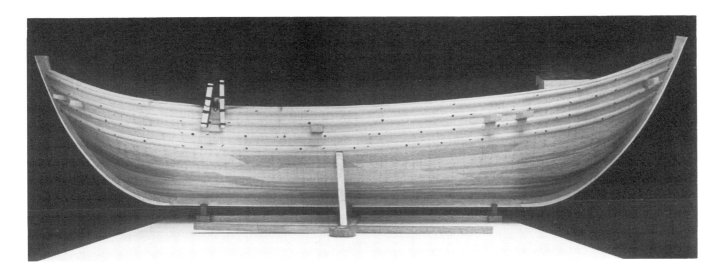

FIG. 8–13. A 1:10 scale half-model of the seventh-century Yassi Ada vessel. (model by J. Richard Steffy; photo by Bobbe Clinton Baker)

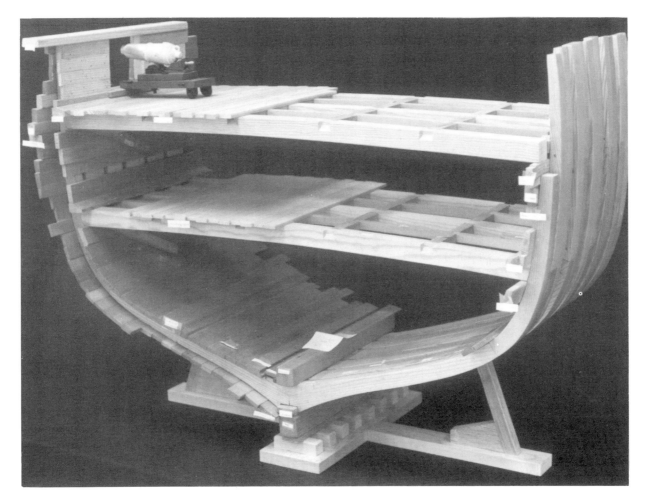

FIG. 8–14. A section model of the U.S. sloop-of-war *Peacock* built to specifications found in a copy of the original builder's contract. (model by K. G. Crisman, C. W. Haldane, and F. M. Hocker; photo by Ralph Pedersen)

FIG. 8–15. A diorama of the partially excavated Serçe Limani site. (photo by J. Richard Steffy)

specifications of the testing laboratory. One series of experiments was made with a 1:5 scale sailing model of the Kyrenia ship (Fig. 8–16), which was crewed by two boys who followed instructions relayed from an accompanying boat. While less scientific than formal tank tests, such models are nevertheless educational and accommodate experiments that are impossible in tanks.

EXHIBITION MODELS

Many lay visitors to a ship reconstruction exhibit will not comprehend the ship as it originally appeared by studying the reassembled remains, even if the remains are extensive. They can be helped by, and your research will greatly benefit from, an exhibition model. The Yassi Ada and Brown's Ferry models mentioned above were not begun as exhibition models; they were made from cheap pine and intended only for research. They were requested later for exhibition by project directors and are, we hope, only temporary museum occupants. It is better to reverse the process, as was done in the case of the Serçe Limani exhibition model (Fig. 8–17). Here a 1:10 scale, highly detailed and rigged model is being made from museum-quality materials. Construction followed the same sequence used on the original vessel. A number of previously unresolved research problems were answered as work on the model reached the appropriate stages.

REPLICAS

It is sometimes necessary to replicate some small part of a ship if that component is to be understood. If you really want to learn the value and strength of mortise-and-tenon joints, cut a row of them and see for yourself

FIG. 8–16. A 1:5 scale experimental sailing model of the Kyrenia ship. (courtesy Kyrenia Ship Project)

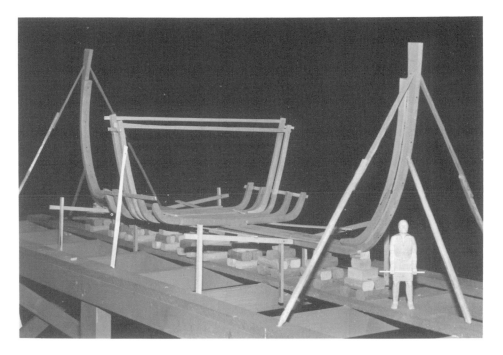

FIG. 8–17. The Serçe Limani exhibition model under construction. (model by F. M. Hocker; photo by Ralph Pedersen)

(Fig. 8–11). You will never understand them as thoroughly by any other means.

Sectional replicas can be used for research and then, because the expense and effort is too great to simply discard them, become museum displays. Two such assemblies are the Kyrenia sectional replica (Fig. 8–18), which stands as a separate museum display, and the Serçe Limani sectional replica (Fig. 8–19), which has been installed within a sparsely preserved area of the reassembled hull. Both were used to answer questions

and are now loaded with original cargo to show visitors how the hold appeared on the final voyages. Both were constructed with the same materials as their prototypes.

By far the ultimate research vehicle is a full-size, faithfully duplicated copy of the original ship. Such a replica was made for the Kyrenia ship (Fig. 8–20; also see Figs. 3–27, 3–32, and 3–36). Replicas are very expensive and time consuming, and they are hardly worth the effort if the prototype is sparsely preserved. If a large part of the hull has been accurately reconstructed, however,

FIG. 8–18. The free-standing Kyrenia ship sectional replica. (courtesy Kyrenia Ship Project)

FIG. 8–19. The Serçe Limani sectional replica being installed within a part of the original hull assembly. (photo by Donald A. Frey)

they have no parallel for studying construction techniques and ship handling. No ship can be precisely replicated; you would need the same trees, the same mentalities, and complete isolation from the modern world for that. But this one was about as close as you can get. More than ten years of study had gone into the Kyrenia ship before the replica was attempted. The hull was built from local pine, fastened with hand-forged, double-clenched copper nails, edge-joined with closely spaced, pegged mortise-and-tenon joints, and sports a linen sail complete with brailing rig. Every step of the construction was documented verbally and photographically, as were the numerous sea trials to test steering, rigging, and other handling details. But don't begin such a project without understanding what it will cost, and don't fail to realize that the operation and maintenance can be as expensive as the construction—or more so.

Reassembling Hull Remains

By the time research has progressed far enough to consider fragment reassembly details, you will have developed quite a few ideas about the ways in which to support and fasten the hull. There is no single outstanding method of reassembling the preserved remains of ships; every hull and every location has its own special problems that demand individual attention. Perhaps the best way to start is to actually write a theme for the reconstruction, listing the most important features of the vessel and the ways in which you want to present them to the world. A reassembled hull, after all, is every bit as important as are all the publications written about it. This is *the* vessel, the focus of all your efforts for the past several years, and you will want to display it so that it does not look like a confusing pile of firewood.

In some museums, the ships themselves are the theme; if well-preserved, they stand by themselves with little need for auxiliary exhibits. The Viking museum at

FIG. 8–20. Kyrenia II in heavy weather. (courtesy of the Kyrenia Ship Project)

FIG. 8–21. The Kyrenia ship reconstruction, showing partial ceiling installation. (courtesy Kyrenia Ship Project)

Roskilde, Denmark, features a variety of vessel types and does a good job of ghosting the more sparsely preserved ones so that everyone knows what they looked like. Their supporting displays compliment the variety of the hulls. In Bodrum, the theme of the Serçe Limani ship museum is medieval ship construction and shipboard life. The hull, itself rather sparsely preserved, has ghosting to highlight the design and a replica of three meters of the starboard side to show how the vessel was ballasted and ladened. Supporting artifact exhibits illustrate shipboard life, ship carpentry, anchors, and other maritime memorabilia.[3]

You can read about all this elsewhere. What should be considered in planning your reconstruction is that all parts of it should be visible and illustrative to scholars and laymen alike. Some of us like to study the bottoms of hulls without lying on our backs, so flat-bottomed hulls shouldn't be set on the floor. Stanchions should not hide important information, nor should all of the frames be covered with ceiling planking so that one of the most vital parts of the hull is hidden from view; display at least some of the ceiling planking separately (Fig. 8–21). It is just a matter of using a little common sense so that all of the interesting features are visible. Don't forget, either,

that the ship will gather dust, so that later cleaning methods must also be considered.

Once the height of the hull is established and centerlines and hull parameters are marked off on the floor, it is time to start building the supporting structure. Where vessels have survived partially intact, such as the Kinneret or Dashur boats, permanent supporting systems can sometimes be installed initially (see Fig. 3–9). These systems must be designed so that they will accommodate further work on the hull, such as minor repairs and cosmetizing, and still be aesthetically pleasing and revealing. Permanent stanchioning of extensively preserved hulls requires a great deal of engineering. Other than aesthetics, the weight of the hull, hull movement (due to possible humidity changes), and any serious geological vibrations must be taken into consideration. The conservator must also be consulted, since all supporting and fastening systems must be compatible with the treated wood.

Where survival consists entirely of relatively small pieces, the problem is more complex. Here you will need temporary supports that can be removed and replaced with permanent ones later (Fig. 8–22). Temporary supporting systems can best be planned with the use of fragment models (as in Fig. 8–1) or other illustrative devices. They can be erected completely before the installation of fragments, or they can expand the ship. I prefer the latter method, starting with the keel supports and then expanding scaffolding and hull in all directions from the midship area. Such a sequence eliminates the need for rebuilding scaffolding if the ship wants to take another direction from the one you planned.

That is an important point. A construction scaffolding must permit flexibility. Always allow the ship to dictate the reconstruction, rather than restricting it to the

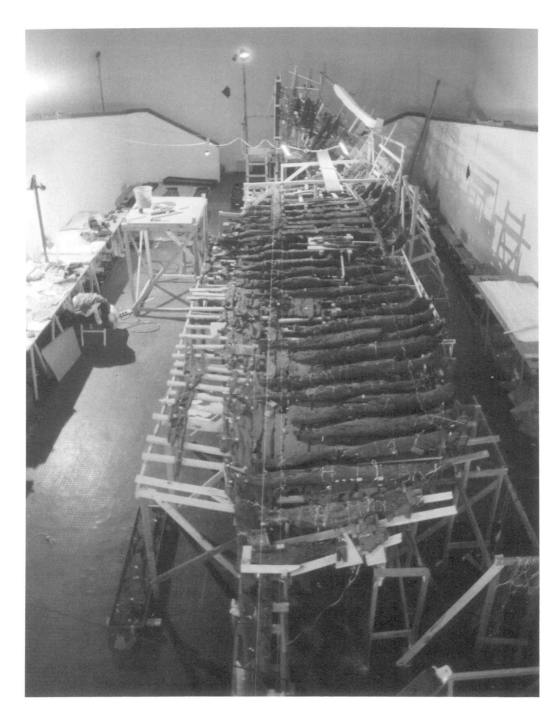

FIG. 8–22. Temporary scaffolding supports the Serçe Limani fragments during reassembly. (photo by Donald A. Frey)

shapes assumed to be proper. Remember, I said that graphic and three-dimensional forms of laboratory reconstruction were never precise because it is impossible to duplicate every break and angle precisely. Sometimes the slightest angular differences between laboratory reconstruction and that of the actual remains will become big variations by the time you reach the stern or caprail.

Consider every possibility for permitting the ship to control the outcome of the assembly.

Joining timbers and fragments is dictated by the condition of the wood, the original fastenings, the museum environment, the form of construction, the supporting system, the type of conservation, and other chemical and physical requirements. There are now bonding agents

FIG. 8–23. Temporary scaffolding supports the Kyrenia ship's frames during reassembly. (courtesy Kyrenia Ship Project)

available for light fragment joinery, but iron bolts and roves, dowels, toothpicks, brass brads, fiberglass rod, stainless steel rod, and other materials have been used successfully. Figures 8–23, 8–24, and 8–25 illustrate methods of attachment and support.

Regardless of fastening methods, however, ship and boat remains seldom fit together in the museum with the same precision the shipwright gave them. You are, after all, working on a wreck. Although every effort should be made to produce as accurate a reassembled hull as possible, seabed distortion, decomposition, breakage due to excavation or handling, and dimensional changes as a result of conservation processes are facts of life that the reconstructor must accept and deal with accordingly.

I cannot overstress the importance of keeping good records of every phase of the research and reconstruction. Remember the publications to follow—the texts, the tables, and the illustrations. Take plenty of photographs of the models in various stages, and copy the sketches; if you are working with computer graphics, print the evolving stages at regular intervals. And by all means, keep a record of every new revelation, no matter how insignificant it may seem. I speak with bitter experience when I say that what may seem irrelevant or unimportant now may someday become a major focus of research.

FIG. 8–24. Joining frame pieces with polyethylene-coated dowels on the Kyrenia ship. (courtesy Kyrenia Ship Project)

FIG. 8–25. Drilling a wire support in place on the Kyrenia reconstruction. (courtesy Kyrenia Ship Project)

9

INTERPRETATION AND DISSEMINATION

By the time recording, research, and reconstruction have been completed, the participants in the project have amassed an enormous amount of information. But at that point, the knowledge is concentrated in only a few minds; until it is shared with the rest of the interested world, not much has been accomplished. For the larger projects, there should have been a series of published reports outlining the progress and results of the project. Such interim reports are vital in maintaining widespread interest in the project, informing those who might be working on parallel material, as well as simply feeding the bank of archaeological knowledge. Eventually, all of the information can and should be made available to others. How that is done is as important as all that has gone on before.

Dissemination of information is the very essence of archaeology. However burdensome it may sometimes seem, it is the crowning glory to an important effort; it legitimizes your intrusion into this public sanctity. There are many ways to distribute this new knowledge effectively: technical or popular publication, lectures, documentary films, museum displays, and controlled mass media releases. This chapter is primarily intended to describe how the results of research and reconstruction can be converted into comprehensible form for technical reports.

The Seven Elements of Good Ship Reporting

Any ship report, whether written or verbal, is only as good as its presenter allows it to be. Regardless of the difficulty of the work or the extent of the research, the presentation is what is finally digested; it is really a vital extension of the excavation and research processes. The following simple guidelines for presentations might prove useful in preparing that next report.

A good ship report should be:

1. *Lively*—Avoid the droll forms of technical language that are often misconstrued as being scholarly. Use a narrative style wherever possible. Attempt to place the reader in the position of an eyewitness, always with plenty of interesting features to observe.
2. *Authoritative*—Present the subject as if you understand it exactly (if you don't, why are you presenting it?) and are completely comfortable with it.
3. *Comprehensible*—Explain things so that they are perfectly understood and so that alternate interpretations are unlikely. Use clear, practical language.
4. *Precise*—Although it isn't always possible, try to avoid words like approximately, about, *circa*, etc. Interpret and present your subject as precisely as possible. Where approximations are necessary, at least define their limits or explain their existence.
5. *Logical*—This applies to both interpretation and presentation. Your hull must adhere to the laws of physics and sound judgment. Follow a common, logical course of presentation. The best reports often relate things as they happened, whether in the shipyard or at the excavation site. A good format for the report is:
    a. background: description of site, excavation, artifacts and other relevant data
    b. method of recording
    c. the hull catalog: description of timbers and hull-related artifacts
    d. interpretation and reconstruction

e. analysis
f. conclusions

In describing the hull remains and analyzing them, the best format follows that of the building process:

a. keel and posts
b. frames
c. planking
d. keelson and ceiling
e. steps, spars, rigging
f. steering
g. anchors and deck machinery
h. other details, including repairs

For vessels with edge-joined planking, frames and planking should be reversed.

6. *Economical*—Don't be wordy. Your readers and listeners will appreciate your conciseness.

7. *Suggestive*—Every worthwhile plant leaves seeds when it has finished its task. So does every good ship report. Leave the reader with something to ponder—the unpreserved but suggestive areas, or perhaps the way earlier or later shipbuilders might have done the job.

Presenting Catalogs and Field Data

After the work has been introduced with enough background information to make the reader familiar with the project, the first logical step is to describe the source material—the hull remains, rigging, and ship-related artifacts. Although this is a relatively uncomplicated procedure for sparsely preserved wrecks, it is an awesome task where thousands of wood fragments or tons of timber survive. All of the information must be dispensed, of course, although considerable alterations should be made to most of it to bring it within practical limits. The publication of details of five thousand individual hull fragments, for instance, would be equally redundant to reader and writer, publication costs would be astronomical, and one would have to question the scholarly nature of such an elementary approach. It would be better to take a cue from the pottery specialists who illustrate and describe their vessels after all the broken shards have been reassembled into their original context. Some people might argue that, unlike pottery shards, perhaps half the hull fragments will bear individual characteristics and even the repetitive ones might have a dozen or more important features to record. This is true, and their surface shapes contribute to the combined shape of a much larger and more complex object, but the overall situation is the same. While wood fragments may be too numerous to be shown individually as parts of the entire hull, they can always be represented collectively as parts of members of that hull, such as planks or frames. Their individuality can still be maintained, and their common details noted, by a combination of graphic and literary descriptions.

DRAWINGS

Figure 9–1 shows the interior surface of one broken bottom plank as it was drawn for publication. Here the fragments have been assembled into what remained of this sternmost section of the strake. They can still be located individually by their shapes and frame numbers, all the

fastenings and important marks are indicated, and special characteristics can be shown on adjacent sketches. A verbal description accompanied the drawing, clarifying any questionable details and supplying information that could not be illustrated. By this method, many hull fragments can be presented on relatively few drawings. Now even the final report can be reduced to manageable size and interesting content.

That same strake could also be drawn as in Figure 9–2, where each fragment is separated from its neighbor to illustrate individuality more clearly. Or it could be shown as in Figure 9–3, where the fragments are assembled and the outline of the entire reconstructed strake is shown in dashed lines. Such an illustration might be used where space is at a premium; both the hull remains and reconstructed information can be shown on a single drawing. Combining catalog information with reconstructed results might be considered a matter of personal preference, although there is a danger of reader misinterpretation, as well as a break in logical report sequence, in combining excavated source material with conclusions resulting from research. If such an illustrative format is used, the drawings should clearly segregate excavated information from reconstructed information.

Long strakes, such as the Kyrenia ship's port strake 6, are difficult to arrange in single lines where publications limit drawings to single page size.[1] If each strake is shown in single length and several strakes are combined to give height to the illustration, the details have to be reduced so much that they are difficult to discern. Therefore, the method shown in Figure 9–4 seems to be the most practical solution. If the publication format permits foldout drawings, flexibility is increased to the point where the planking of an entire side might be shown on one large sheet.

Timbers can be presented in similar fashion, with the necessary cross-sections arranged as shown for keels and frames in Figures 9–5 and 9–6. Hulls or sections of

Fɪɢ. 9–1. Planking fragment drawings assembled to illustrate the entire plank as it survived.

Fɪɢ. 9–2. The same plank drawn with separations between individual fragments.

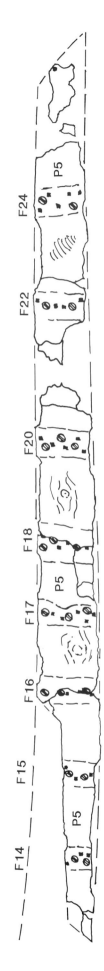

Fɪɢ. 9–3. The assembled plank, as in Fig. 9–1, with its reconstructed original shape in dashed lines.

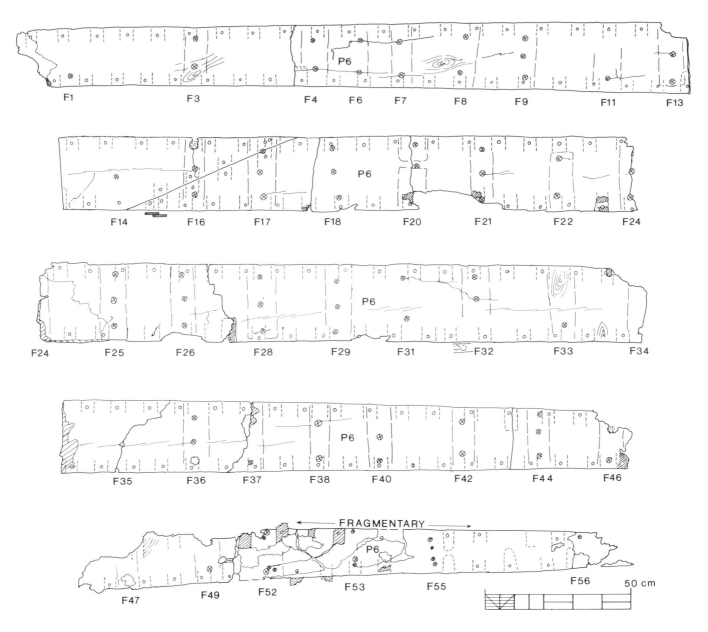

FIG. 9–4. A published drawing of the partially assembled fragments of the Kyrenia ship's port strake 6. (*AJA* 89.1, ill. 5)

hulls that are retrieved intact can be illustrated as was the Brown's Ferry vessel in Figure 5–40, with the details added in separate sketches. Don't forget the details. Detailed sketches can save hundreds of words of text. Note the use of detail sketches in Figure 9–7. Such sketches simplify the writing of the text.

TABLES

Text can also be reduced to manageable size by the use of tables. Tables, like illustrations, are orderly and pleasing to the eye. They say in a few columns what might take many pages to arrange in sentence form. Look what has been done for the planking and mortise-and-tenon joints of the

Kyrenia ship in Tables 9–1, 9–2, and 9–3.[2] Such tables make reference work much easier, too.

VERBAL DESCRIPTIONS

As stated above, ship reports should reflect logic and continuity. Catalogs are best arranged in the sequence of construction, or what you believe to be the sequence of construction, and that sequence should be followed throughout the article or book. Designations for hull timbers should follow some form of logic, too. A report that refers to frame pieces as AXT and BAA is confusing. It forces the reader to revert to the site plan just to identify what sort of timber it is and where it is located. If

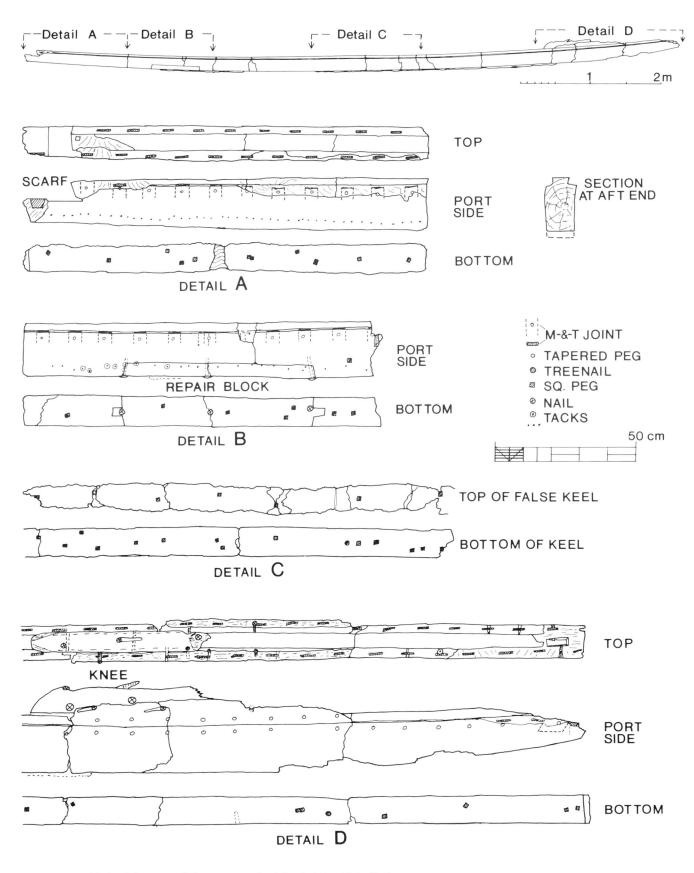

FIG. 9–5. A published drawing of the Kyrenia ship's keel. (*AJA* 89.1, ill.3)

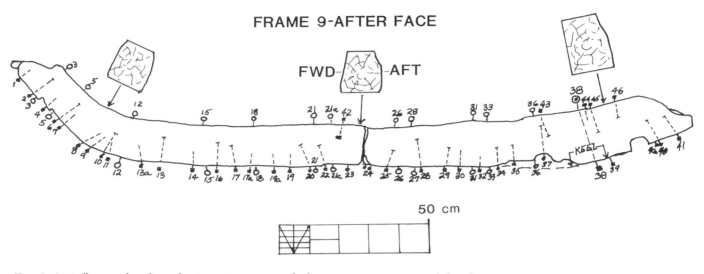

FIG. 9–6. A floor timber from the Serçe Limani vessel, showing cross sections and details.

fragments were so labeled for excavation, convert them or add descriptive prefixes for publication. Use designations similar to those described in chapter 7; they identify the timber and its location precisely.

Regardless of how enlightening drawings and photographs might be, verbal descriptions are always necessary. Describing the hull remains efficiently is the most difficult part of writing a ship report for most authors, perhaps because a more elaborate version of the catalog has already been written at least once and has been examined endlessly. The burden can be eased partially by the challenge of presenting it ingeniously and frugally while still maintaining all the original content.

SCOPE

Publishing a hull catalog, then, is really a matter of good file management, where all of the excavated material is presented as clearly, precisely, and economically as

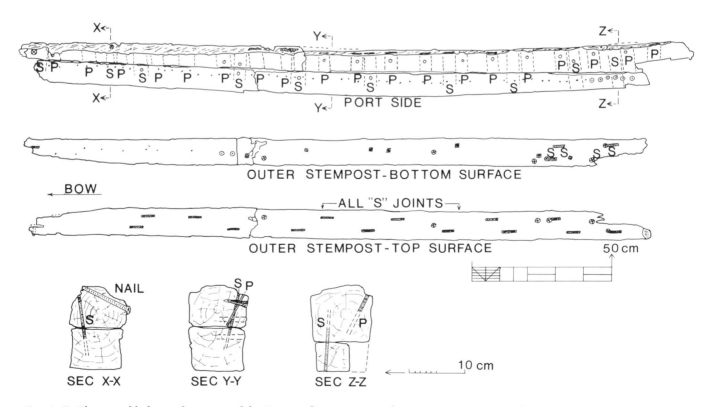

FIG. 9–7. The assembled stem fragments of the Kyrenia ship. Mortise-and-tenon joints connecting the inner and outer posts are labeled S; planking joints are labeled P. (*AJA* 89.1, ill. 4)

TABLE 9–1. Outer planking dimensions

Strake Number	Preserved Length (m)	Maximum Width (cm)	Average Thickness (cm)
P1	6.80*	ca. 20	3.6
S1	9.07†	ca. 20	3.7
P2	9.64	18.5	3.5
S2	7.65†	17 rem.	3.8
P3	10.55	21.7	3.5
S3	9.95†	18.5	3.8
P4	10.43	19.7	3.6
S4	10.40	19.1	3.8
P5	10.27	26.8	3.6
S5	10.07	26.3	3.8
P6	10.22	26.7	3.8
S6	6.40	24.3	3.7
P7	9.90	22.2	3.8
S7	6.24	21.5	3.6
P8	9.80	26.5	3.8
S8	6.35	22.9	3.8
P9	9.34	24.0	3.8
S9	5.71	28.1	4.1
P10	9.32	21.5‡	8.0
S10	4.83	21.8	7.9
P11	8.38	31.5§	3.9
P12	5.73	22.7	6.1
P13	1.95	8.4 rem.	3.2

* there were an additional 2 m of scattered fragments in the stern area

† fragmentary and intermittent preservation

‡ indicates width of 8 cm thick area; aft section is 25 cm wide at junction with strakes 8 and 9

§ indicates width of combined strake sections at frame 40

possible, using whatever combination of words, photographs, and drawings will accomplish the best results. Be aware of what is meant by economically, however; avoid needless repetition or irrelevant information, but don't be frugal to the point of eliminating vital information. The problem with some reports is that their authors ignore many of the important details that are necessary for thorough comparative studies with other vessels of the period. A quick glance at a few journals lying on my desk reveals that one person gave the size of planking mortises on an ancient vessel but neglected to reveal their spacing. Another report on an eighteenth-century ship omits the sizes of frames and their frequency, while still another lists no wood types, planking thicknesses, or frame sizes, nor does it indicate in verbal or graphic form whether or not the vessel had a keelson or ceiling.

One can hardly compare ships and boats thoroughly if half the information is missing. Unfortunately, in many cases this information will be missing forever because it was never recorded or researched. The following list, intended as a guide for all types of vessels, is considered to be the absolute minimum standard for documenting ships and boats. Where some of these categories did not survive and are therefore not part of the hull catalog, they might be determined by research and should be documented in the reconstruction section of the report. Be certain to include all of the categories that apply to the vessel you are recording or reporting.

keels—provide a description to supplement drawings, if necessary; wood type(s); number of pieces in keel; sided and molded dimensions, taken at various applicable locations if dimensions are not constant; scarf and end details; rabbet dimensions; and distance from rabbet to top of keel.

false keels—description; wood type; number of pieces; fore and aft limits; method of attachment to keel; composition, dimensions, and distribution of fastenings.

stems—descriptions to supplement drawings; wood type(s); number of pieces comprising stem; sided and other dimensions, as applicable, including total molded dimensions at key locations; method of attachment to keel; fastening types, composition, dimensions, and distribution; draft marks; head knee and/or figurehead attachments; rigging hardware.

sternposts—supplementary description; wood type(s); number of pieces; sided, molded, and other important dimensions; method of

TABLE 9–2. Planking scarf joints

Strake Number	Boward Angle	Width, Aft End	Diagonal Length	Location	No. of Joints
P1	down	17.0	49.0	F31–F33	3
S2			did not survive		
P2	up	16.5	60.0	F14–F17	3
S2	up		partial survival	F14–F18	?
P3	down	16.0	52.0	F34–F36	4
S3			did not survive		
P4	down	19.0	56.5	F20–F22	4
S4	down	18.3	54.0	F17–F20	3
P4			no evidence for forward scarf		
S4	down	14.8	42.5	F52–F55	2
P5	down	25.7	68.3	F32–F34	6
S5	down		partial survival	? –F34	?
P6	up	25.5	65.1	F14–F17	4
S6	up	22.8	70.0	F16–F18	4
P7	down	22.0	61.0	F37–F40	4
S7			did not survive		
P8	down	26.6	80.0	F20–F24	8
S8	up	21.0	63.0	F13–F16	4
P9	down	23.2	67.0	F32–F34	4
S9	down	27.0	69.5	F33–F35	5
P9	up	15.7	54.0	F52–F55	3
S9			forward scarf did not survive		
P10	up	20.7	81.0	F16–F20	11
S10	up		partial survival	F16–F21	11
P11	down	28.2	71.5	F27–F35	5
P12			none found		
P13			none found		

TABLE 9–3. Mortise-and-tenon joints
(contiguous planking seams only)

Seam	Spaces Measured		Length of Seam (m)		Avg. Joint Spacing (cm)		Joints Recorded	
	port	stbd	port	stbd	port	stbd	port	stbd
K/1	84	84	9.90	9.84	11.8	11.7	85	85
1/2	80	*	9.41	†	11.8	†	81	31‡
2/3	77	21	9.31	2.54	11.9	12.1	79	46‡
3/4	81	67	9.54	8.11	11.8	12.1	87	70
4/5	87	57	9.20	7.94	10.6	14.0	93	59
5/6	92	51	9.92	6.31	10.8	12.4	94	52
6/7	88	67	9.84	7.67	11.2	11.5	91	68
7/8	73	55	8.18	6.25	11.2	11.4	75	59
8/9	78	49	9.01	5.63	11.6	11.5	80	50
9/10	79	45	9.00	5.20	11.4	11.6	82	49
10/11	74	*	8.41	——	11.5	——	77	28
/11A	20	†	2.64	†	13.2	†	21	†
11/12	51	†	6.54	†	12.9	†	55	†
12/13	37	†	4.63	†	12.5	†	38	†
Total	1,001	496	115.53	59.49	11.7	12.0	1,038	597

* unreliable
† did not survive
‡ estimated; several partial joints may belong to the same unit

attachment to keel; fastening types, composition, dimensions, and distribution; draft marks; gudgeon information.

deadwood and *stern knees*—supplementary description; wood type(s); number of pieces; forward and after or upper limits; applicable dimensions; method of attachment to keel, sternpost, or other deadwood pieces; fastening types, composition, dimensions, and distribution; rabbet details, where applicable; description and dimensions of hooks, scarfs, steps, mortises, and frame recesses.

aprons—description; wood type; number of pieces; sided and molded dimensions; rabbet and scarf details; notches and steps for frames.

frames—description; wood type(s); number of pieces in frames; nature of frame composition (or the manner in which detached floors and futtocks are arranged); room-and-space; note whether first futtocks are afore or abaft the floor timbers; sided and molded dimensions over keel, at heads and heels of futtocks, and intermediate dimensions where applicable; butt, scarf, or chock details; method of attaching futtocks to each other in the case of composite frames, including fastening details; method of attachment to keels, deadwood, and aprons, including fastening details; dimensions of deadwood or keelson notches; locations and dimensions of limber holes; edge chamfering details; planking flat information; carpenter marks for assembly, where applicable.

hawse pieces and *knightheads*—same as for frames, but include hawse hole dimensions.

planking—description of planking arrangement; wood type(s); thickness, each strake; applicable widths, especially at midships and ends; stealer dimensions; composition, dimensions, and distribution of fastenings (don't overlook the treenail wedges); scarfs and butts; hooding end details, including fastening patterns and shapes; form of log conversion (quarter sawn, radial, etc.); include stern planking where it exists.

for *edge-joined planking*—mortise dimensions (wide, deep, and thick), taken from numerous, widely scattered locations; tenon dimensions; average center-to-center joint spacing, also noting extreme variations from the average; peg diameters at inner and outer plank surfaces; average distances between peg centers and seams; orientation of mortises at scarfs (perpendicular to scarf or to plank seam); method of cutting mortises, if discernable.

for *clinker planking*—average overlap; composition, dimensions, and distribution of roves, clench-nails, or other lap fastenings; luting coves or channels.

wooden sheathing or *furring*—description; wood type; thicknesses; widths; method of application and fastening details; composition of underlayment; thickness of underlayment; butt and end details; seam details.

metal sheathing—description; type of metal; thickness; size of sheets; pattern of application; sizes and directions of overlaps; fastening dimensions, composition, and distribution; composition and thickness of underlayment; method of tucking around keels and posts.

caulking and *luting*—composition of material; number of threads; depth driven (caulking) or size of coves (luting); description of covering strips, if applicable; thickness and composition of surface caulking, if applicable; caulking repairs or signs of recaulking.

keelsons—description; wood type; length; number of pieces; sided and molded dimensions; notching for frames; end details; mortise, mast step, and other cuttings; method of attachment to keels or frames; description and dimensions of fastenings.

ceiling (includes common ceiling, limber boards, thick stuff, footwales, stringers, clamps, and shelf clamps)—pattern and description; wood type(s); thicknesses; widths; fastenings; butts; end details.

These are the most commonly preserved and recorded members, but you should include similar data for all other existing components, such as transoms, fashion pieces, stemsons and sternsons, riders, mast steps, decks, deck beams, knees of all types, carlings, ledges, breast hooks, waterways, scuppers and drains, caprails, gunports, shot lockers, compartments, pumps, capstans, windlasses, anchors, catheads, bitts, channels, deck houses, and on and on. One way to make certain that you haven't ignored anything is to scan the pages of a good marine dictionary, the index of a book on ship construction, or one of the many builder's contracts listed in publications or on file in various archives.

Interpreting Research and Reconstruction

DESCRIBING PROCEDURE

It is an unfortunate fact that these marvelous methods and devices you have developed to enhance your research, and of which you are now so proud, may be of little interest to many of your readers. Most people are interested in results—what you have found, how it looked, what it did, and so on. They must have some understanding of your methods of interpretation, if only to establish whether or not your research is complete and proper, but they do not want to know all the minor, especially the standard, details.

If you have developed some new research vehicle in the course of your work, perhaps a revolutionary computer process or research model, you may want to enlarge your methodology section. Remember, though, that you are writing a ship report and the ship should remain the major subject. If the research tool description becomes too elaborate, you might consider publishing it separately and merely referring to it in your report.

As was the case with catalog descriptions, use plenty of illustrations to clarify information and reduce text size. Good photographs are important in describing research methods, such as the use of models or testing devices.

LINES DRAWINGS

Lines drawings are graphic descriptions of the shapes of the hull you have reconstructed. Their interpretation was described in chapter 2; now let's consider how they are made and what should or should not be included in them. Drafting methods and drawing formats described below will, in certain cases, apply to many of the other types of drawings presented later in this chapter.

Lines drawings can be produced for publication either manually or by computer assisted drafting (CAD) programs. If CAD systems are used, however, they should be sophisticated enough to produce fair lines in a variety of pen sizes and must be provided with enough data so that false averaging of lines does not occur between documented points. Avoid the packaged systems that produce lines "automatically" based on such data as planking shapes or designated dimensions. They are wonderful programs if you are designing a vessel, but they are not compatible with ships of most periods and tend to overlook repairs and departures from what is today considered sound design and construction. Don't use the computer as a time saver for producing lines drawings, either. A lot can still be learned while drafting the final hull lines, because you are in a sense going through the process of reconstructing the hull once more. New ideas can crop up, or an error in taking lines off models might be detected. Whether your drawings are being produced manually or electronically, proceed slowly and carefully; think of your work as one more step in the research process rather than a production for publication. Figure 9–8 shows the drafting of large-scale hull lines with splines and weights.

Now for the details. If you have been consulting texts on ship drafting or naval architecture, you may have to ignore or revise what you have already learned about the format of lines drawings. While traditional and modern methods, such as showing hulls with their bows to the right of the drawing or using certain numbering systems for stations, serve their intended purposes quite well, they may not be compatible with the artifact you are about to illustrate. Your lines must first of all describe that wreck on the seabed. If your hull was best preserved on the port side and most of the results of research came from that

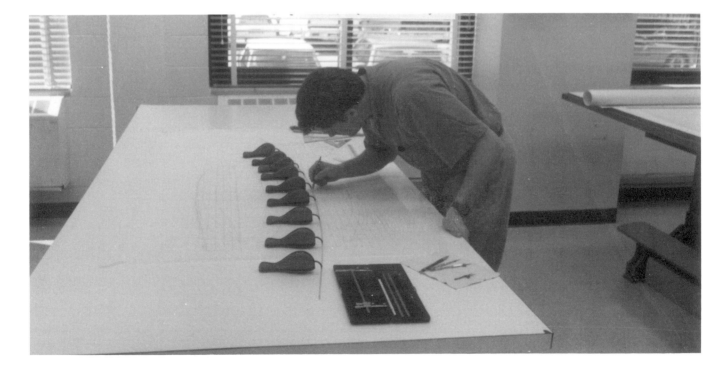

FIG. 9–8. A set of hull lines being produced manually, showing some of the tools of the trade. (photo by Stephen Paris)

side, then your drawings should show the port side on all three views (bow to the left on the sheer and half-breadth plans, after half of the hull to the left of the centerline on the body plan). Lines should be spaced to best illustrate the preserved areas, and numbering systems must be consistent with the published catalog designations wherever possible. There will be more about that later.

In addition, the lines of your shipwreck are limited to the parameters of the reconstruction, and that often results in an incomplete drawing. In short, interpretive (archaeological) ship drawings necessarily differ from developmental (designer's) drawings because their intended purposes are quite different.

It is an unfortunate fact that many publishers fail to recognize the importance of lines drawings. In spite of protests, they will reduce a once-proud ten-foot drawing to three by five inches or place one view on a separate page, sometimes in a different size than the others. Nevertheless, you must aim for perfection, and that means placing all three drawings on one sheet to the same scale. It is inconvenient if one has to flip pages to study waterlines or buttock lines on separated views, even more so if one must keep adjusting dividers to interpret drawings of different scales.

How you select the locations for each of the three views is a matter of personal choice in archaeology, although the size, shape, and extent of preservation of your wreck may automatically dictate the best arrangement. Archives of old ship plans or books of well-executed ship drafts—the publications of Howard I. Chapelle, for instance—contain virtually every possible arrangement. Sometimes all three views are stacked one above the other, or the body plan may be placed to the right or left of one of the longitudinal views, or perhaps the sheer view is at the bottom of one drawing and at the top of another. In some cases space has been saved or a drawing artistically balanced by the addition of a sectional view of the construction. All are acceptable with one exception; none of the three major views should be superimposed over the other. Wherever possible I place the sheer view near the bottom of the drawing, the half-breadth plan above it, and the body plan directly astern of it, with the legend occupying the space above the body plan. If space permits, the diagonals are shown separately between the sheer and half-breadth plans, as in the Kyrenia drawings in Figure 3–38 or the Serçe Limani preliminary lines in Figure 4–9. Where space does not permit a separate diagonal view, they can be superimposed over the half-breadth plan as in the *Eagle* drawings (Fig. 5–61). My only reason for using this format is that I like to work with and interpret drawings this way. Whatever arrangement you choose, the dimensions of the area of the resultant drawing should be proportional to the intended published dimensions. A lines drawing that is four times as long as it is wide makes a poor appearance at any scale.

Ideally, one should space all the stations and water and buttock lines equidistantly. Equal spacing provides balance to the drawing, makes subsequent production of half-models more convenient, and simplifies the calculation of immersed hull volume in case you are interested in determining displacement. But sometimes those minor conveniences must be sacrificed in order to fulfill the primary purpose of your drawings—to explicitly describe your reconstruction of the excavated remains of your vessel. For an example of a balanced set of lines, look again at the Kyrenia drawings in Figure 3–38; the lines are shown in straight configurations only in Figure 9–9. The Kyrenia ship was extensively preserved except in the ends of the hull, and even at the ends there were scattered fragments and artifacts to partially support reconstruction. Because preservation was distributed evenly and hull shapes changed constantly, it was possible to space stations and water and buttock lines evenly. Only near the top of the hull and in the peaks, where reconstruction was supported with little evidence, were the waterline spacings increased.

Not all ships are so evenly or extensively preserved, however. Look at the Serçe Limani lines drawings in Figure 4–9, for instance. The final lines drawing of that reconstruction, now awaiting publication, are even more irregular. The straight lines for this drawing have been isolated in Figure 9–10. Here the hull was extensively preserved to just above the turn of the bilge and in the upper port stern area; survival was sparse elsewhere. The lines drawings reflect this. The lowest water lines are placed at 15, 25, and 50 cm above the keel because this was the area of greatest preservation and, therefore, the area of greatest design substantiation and textual discussion. Buttock lines, however, were all spaced 50 cm apart because the shape of the bottom of the hull did not change much except toward the ends of the hull. In fact, were it not for the increased curvatures in the stern, they could have been placed a meter apart. Now look at the body station spacings. They were a meter apart except at the stern; this was more than enough to reveal how little the hull changed shape in its central areas and how little evidence there was for more precise reconstruction in the bow. In the stern, however, because the side survived, the spacing is halved to indicate all the design information we have accumulated and analyzed in the text.

The point is that the lines drawings are an expression of the results of your research. If an area is well preserved and a lot has been learned about its changing hull shapes, then the lines should be spaced as closely as is necessary to illustrate those shapes. Where survival is sparse and reconstruction remains in doubt, there is little value in spacing stations and longitudinal lines closely, especially where such a practice might be misleading.

That raises a question concerning the extent to which lines drawings and construction plans should be produced and, in a sense, this is a moral question. On

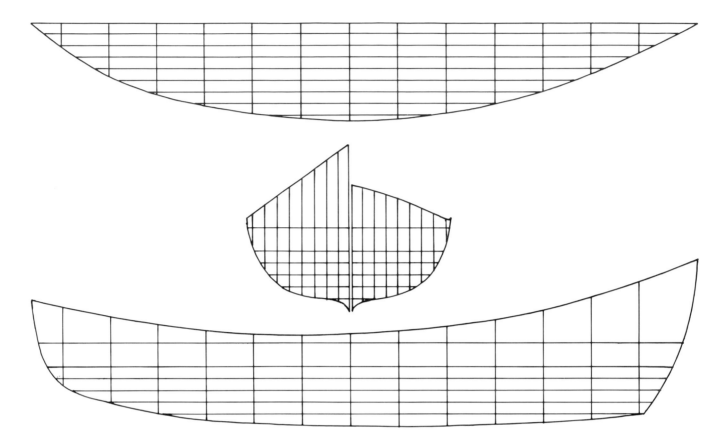

FIG. 9–9. Typical line spacings for extensively preserved vessels.

most shipwrecks there are areas that are fairly intact and can be reconstructed reliably, while other locations are so poorly represented that although hull shapes and features can be discerned and reproduced, any reconstruction will always be clouded with doubt or the possibility of alternatives. Certainly one should not draw a deckhouse if there is no evidence for a deckhouse; that is not the problem. The difficulty lies in those gray areas where limited survival provides suggestions but not proven facts. Reconstructors must ponder these areas and decide whether their interpretations of them would be helpful or misleading to others.

I believe ship researchers have a duty to divulge *all* of the new information they have acquired, and this includes the gray areas. In the course of their work they have developed a familiarity with the hull remains that could only be accumulated through months or years of intensive study; they have a familiarity no one else is ever likely to achieve for that particular hull. Even for those gray areas, the opinions they form are shaped by an understanding of the shipwright's discipline, a thorough knowledge of patterns of construction and design, a familiarity with the applications of materials and processes and the limits of technology. Consequently, that reconstructor's projections and hypotheses are far more reliable than ours would be. They should be shared with us,

but it must be done in such a way that hypothesis and fact do not become confused.

There are numerous ways to configure drawings so that the reader can readily separate fact from theory. Dashed lines are sometimes used to represent sparsely preserved or nonexistent areas on lines drawings and construction plans. There is nothing wrong with that, although a lines drawing of a hull such as the Serçe Limani merchantman would have at least half of its lines dashed, since more than half of the reconstruction resulted from limited information. Such drawings never look quite right, are difficult to interpret and produce, and they still cannot separate the areas that are based on different levels of substantiation. Another method that is less cumbersome uses a dashed line to describe the limits of concentrated preservation (e.g., Fig. 3–38). Below this line the hull was well preserved and reconstruction is reliable. Beyond it solid lines are still used for the gray areas, but dashed lines in the extremities are based entirely on secondary evidence, such as construction patterns, archival information, or artifact and cargo distribution. In addition, a verbal description of what those lines represent and the methods used to derive them must be included in the text, so that the reader understands precisely which parts of your reconstruction are in doubt and to what extent your theories are substantiated.

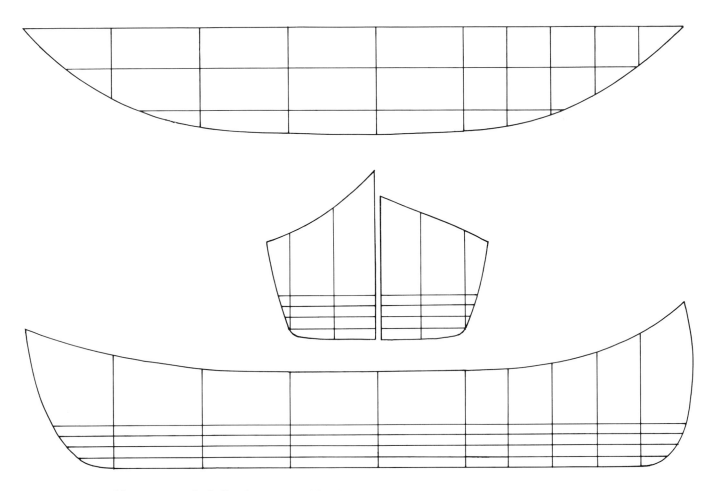

Fig. 9–10. Typical line spacings for hulls whose survival has been limited to specific areas.

All ship and boat drawings must have scales, and for lines drawings they should be elaborate enough to make interpretation convenient for the reader. The checkerboard or integrated scales used to illustrate artifacts will not normally suffice. Nor are notations such as "1:10 scale" or "scale ¹⁄₁₀th" satisfactory; published drawings might be altered in size to fit publication format, in which case that is not the scale at all. Scales for lines drawings must permit measurement over the entire length of the hull or some very small increment of it, at times simultaneously. Figure 9–11 shows several types and arrangements of scales; they can be seen in use in the various lines drawings in this book.

Some form of scale should extend over the entire length of the hull, preferably below the sheer plan or between the sheer and half-breadth plans. These scales are convenient when determining distances between stations or when locating gunports or masts if these have been included in your lines drawings; they are also useful for aligning a point on one plan to the other. They can be elaborate full-length scales, as in the *Charon* and *Eagle* drawings (Figs. 5–56 and 5–61), or simple incremental lines, as in the Kyrenia drawing (Fig. 3–38). It is

advisable to include a scale in feet and inches for drawings of ships known to have been built to English measurements, but in this day of almost universal use of the metric system, it is advisable to include a metric scale with such drawings, such as was done for the Brown's Ferry vessel drawings in Figures 5–41, 5–42, and 5–43.

Very small increments may also have to be measured, such as the width of a garboard rabbet or the thickness of a false keel. For this an incremental scale must be provided, either within the base scale (the *Charon, Eagle,* and Brown's Ferry vessel drawings) or in some remote configuration (the Kyrenia drawing). Figure 9–11 shows how such scales are made and used in both metric and English versions.

A legend is imperative. It guarantees identification of the drawing in publication formats where captions might be separated from drawings, and it prevents publication mixups. Additionally, legends quickly identify drawings on file to those unfamiliar with them. A legend should include the name and type of the vessel, its date or period, and principal dimensions if known. You may also want to include the project name or other pertinent information, but keep legends as short as possible.

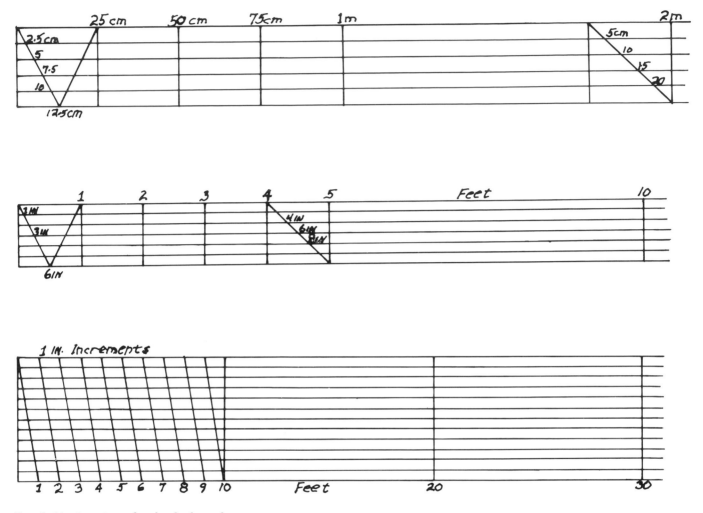

Fig. 9–11. A variety of scales for lines drawings.

Lengthy descriptions belong in the text. Stations should be identified so that they can easily be located on all views, but it is usually unnecessary to identify waterlines and buttock lines. Specific details or special construction referred to in the text might be noted, and the drawing should be signed by its creator and dated.

Except for those requirements, the drafting of hull lines is a purely mechanical operation. Most drawings can be enhanced through the use of lines of varying thicknesses. For all but the simplest drawings, I prefer to use three or four pen sizes; their thicknesses vary according to the type of drawing or the magnitude of reduction for publication. This has nothing to do with artistic values, although drawings with multiple line thicknesses are more pleasing to the eye. Hull lines are easier to interpret if varying pen sizes are used, as long as those thicknesses are consistent in all views. Centerlines, scales, and the like are made the thinnest; straight hull lines are made slightly heavier but one size thinner than their curved representations, as in Figure 3–38. Designed waterlines, and hull outlines where practical, are highlighted with the heaviest

lines. None of them should be so thick that intersecting points lose their sharpness or that reduction of the drawing results in dark areas.

For additional information relating to documentation of vessels of the last few centuries, refer to the two manuals cited previously—*Guidelines for Recording Historic Ships* and *Boats: A Field Manual for their Documentation* (see chap. 7, note 7).

CONSTRUCTION DRAWINGS

Lines drawings illustrate design; construction drawings reveal structural details and relate the construction to the design. There are many forms of construction drawings, one of the most informative being the section drawing (Figs. 3–31 and 5–62). Section drawings illustrate all of the construction at a given cross-section of the hull. They should also be enhanced with good incremental scales so that planking thicknesses and nail spacings can be measured directly. Other forms of construction drawings include interior views (Fig. 4–26), exterior views with frame locations superimposed (Fig. 9–12), and various forms of

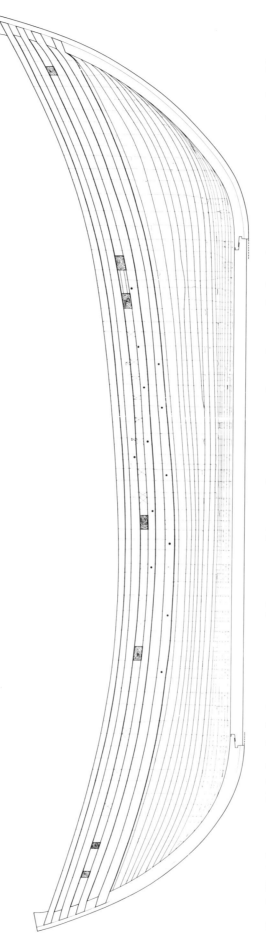

Fɪɢ. 9–12. A drawing, published in the final project report, of the exterior of the seventh-century Yassi Ada vessel's port side; frame locations are superimposed in dotted lines.

planking drawings, such as in Figure 3–3. Details can be included with an overall construction plan, or they can be drawn separately, as in Figure 3–40.

Shipwrecks seldom survive extensively above deck level, and thus topside drawings are used infrequently in archaeological reports. If the evidence exists, however, by all means include sail or rigging plans (Fig. 5–67), deck plans (Fig. 5–50), interior arrangements (Fig. 5–30), and any other form of illustration that might enhance the report.

CALCULATIONS AND PHYSICAL PROPERTIES

If shipwrecks are extensively preserved to the designed waterline or above, it is sometimes possible to determine many of their physical characteristics, such as principal dimensions, tonnages, and hydrostatic properties. It is a good idea to accumulate these data, even for vessels with no extant parallels, since the information might be useful in comparing the wreck with craft of other periods or for comparisons with future parallels. Extreme caution must be used in reporting such data, however. A hull whose survival was limited to only 5 percent of its original structure can hardly be calculated for coefficients or lateral resistance, nor can one that was complete only to the waterline supply accurate stability data.

The first two appendixes contain information about the physical properties of hulls and methods of determining them. Relatively few excavated hulls qualify for such detailed documentation. Use them conservatively.

The rest of it is up to you—providing the wreck, recording it, researching and reconstructing it, and most importantly of all, sharing everything you have learned with the rest of us. In parting, it might be advantageous to briefly consider that last step once more. Think again about your research goals; have you exploited them adequately, and have you included all of them in your final report?

Has the design been analyzed sufficiently? Do you know how the body shapes were acquired and what sort of geometry was used to determine them, if any? Did you question, in your analysis, why the bottom and sides were shaped as they were, or how this design compared to others in the same period or trade?

Have you considered why the hull was constructed as you determined, and why such wood types were used? Could you tell how the logs were converted into timbers and planks, and what tools were used in the process? Where and why are there weaknesses in the hull? Did the tool marks indicate well-disciplined shipwrightery? Were there repairs? If so, how did their application differ from the workmanship of the original builders?

What did you learn about the limits of the hold, its volume and configuration, and telltale signs of stowage arrangements? And how did that hold relate to the cargo and artifacts, and to the rest of the hull? Were there signs of people? Ah yes, how much did you learn about the shipwrights, the crew, the passengers? You should be asking yourself these questions, and hundreds more, as you prepare the final report. These are the types of questions that supplied the information for the history chapters, with enough left over for several more volumes. Now it is your turn. Bon voyage.

APPENDIX A
DISPLACEMENT

Displacement, the weight of a vessel and all of its burden, can be calculated for certain well-preserved hulls. Displacement calculations, in turn, can sometimes be used to determine the tonnage, or tons burden, of excavated hulls dating to periods before tonnage rules were established. Such calculations must be used with caution, however, and the resulting values will nearly always be approximations. The *Vasa* is so nearly complete that both displacement and tonnage can be determined with almost as much accuracy as newly designed vessels. But there are few *Vasas;* for most excavated examples, the degree of reliability will be something less.

The weight of a vessel and all of its cargo, passengers and crew, ballast, artifacts, and gear determined its displacement before it sank. But "souvenirs" may have been taken from the site, perishable items may have disappeared without a trace, or some of the cargo and gear may have been jettisoned before the ship sank. Hull weight estimates may also be misleading unless survival is extensive. However, where the cargo is well protected and undisturbed and enough of the hull is preserved to determine submerged volume or ship weight with a fair degree of accuracy, acceptable displacement estimates are a possibility.

The Kyrenia ship was preserved extensively, and most of its cargo was covered with a heavy layer of overburden. Hull weight could be estimated rather accurately from the reconstruction, as could the number and capacity of its cargo of amphoras. Similarly, the Brown's Ferry vessel was well enough preserved to determine principal dimensions rather reliably. Although some of its brick cargo may have been removed by souvenir hunters, the 25 tons that survived must have been nearly a full load for this little vessel. But even such extensively preserved examples must be regarded with caution.

For the archaeologist, one of two goals is possible—the determination of a flotation line by measuring displacement, or the determination of displacement from a given flotation line. In the first case, the hull weight must be calculated by finding the volume of all the scantlings in the construction plan and multiplying this by the weight(s) of the given wood type(s). To this product must be added the combined weights of fastenings, sheathing, fittings, etc. This is a big job, and it should not be attempted where the reconstructed hull is largely hypothetical.

To the vessel weight must be added the weight of cargo, gear, rig, anchors, ballast, stores, and people. Don't forget the people. On a trireme they could account for an additional 15 tons or so, a large proportion of the displacement. The flotation line can then be determined from the lines drawing by reversing the process described below.

For the second procedure, flotation lines are sometimes evident or can be estimated reasonably well. In the last few centuries, copper or zinc sheathing was applied only a foot or two above the full-load waterline. Marine growth tends to reflect a certain flotation line, although one cannot be certain that this line was not created at a dock while unloaded just before the vessel sank. On rare occasions, waterlines are painted or inscribed on hulls. From these indicators, the displacement can be calculated as follows.

Determining displacement is merely a matter of calculating the volume of the submerged part of the hull. Unfortunately, immersed shapes of all except barge hulls are complex and the calculations somewhat involved. The following examples are given in the English system; convert to metric values if you are using that system for your reconstruction. Regardless of the system you use, however, a result in long tons (2,240 lbs) is advisable for comparative purposes, since wooden ships in the documented periods were most frequently rated in long tons. Additional values in botte, lasts, or other applicable ratings will enhance the value of your study.

You will need an accurate lines drawing of the immersed portions of your reconstructed hull. For the most convenient calculations, body stations must be spaced equidistantly. First find the area of the submerged part of each body station to the *outside* of the hull planking (you will have to add this planking thickness if your body stations are molded). This can be done most accurately by using a planimeter or computer program to determine the area directly. If you don't have one of these devices at your disposal, use a system followed by many ship and boat builders of the past and illustrated in Figure A–1, whereby the sum of the areas of appropriately inscribed triangles (area equals the base multiplied by one-half of the altitude) is equal to the submerged station area. The method is sufficiently accurate for archaeological finds.

Total volume is then determined by adding one-half of the areas of the two end stations to the areas of all the others and multiplying this sum by the common distance between stations. This is known as the Trapezoidal Rule. In practical application it works as in Figure A–2, where there are nine equally spaced stations. For displacement calculations, the station areas are the ordinates and the common spacing, d, is the multiplier. Thus

$$\text{volume} = d(\tfrac{1}{2}[D] + [C] + [B] + [A] + \otimes + [1] + [2] + [3] + \tfrac{1}{2}[4]).$$

This, of course, is only half the immersed volume and must be multiplied by 2 for full displacement. That value, in turn, must be multiplied by 64 lbs, the weight of a cubic foot of saltwater, and divided by 2,240 to arrive at the displacement in long tons. Since $^{64}/_{2,240}$ can be simplified to $^{1}/_{35}$, the calculations can be simplified by dividing cubic feet by 35.

Thus if D = 6 sq ft, C = 12 sq ft, B = 16 sq ft, A = 20 sq ft, $\otimes$ = 22 sq ft, 1 = 20 sq ft, 2 = 16 sq ft, 3 = 9 sq ft, and 4 = 4 sq ft, and the interval between stations is 5 ft, then

$$5(3 + 12 + 16 + 20 + 22 + 20 + 16 + 9 + 2) = 605 \text{ cu ft};$$

and 605 × $^{2}/_{35}$ = 34.5 long tons displacement.

Naval architects sometimes use Simpson's Rules for such calculations. They require an even number of stations, and they are more complex, yet no more accurate for our purposes, than the Trapezoidal Rule. Although

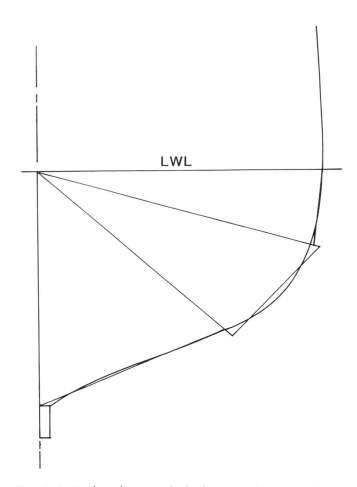

FIG. A–1. Finding the area of a body section by means of superimposed triangles.

displacement calculations are included in any good book on naval architecture, Chapelle's *Yacht Designing and Planning* and Gillmer and Johnson's *Introduction to Naval Architecture* are probably the best sources for archaeologists.[1] Chapelle includes a formula for converting molded body station areas to those including planking.

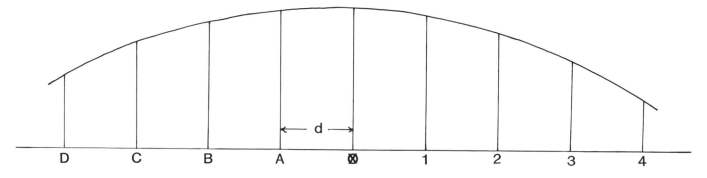

FIG. A–2. Using the Trapezoidal Rule to determine displacement.

APPENDIX B
DIMENSIONS AND PROPORTIONS

When a hull is preserved extensively enough to permit an accurate reconstruction—or at least a reliable reconstruction of its underwater portion—certain proportions and hydrostatic and hydrodynamic properties can be determined for comparison with other documented vessels. While such comparisons may be of limited value at present, especially in the case of ancient and medieval craft where approximate parallels are nonexistent, the prospect of future parallels due to expanding archaeological activity makes the calculation of such properties advisable. At the very least, enough information should be provided in final reports so that these values can be calculated in the future.

The following proportions and hydrodynamic properties are considered to be the most useful in archaeological studies. Additional information can be found in textbooks on naval architecture.[2]

Principal Dimensions: lengths (Fig. B–1)

L_k—length of the keel; generally, the bottom length of the keel or "the part that treads the ground," regardless of the location of scarfs.

L_{wl}—length of the waterline at full load.

L_{bp}—length between perpendiculars; wherever possible, the perpendiculars should be located at the upper extremities of the stem and sternpost rabbets.

L_d—length of the upper deck.

L_h—overall hull length.

L_{oa} (not shown)—extreme length, including bowsprit and rudder.

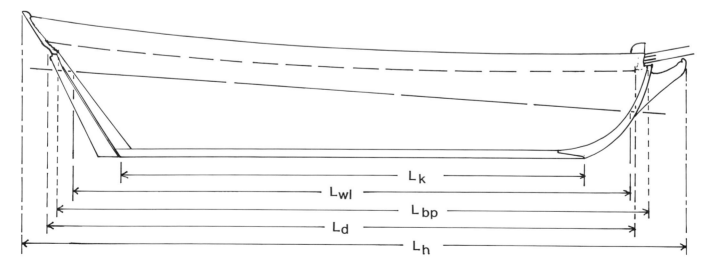

FIG. B–1. Principal dimensions: lengths.

Principal dimensions: breadths and depths
(Fig. B–2)

    B—maximum breadth.

    B_m—molded breadth (to inside of planking).

    Draft—from full-load waterline to the bottom of the keel.

    Draft, molded—distance from the waterline to a plane coinciding with the bottom of the garboard at the keel.

    D_{max}—maximum depth, taken from the upper deck at the side to the bottom of the keel amidships.

    D_m—molded depth, taken from the upper deck at the side to the bottom of the garboard at the keel.

    D (or D_h)—depth of hold, as used for tonnage calculations; the depth at amidships from the bottom of the upper deck beam to the top of the limber board.

Length/Beam Ratio—normally stated as the ratio of the hull's length between perpendiculars to the maximum breadth, but performance comparisons are sometimes made using waterline values.

Waterplane Area (Fig. B–3)—area of the hull at the plane of full-load immersion.

    Four coefficients can be determined that might prove helpful in comparing hull proportions as they apply to displacement, capacity, or performance of excavated vessels. They are dimensionless ratios and are therefore useful in comparing hulls of varying sizes and proportions.

Waterplane coefficient—if the waterplane area in Figure B–3 is enclosed with a rectangle (shown in dashed lines) whose sides are equal to the hull's length and breadth at the load waterline, the ratio between the areas of the waterplane and rectangle is called the waterplane coefficient. The fuller the hull at the waterline, the larger the coefficient. For instance, the waterplane coefficient of the full-hulled, flat-bottomed Zuyderzee *buertschip* (Fig. 5–30) has been calculated at 0.87 and the earlier Almere cog (Fig. 4–46) at 0.85.[3]

Midship coefficient (Fig. B–4)—ratio of the molded area of the immersed midship section at full load to the area of a rectangle whose sides represent molded draft and breadth. The midship coefficient of the *buertschip* was 0.96; for Donald McKay's *Lightning*, a sleek clipper ship with a waterline length of 228 ft and a displacement of 2,661 tons, the midship coefficient was 0.75.[4]

Block coefficient (Fig. B–5)—relationship between the displacement volume of a hull and that of a block whose volume is the product of the draft, beam, and waterline length, using molded dimensions throughout. The block

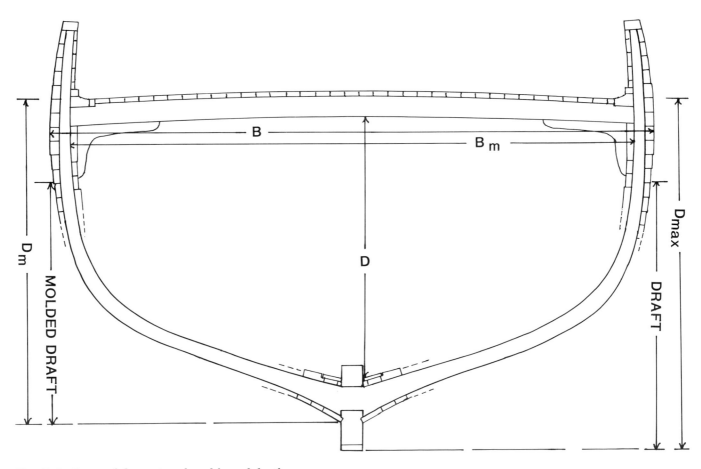

FIG. B–2. Principal dimensions: breadths and depths.

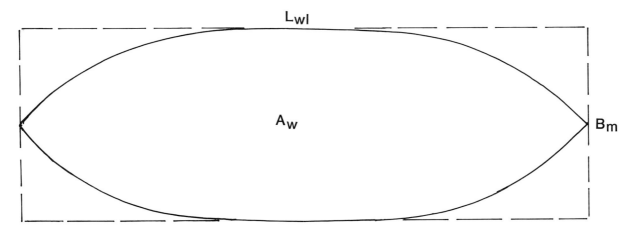

FIG. B–3. Waterplane area: its enclosing rectangle, representing maximum hull dimensions at the waterline, is shown in dashed lines.

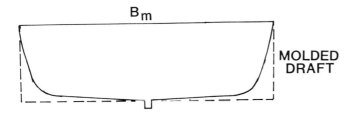

FIG. B–4. Midship coefficient.

coefficient for the *buertschip* was 0.73; for the *Lightning* it was 0.54.

Prismatic coefficient (Fig. B–6)—relationship between the displacement volume of a hull and that of a prism whose sides are equal to the full-load waterline length, using molded dimensions throughout. The prismatic coefficient of the *buertschip* was 0.75; for the *Lightning* it was 0.61.

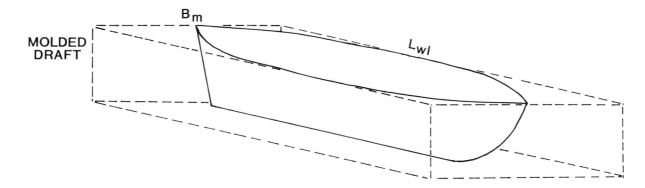

FIG. B–5. Block coefficient.

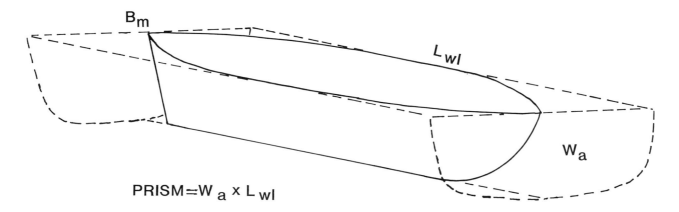

FIG. B–6. Prismatic coefficient.

APPENDIX C
CHARACTERISTICS OF COMMON SHIPBUILDING TIMBER

A search of archaeological reports, contemporary literature, and archival material, such as shipbuilding contracts and naval inventories, reveals that an extremely large variety of wood types was utilized in the construction of the world's ships and boats. Acacia, ash, balsa, hornbeam, larch, locust, juniper, mahogany, maple, mulberry, plane, sidder, spruce, sycamore, teak, and walnut are but a few of the species of trees that were harvested in the production of waterborn vessels. Sometimes exotic or unlikely wood types appear in the analyses of shipwrecks—hawthorne, jujube, olive, and rosebud on Mediterranean and Galilee wrecks, for instance. However, a check of about five hundred reports, contracts, and literary descriptions of ships of all periods indicated that by far the softwoods most frequently mentioned were cedar, cypress, fir, and pine; beech, elm, and oak dominated the hardwoods, with oak being mentioned the most frequently.

Both the archives and archaeological studies have produced vessels that were fabricated exclusively, or nearly so, from a single species of wood. More often, however, specific wood types were selected for specific tasks. A typical example is this excerpt from the contract of the United States ship *Peacock*, a 20-gun ship-sloop built in 1813.

> The Vessel is to be built of the best materials cut when the Sap was down, her frame, bottom, planks, wales and thick stuff, the clamps, spirkettings and thick stuff of the deck of White Oak, free from defects, except the Apron, Knight heads, Hawse pieces and main Transom which are to be of Live Oak, the Ceiling deck plank, Beams, Ledges, and plank of the Topsides of Yellow pine, free from Sap and all other defects, the top timbers on each side of the ports to be locust, as also the timber heads, all the other top timbers and half top timbers to be of red cedar. . . . It is understood between the parties, that the Navy Department has the privilege to substitute Mahogany in the place of White Oak for any part of the Ship's construction. . . .[5]

A few of the more popular species of shipbuilding timber are discussed briefly below. They are listed by their common names ascribed to them in the documentation.[6]

Beech

European Beech (*Fagus sylvatica*)—grows over a wide area of Europe and western Asia. Although rather difficult to work, it is straight-grained and very strong, hard, and dense; it was therefore desirable for keels, keelsons, and other long timbers requiring strength. The keel of the Red Bay galleon is one example. The weight of northern European beech averages 720 kg/cu m (45 lb/cu ft) at 12 percent moisture content; more southerly stands produced slightly less dense timber.

Cedar

Cedar of Lebanon (*Cedrus libani*)—widely touted in early literature, it was found on the Athlit ship, the Kinneret boat, and several Egyptian funerary vessels. A true cedar, it grows in the Middle East to heights sometimes exceeding 45 m and is strongly scented. It is fairly light (560 kg/cu m [35 lb/cu ft]), is durable, is said to be resistant to marine biological attack, and is easily worked. Most so-called cedars, however, are not true cedars but derive their designations from their fragrance or other similar properties. An example follows.

Eastern Red Cedar (*Juniperus virginiana*)—also known as "pencil cedar" or "Virginia cedar," this was probably the wood requested for top timbers in the *Peacock* contract cited above. Distributed over much of the eastern United States and southeastern Canada, the wood was a favorite for cedar chests because of its strong aroma, for pencils, and of course, as a shipbuilding timber. It is durable, resistant to splitting, and weights only about 530 kg/cu m (33 lb/cu ft).

Port Orford Cedar (*Chamaecyparis lawsoniana*)— found in lengths exceeding 60 m and with diameters of 3.5 m and more, it grows along the Oregon and California coasts. It is very similar to Yellow, or Alaska, cedar, which is slightly heavier than the cured weight of 430 kg/cu m (27 lb/cu ft) for cured Port Orford timbers. A durable wood, its light weight made it desirable for planking and topside construction.

These are but a few of the many so-called cedars converted into timbers in boatyards and shipyards worldwide. The big thirteenth-century Quanzhou vessel, excavated recently in Fujian province in China, was found to be double and triple planked in cedar.

Cypress

True cypress (*Cupressus* spp.), such as was found on late classical and medieval vessels in the Mediterranean, it is a strong, durable softwood with an average weight of 450 kg/cu ft (28 lb/cu ft). A more highly documented wood carrying the name of cypress was that used for the keelson of the Brown's Ferry vessel and for all manner of ship and boat construction, especially in coastal and local craft, from the early colonial period to the present century. A few details follow.

Baldcypress (*Taxodium distichum*)—commonly called cypress, it is also known as southern, white, red, and yellow cypress, and half a dozen other designations. Although it grew over a large area of the United States, its greatest concentration was in the southern coastal states. Baldcypress is relatively easy to work, is moderately strong and hard, and is highly resistant to decay. Its cured weight averages around 510 kg/cu m (32 lb/cu ft).

Elm

English Elm (*Ulmus procera*); **Dutch Elm** (*Ulmus hollandica*)—although numerous species of elm can be found worldwide (six in the United States alone) and elm frames were found on Roman wrecks, the English and Dutch species seem to be documented most frequently for shipbuilding. Elm was frequently the preferred wood for keels on English warships, but it was by no means limited to use for keels. The *Dartmouth*, for instance, had planks as well as keel and deadwoods made from elm. Both species weigh about 550 kg/cu m (34 lb/cu ft) at 12 percent moisture content and are similar in strength factors, although Dutch elm is said to be about 40 percent tougher than English elm.

Fir

Fir was documented for hull members on wrecks ranging from the Bronze Age Ulu Burun wreck to abandoned schooners on the Pacific coast of the United States. It enjoys literary coverage for nearly as long a period. Only two types are discussed here.

Silver Fir (*Abies alba*)—one of several species of fir used for ancient Mediterranean shipbuilding. Theophrastus said fir was used for triremes because of its lightness; modern silver fir weights average about 480 kg/cu m (30 lb/cu ft) when seasoned. Fir was also available in great lengths, again making it desirable for galleys, but it was not nearly as resistant to decay as the pines found in wrecks of ancient merchant vessels.

Douglas Fir (*Pseudotsuga menziesii*)—not a true fir, it is also known as Oregon pine, yellow fir, and red fir. Douglas fir ranges from the Rocky Mountains to the Pacific coast, and from central British Columbia to Mexico. This rapidly growing tree sometimes reaches heights in excess of 90 m and diameters of 4.5 m or greater; straight boles are said to be commonly free of branches for 20 m or more. In addition to great timber lengths, the wood works well with hand and power tools. Moderately durable, its weight and strength vary widely among samples; extant shipbuilding tables list its weight at 550 kg/cu m (34 kg/cu ft) with 15 percent moisture content. Contracts for large sailing ships built on the Pacific coast early in this century specify yellow fir for nearly all construction.[7]

Oak

Oak (*Quercus* spp.) was probably the most commonly used wood throughout history. It appears on a Bronze Age wreck (Ulu Burun tenons), secured the seams of countless classical vessels, and still exists in the "wooden walls" that survive—the *Vasa,* the *Victory,* the *Constitution,* and many more. It was the mainstay of the Viking world and dominated the construction of warships and transoceanic carriers. Many species of oak were used in the construction of ships and boats, but the ones listed below seem to surpass all others in the literature and archaeological reports.

American White Oak—true white oak (*Quercus alba*), chestnut oak (*Q. prinus*), and half a dozen other predominant white oak species range over the eastern half of the United States and southeastern Canada. Strong, straight-grained, hard, and durable, it was ideal for ship and boat construction. Although its hardness required a bit more effort to work, it took fastenings well and could be shaped readily. It was a heavy wood, most species averaging around 750 kg/cu m (47 lb/cu ft) at 12 percent moisture content.

European Oak (*Quercus robur* and *Q. petraea*)—found on numerous wrecks, this wood played a major role in European commerce and warfare as well as the colonization of the Americas. It is slightly lighter than American white oak, averaging about 720 kg/cu m (45 lb/cu ft), but has approximately the same grain and strength properties. Both species grow throughout Europe and in Asia Minor and North Africa.

Turkey Oak (*Quercus cerris*)—best known for its widespread use as tenon wood on ancient ships, it was used for other hull timbers as well. Turkey oak grows in southern Europe and southwestern Asia. It is stronger and heavier than European oak, weighing as much as 870 kg/cu m (54 lb/cu ft) when seasoned. Although difficult to work, Turkey oak's strength gave it great resistance against tenon shear and made it ideal for the tenons, treenails, false keels, and other assignments it fulfilled.

Live Oak (*Quercus virginiana*)—also a white oak, this species is far heavier and stronger than any of the other American white oaks. So named because it is a semi-evergreen, live oak is found along the Atlantic and Gulf coasts of the United States from Virginia to Texas and in a small area of western Cuba. Its branches sometimes span areas as much as 50 m wide, more than twice the tree's normal height. Trunks frequently exceed 6 m in circumference. Much heavier, harder, and stronger than the other oaks, its great tensile strength, resistance to rot, and large, curved branches made it extremely desirable for large warships and merchantmen. Due to its hardness, timbers were roughly shaped as soon as they were felled (they weighed about 75 lb/cu ft at this stage), then shipped to yards as far away as New England. The result was a live oaking industry that survived for more than a century and has been documented thoroughly.[8]

Pine

The durability, strength, availability, resistance to rot and biological attack, and the ease with which they could be worked and bent made a great variety of pines ideal for shipbuilding. Two applications are listed below.

Mediterranean Pines—several species that grew conveniently close to the shore and possessed the above characteristics are frequently recorded on shipwrecks and can still be found in watercraft of the Mediterranean and Aegean. All have similar features, and all are resinous, which is a characteristic that ancient shipbuilders exploited for surface applications of caulking and underlayments. **Aleppo pine** (*Pinus halepensis*) grows along much of the northern Mediterranean coast and northwestern Africa. Except for tenons and a false keel, the Kyrenia ship was built entirely of this material. East of Greece, especially in Cyprus and Turkey, a variation of this species known as **Cyprus pine** (*Pinus brutia*) can be found in greater concentrations. **Maritime pine** (*Pinus pinaster*) is a more westerly variety concentrated mainly along the Mediterranean coast from Italy to Portugal and along the Atlantic coasts of Portugal and France. It grows longer and straighter than the more easterly varieties. All three woods were ideal for cutting the thousands of mortises found in the edges of ancient ships. Weights varied according to resin content; seasoned values have been documented ranging from as low as 510 kg/cu m (32 lb/cu ft) for maritime pine to 580 kg/cu m (36 lb/cu ft) for Cyprus pine.

Southern Pine—known by various names, such as southern yellow pine, longleaf yellow pine, and as American pitch pine in Europe, it includes **longleaf pine** (*Pinus palustris*), which grows from eastern North Carolina southward to Florida and westward to Texas, **loblolly pine** (*P. taeda*), and several allied species, all of which are found in the southeastern or south central United States. Longleaf pine is classified as strong, stiff, hard, and relatively heavy at about 660 kg/cu m (41 lb/cu ft) when seasoned. Loblolly pine is somewhat lighter. Because they could be worked readily and had such excellent characteristics, southern pines were used extensively for ship and boat timbers, as well as for masts and spars. The Brown's Ferry vessel was planked in southern yellow pine.

NOTES

1. Introduction

1. J. Richard Steffy, "The Kyrenia Ship: An Interim Report on Its Hull Construction," *AJA* 89.1 (1985): 71–101.

2. Lionel Casson and J. Richard Steffy, eds., *The Athlit Ram.*

3. Angela Care Evans and Rupert Bruce-Mitford, "The Ship," in *The Sutton Hoo Ship-Burial,* vol. 1, Rupert Bruce-Mitford et al., pp. 345–435.

2. Basics

1. Lionel Casson and J. Richard Steffy, eds., *The Athlit Ram.*

2. Cheryl Ward Haldane, "The Dashur Boats" (Master's thesis, Texas A&M University, 1984).

3. J. Richard Steffy, "The Kyrenia Ship: An Interim Report on Its Hull Construction," *AJA* 89.1 (1985): 71–101.

4. Steffy, "The Reconstruction of the Eleventh Century Serçe Liman Vessel: A Preliminary Report," *IJNA* 11.1 (1982): 13–34.

5. Steffy et al., "The *Charon* Report," in *Underwater Archaeology: The Challenge before Us,* ed. Gordon P. Watts, pp. 114–43.

3. Ancient World

1. For excavation and conservation details, as well as a catalog of the finds, see Mohammad Zaki Nour et al., *The Cheops Boats,* Part I. Paul Lipke, *The Royal Ship of Cheops.*

2. Björn Landström, *Ships of the Pharaohs,* p. 35.

3. Lipke, *Cheops,* p. 117.

4. Landström, *Pharaohs,* p. 38.

5. Henri Wild, *Le Tombeau de Ti, Fascicule II: La Chapelle (Première partie),* pls. 128 and 129.

6. This brief study deals only with the two lower registers. For a detailed examination of the mastaba of Ti shipbuilding scenes, see Wild, *Le Tombeau* (note 5), and Edward M. Rogers, "Boat Reliefs in the Tomb of Ti and Mastaba of Mereruka," *INA Quarterly* 19.3 (1992): 8–13.

7. Jean-Jacques de Morgan, *Fouilles à Dâhchour: Mars–juin 1894,* pp. 81–83.

8. Cheryl Ward Haldane, "The Dashur Boats" (Master's thesis, Texas A&M University, 1984). See also Haldane, "A Fourth Boat from Dashur," *AJA* 88.3 (1988): 389; and Haldane, "Boat Timbers from El-Lisht: A New Method of Ancient Egyptian Hull Construction, Preliminary Report," *MM* 74.2 (1988): 141–52.

9. For an interesting popular account of the Pittsburgh boat, see Diana Craig Patch and Cheryl Ward Haldane, *The Pharaoh's Boat at The Carnegie.*

10. Cheryl Ward Haldane, personal communication.

11. Cheryl Ward Haldane and Cynthia W. Shelmerdine, "Herodotus 2.96.1–2 Again," *Classical Quarterly* 40.4 (1990): 535–39.

12. Lionel Casson, *Ships and Seamanship in the Ancient World,* p. 14, n. 15.

13. James Hornell, *Water Transport: Origins and Early Evolution,* pp. 215–17 and pl. 35.

14. Cemal Pulak, "The Bronze Age Shipwreck at Ulu Burun, Turkey: 1985 Campaign," *AJA* 92.1 (1988): 1–37.

15. E. V. Wright, *The North Ferriby Boats.* Subsequent studies were published in "The North Ferriby Boats: A Revised Basis for Reconstruction," in *Sewn Plank Boats,* ed. Sean McGrail and Eric Kentley, 105–44. A definitive book on the entire Ferriby project by E. V. Wright has been released recently: *The Ferriby Boats: Seacraft of the Bronze Age.* See also "The North Ferriby Boats: A Final Report" (Paper presented at the Sixth International Symposium on Ship and Boat Archaeology, Roskilde, Denmark, 1991; publication forthcoming).

16. For dating information, see V. R. Switsur and E. V. Wright, "Radiocarbon Ages and Calibrated Dates for the Boats from North Ferriby, Humberside: A Reappraisal," *The Archaeological Journal* 146 (1989).

17. See Wright's latest book, *The Ferriby Boats: Seacraft of the Bronze Age,* for such details.

18. Patrice Pomey, "L'épave de Bon-Porté et les bateaux cousus de Méditerranée," *MM* 67.3 (1981): 225.

19. Jean-Pierre Joncheray, "L'épave grecque, ou etrusque, de Bon-Porté," *Cahiers d'Archéologie Subaquatique* 5 (1976): 5–36.

20. Pomey, "L'épave de Bon-Porté," *MM* 67.3 (1981): 225–42. See also Lucien Basch, "The Sewn Ship of Bon-Porté," *MM* 67.3 (1981): 244.

21. The information on the Ma'agan Michael vessel has been graciously supplied by Elisha Linder, project director, and Jay Rosloff, field director. Papers with more extensive details have been submitted for publication. See also Elisha Linder, "The Ma'agan Michael Shipwreck: First Season, 1988," *CMS News* 16 (1989): 5–7; and Jay Rosloff, "The Ma'agan Michael Shipwreck Excavation Report: 1989 Season," *CMS News* 17 (1990): 3–4.

22. Helena Wylde Swiny and Michael L. Katzev, "The Kyrenia Shipwreck: A Fourth-Century B.C. Greek Merchant Ship," in *Marine Archaeology*, ed. David J. Blackman, pp. 339–59.

23. J. Richard Steffy, "The Kyrenia Ship: An Interim Report on Its Hull Construction," *AJA* 89.1 (1985): 71–101. Michael L. Katzev and Susan Womer Katzev, "Kyrenia II: Building a Replica of an Ancient Greek Merchantman," *Tropis I*, pp. 163–75. See also M. and S. Katzev, "Voyage of Kyrenia II," *INA Newsletter* 16.1 (1989): 4–10; M. Katzev,"An Analysis of the Experimental Voyage of Kyrenia II," *Tropis II*, pp. 245–56; and J. R. Steffy, "The Role of Three-Dimensional Research in the Kyrenia Ship Reconstruction," *Tropis I*, pp. 249–62.

24. Honor Frost et al., *Lilybaeum*.

25. Lionel Casson and J. Richard Steffy, eds., *The Athlit Ram*.

26. P. Pomey, "La coque," in *L'épave romaine de la Madrague de Giens (Var)*, *Gallia* suppl. 34, ed. A. Tchernia, P. Pomey, et al., pp. 75–107. For supplemental information, see Pomey, "Le navire romaine de la Madrague de Giens," *Comptes rendus de l'académie des inscriptions* (Jan.–Mar., 1982): 133–54; and B. Liou and P. Pomey, "Direction des recherches archéologiques sous-marines," *Gallia* 43 (1985): 564–65.

27. Michel Rival, *La charpenterie navale romaine*, p. 132.

28. Shelley Wachsmann et al., *The Excavations of an Ancient Boat in the Sea of Galilee (Lake Kinneret)*.

29. Steffy, "The Herculaneum Boat: Preliminary Notes on Hull Details," *AJA* 89.3 (1985): 519–21.

30. Guido Ucelli, *Le navi di Nemi*.

31. Peter Throckmorton, "The Antikythera Ship," in Gladys Davidson Weinberg et al., *The Antikythera Shipwreck Reconsidered*, *TAPS* 55.3 (1965): 40–47. Michael A. Fitzgerald, "The Ship," in *The Harbours of Caesarea Maritima: Results of the Caesarea Ancient Harbour Excavation Project, 1980–1985*, vol. 2, *The Small Finds and the Ship*, ed. John P. Oleson, BAR-S, forthcoming.

32. Jean-Marie Gassend, Bernard Liou, and Serge Ximénès, "L'épave 2 de l'anse des Laurons (Martigues, Bouches-du-Rhône)," *Archaeonautica* 4 (1984): 75–105.

33. Peter Marsden, "The County Hall Ship, London," *IJNA* 3.1 (1974): 55–65.

34. Marsden, *A Roman Ship from Blackfriars, London*.

35. Ibid., p. 34.

36. Olaf Höckmann, "Zur Bauweise, Funktion und Typologie der Mainzer Schiffe," in *Die Mainzer Römerschiffe*, ed. Gerd Rupprecht, pp. 44–77.

4. Medieval Vessels

1. George F. Bass and Frederick H. van Doorninck, Jr., "An Eleventh Century Shipwreck at Serçe Liman, Turkey," *IJNA* 7.2 (1978): 119–72.

2. See *INA Newsletter* 15.3 (1988) for a report of the anticipated museum displays, the hull reconstruction process, and descriptions of the cargo and artifacts. A multivolume final report on the entire project is now in preparation.

3. F. H. van Doorninck, Jr., "The Fourth Century Wreck at Yassi Ada: An Interim Report on the Hull," *IJNA* 5.2 (1976): 115–31.

4. G. F. Bass, F. H. van Doorninck, Jr., et al., *Yassi Ada: A Seventh-Century Byzantine Shipwreck*. For a detailed description of the hull remains, see van Doorninck, "The Hull Remains," pp. 32–63, of *Yassi Ada*. The construction process outlined here is described and illustrated in J. Richard Steffy, "Reconstructing the Hull," pp. 65–86, of *Yassi Ada*.

5. Marie-Pierre Jézégou, "Elements de construction sur couples observes sur une épave du haut moyen-age decouverte a Fos-sur-mer (Bouches-du-Rhône)," *VI Congreso Internacional de Archqueologie Submarina*, pp. 351–56. Peter Throckmorton and Joan Throckmorton, "The Roman Wreck at Pontano Longarini," *IJNA* 2.2 (1973): 243–66.

6. Robert S. Lopez, "The Role of Trade in the Economic Readjustment of Byzantium in the Seventh Century," *Dumbarton Oaks Papers XIII* (1959), pp. 69–85.

7. Much of the following information about the Serçe Limani hull construction has been published in various papers and articles, including the following: J. Richard Steffy, "The Reconstruction of the Eleventh Century Serçe Liman Vessel: A Preliminary Report," *IJNA* 11.1 (1982): 13–34; J. Richard Steffy, "Reconstructing the Hull," *INA Newsletter* 15.3 (1988): 14–21; J. Richard Steffy, "The Mediterranean Shell to Skeleton Transition: A Northwest European Parallel??" in *Carvel Construction Technique*, ed. R. Reinders and K. Paul, pp. 1–9.

8. For details of rigging remains and sail plan evidence, see Sheila D. Matthews, "The Rig of the Eleventh-Century Ship at Serçe Liman, Turkey" (Master's thesis, Texas A&M University, 1983).

9. S. D. Goitein, *A Mediterranean Society*, vol. 1, p. 305. See also Abraham L. Udovitch, "Time, the Sea, and Society: Duration of Commercial Voyages on the Southern Shores of the Mediterranean during the High Middle Ages," in *La navigazione mediterranea nell'alto medioevo (1977 Settimane)*, 2: 503–46.

10. Goitein, *Mediterranean Society*, vol. 1, pp. 305–308.

11. Ibid., p. 306.

12. Marco Bonino, "Lateen-rigged Medieval Ships: New Evidence from Wrecks in the Po Delta (Italy) and Notes on Pictorial and Other Documents," *IJNA* 7.1 (1978): 9–28.

13. Relazione, *Sulla scoperta di due barche antiche nel territorio del comune di Contarina in provincia di Rovigo nel gennaio 1898*, Commissione della R Deputazione di Storia patria per le Venezie (Venice, 1900).

14. Among the many contracts, letters, notes, and treatises relating to shipbuilding and maritime activities in the late medieval period, two have made elaborate contributions to our understanding of early naval architectural developments in the Mediterranean area. The first is a manuscript written in 1444 by Giorgio Timbotta of Modon (British Museum, MS Cotton Titus, A. 26), a Venetian merchant of many interests. The parts on shipbuilding have been translated and analyzed by R. C. Anderson in "Italian Naval Architecture about 1445," *MM* 11 (1925): 135–63. The manuscript covers a variety of subjects, including an extensive section on shipbuilding, sailmaking, and arithmetic of a nautical nature.

The second is the *Fabrica di galere*, an anonymous fifteenth-century Venetian manuscript now in the Magliabecchiana Library in Florence (Bibl. Naz. Florence, MSS, Coll. Magliabecchiana, classe 19, palco 7). It was partially translated into French and analyzed by A. Jal in "Fabbrica di galere," *Archéologie navale* 2, (Paris, 1840), 1–106. An excellent interpretation of the square-rigged ships not included by Jal was published recently by Sergio Bellabarba in "The Square-rigged Ship of the *Fabrica di galere* Manuscript," *MM* 74.2 (1988): 113–30 and *MM* 74.3 (1988): 225–39.

Two modern sources, which provide excellent insights to medieval and renaissance ship architecture and construction methods, are *Venetian Ships and Shipbuilders of the Renaissance* (Baltimore, 1934) by Frederic C. Lane and "The Naval Architecture of Crusader Transport Ships," a series of three articles by John H. Pryor in *MM* 70.2, 70.3, and 70.4 (1984). Pryor includes a commendable analysis of the dimensions listed in various contracts for the lease or purchase of Crusader vessels from the maritime republics of Genoa, Marseilles, and Venice between 1246 and 1320.

15. Bellabarba, "The Square-rigged Ship," *MM* 74.2, p. 116.

16. Lane, *Venetian Ships*, p. 89.

17. Interpreted by Anderson in *MM* 11 (1925): 142.

18. Ibid., p. 154. Bartolomeo Crescentio, *Náutica Mediterránea*, pp. 21, 47.

19. The two-stave method, which may have been unknown to the earlier Venetian authors cited here, was based on geometric progressions similar to the triangles described below. For an excellent description of the two-stave method, see John Patrick Sarsfield, "Mediterranean Whole Moulding," *MM* 70.1 (1984): 86–88.

20. Crescentio (quoted in Anderson, "Italian Naval Architecture," *MM* 11 (1925): 154) states that the geometric progression for locating individual bases should be at 1, 2, 4, 7, 11, 16, 22, and onward, each interval being one more than the last. But Sarsfield ("Mediterranean Whole Moulding," *MM* 70.1 (1984): 87) rightly suggests that the progression actually should follow the formula

$$S = \frac{n(n+1)}{2},$$

a progression that seems to produce much more satisfactory rising and narrowing lines. My illustration uses that formula.

21. Lane, *Venetian Ships*, p. 95.

22. Sarsfield, "Survival of Pre–Sixteenth-Century Mediterranean Lofting Techniques in Bahia, Brasil," in *Local Boats: Fourth International Symposium on Boat and Ship Archaeology, Porto, 1985*, ed. Octavio Lixa Filgueiras, pp. 63–88.

23. Bellabarba, "The Square-rigged Ship," p. 120.

24. Peter Marsden, *A Roman Ship from Blackfriars, London.*

25. Sean McGrail, "Further Aspects of Viking Age Boatbuilding," in *Archaeology of the Boat*, Basil Greenhill, pp. 241–44.

26. G. Rosenberg, "Hjörtspringfundet," *Nord Oldtideminder*, vol. 3, part 1. See also Ole Crumlin-Pedersen, "Skin or Wood? A Study of the Origin of the Scandinavian Plank-Built Boat," in *Ships and Shipyards, Sailors and Fishermen*, ed. Olof Hasslöf et al., pp. 208–34.

27. Basil Greenhill, *Archaeology of the Boat*, pp. 82, 178–80.

28. Haakon Shetelig and H. Falk, *Scandinavian Archaeology*, p. 353.

29. Angela Care Evans and Rupert Bruce-Mitford, "The Ship," in Rupert Bruce-Mitford et al., *The Sutton Hoo Ship-Burial*, vol. 1, pp. 345–435.

30. A. W. Brøgger and Haakon Shetelig, *The Viking Ships: Their Ancestry and Evolution*, pp. 79–103. Shetelig additionally credits Fr. Johannessen, a naval engineer who made a lifelong study of Viking ships and navigation, for his contributions to this analysis. Werner Dammann, *Das Gokstadschiff und seine Boote.* Most of the dimensions cited have been derived from this work.

31. Arne Emil Christensen, "Viking Age Boatbuilding Tools," in *Woodworking Techniques before A.D. 1500*, ed. Sean McGrail, p. 331.

32. Also illustrated in Douglas Phillips-Birt, *The Building of Boats*, Figs. 87–90.

33. Brøgger and Shetelig, *The Viking Ships*, pp. 108–15.

34. Olaf Olsen and Ole Crumlin-Pedersen, "The Skuldelev Ships. (II)," *Acta Archaeologica* 38 (1967): 75–170. See also Olsen and Crumlin-Pedersen, *Five Viking Ships from Roskilde Fjord.*

35. J. T. Tinniswood, "English Galleys, 1272–1377," *MM* 35 (1949): 276–315.

36. R. C. Anderson, "The Bursledon Ship," *MM* 20 (1934): 158–70; see also M. W. Prynne, "Henry V's *Grace Dieu*," *MM* 54 (1968): 115–28.

37. Alexander McKee, "The Influence of British Naval Strategy on Ship Design: 1400–1850," in *A History of Seafaring Based on Underwater Archaeology*, ed. George F. Bass, pp. 227–28.

38. Sir Westcott Abell, *The Shipwright's Trade*, pp. 20–22.

39. For an excellent description of the logic of cog construction and various aspects of methodology, see Frederick M. Hocker, "The Development of a Bottom-based Shipbuilding Tradition in Northwestern Europe and the New World," (Ph.D. diss., Texas A&M University, 1991).

40. Crumlin-Pedersen, "Danish Cog-Finds," in *The Archaeology of Medieval Ships and Harbours in Northern Europe*, ed. Sean McGrail, pp. 17–34. Reinder Reinders, *Cog Finds from the IJsselmeerpolders*, Flevobericht 248, p. 31.

41. Detlev Ellmers, "The History of the Cog as a Ship Type," in *The Hanse Cog of 1380*, ed. Klaus-Peter Kiedel and Uwe Schnall, pp. 60–73.

42. Aleydis M. Van de Moortel, *A Cog-like Vessel from the Netherlands*, Flevobericht 331.

43. Kiedel and Schnall, *The Hanse Cog*. The construction sequence I use follows that suggested by Werner Lahn, pp. 52–59, of *The Hanse Cog*. See also D. Ellmers, "The Cog of Bremen and Related Boats," in *The Archaeology of Medieval Ships and Harbours in Northern Europe*, ed. Sean McGrail, pp. 1–15.

44. Hocker, "The Development of a Bottom-based Shipbuilding Tradition," pp. 127–52.

45. Hocker, "The Development of a Bottom-based Shipbuilding Tradition."

46. Donald H. Keith and Christian J. Buys, "New Light on Medieval Chinese Seagoing Ship Construction," *IJNA* 10.2 (1981): 124.

47. Jeremy Green, "The Song Dynasty Shipwreck at Quanzhou, Fujian Province, People's Republic of China," *IJNA* 12.3 (1983): 253–61.

48. Ibid., p. 255.

49. Li Guo-Qing, "Archaeological Evidence for the Use of Chu-nam on the Thirteenth Century Quanzhou Ship, Fujian Province, China," *IJNA* 18.4 (1989): 277–83.

50. The articles cited above (notes 46, 47, and 49) are in part based on an earlier report in the Chinese archaeological journal *Wen Wu*, which has been translated into English by Douglas Merwin and published in *Studies in Chinese Sociology and Anthropology* (1977): 6–106.

51. Green and Zae Geum Kim, "The Shinan and Wando Sites, Korea: Further Information," *IJNA* 18.1 (1989): 33–41. See also Green, "The Shinan Excavation, Korea: An Interim Report on the Hull Structure," *IJNA* 12.4 (1983): 293–301.

5. *Age of Global Seafaring*

1. Frederic C. Lane, "Venetian Naval Architecture about 1550," *MM* 20 (1934): 24–49.

2. Richard A. Barker, "Fragments from the Pepysian Library," *Revista da Universidade de Coimbra* 32 (1986): 161–78.

3. Donald H. Keith, "Shipwrecks of the Explorers," in *Ships and Shipwrecks of the Americas*, ed. George F. Bass, pp. 66–67.

4. Some of Oliveira's drawings and textual material have been published and discussed by Eric Rieth in *Neptunia* 165 (1987): 18–25, *Neptunia* 166 (1987): 16–31, and *Neptunia* 169 (1988): 36–43.

5. An English language translation has been published by J. Bankston, *Nautical Instruction, 1587, by Dr. Diego García de Palacio*.

6. See René Burlet and Eric Rieth, "Outils et Démarches," *Histoire et Mesure* III.4 (1988): 463–89 for an interesting three-dimensional reconstruction of a 400-ton ship listed in García de Palacio's text. Their research was developed using mold-and-batten and half-models as are described in chapter 8.

7. Roger C. Smith, *Vanguard of Empire: Ships of Exploration in the Age of Columbus*.

8. Keith, "Shipwrecks of the Explorers," pp. 60–64.

9. Thomas J. Oertling, "The Molasses Reef Wreck Hull Analysis: Final Report," *IJNA* 18.3 (1989): 229–43.

10. Like the Molasses Reef wreck, the Highborn Cay wreck was excavated by the Institute of Nautical Archaeology under the direction of Donald Keith and the hull was interpreted by Thomas Oertling. For hull details, see Oertling, "The Highborn Cay Wreck: The 1986 Field Season," *IJNA* 18.3 (1989): 244–53.

11. M. Redknap, *The Cattewater Wreck*.

12. H. Lovegrove, "Remains of Two Old Vessels Found at Rye, Sussex," *MM* 50.2 (1964): 115–22.

13. Mac Guérout, Eric Rieth, and Jean-Marie Gassend, "Le Navire Génois de Villefranche un naufrage de 1516 (?)," *Archaeonautica* 9 (1989).

14. Cemal Pulak, personal communication.

15. The following information was derived from a study by Jay Rosloff. For structural details, see Jay P. Rosloff and J. Barto Arnold III, "The Keel of the *San Esteban*: Continued Analysis," *IJNA* 13.4 (1984): 287–96.

16. Warren Blake and Jeremy Green, "A Mid–Sixteenth Century Portuguese Wreck in the Seychelles," *IJNA* 15.1 (1986): 5–7.

17. The excavations were conducted by a Parks Canada team under the direction of Robert Grenier. See Robert Grenier, "Basque Whalers in the New World: The Red Bay Wrecks," in *Ships and Shipwrecks of the Americas*, ed. George F. Bass, pp. 69–84.

18. Peter J. A. Waddell, "The Disassembly of a Sixteenth Century Galleon," *IJNA* 15.2 (1986): 137–48.

19. Redknap, *Cattewater Wreck*, pp. 95, 98, raises the possibility of Ibernian origins for the Cattewater vessel.

20. W. Salisbury, "The Woolwich Ship," *MM* 47.2 (1961): 86.

21. Margaret Rule, *The Mary Rose: The Excavation and Raising of Henry VIII's Flagship*.

22. Ibid., pp. 21, 22.

23. Eric Rieth, "La question de la construction navale à franc-bord au Ponant," *Neptunia* 160 (1985): 8–21.

24. M. Oppenheim, *A History of the Administration of the Royal Navy and of Merchant Shipping in Relation to the Navy from 1509 to 1660*, p. 54.

25. Rieth, "La question de la construction," p. 21.

26. Sir Wescott Abell, *The Shipwright's Trade*, pp. 26–38.

27. Barker, "Fragments," pp. 161–63.

28. William A. Baker, who designed *Mayflower II* and many other colonial replicas, determined that the length occupied by the stem and sternpost usually were approximately equal to the maximum breadth of the hull. See Baker, *The Mayflower and Other Colonial Vessels*, p. 13.

29. An excellent discussion of the sequential projection of body shapes by several methods is given by Richard Barker in "Design in the Dockyards, about 1600," in *Carvel Construction Technique*, ed. R. Reinders and K. Paul, pp. 61–69.

30. Barker, "Fragments," p. 161.

31. The best sources for relating tonnage to maritime trade, naval activity, and shipbuilding are a series of four articles by William Salisbury, "Early Tonnage Measurement in England," *MM* 52 (1966) and *MM* 53 (1967); and Dorothy Burwash, *English Merchant Shipping, 1460–1540*. A broader geographical area is addressed by Frederic C. Lane, "Tonnages, Medieval and Modern," *The Economic History Review*, Second Series, 17.8 (1964): 213–33. See also W. A. Baker, *The Mayflower and Other Colonial Vessels*, pp. 13, 14.

An excellent account of the application of tonnage, especially for later sailing ships, can be found in a series of articles by John Lyman in *The American Neptune*: "Register Tonnage and Its Measurement, Part I," 5.3 (1945): 223–34; "Register Tonnage and Its Measurement, Part II," 5.4 (1945): 311–25; "Tonnage—Weight and Measurement," 8.2 (1948): 99–113.

32. Lane, "Tonnages, Medieval and Modern," p. 226.

33. Barker, "Fragments," p. 163.

34. Allan J. Wingood, "*Sea Venture*: An Interim Report on an Early Seventeenth Century Shipwreck Lost in 1609," *IJNA* 11.4 (1982): 333–47.

35. Ibid.

36. Jonathan Adams, "*Sea Venture*: A Second Interim Report—Part I," *IJNA* 14.4 (1985): 275–99.

37. Ibid., p. 291.

38. Wingood, "*Sea Venture*: An Interim Report," p. 335.

39. William Salisbury had edited and published it under the title "A Treatise on Shipbuilding, c. 1620," along with some interesting commentary. See *A Treatise on Shipbuilding and a*

Treatise on Rigging Written about 1620–1625, ed. W. Salisbury and R. C. Anderson.

40. Baker, *The Mayflower and Other Colonial Vessels,* pp. 16, 17. Figure 5–26 combines Baker's illustration with a somewhat more complex drawing for molding a British longboat of 1715 as described by Howard I. Chapelle, *American Small Sailing Craft,* pp. 11, 12. The works of William A. Baker, incidentally, are indispensable for anyone studying early seventeenth-century ships and boats. His articles on design, whole molding, rigging, and construction provide an overview of the contemporary treatises cited above. They remain the best general study on small craft of the period. Shortly before his death in 1981, Baker wrote *The Mayflower and Other Colonial Vessels,* in which he revised and combined many of his earlier works.

41. Carl Olof Cederlund, "Shipbuilding in the Seventeenth and Eighteenth Centuries: The *Wasa* as a Product of Dutch Shipbuilding," in *The North Sea: A Highway of Economic and Cultural Exchange,* ed. A. Bang-Andersen, B. Greenhill, and E. H. Grude, pp. 167–80.

42. Anders Franzen, *The Warship VASA.* A reconstruction drawing by N. G. Kowarsky accompanying the architectural drawings published by the museum (see n. 43) list hull length at 200 ft, which appears to include the beakhead, stern height at 65 ft, and the tonnage at 1,300.

43. Statens Sjöhistoriska Museum, Stockholm, *Drawings: Wasa 1628.*

44. The hull was partially recorded during excavation; final recording and hull analysis was done by Frederick M. Hocker. See Hocker, "The Development of a Bottom-based Shipbuilding Tradition in Northwestern Europe and the New World" (Ph.D. diss., Texas A&M University, 1991), pp. 181–219. See also Hocker, "The Lelystad *beurtschip:* Preliminary report on the hull construction," in *Scheepsarcheologie: prioriteiten en lopend onderzoek,* ed. Reinder Reinders and Rob Oosting, Flevobericht 322, n.p.

45. All information on the *Dartmouth* was extracted from the report by Colin J. M. Martin, "The *Dartmouth,* A British Frigate Wrecked off Mull, 1690; 5. The Ship," *IJNA* 7.1 (1978): 29–58.

46. In recent correspondence, Martin suggested the extant framing plan may be the result of re-keeling. Consequently, his research continues on the hull remains and in the archives.

47. John Franklin discusses twelve of the better models in his *Navy Board Ship Models, 1650–1750.*

48. Brian Lavery, ed., *Deane's Doctrine of Naval Architecture, 1670.*

49. For an excellent description of English warship framing, see Peter Goodwin, *The Construction and Fitting of the English Man-of-War, 1650–1850,* pp. 13–28.

50. A brief preliminary study of the Brown's Ferry vessel's remains was made by the author shortly after the excavation. The hull has since undergone a lengthy conservation process and was recently analyzed thoroughly by Frederick M. Hocker. The information provided here has been taken from parts of both of their reports on the hull's construction: Alan B. Albright and J. Richard Steffy, "The Brown's Ferry Vessel, South Carolina: Preliminary Report," *IJNA* 8.2 (1979): 121–42; and Hocker, "The Development of a Bottom-based Shipbuilding Tradition," pp. 227–48. See also "The Brown's Ferry Vessel: An Interim Report," in *Underwater Archaeology Proceedings of the Society for Historical Archaeology Conference, Kingston, 1992,* ed. D. H. Keith and Toni Carrell, pp. 20–25.

51. Rusty Fleetwood, *Tidecraft,* pp. 31, 48.

52. Warren C. Riess, "Design and Construction of the Ronson Ship," in *Carvel Construction Technique,* ed. R. Reinders and K. Paul, pp. 176–83.

"The Ronson Ship: The Study of an Eighteenth Century Merchantman excavated in Manhattan, New York in 1982," (Ph.D. diss., University of New Hampshire, 1987).

In "Design and Construction of the Ronson Ship," Riess discusses some interesting features about the hull's design and compares it with contemporary documentation. One of his most interesting discoveries centers around the projections of the stem and breast hook, which are curved to radii of 16 ft and 8 ft respectively.

53. Jay P. Rosloff, "The Water Street Ship: Preliminary Analysis of an Eighteenth-Century Merchant Ship's Bow," (Master's thesis, Texas A&M University, 1986).

54. Kevin J. Crisman, "The Construction of the *Boscawen,*" *The Bulletin of the Fort Ticonderoga Museum* 14.6 (1985): 356–70.

55. The excavation team consisted of field students from the Nautical Archaeology Program at Texas A&M University and archaeologists from the Virginia Historic Landmarks Commission. For details, see Steffy et al., "The *Charon* Report," in *Underwater Archaeology: The Challenge before Us,* ed. Gordon P. Watts, Jr., pp. 114–43.

56. Thomas J. Oertling, "The History and Development of Ships' Bilge Pumps, 1500–1840," (Master's thesis, Texas A&M University, 1984).

57. Jean Boudriot provides an excellent illustrated description for the coppering of French hulls in his *The Seventy-four Gun Ship,* vol. 3, pp. 241–45.

58. The excavation was conducted by the Virginia Division of Historic Landmarks under the direction of John D. Broadwater. See Broadwater, Robert M. Adams, and Marcie Renner, "The Yorktown Shipwreck Archaeological Project: An Interim Report on the Excavation of Shipwreck 44YO88," *IJNA* 14.4 (1985): 301–14.

59. Currently, there is an unpublished hull construction report on the Yorktown wreck: John William Morris III, "Site 44YO88: The Archaeological Assessment of the Hull Remains at Yorktown, Virginia," (Master's thesis, East Carolina University, 1991). Figures 5–58 and 5–59 are from this thesis.

60. David C. Switzer, "Nautical Archaeology in Penobscot Bay: The Revolutionary War Privateer *Defence,*" in *New Aspects of Naval History,* ed. Craig L. Symonds, pp. 90–101.

61. Information and illustrations dealing with the *Eagle* (through the end of this chapter) are from the reconstruction report by Kevin Crisman, published in book form as his *The Eagle: An American Brig on Lake Champlain during the War of 1812.*

62. Kevin J. Crisman, "The *Jefferson:* The History and Archaeology of an American Brig from the War of 1812," (Ph.D. diss., University of Pennsylvania, 1989). See also Crisman, "The Lake Brigs *Jefferson* and *Eagle,*" *Seaways* 2.4 (1991): 5–9.

63. Christopher F. Amer, "The Construction of the Browns Bay Vessel," (Master's thesis, Texas A&M University, 1986).

7. Recording

1. John O. Sands, *Yorktown's Captive Fleet.*

2. On occasion, they are still doing it this way. See the excellent account on frame assembly in Andy Davis, "Double-Sawn Framing," *WoodenBoat* 82 (May/June 1988): 48–59, where a somewhat different but equally functional method of timber designation is used. See also Howard I. Chapelle, *Boatbuilding: A Complete Handbook of Wooden Boat Construction.*

3. To the best of my knowledge, the UM designation was first used on the Kyrenia ship project. The expanded version described here was developed for the Serçe Limani project by Sheila Matthews, who recorded most of the hull remains.

4. See Sean McGrail, ed., *Sources and Techniques in Boat Archaeology,* pp. 165–72, where Ole Crumlin-Pedersen describes and illustrates this method as it was used to record the fragments of the Skuldelev ships in Denmark. Crumlin-Pedersen further discusses photographic reduction of such drawings to 1:10 scale. *Sources and Techniques,* incidentally, is highly recommended to readers interested in recording and researching hull remains. Although published in 1977, most of the methodology described in this collection of papers is still reliable and timely.

5. D. L. Hamilton, "INA Enters the SHARPS Era," *INA Newsletter* 15.2 (1988): 6, 7.
Peter J. A. Waddell, "Electronic Mapping of Underwater Sites," in *Underwater Archaeology Proceedings from the Society for Historical Archaeology Conference (1990),* ed. Toni Carrell, pp. 57–62.

6. Nick Rule, "The Direct Survey Method (DSM) of Underwater Survey, and Its Application Underwater," *IJNA* 18.2 (1989): 157–162.

7. Richard K. Anderson, Jr., *Guidelines for Recording Historic Ships.* This volume is a publication of the Historic American Buildings Survey/Historic American Engineering Record Division of the National Park Service, U.S. Department of the Interior. Paul Lipke, ed., *Boats: A Field Manual for Their Documentation.* Forthcoming.

8. Research and Reconstruction

1. René Burlet and Eric Rieth, "Outils et Démarches," *Histoire et Mesure* III.4 (1988): 463–89.

2. See Aleydis M. Van de Moortel, *A Cog-like Vessel from the Netherlands,* Flevobericht 331. The model was used to reconstruct the Zuyderzee vessel NZ43.

3. My involvement in the Serçe Limani project was limited to research, laboratory reconstructions, and occasional visits to the site. Actual recording and reassembly were supervised by Sheila Matthews, who did much of the work on both. The final supporting structure was designed and built by Robin C. M. Piercy; the sectional replica was designed and built by F. M. Hocker; and the theme of the museum as described here was largely the brainchild of F. H. van Doorninck, Jr.

9. Interpretation and Dissemination

1. J. Richard Steffy, "The Kyrenia Ship: An Interim Report on Its Hull Construction," *AJA* 89.1 (1985): 78.

2. Ibid., pp. 79, 80, 82.

Appendixes

1. Howard I. Chapelle, *Yacht Designing and Planning,* pp. 142–44, 203–207. Thomas C. Gillmer and Bruce Johnson, *Introduction to Naval Architecture,* pp. 291–96.

2. Howard I. Chapelle has some interesting commentary on dimensions and proportions of sailing ships in *The Search for Speed under Sail;* see especially his "Conclusions and Comments," pp. 398–414. See also Gillmer and Johnson, *Naval Architecture,* pp. 37–58, for more modern applications.

3. These coefficients and the *buertschip* coefficients to follow can be found in Frederick M. Hocker, "The Development of Bottom-based Shipbuilding Tradition in Northwestern Europe and the New World," (Ph.D. diss., Texas A&M University, 1991): table 1, table 2.

4. Chapelle, *Search for Speed,* p. 407.

5. The contract of the *Peacock* has been reprinted in H. I. Chapelle, *The History of American Sailing Ships,* pp. 365–76.

6. Most of the descriptions, weights, and other technical information provided here comes from the following publications: Gwendoline M. Lavers, *The Strength Properties of Timbers,* Forest Products Research Bulletin no. 50 (2d ed.); Department of the Environment (U.K.), *Handbook of Hardwoods* (2d ed.), rev. R. H. Farmer; Department of the Environment (U.K.), *A Handbook of Softwoods* (2d ed.); U.S. Forest Products Laboratory, *The Encyclopedia of Wood;* Russell Meiggs, *Trees and Timber in the Ancient Mediterranean World.*

7. For instance, the 200-ft, four-masted barkentine *James Tuft* and the four-masted schooner *Caroline,* contracted in Puget Sound in 1902, were both built almost exclusively of yellow fir. Their contracts can be found in Chapelle, *History of American Sailing Ships,* pp. 376–86.

8. For an especially fascinating and thorough account of the live oaking industry that served shipbuilding, see Virginia Steele Wood, *Live Oaking: Southern Timber for Tall Ships.* Much of the information in this listing was derived from her book.

ILLUSTRATED GLOSSARY OF SHIP AND BOAT TERMS

This glossary is intended to define the terminology used in this text, as well as that which researchers might be required to apply or interpret in their studies of shipwrecks and archives. It is limited to construction terminology. The reader is advised to consult one of the dictionaries listed in the bibliography for shiphandling, maneuvering, and general nautical terms. The same advice applies to specialized rigging terminology and details, although the text addresses or illustrates many of the most common rigs.

Words set in **bold type** are defined elsewhere in the glossary. Entries have been illustrated wherever possible, either within the glossary or in the text. Alternate terms or spellings are listed in brackets after the entry. Alternate definitions for a single entry are commonplace; this is the result of diffusion, varying localities, and technological progress. However, the reader is cautioned that many of the timbers and devices listed here might have had additional identifications, often the invention of the writer or in local slang; some difficulty may be experienced in identifying such entries in various documents. The confusion extends to modern publications. One marine dictionary shows the knee of the head as being located behind the gripe, while most of the others call this timber an apron and properly place the knee of the head just below the bowsprit. I have tried to sort out this confusion where possible.

Ancient ships contained structural arrangements that had disappeared by the medieval period, and therefore they remain unlisted in publications. A few of them have been assigned terms in archaeological publications; the rest I hope I have anticipated and defined accurately.

One more word of caution. Many of the illustrations in the glossary are composite drawings, in some cases including features of several vessels or vessel types in the same drawing. Unless otherwise stated, these illustrations are not intended to represent construction details of specific watercraft.

Adze [Adz] (Fig. G–8). An axe-like tool with its blade at right angles to the handle, used for shaping and dressing wood.

Amidships. The middle of a vessel, either longitudinally or transversely.

Anchor (Figs. G–1 and G–2). A wooden, stone, or metal device that, when connected to a vessel with a cable or chain, was used to secure the vessel to the bed of a waterway to prevent it from drifting.

    Anchor bed. A reinforcement or platform, fitted on the side or deck of a vessel, on which an anchor or stack of anchors was stowed.

    Best bower. One of the principal anchors of a ship, normally the one used first; in the last several centuries, it was usually the second largest anchor and was carried on the starboard bow.

    Bill. The tip of the anchor's palm; also called a *pea*, **peak**, or *pick*.

    Bower. One of the principal anchors of a vessel, permanently attached to a cable or chain and stowed ready for immediate use.

    Crown. That portion of an anchor where its arms joined the shank.

    Fluke. The pointed or chisel-shaped end of an anchor arm, which was designed to dig into the bottom.

    Grapnel (Fig. G–2h). A relatively small anchor, usually fitted with four or five arms, used variously for making fast to other vessels, snagging cables, or anchoring small boats.

    Kedge. A light anchor used for moving a vessel or temporarily holding it in a waterway.

    Palm. The triangular flat face of an anchor's fluke.

    Shank. The shaft of an anchor.

    Sheet anchor. The heaviest anchor of a large vessel, shipped in a ready position to be used for any emergency. In the later years of large sailing ships, this was the third bower and was usually carried in the starboard bow next to the best bower. It was also called the *sacred anchor*.

Shoe. A convex block of wood into which an anchor bill could be fitted to prevent damage to the ship's side when the anchor was hoisted.

Stock. A wooden, stone, or metal crosspiece near the top of and perpendicular to the shank; it was designed to cant one of the arms so that its fluke dug into the bottom.

Stream anchor. A smaller anchor, often about one-third the weight of the best bower, which was carried in the stern and used to prevent a vessel from swinging in narrow waterways.

Anchor stock planking (Fig. G–11a). A form of planking in which the longitudinal shapes of the planks resembled anchor stocks. It was similar to the **top and butt** method of planking and was intended to prevent shifting and increase the longitudinal strength of wales and other stress-bearing planks.

Apron (Fig. G–3). A curved piece of timber fixed to the after surface of the stem or to the top of the forward end of the keel and the after surface of the stem; an inner stempost.

Athwartships. Across the ship from side to side; perpendicular to the keel.

Auger (Fig. G–8). A tool used for boring holes.

Average frame spacing. *See* **Room and space**.

Back piece (Fig. G–18b). The aftermost piece of a rudder.

Back rabbet (Fig. G–4c). The upper surface of a keel rabbet or the nesting surface of a post rabbet.

Back rabbet line (Fig. G–4d). The line formed by the junction of the inner plank surface and the upper, or inner, rabbet surface.

Balanced rudder (Fig. G–18a). A rudder whose stock is placed aft of its leading edge so that the water pressure is approximately equal on its forward and after surfaces; balanced rudders require less turning power than conventional rudders.

Ballast. Heavy material, such as iron, lead, or stone, placed low in the hold to lower the center of gravity and improve stability.

Batten. A thin plank or strip of wood used to determine hull curvatures or to temporarily connect timbers during construction.

Batten clamp. *See* **Sintel**.

Baulk (balk). *See* **Beam**.

Beakhead (Fig. 5–25). A platform or projecting structure forward of the forecastle.

Beam (Figs. G–5 and G–7a–G–7e). A timber mounted athwartships to support decks and provide lateral strength; large beams were sometimes called *baulks*. See also **Breadth**.

Beam arm [Curved half-beam] (Fig. G–7a). A curved partial beam whose inboard end was scarfed or tenoned into the side of a deck beam and outboard end terminated at the shelf clamp. Beam arms were used to reinforce potentially weak areas adjacent to hatches, bitts, masts, etc. They were essentially long knees laid as half beams.

Bearding line (Fig. G–4d). The line formed by the junction of the outer garboard surface with the keel, or the outer surfaces of planking ends with the posts.

Beetle (Fig. G–8). A heavy wooden mallet used to drive treenails, wedges, etc. See also **Mallet**.

Belfry. The structure in which the ship's bell was hung. Belfries were usually mounted in the forecastle, although they sometimes appeared near the helm or mainmast; in some instances they were elaborate and ornate.

Berth deck [Birth deck] (Fig. G–5). The deck immediately below the **gundeck**.

Bevel (Fig. G–12f). The fore-and-aft angle or curvature of an inner or outer frame surface.

Beveled edge. *See* **Chamfer**.

Bevel gauge (Fig. G–8). A tool used to determine frame face bevels.

Beveling. The technique of shaping a frame timber to its correct fore-and-aft curvature.

Bilge. The area of the hull's bottom on which it would rest if grounded; generally, the outer end of the floor. When used in the plural, especially in contemporary documents, **bilges** refers to the various cavities between the frames in the floor of the hold where bilge water tends to collect.

Bilge boards. Loose boards placed over the bilges to protect cargo from bilgewater damage; see Figure 4–10 for an example of transverse bilge boards on the Serçe Limani vessel.

Bilge clamp. On ancient ships, a thick strake of ceiling fastened to the inner frame faces at or just above the turn of the bilge; thick ceiling opposite a bilge wale. See also **Ceiling**.

Bilge keel (Fig. 3–7). A secondary keel placed beneath the bilge or at the outer end of the floor. Sometimes called a **sister keel**.

Bilge ledge (Fig. 4–10). A rabbeted longitudinal timber fastened over the frames above the bilge to support transverse ceiling planking.

Bilge strake [Bilge plank] (Fig. G–5). A thick strake of planking placed at or below the turn of the bilge; its purpose was to reinforce the area of the bilge or floor heads. Infrequently it is called a bilge wale.

Binding strakes (Fig. G–5). The closest full-length strakes, or belts of strakes, to the middle of the deck. They reinforced the many openings (hatches, mast steps, pumps, etc.) between them. Binding strakes were so named only when they were thicker than the rest of the deck planks, being fitted into notches in the tops of deck beams.

Bite [Bitar (pl.)] (Fig. 4–32). An athwartship beam in a Viking vessel.

Bitt [Bit] (Fig. G–10). A strong upright post used for securing lines and cables. Figure G–10 shows several bitt arrangements.

Boat. An open vessel, usually small and without decks, intended for use in sheltered water. This term is discussed in the introduction.

Bobstay piece (Fig. G–13d). Part of the knee of the head.

Body lines. *See* **Station lines**.

Bollard timbers. *See* **Knightheads**.

Bolt. A cylindrical metal pin used to fasten ships' timbers together.

Boss. *See* **Wart**.

Bottom. The underwater portion of a fully loaded hull; also used as a general designation for a seagoing vessel.

Bow. The forward part of a hull, specifically, from the point where the sides curve inward to the stem.

Bow drill [Fiddle drill] (Fig. G–8). A device with a hollowed handle in which a spindle rotates; the spindle is connected to a drum, around which a cord is wrapped and run back and forth by means of a bow to rotate the drill bit.

Bowsprit (Figs. G–3, G–15d, G–15e, and G–15f). A spar projecting forward from the bow.

Boxing [Boxing joint] (Fig. G–11b). A type of scarf used primarily to join the keel to the stem or keel timbers to each other.

Brace (Fig. G–18). A metal housing and straps used to secure the stock of a quarter rudder to its blade. Also, the straps of a **pintle** or **gudgeon**.

Bracket. A small brace or knee used to support the gratings in the head of a ship.

Breadth. The width of a hull; sometimes called **beam**, which is technically the length of the main beam.

Breaming. *See* **Graving**.

Breast hook (Figs. G–3 and G–13). A large, horizontal knee fixed to the sides and stem to reinforce and hold them together.

Breastwork. Ballustrades along the upper decks.

Bulkhead. A vertical partition, either fore-and-aft or athwartships.

Bulwark (Fig. G–5). The side of a vessel above its upper deck.

Burden [Burthen]. The cargo capacity of a vessel.

Butt (Fig. G–11b). The lateral end of a hull plank or timber.

Butt joint (Fig. G–11b). The union of two planks or timbers whose ends were cut perpendicularly to their lengths; sometimes called *carvel joint*.

Buttock. The convex part of the hull beneath the stern deck.

Buttock lines (Figs. 2–10 and 2–11). Projections on a lines drawing that reveal vertically oriented longitudinal hull shapes. A complete description of their function is found in chapter 2.

Cable locker [Cable tier]. The compartment where the anchor cable was coiled and stored. Large vessels often had elaborate drainage systems for disposing of the seawater that seeped from recently hauled cables, including tier decks with raised beams that allowed the water to pass beneath the coils.

Caboose [Camboose]. A vessel's galley, or kitchen.

Camber [Crown] (Fig. G–5, no. 31). The arch, or convexity, of a timber; decks were usually cambered so that water would run to the sides and out the scuppers.

Cant frame [Cant timber] (Figs. G–13a and 5–59). A framing member mounted obliquely to the keel centerline in the ends of a vessel; canting provided better frame distribution and permitted more nearly rectangular cross sections of the timbers along the vessel's incurving ends.

Cap [Capping piece]. A block used to cover the exposed ends of timbers and spars.

Caprail [main rail, cap] (Fig. G–5). A timber attached to the top of a vessel's frames.

Capstan [Capstern] (Figs. 5–51, 5–56, and 8–10). A spool-shaped vertical cylinder, mounted on a spindle and bearing, turned by means of levers or bars; used for moving heavy loads, such as hoisting anchors, lifting yards, or careening vessels.

Careen. To deliberately list a vessel so that part of its bottom was exposed for caulking, cleaning, repairing, etc.

Carling [Carline] (Figs. G–7a–G–7d). Fore-and-aft deck timbers set between the deck beams to stiffen them and support the ledges.

Carrick bitt (Fig. G–10). An upright timber supporting the shaft of a windlass; also called a **carrick head** or **windlass bitt**.

Carvel-built (Fig. G–5). Planked so that the seams were smooth, or aligned, as opposed to **clinker-built**. Northern European scholars reserve "carvel-built" for frame-first forms of construction; thus, the flush-laid bottom planks of a cog are not described as "carvel" laid planks.

Carvel joint. *See* **Butt joint**.

Cathead (Fig. G–3). A beam, or crane, projecting from the bow and used for hoisting the anchor clear of the bow after it had surfaced.

Cattail. The inboard end of a cathead.

Caulk [Calk]. To drive oakum, moss, animal hair, or other fibrous material into the seams of planking and cover it with pitch to make the seams watertight. See also **luting**.

Caulking batten [Caulking lath]. A thin wooden strip used to close caulked seams and hold the caulking material in place. See also **Ribband carvel**.

Caulking iron (Fig. G–8). A chisel-shaped tool used to drive caulking into seams.

Caulking mallet (Fig. G–8). A short-handled mallet used to strike caulking irons.

Ceiling (Fig. G–5, nos. 9, 11, 12, 15, and 23). The internal planking of a vessel.

Centerboard [Drop keel, Sliding keel] (Fig. 5–67, bottom). A wooden or iron plate that could be raised and lowered within a watertight housing called the **trunk**; the trunk was built over a slot in the keel or in the hull bottom next to the keel. Centerboards increased lateral resistance and therefore reduced **leeway** when tacking or sailing off the wind.

Chamfer [Beveled edge] (Fig. G–12f). The flat, sloping surface created by slicing the edge off a timber.

Channel [Chain wale] (Fig. 5–62a). A thick, horizontal plank projecting from the side of a vessel and used to support the shrouds and keep them clear of the bulwarks.

Channel wale (Fig. 5–62a). A wale, or belt of wales, located at the line of the channels, to which the chains of the shrouds were fastened.

Charley Nobel (Fig. G–3). The chimney, or flue, of the galley hearth or stove.

Chase port (Figs. 5–56 and 5–61). A gunport placed in the bow or stern to accommodate fore-and-aft mounted guns.

Check. *See* **Shake**.

Cheek [Cheek knee] (Figs. G–3 and 3–48). On later vessels, a knee or brace between the side of the bow and the knee of the head; on ancient warships, a protuberance at the side of the stem against which the side planking was stopped.

Chine (Fig. 3–62). The angular junction of the bottom and side of a vessel; usually found on flat-bottomed hulls, or those with little deadrise. Can also refer to a longitudinal timber located just inside the junction, to which athwartships bottom planks are fastened.

Chock (Figs. G–3 and G–13). An angular block or wedge used to fill out areas between timbers or to separate them; chocks were used to fill out deadwoods and head knees, separate frames and futtocks, etc.

Cistern. A term applied variously to pump wells or to collecting basins at the discharge ends of pumps.

Clamp (Fig. G–5, nos. 18 and 25). A thick ceiling strake used to provide longitudinal strength or support deck beams; clamps were often located directly opposite the wales and acted as internal wales; a clamp that supported a deck beam was called a *shelf clamp*.

Clench [Clinch] (Fig. G–9g). To secure a nail or bolt by bending or flattening its projecting end over the surface it last penetrated; a nail whose tip and shaft were both clenched is said to be *double-clenched,* as in the fastening of ancient ship frames and planks (Fig. 3–28).

Clenched lap [Lapstrake]. *See* **Clinker-built**.

Clinker-built [Clincher-built, Clencher-built] (Figs. 4–24 and 4–32). A vessel constructed so that its outer planking overlaps, and is fastened to, the plank immediately below it. Where planks overlap the ones above them (there have been no European vessel finds to support this alleged method), the procedure is known as *reverse clinker*. The surface of a plank overlapped by a neighbor is called a **land**, and this double thickness is normally held together with closely spaced rivets or nails clenched over metal washers called **roves**. Northern European specialists limit the term "clinker-built" to vessels whose planks are rivetted together; hulls whose overlapping planks are fastened with clenched nails, as in most cog construction, are called *clenched lap* or *lapstrake* hulls.

Coak (Figs. G–9m and G–9n). A rectangular or cylindrical pin let into the ends or seams of timbers about to be joined in order to align or strengthen the union.

Coaming [Combing] (Fig. G–7c). A raised border at the edge of a hatch whose function was to prevent water from entering the space below.

Cockpit. The surgeon's compartment; the sick bay. On yachts, the well from which the vessel is directed.

Common ceiling (Fig. G–5, no. 12). The ordinary ceiling used to prevent cargo and ballast from falling between the frames; common ceiling was usually made from relatively thin planking and seldom contributed longitudinal strength to the hull structure.

Companion. A covering over a cabin hatchway.

Companion way. A stairway or ladder leading from one deck to another.

Compass timber [Compassing]. Naturally curved timbers used for frames and construction in the ends of a hull.

Copper-bottomed [Coppered]. A vessel whose bottom was sheathed in copper to prevent fouling and worm infestation.

Copper fastened. A vessel whose fastenings were made of copper.

Cordage. A general term for ropes and cables.

Counter (Fig. G–14). Technically, the transverse section between the bottom of the stern and the wing transom. However, many documents and drawings refer to the counter as the entire transverse area between the top of the sternpost and the rail or taffrail.

Counter timbers (Figs. G–14a–G–14c). Vertical timbers framing the counter.

Crab. A small capstan, usually portable and lacking a drumhead at the top of its barrel.

Cradle. A structure for supporting a vessel out of water.

Crone (Fig. 4–26). An English translation of an old Norse term denoting the elongated mast steps on Viking vessels.

Crossbeam (Fig. G–10). A substantial timber placed across a pair of bitts.

Cross pillar. *See* **Pillar**.

Crotch [Crotch timber] (Fig. 5–17). A V-shaped or Y-shaped frame or floor timber made from the crotch of a tree; usually mounted on the keel or deadwood in the ends of a vessel.

Crow [Crow bar] (Fig. G–8). A strong iron bar, pointed or chisel-shaped at one end, used for prying or moving heavy timbers.

Crown. *See* **Camber**.

Crutch (Figs. G–3 and G–15a). A bracing timber used to prevent a mast step from shifting laterally; also, a curved or angular timber, similar to a breast hook and used for a similar purpose in the lower part of the stern. On modern vessels, a support for booms at rest.

Cuddy. A cabin or shelter in the forward part of a small vessel.

Curved scarf [Curved butt, S-scarf] (Fig. G–11). The union of two planks or timbers whose ends were canted in the shapes of reverse curves.

Cutting-down line. The elevations of the tops of the floor timbers and deadwoods; in most cases, the curved line formed by the bottom of the keelson, stemson, and sternson.

Cutwater (Fig. G–3). The forwardmost part of the stem; the stem piece or nosing that parts the water.

Dagger knee (Figs. G–3 and G–5). A knee set angularly on the inside of the hull; a knee that is neither vertical or horizontal.

Dagger piece. Any piece of timber, but usually a frame timber, mounted at an angle to the vertical or horizontal planes.

Dead flat. The flat part of the hull in the area of the midship frame; generally, the widest part of the hull, which separated the forward part from the after part.

Deadrise (Fig. G–5). The amount of elevation, or rising, of the floor above the horizontal plane; the difference between the height of the bilge and the height of the keel rabbet.

Deadwood (Fig. G–3). Blocks of timber assembled on top of the keel, usually in the ends of the hull, to fill out the narrow parts of a vessel's body. See also **Rising wood**.

Deadwood knee (Fig. G–3). A knee placed within the deadwood to support the sternpost.

Deadwork. The part of the hull above the full-load waterline.

Deal. A thin plank of fir or pine, most commonly used to sheath hulls.

Deck beam. *See* **Beam**.

Deck hook. (Figs. 5–50 and G–13b). A breast hook placed beneath a deck to support it at or near the stem.

Deck transom (Fig. G–14d). A transom that supported the after ends of deck planks.

Depth of hold. The distance between either the bottom of the main deck or the bottom of its beams and the limber boards, measured at the midship frame.

Diagonal braces (Fig. 5–20). Pillars or posts set angularly in the hull to stiffen it; although used in pairs, they differed from cross pillars in that each brace occupied only one side of the hull.

Diagonal framing. Frames or riders placed diagonally over the regular frames or ceiling to provide additional stiffening to a hull.

Diagonals (Fig. 2–10). Lines on a hull drawing representing specific oblique sections of the hull. Chapter 2 has a complete description of their functions.

Diagonal scarf [Diagonal butt] (Fig. G–11b). An angular junction of two planks or timbers.

Diminishing strakes (Fig. G–5). Belts of outer planking above and below the wales that were successively reduced in thickness, providing a more gradual transition from the protrusion of the wales to the thickness of the side planking.

Double-ender. A vessel whose bow and stern have approximately the same horizontal shape, such as rounded, pointed, or square ends.

Double framing (Fig. G–12). A general term signifying frames composed of two rows of overlapping futtocks.

Dowel [Dowel pin] (Fig. G–9n). A cylindrical piece of wood (of constant diameter) used to align two members by being sunk into each. A cylindrical coak. Unlike treenails and pegs, dowels served an alignment function only, additional fastenings being necessary to prevent separation of the joint.

Draft [Draught]. The depth to which a hull is immersed; also, a drawing or plan.

Draft marks [Draught marks, Load lines] (Fig. 5–58). Figures or lines cut into, or attached to, the stem and sternpost to indicate the depth at which each end of the hull is immersed.

Drag. The difference between the draft of a vessel's stern and its bow.

Drawknife (Fig. G–8). A knife with two handles mounted at right angles to the blade; drawknives are used for shaping and beveling.

Drift. The difference between the diameters of a bored hole and the bolt that is driven into it.

Drift bolt. A cylindrical bolt, headed on one end, that is slightly larger in diameter than the hole into which it is driven.

Drop keel [Sliding keel]. *See* **Centerboard**.

Drop strake (Fig. G–11). A strake of planking that is discontinued near the bow or stern because of decreasing hull surface area. A central stealer.

Dunnage. Brushwood, scrapwood, or other loose material laid in the hold to protect the cargo from water damage or prevent it from shifting, or to protect the ceiling from abrasion.

Ekeing [Lengthening piece] (Fig. G–13b). A timber used to lengthen another timber, such as the extension of a deck hook or knee.

Entrance [Entry]. The foremost underwater part of a vessel.

Eye bolt (Fig. G–9i). A bolt with a circular opening at one end.

Eyes. A name sometimes given to the hawse holes or the areas around them; on ancient ships, ocular decorations at the same locations.

Fair. To shape or adjust a timber or timbers to the correct curvature or location; also, to correct discrepancies in a ship's drawings.

Fair curve [Fair line]. A shape or line whose curvature agrees with the mold loft or that is mechanically acceptable and seaworthy.

Fall home. *See* **Tumblehome**.

False keel [Shoe] (Figs. G–3, G–4a, G–4b, and G–5). A plank, timber, or timbers attached to the bottom of the keel to protect it in the event of grounding or hauling; on large ships, false keels were sometimes made quite thick in order to increase the size and strength of the keel. In North America from the eighteenth century onward, and perhaps in other areas, false keels were called **shoes**.

False keelson. *See* **Rider keelson**.

False stem (Fig. 5–42). An outer timber fixed to the forward surface of the stem to strengthen or protect it, or to provide better symmetry to the cutwater. Also, a name sometimes given to the apron in English documents.

False sternpost (Fig. 3–38). A member attached to the after surface of the sternpost to reinforce or protect it.

Fashion piece [fashion timber] (Fig. G–14a). A timber that framed the shape of the stern.

Fay. To fit or join timbers closely together.

Figure piece (G–13d). A name sometimes given to the upper piece of the knee of the head, upon which the figurehead rested.

Filling frame (Fig. G–12e). A frame composed of a single row of timbers, usually scarfed together, that filled the space between the main, or double-rowed, frames of a large ship.

Filling piece [Filler] (Fig. G–12e). A single timber or block used to fill out an area, such as the side of a gunport where it did not coincide with a frame, or in the spaces between frames to maintain rigidity.

Fine lines. A descriptive term applied to a vessel with a sharp entrance and a narrow hull.

Fish (Fig. 4–26). An English term for the modern Norwegian word describing the fishtail-shaped mast partners on Viking vessels.

Fish plate (Fig. G–9). A metal plate used to join two timbers externally.

Flare. The upward and outward curvature of a vessel's bows; a curved outfall.

Flat scarf (Fig. G–11b). The union of two planks or timbers whose diagonal ends were nibbed (cut off)

perpendicular to their lengths. When planking is scarfed vertically, the ends are not nibbed.

Floor. The bottom of a vessel between the upward turns of its bilges.

Floor head. The outer extremity of a floor timber.

Floor head line. *See* **Rising line**.

Floor ribband [Floor ribbon]. The floor rising line; specifically, a ribband or batten fastened to the outside of the frames at the heads of the floor timbers; used for fairing and to determine the shapes and lengths of intermediate frames.

Floor timber (Fig. G–12). A frame timber that crossed the keel and spanned the bottom; the central piece of a compound frame.

Flush deck. A deck running continuously from bow to stern, without breaks or raised elements.

Foot wale [Footwaleing] (Fig. G–5, no. 15). Thick longitudinal strakes of ceiling located at or near the floor head line or turn of the bilge. Some eighteenth-century English documents called the thick strakes next to the limber strake, or sometimes all of the ceiling, **footwaleing**, in which case the heavy strakes near the turn of the bilge were known as **thick stuff**.

Forecastle. Variously, a short, raised foredeck, the forward part of the upper deck between the foremast and the stem, or the quarters below the foredeck.

Forefoot (Fig. G–3). A curved piece between the forward end of the keel and the knee of the head; the **gripe**. In some documents describing large ships, it is the name given to the rounded forward portion of the gripe, inserted as a separate piece.

Fore hood. The end of a plank at the stem rabbet.

Forelock bolt (Fig. G–9h). An iron bolt with a head on one end and a narrow slot at the other; secured by placing a washer over its protruding end and driving a flat wedge, called a **forelock**, into the slot. Forelock bolts were one of the most popular of shipbuilding fastenings, being commonly used to secure major timbers from Roman times until the nineteenth century.

Forepeak. The forward extremity of the hold.

Frame (Fig. G–12). A transverse timber, or line or assembly of timbers, that described the body shape of a vessel and to which the planking and ceiling were fastened. Frames were sometimes called **timbers** or, erroneously, ribs (*see* **Rib**). Ancient ships often had frames composed of lines of unconnected timbers; later ships usually had compound frames composed of **floor timbers**, **futtocks**, and **top timbers**. **Square frames** were those set perpendicular to the keel; in the bow and stern there were **cant frames**, running obliquely to the keel. Forward of the cant frames and fayed to them, in large round-bowed vessels, were the frames running parallel to the keel and stem, sometimes called **knuckle timbers**; more accurately, these were the **hawse pieces** and **knight heads**, the latter being the frames adjacent to the apron or stemson that extended above the deck to form bitts and support the bowsprit. The aftermost frames were the **fashion pieces**, which shaped the stern. Frame details are illustrated in Figs. G–3, G–5, G–12, G–13, and G–14.

Frame head. *See* **Timber head**.

Frame heel. *See* **Timber heel**.

Freeboard. The distance between the waterline and upper deck.

Furring. *See* **Sheathing**.

Futtock (Fig. G–12). A frame timber other than a floor timber, half-frame, or top timber; one of the middle pieces of a frame.

Futtock plank. In English shipbuilding, the first ceiling plank next to the limber strake.

Gallery. A balcony projecting from the stern or quarter of a large ship.

Galley. A seagoing vessel propelled primarily by oars, but usually one that also could be sailed when necessary. Also, a name given to a vessel's kitchen.

Gammoning hole [Gammoning slot] (Fig. G–13d). An opening in the knee of the head through which the bowsprit gammoning (lashing) passed.

Gammoning knee. A curved timber attached to the top of a vessel's stem, to which the bowsprit was lashed; sometimes used in lieu of a more elaborate knee of the head.

Gammon piece (Fig. G–13d). The part of the knee of the head containing the gammoning hole.

Garboard strake [Garboard] (Figs. G–4 and G–5). The strake of planking next to the keel; the lowest plank. Also, the lowest side strake of a flat-bottomed hull.

Girdling [Girding]. The practice of adding timber to the sides of ships to increase their breadth and thereby improve stability. The practice was most common on sixteenth- and seventeenth-century British vessels and was employed to overcome design flaws due to inability to calculate metacentric height.

Grating. A latticework hatch cover used for light and ventilation. Also, a term applied to the latticework deck in the heads of large ships.

Graving [Breaming]. The practice of cleaning a hull's bottom by burning barnacles, grass, and other foul material preparatory to recoating it with tar, sulphur, etc. The vessel was careened or drydocked to perform this task.

Graving iron (Fig. G–8). A hook-like tool used for removing old caulking.

Graving piece (Fig. G–11a). A wooden patch, or insert, let into a damaged or rotted plank.

Gripe (Fig. G–3). A curved piece joining the forward end of the keel to the lower end of the knee of the head. Generally, the same as **forefoot**.

Gudgeon (Fig. G–18b). A metal bracket attached to the sternpost into which a rudder **pintle** was hung; the female part of a rudder hinge.

Gundeck (Fig. G–6). The deck where the guns were located; large ships had as many as three gundecks (a three-decker), called the lower, middle, and upper gundecks.

Gunport framing. (Fig. G–3). The **sills**, **lintles**, and **filling pieces** that shape and reinforce the gunports.

Gunwale [Gunnel] (Fig. G–5, no. 35). The upper edge of a vessel's side. In sixteenth-century vessels, the wale against which the guns rest.

Half beam (Figs. G–7c and G–7d). A beam extending from the side to a hatch or other obstruction. See also **beam arm**.

Half-frame (Figs. 3–34, 4–5, and 5–53). A frame whose heel began at or near one side of the keel or deadwood and spanned part or all of that side of the hull; half-frames normally were used in pairs.

Hanging knee (Fig. G–5, no. 29). A vertical angular timber used to reinforce the junction of a beam and the side.

Harpins [Harpings]. The forward planks of wales that were strengthened by increased thickness near the stem; usually found on large, round-bowed vessels. Also, a term applied to specially shaped battens fitted to the cant frames or other areas of extreme curvature during construction; used to check and adjust frame bevels.

Hatch [Hatchway] (Fig. G–7c). A rectangular opening in a vessel's deck.

Hatch beam (Fig. G–7c). A removable beam that supported the hatch cover and provided lateral strength when the hatch was not in use.

Hatch coaming. *See* **Coaming**.

Hawse block. A wooden plug used to close a hawse hole in heavy weather.

Hawse bolster. One of the heavy planks fixed around or below the hawse holes to protect the hull planking.

Hawse hole (Fig. G–3). A cylindrical hole in the bow through which the anchor cable passed.

Hawse hook. A breast hook above the upper foredeck; usually, the highest breast hook.

Hawse piece [Hawse timber] (Figs. G–3 and G–13a). A fore-and-aft framing timber whose heel was fayed to the forwardmost cant frame and which reinforced the bow of a large, round-bowed vessel; hawse pieces were so named because the hawse holes were partially cut through them.

Hawse pipe. The tube through which the anchor cable passed between the hawse hole and windlass or capstan deck.

Hawser. A strong rope used to tow or tie up a vessel.

Head. In a general sense, the forward part of a vessel; the extreme bow area; also, a name sometimes given to the **figurehead** or, on later vessels, to the latrine. See also **Timber head**.

Head knee. Sometimes a designation for **cheek knee** (**cheek**), but more frequently an alternate term for **knee of the head**.

Head ledge (Fig. G–7c). An athwartships hatch coaming.

Headrails (Fig. G–3). Curved rails extending from the bow to the knee of the head.

Head timber. Any small timber in the head, but usually those supporting the gratings.

Heel (Fig. 5–17). The junction of the keel and sternpost; also, an angular timber connecting the keel to the sternpost. Separate heel timbers on cogs and cog-like vessels are most frequently called **hooks**.

Heel knee [Stern knee] (Fig. 5–17). An angular timber reinforcing the junction between the keel and the sternpost.

Helm. The tiller or steering wheel; in a general context, the wheel, tiller, and rudder.

Helm port [Rudder hole] (Figs. G–14a and G–14c). The opening in the stern where the rudder stock entered the hull.

Helm port transom (Figs. G–14a and G–14c). The timber reinforcing the helm port.

Hog [Hogging]. The strain on a hull that causes its ends to droop.

Hog [Hog timber]. *See* **Rising wood**.

Hogging truss [Hogging frame]. A strong fore-and-aft framework built into a vessel to prevent hogging; hogging trusses were most commonly seen in canal boats and other long inland vessels. In ancient vessels, it was a strong cable supported by forked posts and attached to the ends of the hull to serve the same purpose (see Fig. 3–6).

Hold (Fig. G–6). In a general sense, the interior of a hull. The term is more commonly used to describe the part of a merchant ship's interior where the cargo and ballast were stowed or, on a warship, the room below the deck where stores and ballast were kept.

Hooding ends [Hoods, Hood ends]. The ends of planks that fit into the stem and sternpost rabbets; hooding ends were sometimes reduced in thickness to permit a better join with the posts.

Hook (Fig. 4–40a). A knee-like timber that connected the keel or central plank to the stem or sternpost. A northern European designation, it is used almost exclusively in reference to cogs and cog-like vessels. In later English documents, bow hooks were called **gripes**; stern hooks were called **heels**.

Hook and butt (Fig. G–11a). A method of planking whereby one edge of the plank was straight while its opposite side had sloping edges locked by a hook. Infrequently, the term was also used to denote a hook scarf.

Hook bolt (Fig. G–9). A bolt with a hook-shaped head used for securing detachable lines, tackle, and other gear.

Hook scarf (Fig. G–11b). The union of two planks or timbers whose angular ends are offset to lock the joint. Hook scarfs are sometimes locked with wedges, or keys.

Horning [to horn]. A process by which frames were aligned to assure that they were level and exactly perpendicular to the keel. *See* **Horning pole** for a description of the process.

Horning pole (Horning board, Horning line). A batten, pole, or line used to align frames; one end was mounted over the keel centerline, or atop the stem or sternpost, while the other end was marked and swung across each frame head to ensure that each side of the frame was equidistant from, and perpendicular to, the keel centerline.

Horseshoe [Horseshoe clamp, plate] (Figs. G–3 and G–9l). A U-shaped iron plate fastened across the seam of the stem and forefoot to strengthen it.

Horsing. A term used to describe the process of driving caulking into planking seams.

Hypozomata. A cable or assembly of cables installed in ancient galleys to overcome hogging.

Inner stempost. The inner timber or timbers of a double-layered stem; unlike an apron, an inner stempost ends at the keel-stem scarf; see Figure 3–24 for an example of the Kyrenia ship's inner stempost.

Inner sternpost (Fig. G–14). A vertical timber attached to the forward surface of the sternpost to increase its strength, and in some cases, to support the transoms.

Intermediate timbers (Figs. 3–23 and 3–34). Those individual timbers installed between the sequential frames for additional localized strength. They could span part of the bottom, turn of the bilge, or side. The term applies primarily to ancient ships and inshore craft, where they reinforced the areas around beams, mast steps, bilge sumps, etc., or extended upward as frames for bulkheads and weather screens.

Inverted knee. *See* **Standing knee**.

Iron knee. *See* **Plate knee**.

Jeer bitts (Fig. G–10). Upright posts used for staying the various courses or halyards.

Jib-boom. A spar extending the length of the **bowsprit**.

Joggles (Fig. 3–3). Notches cut into the surface or edge of a timber, as in the exterior frame surfaces of clinker-built hulls or in the edges of some ancient Egyptian hull planks.

Keel (Figs. G–3 and G–4). The main longitudinal timber of most hulls, upon which the frames, deadwoods, and ends of the hull were mounted; the backbone of the hull.

Keel plank [Central plank, Kingplank]. A central hull plank that was substantially thicker than the rest of the bottom planking and whose breadth was at least twice as great as its thickness; a thick bottom plank used in lieu of a **keel**.

Keelson [Kelson] (Figs. G–3, G–4a, and G–4b). An internal longitudinal timber or line of timbers, mounted atop the frames along the centerline of the keel, that provided additional longitudinal strength to the bottom of the hull; an internal keel.

Most commonly, a single keelson was installed that was no larger than the keel. On very large vessels, however, various combinations of as many as a dozen keelsons were assembled. Where extra molding was required, one or more additional keelsons, called **rider keelsons** or **false keelsons**, were bolted to the top of the main keelson. They could be of identical size to, or smaller than, the main keelson. Auxiliary keelsons bolted along-side the main keelson were known as *sister*, (U.S.), *side, auxiliary*, or *assistant keelsons*. However, care should be exercised in interpreting the various keelsons from contracts. For instance, some nineteenth-century American contracts for large schooners refer to the keelson above the main keelson as the sister, and the one above that as the assistant sister keelson. On occasion, large square timbers were placed at the floor head line or near the bilge, usually above the bilge keels. These were called **bilge keelsons** or, in some British document, **sister keelsons**. Secondary keelsons did not necessarily run the full length of the hull, terminating at the ends of the hold, the last square frames, or some other appropriate location. Figure G–4 illustrates some typical arrangements.

Keel staple [Keel clamp] (Figs. G–3 and G–4a). A large metal staple used to attach the false keel to the keel.

Kevel head. The extension of a frame or top timber above the bulwarks to form a bitt, to which ropes were secured.

Kingplank [Central strake, Kingstrake]. Variously, the central strake of a flush deck or the central strake of a hull without a keel.

Knee [Knee timber] (Figs. G–5, nos. 17, 19, and 29; G–7a, G–7b, G–7c, and G–7e). An angular piece of timber used to reinforce the junction of two surfaces of different planes; usually made from the crotch of a tree where two large branches intersected, or where a branch or root joined the trunk. See also **Dagger knee, Hanging knee, Lodging knee**, and **Standing knee**.

Knee of the head [Head knee] (Fig. G–13d). A knee or knee-shaped structure, fixed to the forward surface of the stem, that formed the cutwater at its lower end and supported the headrails and figurehead at its upper end.

Knightheads (Figs. G–3 and G–13a). The forwardmost frame timbers, which ran parallel to the stem, their heels being fayed to the forwardmost cant frames

and their heads extending above deck level to form bitts that supported the bowsprit between them. Also, a name given to a pair of bitts, located just aft of the foremast on merchant ships, that supported the ends of the windlass, or to any bitt whose upper end was carved in the shape of a human head.

Knuckle. A sharp angle in a frame.

Knuckle timbers (Fig. G–13a). A name sometimes applied to the fore and aft frames in the bow of a round-bowed ship. The **hawse pieces** and **knightheads**.

Land. The portion of a plank that is overlapped by another on a clinker-built vessel.

Lapstrake [Clenched lap]. *See* **Clinker-built**.

Larboard. *See* **Port**.

Ledge (Figs. G–7a and G–7b). A short beam set between and parallel to the deck beams to provide intermediate support of the deck; the ends of ledges were supported by **carlings, clamps**, or **lodging knees**.

Leeboard. A large plate, or assembly of timbers, mounted on the side of a hull and lowered when sailing off the wind to increase lateral resistance and reduce **leeway**.

Leeway. The sideways drift of a vessel when sailing with the wind abeam.

Lengthening piece. *See* **Ekeing**.

Level lines. Another name for the **waterlines** on hull plans; they described the horizontal sections of the hull.

Light [Light port]. An opening in a vessel's side or deck, usually glazed, to let light into a compartment.

Limber boards (Fig. G–5, no. 8). Ceiling planks next to the keelson which could be removed to clean the limbers; on some ancient vessels, limber boards were laid transversely above the centerline of the keel (see Fig. 3–31). Holes or slots were sometimes cut into limber boards so that they could be lifted more easily.

Limber holes [Watercourses] (Figs. G–5, no. 10, and G–12). Apertures cut in the bottom surfaces of frames over, or on either side of, the keel to allow water to drain into the pump well.

Limber ledges (Fig. 3–31). Rabbeted timbers running parallel to the keel and atop the floor timbers for the purpose of supporting transverse ceiling planks.

Limbers. Watercourses or channels alongside or central to the keel or keelson, through which water could drain into the pump well.

Limber strake (Fig. G–5, no. 9). The lowest permanent ceiling strake, fastened to the tops of the frames next to the limber boards and keelson.

Lines [Hull lines]. The various shapes of a hull; expressed graphically, a set of geometric projections, usually arranged in three views, that illustrates the shape of a vessel's hull. A description of lines drawings is in chapter 2.

Lining (Fig. G–5). The common ceiling of the orlop, berthing, and gun decks of ships, set between the spirketting and the clamps. The lining was frequently called **quickwork**, a term more commonly used in British documents.

Lintle (Fig. G–3). The upper horizontal timber framing a gunport, large square light, or gallery door.

Load line. In some cases the term **load line** denoted full-load draft. *See* **Draft marks**.

Locked pintle. A **pintle** that was flanged or keyed in order to prevent the rudder from accidentally unshipping.

Lodging knee [Lodge knee] (Figs. G–5, no. 19, G–7a, and G–7b). A horizontal, angular timber used to reinforce two perpendicular beams or the junction of a beam and the side of the hull.

Longitudinal. *See* **Stringer**.

Loof. The after part of the bow, where the side began curving inward toward the stem.

Loom. Another term for the stock of a quarter rudder. Also, the stock, or pole piece, of an oar or sweep.

Luting. A term used frequently to describe the caulking of lapstrake (clinker-built) hulls. In most cases, animal hair, wool, or moss was soaked in pitch or resin and laid in a **luting cove**, which was cut in the lower inside surface of the overlapping plank. Luting generally refers to caulking inserted between two hull members before they were assembled, as opposed to driven caulking (see **Caulk**). The term is also applied to any plastic material used between two adjacent members.

Main. In shipbuilding, the adjective applied to the most important timbers, or those having the greatest cross-sectional area; thus, on ancient vessels the main wale was usually the lowest and largest, while on later warships it was the one below the gunports; also, main breadth, main hatch, main hold, main keelson, etc.

Main frame. A term sometimes applied to frames composed of two rows of futtocks to distinguish them from filling frames, the single-rowed frames placed between them; it applies to larger vessels of the last few centuries. The term was also used infrequently to denote the **midship frame**.

Main piece (Fig. G–13). The longest and largest timber in the knee of the head. Also, a term sometimes applied to the main vertical timber, or stock, of a rudder (Fig. G–18b).

Mallet (Fig. G–8). A large hammer with a short handle and a cylindrical wooden head, sometimes hooped with iron to prevent it from splitting, used for caulking (caulking mallet) and general shipwrightery. The heaviest mallets were also called **beetles**.

Manger. A small compartment, located just inside the hawse hole, whose after bulkhead (called a **manger board**) diverted water entering the hawse hole into the limbers.

Margin plank. *See* **Nibbing strake**.

Mast carlings (Fig. G–7d). Fore-and-aft beams that helped support a mast where it pierced a deck; also called **mast partners**. *See* **Partners**.

Mast partner (Figs. G–7d and 5–50). *See* **Partners** and **Mast carlings**.

Mast step (Figs. G–15a–G–15c). A mortise cut into the top of a keelson or large floor timber, or a mortised wooden block or assembly of blocks mounted on the floor timbers or keelson, into which the tenoned heel of a mast was seated. Various types of mast steps are shown in Figure G–15 and throughout chapters 3, 4, and 5.

Maul (Fig. G–8). A heavy wood or iron hammer, primarily used to drive large bolts.

Meginhufr (Figs. 4–27 and 4–31). A thick plank separating the bottom, or *lower ship*, of a Viking hull from its sides. Either rectangular or L-shaped in cross-section, meginhufrs evolved from the triangular-sectioned sheer strakes of earlier, simpler Norse hulls.

Metacenter. The intersection of a vertical line drawn through the center of gravity of a vessel when it is stable with a vertical line drawn through its center of buoyancy when the vessel is heeled. See chapter 2 for a description of its application.

Midship [Midships]. A contraction of **amidships** and consequently, in a general sense, it refers to the middle of the ship. In construction, however, it is often used as an adjective referring to the broadest part of the hull, wherever it may be.

Midship beam (Fig. G–5, no. 30). The longest beam in a vessel, located at or near the **midship bend**.

Midship bend (Fig. G–5). The broadest part of the hull; the widest body shape, formed by the centerline of the **midship frame**.

Midship flat [Midship body, Midsection, Midship section]. The extent of the broadest part of the hull, formed by the midship frame and all adjacent frames of the same breadth.

Midship frame (Fig. G–5). The broadest frame in the hull; the frame representing the midship shape on the body plan.

Mold [Mould] (Fig. G–16). A pattern used to determine the shapes of frames and other compass timbers. Molds were usually made from thin, flexible pieces of wood. Convex molds were called *bend molds,* concave molds were known as *hollow molds,* and *compound* or *reverse molds* included entire frame shapes. The degree of bevel and other pertinent information was written on the molds. The process of shaping outer frame surfaces with molds was known as **beveling**. Figure G–16 illustrates several types of molds. See also **Whole molding**.

Molded [Molded dimension]. The various dimensions of timbers as seen from the sheer and body views of construction plans; the dimensions determined by the molds. Thus, the vertical surfaces (the sides) of keels, the fore-and-aft sides of the posts, the vertical or athwartships surfaces of frames, etc. Normally, timbers are expressed in sided and molded dimensions, while planks and wales are listed in thicknesses and widths. Molded and sided dimensions are used because of the changing orientation of timbers, such as frames, where "thick" and "wide" or "height" and "depth" become confusing.

Molded depth. The depth of a hull, measured between the top of the upper deck beams at the side and a line parallel to the top of the keel.

Molding. *See* **Mold** and **Whole molding**.

Mold loft. A protected area or building in a shipyard where the hull lines, from which the molds were produced, were drawn full size on a specially prepared flat surface.

Mortise (Fig. G–17). A cavity cut into a timber to receive a tenon. Large mortises were sometimes referred to as *steps*.

Mortise-and-tenon joint (Fig. G–17). A union of planks or timbers by which a projecting piece (tenon) was fitted into one or more cavities (mortises) of corresponding size. The most common types are:

Fixed tenon and single mortise (Fig. G–17a). A tenon was shaped from the end on one timber and inserted into the mortise of the other. When the tenon of a large vertical timber was left unlocked, as in masts, and sternposts, it was said to be stepped.

Free tenon and two mortises (Fig. G–17b). The most common method of edge-joining planking in ancient and early medieval vessels in the Mediterranean area, it also was used to secure adjoining surfaces of parallel timbers, such as stems and floor timber chocks. Corresponding mortises were cut into each planking edge; a single hardwood tenon was inserted into the lower plank and the adjacent plank fitted over the protruding tenon. In many instances, the joint was locked by driving tapered hardwood pegs into holes drilled near each strake or timber edge.

Free tenon and three or more mortises (Fig. G–17c). Used in superstructure fabrications or places where hull planking was too narrow to provide sufficient seating for the desired tenon length.

Although small planking joints whose tenons are unpegged and contribute no structural strength are essentially **coak joints**, the term mortise-and-tenon joint has become universally accepted for all such forms of edge joinery.

Mortising chisel (Fig. G–8). A specialized chisel used for shaping narrow mortises.

Narrowing line (Fig. 5–19). A curved line on the half-breadth drawing of a hull, designating the curve of maximum breadth or the ends of the floor timbers throughout the length of the hull. The former was called the *maximum breadth line;* the latter was known as the *breadth of floor line*. See chapter 5 for details.

Nib [Nibbing end] (Fig. G–7f). The practice of squaring the ends of deck planks where they terminated at the sides of the hull to avoid fine angles and subsequent splitting and distortion.

Nibbing strake [Margin plank] (Fig. G–7f). A plank running adjacent to the waterways in the ends of a vessel, into which the nibbed ends of deck planks were fitted. English documents most frequently referred to this timber as a margin plank; American contracts more commonly called it a nibbing strake.

Oakum [Oakham]. Caulking material made from rope junk, old rope, and rope scraps; it was unwound, picked apart, and the fibers were rolled and soaked in pitch before being driven into planking seams.

Oar port (Fig. G–3). An opening in a vessel's side through which the looms of oars or sweeps passed. See also **sweep port**.

Orlop deck (Fig. G–6). The lowest deck of a large ship.

Outboard. Situated near or on the outer side of a vessel; toward the outer side.

Outer stem. (Fig. 3–24). A name sometimes given to the main stempost or to the forward layer of timbers in a double-layered stem.

Outfall. The outward slant of a vessel's sides. See also **flare**.

Overhang. The part of a vessel's stern that projects aft of the rudder stock.

Packing piece (Fig. G–7a). A short piece of timber used to fill open areas between structural timbers; used most frequently at the sides between deck beams or lodging knees.

Parcel (Fig. 5–14b). To surround or enclose with strips of flexible material, as in the reinforcement of caulked planking seams (usually lead strips) or between ropes and their servings (usually strips of canvas).

Partners (Fig. G–7d). The timbers surrounding the deck openings for masts, pumps, bitts, and capstans; their primary purpose was to strengthen the deck around the opening and counteract strain. Partners were also used on occasion to steady masts on undecked vessels.

Patch tenon (Fig. G–17d). In ancient vessels, a headed tenon inserted from the exterior or interior surface of a plank. Patch tenons were normally used in the replacement of rotten or damaged planking. The name comes from their installed appearance as square patches in the sides of hulls.

Pay. To coat; to cover a hull bottom with a protective layer of pitch, resin, sulphur, etc.

Peak. The upper portions of the narrow ends of a vessel; cited individually in some documents as **forepeak**

and **afterpeak**. Also, a term used to designate the tip of an **anchor palm**.

Peg [Tenon peg] (Fig. G–17b–d). A tapered wooden pin driven into a pre-drilled hole to fasten two members or lock a joint. Pegs came in a variety of sizes and tapers; they could have square, round, or multi-sided cross sections. The important difference between dowels and pegs in ancient construction was that the former were of constant diameter and lightly set, while the latter were tapered and driven with appreciable force. The most common use of pegs in ancient construction was the locking of mortise-and-tenon joints.

Pillar (Fig. G–6). Large vertical stanchion, usually turned or dressed for aesthetic reasons, used to support deck beams or reinforce potentially weak areas. By the seventeenth century, pairs of pillars, called **cross pillars**, were set diagonally across the hull to provide transverse strength.

Pin rail. A long rack, usually attached to the inside of bulwarks, for holding belaying pins; a short pin rail was called a pin rack.

Pintle (Fig. G–18). A vertical pin at the forward edge of a stern-hung rudder that fit into a gudgeon on the sternpost to form a hinge. On most vessels, they were welded or cast to a bracket whose arms were fastened to the sides of the rudder.

Pitch [Tar]. A dark, sticky substance used in caulking seams or spread over the inner or outer surfaces of hulls as waterproofing and protection against some forms of marine life. Pitches were variously derived from the resins of certain evergreen trees; from bitumens, such as mineral pitches; or from the distillation of coal tar, wood tar, etc.

Planking (Fig. G–5). The outer lining, or shell, of a hull.

Planking strake [Strake, Streake]. A continuous line of planks, usually running from bow to stern; the sum of a row of planks.

Planksheer [Sheer plank] (Fig. G–5). The strake that described the sheer line of a vessel, attached to the toptimbers from stem to stern at the level of the upper deck. Also, in various times and places, the name given to the uppermost continuous strake of side planking or the upper edge of the uppermost strake. In later English documents, a sheer rail or one of the drift rails.

Plate knee [Plate] (Fig. G–7e). A knee made from iron plate. Normally superimposed over a timber or wooden chock, iron knees were introduced in the latter part of the eighteenth century.

Plug treenail (Fig. 3–28). A piece of straight-grained wood through which metal fastenings were driven. In some cases, pilot holes are said to have been pre-bored through their lengths. They were not driven into the holes of the planks, but fit rather loosely and expanded tightly when the nails were driven through them. Plug treenails were commonly used on the exterior hull surfaces of ancient ships to prevent leakage and splitting of the planks around the fastenings.

Poop [Poopdeck]. The highest and aftermost deck of a ship.

Port [Port side, Larboard]. The left side of a vessel when facing forward.

Pump well [Sump] (Fig. G–3). The cavity or compartment in the bottom of a hull, usually near amidships, where bilgewater collected and from which it was pumped out or bailed. Wells ranged from simple sumps between frames to watertight compartments extending the full height of the hold.

Quarter. The after part of a vessel's side.

Quarterdeck. The after part of the upper deck, from the mainmast to the poop.

Quarter gallery. A small balcony on the side of a ship near its stern.

Quarter rails: Rails, balustrades, or planking running along the quarterdeck.

Quarter rudder. *See* **Rudder**.

Quarter timber. A frame in a vessel's quarter.

Quickwork (Fig. G–5). The common ceiling of the orlop, berthing, and upper decks as well as the gundeck. It was so named because it did not require caulking or precision joinery and therefore could be erected comparatively quickly. See also **Lining**.

Rabbet (Figs. G–3 and G–4). A groove or cut made in a piece of timber in such a way that the edges of another piece could be fit into it to make a tight joint. Generally, the term refers to the grooves cut into the sides of the keel, stem, and sternpost, into which the garboards and hooding ends of the outer planking were seated.

Rabbet plane (Fig. G–8). A plane used in smoothing rabbets.

Rag bolt (Fig. G–9). A bolt whose shaft was barbed to prevent it from working out of its hole.

Rail of the head. *See* **Headrails**.

Rake. The inclination of the stem and sternpost beyond the ends of the keel; also, the inclination of the masts from the perpendicular.

Ram (Fig. 3–44). A strong projection on the bow of an ancient warship, usually sheathed in metal, used as a weapon to strike another vessel. Specifically, the ram included the ramming timber, the forward bow timbers configured to reinforce the ramming timber, and a metal sheath; in actual practice, the metal sheath is usually called the **ram**. The **Athlit ram** is discussed in chapter 3. Rams were also used, with little success, on iron warships after the middle of the nineteenth century.

Ram bow. Any bow with a projecting forefoot or ram. Ram bows sometimes served non-military functions: a means of reinforcing the bow construction externally, a method of lengthening the waterline to improve lateral resistance and maneuverability, or a decoration or symbol.

Ramming timber (Figs. 3–45 and 3–46). The main timber of an ancient ram, projecting forward from its envelope of bow planks and timbers to reinforce the head of the ram.

Reaming beetle [Reeming beetle] (Fig. G–8). The heaviest caulking mallet, used with a **reaming iron** for opening seams so that caulking could be driven into them.

Reaming iron [Reeming iron] (Fig. G–8). An iron chisel used for opening planking seams for caulking.

Rib. A small transverse member, often flexible and composed of one or several pieces, that stiffened the outer skin of a hull. Although often a layman's term for **frame**, rib is more properly applied to small craft, such as canoes, small boats, certain heavy frames that run from gunwale to gunwale in clinker-built vessels, or vessels whose skin is made of material other than wood.

Ribband carvel. The designation for a carvel-planked hull whose seams were covered with battens, or ribbands, to prevent the caulking from working out.

Ribbands [Ribbons, Battens]. Long, flexible strips of wood most commonly used as temporary keepers by nailing them across the outside of standing frames while the vessel was being built. When the term *framed on ribbands* was popular in the last few centuries of wooden shipbuilding, the ribbands were sometimes carefully arranged to represent certain rising and narrowing lines, from which planking and intermediate frame shapes were derived.

Rider [Rider frame] (Fig. G–6). An internal frame seated atop the ceiling, to which it was fastened; riders could be single pieces, but more often they were complete frames composed of floor timbers, futtocks, and top timbers. Installed either transversely or diagonally, they provided extra stiffening.

Rider keel (Fig. G–4b). One or more additional keels bolted to the bottom of the main keel to increase its strength. It should not be confused with a **false keel**, whose primary purpose was to protect the keel's lower surface.

Rider keelson (Fig. G–4b). An additional keelson, or one of several additional keelsons, bolted to the top of the main keelson of a large ship. In some documents, it was called a *false keelson*. See also **Keelson**.

Riding bitts (Fig. G–10). Strong, upright timbers in the bow of a ship, to which the anchor cables and hawsers were secured.

Ripping iron (Fig. G–8). A claw-like tool used for removing old copper or wooden sheathing.

Rising line (Fig. 5–19). A curved line on the sheer drawing of a ship, designating the outer ends of the floor timbers or the height of maximum breadth throughout the length of the hull. The former line was called the *rise of floor line* or the *floor head line;* the latter was known as the *height of breadth line*. See also **Narrowing lines**.

Rising wood [Deadwood, Hog] (Figs. G–3 and G–4a). Timbers fastened to the top of the keel and notched into the bottom of the floor timbers to better secure those members to each other and give the proper rising to the floor timbers. Rising wood was located between the apron or forward deadwood and the after deadwood, and was sometimes referred to as the central or keel deadwood.

Rockered keel (Fig. 3–24). A keel that is curved longitudinally so that it is deeper at its middle than at its ends. The term also refers to keels that are molded to a greater dimension amidships than at their ends. *Rocker* should not be confused with **sag**, which is an accidental rocker.

Room and space (Fig. G–12c). The distance from a molded edge of one frame to the corresponding point on an adjoining frame, usually measured at or near the keelson. The part occupied by the frame is called the *room,* while the unoccupied distance between it and the adjacent frame is called the *space*. On large ships of the last few centuries, where filling frames were placed between double frames, the term applied to the distance between the molded edge of one double frame to the corresponding point on the next double frame. Because of the uneven siding of forward frame faces, irregular spacing, and varying methods of fabrication, **room and space** is often a meaningless term in ancient hull documentation. A more definitive designation for ancient ships is **average frame spacing**, the average of distances between frame centerlines at a common appropriate location, taken throughout the hull or hold.

Round tuck stern. *See* **Tuck**.

Rove [Roove] (Fig. G–9). A small metal washer, used in clinker-built hulls, over which nail or rivet ends are flattened to lock the fastening. The term was also applied to washers used in bolting scarfs, floor timbers, etc.

Roving iron (Fig. G–8). An iron, hollow-ended tool used to drive **roves** over the ends of nails and bolts before clenching.

Rudder (Fig. G–18). A timber, or assembly of timbers, that could be rotated about an axis to control the direction of a vessel underway. Until the middle of the medieval period, the practice was to mount rudders on one or both stern quarters; these were known as *quarter rudders*. By the late medieval period, however, it appears that most vessels of appreciable size were steered by a single rudder hung at the sternpost; these were known as *stern-hung rudders*. For a brief period, the two types were sometimes used in combination. Rudders were designed for the vessel and type of duty they served. In protected waters they could be made quite broad, while seagoing ships utilized longer, more narrow rudders. For the largest seagoing ships, rudder construction was complex and required huge timbers, the assembly sometimes weighing several tons.

Rudder blade (Fig. G–18). The flat part of the rudder that diverts the water.

Rudder breeching. A strong rope with one end attached to the rudder and the other inside the stern, used to relieve some of the weight on the **gudgeons**.

Rudder chains. Chains or ropes attached to each side of the rudder and to the stern, used to prevent the loss of a rudder if it accidentally became unshipped.

Rudder head (Fig. G–18). The upper part of the rudder stock.

Rudder hole (Fig. G–18). An opening in the stern through which the rudder stock passed.

Rudder post. A term infrequently used to describe either the outer sternpost or the rudder stock.

Rudder sheath (Fig. G–18). A wooden or metal protective covering placed over the leading edge of a quarter rudder blade.

Rudder stock (Fig. G–18). A strong vertical piece to which the tiller was fitted; on large, post-medieval vessels it was the main vertical timber of the rudder, and it was also known as the **mainpiece**.

Rudder trunk. A housing for the rudder stock, usually extending from the counter to the steering deck.

Runghead. *See* **Wronghead**.

Sag [Sagging]. The accidental rocker formed in a keel and bottom due to insufficient timbering or improper loading.

Scantlings. The principal timbers of a vessel.

Scarf [Scarph]. An overlapping joint used to connect two timbers or planks without increasing their dimensions. Figure G–11 illustrates various scarfs used throughout shipbuilding history.

Scroll [Scroll head, Fiddlehead]. Ornamental molding used in place of a figurehead.

Scupper (Fig. G–3). A hole or channel cut in a vessel's side or waterway to drain off deck water.

Scuttle. A small opening, usually covered with a lid, in the side or deck for utilitarian purposes, such as a ballast port.

Seam. The longitudinal joint between two timbers or planks; the term usually refers to planking seams, the longitudinal juxtaposition of the edges of planks in the sides or decks, which were made watertight.

Shake. A longitudinal crack or distortion in a timber, caused by sun, weather, or improper curing. Cracks occurring during curing are also referred to as *checks*.

Sheathing. A thin covering of metal or wood, to protect hulls from marine life or fouling, or to stabilize and protect surface material applied for that purpose. Sheathing was most commonly used in the form of copper, lead, zinc, or alloy sheets, or thin wooden planks known as *furring* or *deals*. Chapters 3 and 5 have more on sheathing.

Sheathing nail (Figs. G–9c and G–9d). A small nail or tack used to attach sheathing to a hull.

Sheer. The longitudinal sweep of a vessel's sides or decks.

Sheer line. Specifically, the line of the upper or main deck where it meets the side, but the term is often used to describe the sweep of the bulwarks or weather rail.

Sheer plan. The side view of a vessel's hull plan.

Sheer plank. *See* **Planksheer**.

Shelf [Shelf clamp, Shelf piece]. *See* **Clamp**.

Shelf wale. On ancient and early medieval ships, a thick strake of external planking that supported through-beams and other timbers penetrating the outer planking.

Shell. The external planking of a vessel.

Shell-first construction [Shell-built]. A modern (sometimes misleading) term used to describe the process by which all or part of the outer hull planking was erected before frames were attached to it. In pure shell-built hulls, outer planking was self-supporting and formed the primary structure; the framework fastened to it formed the secondary, or stiffening, structure.

Shift. The act of arranging butts and scarfs so that adjacent joints are not in vertical alignment, thereby avoiding possible hull weaknesses.

Shim. A thin piece of wood used to fill a separation between two timbers or a frame and a plank.

Shipwright. A master craftsman skilled in the construction and repair of ships. In many instances, the person in charge of a ship's construction, including the supervision of carpenters and other personnel, control of expenditures and schedules, and acquisition of materials. Probably in many more areas and periods than have been documented, the term designated a formal title, such as the shipwrights to the English monarchs, or a level of expertise qualifying admission to a guild or association.

Shoe (Figs. G–4 and G–5). A term variously applied to the cover for an anchor fluke or a protecting piece at the bottom of a keel or rudder. *See* **Anchor** and **False keel**.

Shole [Sole, Shoe] (Fig. G–18b). A horizontal piece of wood or metal fixed along the bottom of a rudder to protect the lower ends of the vertical rudder pieces and align the bottom of the rudder with the bottom of the false keel.

Shore. A prop or pole used to brace a vessel in an upright position when not afloat or supported by a cradle.

Shot garland. A rack with hollows cut into it for supporting a row of cannon shot.

Shot locker (Fig. G–3). A small compartment, usually located near the foot of the mainmast, where round shot was stored.

Shroud. A rope or wire support used to steady a mast to the side of a hull.

Side. Described variously as the part of a hull above the waterline or the part above the turn of the bilge.

Sided [Sided dimension]. The dimension of an unmolded surface; the distance across an outer frame surface, the forward or after surface of a stem or sternpost, or the upper surface of a keel or keelson. *See* **Molded** for further information on timber dimensions.

Side keelson. *See* **Keelson**.

Side timbers (Fig. 3–34). In ancient and medieval vessels, one of a series of **intermediate framing timbers** inserted to provide stiffness along the line of wales. *See also* **intermediate timbers**.

Sill (Fig. G–3). The lower horizontal timber framing a gunport, large square light, or gallery door.

Sintel [Batten clamp] (Fig. 4–49). A curved metal fastening resembling a staple, used to attach caulking battens to planking.

Sister keel. *See* **Bilge keel**.

Sister keelson. *See* **Keelson**.

Skeg (Figs. G–14e and G–14f). A triangular piece, resembling external **deadwood** placed above the after end of the keel; used to reinforce the sternpost and improve sailing qualities of small craft and flat-bottomed vessels. Alternately, the angular after end of the keel, or an extension of the keel, on which the rudder post was mounted or which was used to protect the forward edge of the rudder.

Skeletal construction [Frame-first construction]. A modern (sometimes misleading) term used to describe the procedure in which hulls were constructed by first erecting frames and then attaching the outer skin of planking to them.

Sleeper. A seventeenth-century term for thick ceiling; a bilge stringer or footwale. In eighteenth-century English documents, a transom knee.

Sliding keel. *See* **Centerboard**.

Snelle (Fig. 4–32). A winged, or partition-like, stanchion used to support beams in Viking vessels.

Sny. An archaic term used to describe the upward sweep of bow and stern planking.

Spirketting (Fig. G–5, no. 23). Thick interior planks running between the waterways and the **lining** or **quickwork**.

Square frame. *See* **Frame**.

Square tuck stern. *See* **Tuck**.

Stanchion (Fig. G–5, no. 7). An upright supporting post, including undecorated supports for deck beams and bulkheads.

Standard. *See* **Standing knee**.

Standing knee [Standard] (Figs. G–7e and 5–21). A knee mounted on a deck with its vertical arm pointed up-

ward; most commonly used to reinforce the junction of the deck and side.

Staple (Figs. G–3 and G–4). A metal rod or bar whose sharpened ends were bent at right angles, used to fasten false keels to keels or to secure planking seams that tended to separate. Staples were used from the classical period to the present century.

Starboard. The right side of a vessel when facing forward.

Station lines [Body lines, Section lines] (Fig. 2–11). The projections on a lines drawing that represent the various body shapes of a hull. Chapter 2 includes a complete description of their functions.

Stealer (Fig. G–11a). A short plank inserted between two strakes of planking so that the regular strakes did not have to be made too wide; usually located at the bow or stern ends of bottom or lower side strakes.

Steering gear (Fig. G–18). The mechanism, consisting of chains, ropes, blocks, etc., used to transfer movement of the wheel to the tiller. In more general terms, the various components composing any steering mechanism.

Steering oar. An oar used to steer a small vessel, either from the side or the stern. A steering oar should not be confused with a **quarter rudder**, which is the device commonly used to steer ancient vessels and is permanently mounted and turns about a fixed axis.

Stem [Stempost] (Fig. G–3). A vertical or upward curving timber or assembly of timbers, scarfed to the keel or central plank at its lower end, into which the two sides of the bow were joined.

Stem head (Fig. G–13d). The upper end of the stem.

Stemson (Fig. G–3). A curved timber mounted on the inner surface of the apron; usually, the forward and upward extension of the keelson.

Stern. The after end of a vessel.

Stern framing (Fig. G–14). The assembly of timbers consisting of the sternpost, transoms, and fashion pieces.

Stern knee (Fig. G–14e). An angular timber that reinforced the joint between the keel or lower deadwoods and the sternpost or inner sternpost. Also known as the **knee of the post**.

Stern port (Figs. 5–56 and 5–61). An opening in the stern for guns, cargo loading, or light and ventilation.

Sternpost (Figs. G–14a, b, d). A vertical or upward-curving timber or assembly of timbers stepped into, or scarfed to, the after end of the keel or heel.

Sternson (Fig. G–14a). A curved timber joining the keelson and inner sternpost; usually an extension of the keelson and was mounted on top of the deadwood.

Sternson knee. A knee fitted atop or abaft the sternson to reinforce the upper part of the sternpost.

Stern walk [Stern gallery]. A balcony mounted across the stern.

Stocks. A structure supporting a vessel under construction or repair.

Stopwater (Fig. G–11b). A wooden dowel inserted athwartships in the scarf seams of external timbers to prevent shifting of the joint or to discourage water seepage along the seams.

Strake [Streake]. A continuous line of planks, running from bow to stern.

Stringer [Longitudinal]. A general term describing the longitudinal timbers fixed to the inside surfaces of the frames; the ceiling, other than the common ceiling.

Sump. *See* **Pump well**.

Surmark [Sirmark]. A mark denoting the location or sweep of a ribband or batten.

Sweep port (Fig. G–3). An opening in the bulwarks to accommodate a sweep (large oar).

Tabernacle. A timber assembly or housing that supported a mast or post at deck level. A common support for a hinged mast.

Taffrail [Tafferal] (Figs. G–14a–c). Variously, the upper part of the stern or the rail on top of the stern.

Tenon (Figs. G–14e and G–17). A wooden projection cut from the end of a timber or a separate wooden piece that was shaped to fit into a corresponding mortise. *See* **Mortise-and-tenon joint**.

Tenon-built. A term used to denote vessels whose planking edges were joined by means of **mortise-and-tenon joints**.

Thick stuff (Fig. G–5). A term referring to the thick ceiling of the bottom.

Thole [Tholepin]. A pin, or one of a pair of pins, set vertically in the gunwale to serve as the fulcrum for an oar.

Through-beam (Fig. G–18a). An athwartships timber that extended through and beyond the outer hull planking. Through-beams were most common on ancient and medieval hulls, where they supported the quarter rudders or provided athwartships stiffness to the upper part of the hull.

Thwart. A transverse plank in a boat or galley; used to seat rowers, support masts, or provide lateral stiffness.

Tiller (Fig. G–18). A wooden or metal level fitted into the rudder head, by which the rudder could be moved from side to side.

Timber and room. *See* **Room and space**.

Timber head (Fig. G–12a). The upper extremity of a hull timber.

Timber heel (Fig. G–12a). The lower extremity of a hull timber.

Timbers. In general context, all wooden hull members; specifically, those members that formed the frames of a hull.

Tons burden. *See* **Burden**.

Top and butt (Fig. G–11a). A method of planking whereby one edge of the planks were straight while their opposite sides had two sloping edges of unequal length, reducing the plank widths to half. It was used to increase longitudinal strength and to

prevent shifting of wales and other stress-bearing planks.

Top timber (Fig. G–12a). The uppermost member of a frame.

Transom (Figs. G–14a–d). One of the athwartship members, fixed to the sternpost, that shaped and strengthened the stern.

Transom beam. *See* **Transom**.

Transom knee (Fig. G–14c). An angular, horizontal reinforcing timber bolted to a transom and the side.

Treenail [Trunnel, Trennal] (Figs. G–9o and G–9p). A round or multi-sided piece of hardwood, driven through planks and timbers to connect them. Treenails were employed most frequently in attaching planking to frames, attaching knees to ceiling or beams, and in the scarfing of timbers. They were used in a variety of forms: with expanding wedges or nails in their ends, with tapered or square heads on their exterior ends, or completely unwedged and unheaded. When immersed, treenails swelled to make a tight fit.

Tuck (Fig. G–14d). The place where the ends of the bottom planks terminated under the stern or counter. When planks ended in a convex curvature, a vessel was said to have a round tuck; when the stern and counter lay perpendicular to the posts, the vessel was said to have a square tuck.

Tumblehome [Fall home] (Fig. G–5). The inward curvature of a vessel's upper sides as they rose from the point of maximum breadth to the bulwarks. Tumblehome reduced topside weight and improved stability.

Turn of the bilge. The outboard part of the lower hull where the bottom curved toward the side.

Underwater body. The portion of the hull below the waterline.

Upper deck (Fig. G–6). The highest deck extending unbroken from bow to stern.

Upper wale (Fig. 3–31). The highest wale.

Waist. The part of a vessel between the quarterdeck and the forecastle.

Wale. A thick strake of planking, or a belt of thick planking strakes, located along the side of a vessel for the purpose of girding and stiffening the outer hull.

Wart [Boss] (Fig. 4–29). A horizontal hardwood block or projection, attached to the starboard side of a Viking ship's stern, upon which the rudder post rotated.

Waterlines [Level lines] (Figs. 2–10, 2–11). Lines on a hull drawing representing the horizontal sections of the hull. Chapter 2 completely describes their function.

Waterway (Fig. G–5). A timber or gutter along the side of a deck whose purpose was to prevent the deck water from running down between the frames and to divert it to the scuppers.

Way. The stocks; a structure on which a vessel was built.

Weather deck. Any exposed deck.

Well. *See* **Pump well**.

Wheel [Steering wheel] (Fig. G–18c). A vertical steering device, fixed to a deck and linked to the tiller by ropes, chains, or gear.

Whipstaff (Fig. G–18d). A vertical steering lever that preceded the wheel; it was connected to the tiller by a toggle arrangement, and it was mounted in a bearing on the deck above the tiller.

Whole molding (Fig. 5–24). A process to determine the transverse shapes of hulls by means of one or more standard molds, which were shifted as necessary to produce fair shapes without the use of compasses and complex drafting methods. The process was not as precise as determining individual hull shapes from lines drawings or with compasses and scales, and it was usually limited to the production of small craft after the seventeenth or early eighteenth century.

Windlass (Fig. G–10). A horizontal cylinder, supported by bitts or brackets, used to haul anchors and hawsers.

Wing transom (Figs. G–14a, c, d). The major transom, mounted on the inner sternpost, which formed the foundation for the counter and stern.

Withy. A flexible twig or root, most frequently worked by hammering to make it more pliable, used for binding the seams of planks and timbers.

Wronghead [Runghead] (Fig. G–12a). The head, or extremity, of a floor timber.

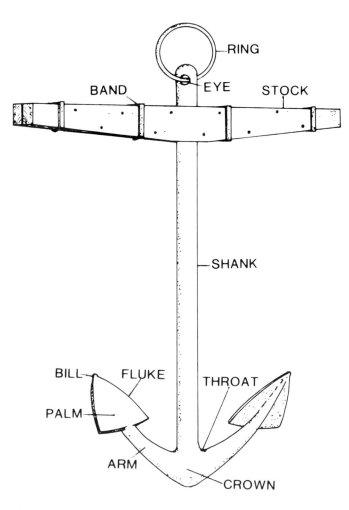

Fig. G–1. The parts of an Admiralty anchor.

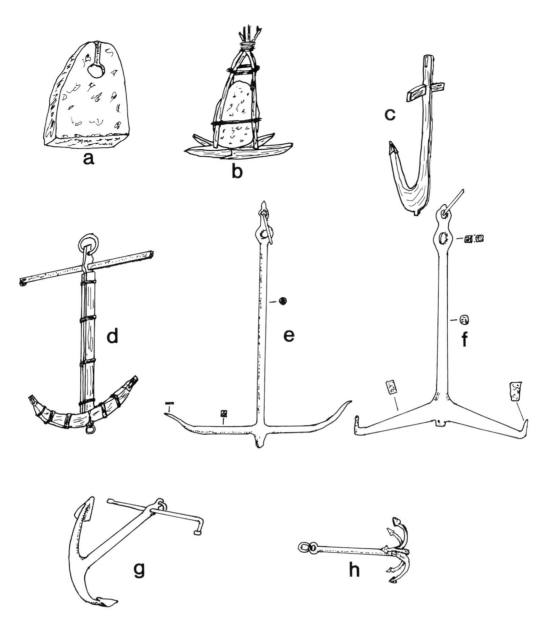

FIG. G–2. Selected anchor types: (a) one of a great variety of Bronze Age stone anchor shapes; (b) a primitive stone and wood grapnel; (c) a large, one-armed wooden anchor with a lead-filled stock and copper fluke tip from the Ma'agan Michael wreck (ca. 400 B.C.) in Israel [after Rosloff, *IJNA* 20.3: 224]; (d) a Roman iron anchor cased in wood, with removable iron stock, from the first-century Nemi excavations [after Ucelli, fig. 270]; (e) a seventh-century Byzantine anchor from Yassi Ada, Turkey [after van Doorninck, fig. 6-15]; (f) an eleventh-century iron anchor from the wreck at Serçe Limani, Turkey [sketched from a replica by F. H. van Doorninck, Jr.]; (g) a nineteenth-century iron anchor most commonly known as a fisherman's anchor; the iron stock could be partially withdrawn and stored adjacent to the shank to save deck space; (h) an eighteenth-century grapnel with five flukes.

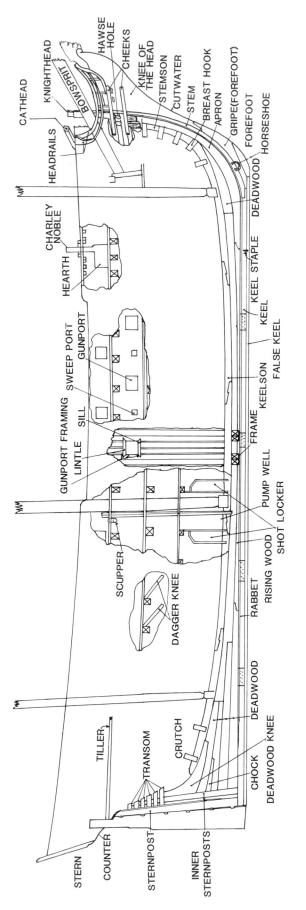

CATHEAD

KNIGHTHEAD

BOWSPRIT

HAWSE HOLE

CHEEKS

KNEE OF THE HEAD

STEMSON

CUTWATER

STEM

BREAST HOOK

APRON

GRIPE(FOREFOOT)

FOREFOOT

HEADRAILS

DEADWOOD

HORSESHOE

CHARLEY NOBLE

HEARTH

KEEL STAPLE

KEEL

GUNPORT FRAMING

SWEEP PORT

GUNPORT

SILL

LINTLE

FALSE KEEL

FRAME

KEELSON

PUMP WELL

SHOT LOCKER

SCUPPER

DAGGER KNEE

RABBET

RISING WOOD

DEADWOOD

DEADWOOD KNEE

TILLER

TRANSOM

CRUTCH

CHOCK

STERN

COUNTER

STERNPOST

INNER STERNPOSTS

Fig. G–3. Hull timbers; side views.

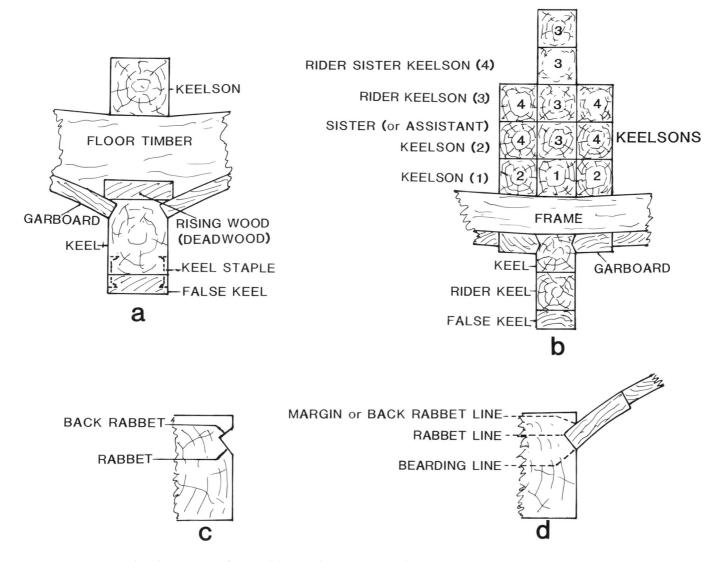

FIG. G–4. Principal timbers; sectional views: (a) a popular arrangement for small and medium sized craft; (b) a typical arrangement of principal timbers for large vessels, this for an early twentieth-century four-masted schooner with a 200-ft-long double keel; (c) the designations of keel and post rabbet surfaces; and (d) the designations of the lines formed by the junction of the rabbet and garboard surfaces.

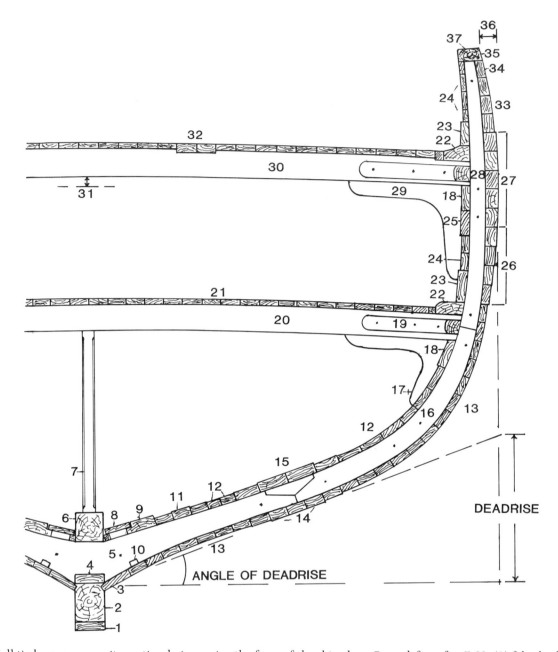

FIG. G–5. Hull timbers; a composite sectional view, using the form of the ship-sloop *Peacock* from fig. 5-62: (1) false keel; (2) keel; (3) garboard; (4) rising wood [deadwood]; (5) floor timber; (6) keelson; (7) stanchion; (8) limber board; (9) limber strake; (10) limber hole; (11) thick stuff [footwaling]; (12) common ceiling; (13) bottom planking; (14) bilge strakes; (15) footwale; (16) second futtock; (17) dagger knee; (18) shelf clamp; (19) lodging knee; (20) lower [or berthing] deck beam; (21) lower deck planking; (22) waterway; (23) spirketting; (24) lining [quickwork]; (25) clamp; (26) diminishing strakes; (27) wale; (28) top timber; (29) hanging knee; (30) upper deck beam; (31) camber; (32) binding strake; (33) bulwark; (34) planksheer; (35) gunwale; (36) tumblehome; (37) caprail.

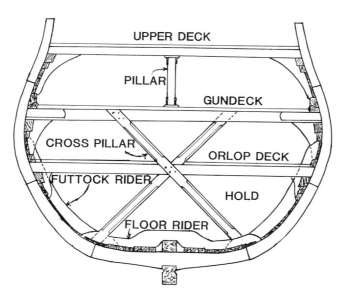

FIG. G–6. Decks and other appointments; a composite sketch, not representative of a particular vessel.

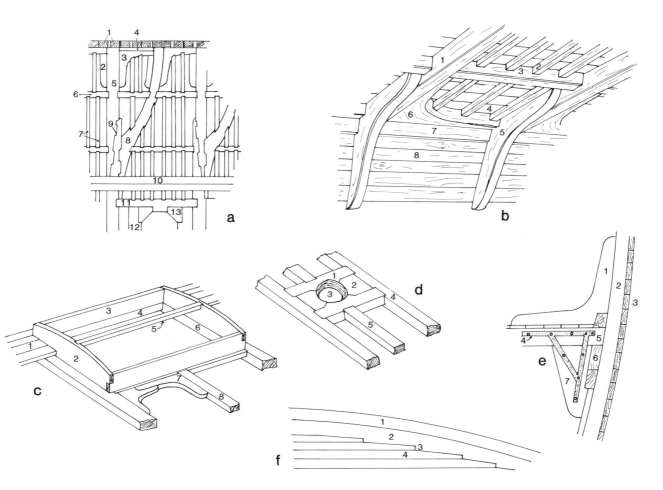

FIG. G–7. Deck framing and details. [a] deck framing at the mainmast of a large warship: (1) frames; (2) hanging knee; (3) lodging knee; (4) packing piece; (5) deck beam; (6) carlings; (7) ledges; (8) beam arm; (9) deck beam scarf; (10) binding strake; (11) mast carling; (12) mast partner; (13) chock; [b] typical deck framing and supporting features (after John R. Stevens, p. 29): (1) deck beam; (2) ledge; (3) carling; (4) deck planking; (5) hanging knee; (6) lodging knee; (7) shelf clamp; (8) ceiling [quickwork]; [c] a common form of hatch construction; (1) deck planking; (2) head ledge; (3) hatch coaming; (4) carling; (5) hatch beam; (6) deck beam; (7) lodging knee [only one set shown]; (8) half beam; [d] a typical mast partner for small merchant ship: the partners are (1) carlings and (2) chocks; (3) mast hole; (4) deck beam; (5) half beam; [e] standing and plate knees: (1) standing knee; (2) frame; (3) outer planking; (4) plate knee; (5) deck beam; (6) shelf clamp; (7) chock; [f] a method of terminating deck planks at the incurving sides of ships: (1) waterway; (2) nibbing strake [margin plank]; (3) nibbed end; (4) deck plank.

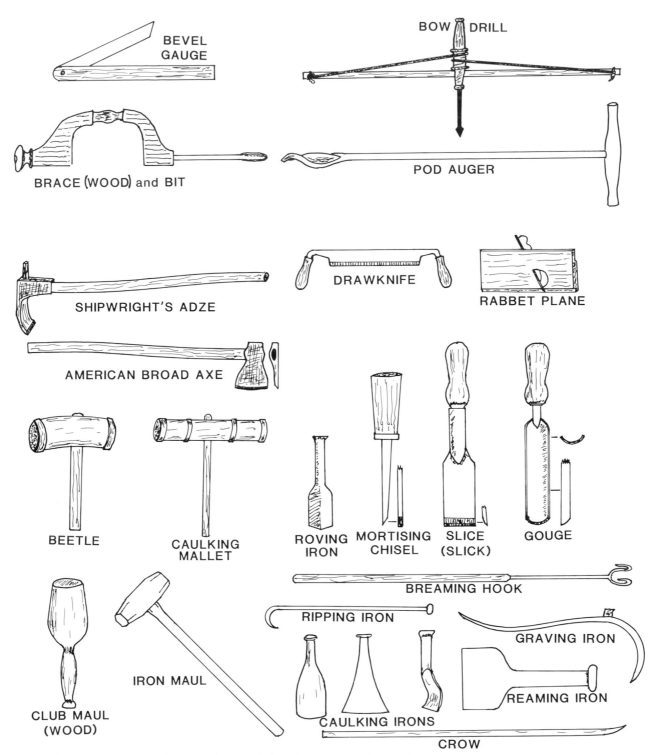

BEVEL
GAUGE

BOW DRILL

BRACE (WOOD) and BIT

POD AUGER

SHIPWRIGHT'S ADZE

DRAWKNIFE

RABBET PLANE

AMERICAN BROAD AXE

BEETLE

CAULKING
MALLET

ROVING
IRON

MORTISING
CHISEL

SLICE
(SLICK)

GOUGE

BREAMING HOOK

CLUB MAUL
(WOOD)

IRON MAUL

RIPPING IRON

CAULKING IRONS

GRAVING IRON

REAMING IRON

CROW

FIG. G–8. An assortment of shipwright's tools likely to be found on shipwrecks.

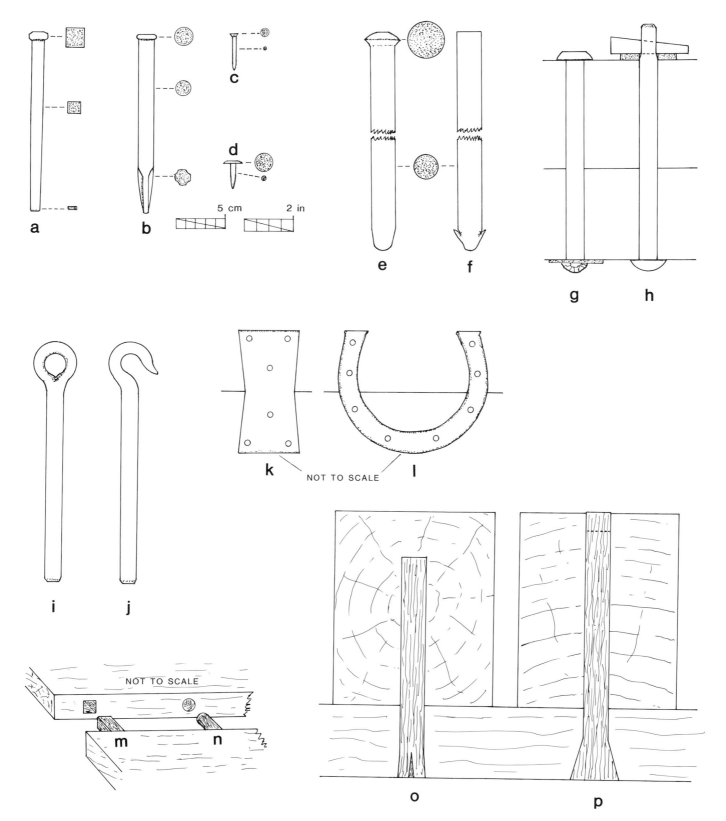

Fig. G–9. Typical fastenings: (a) square-headed spike used for planking and general fastening; (b) round-headed dump used for similar fastening; (c) nineteenth-century copper nail used to attach copper sheathing to hull bottoms; (d) fourth-century B.C. copper nail used to fasten lead sheathing to hull bottoms; (e) a short drift bolt; (f) unheaded rag bolt, barbed with a chisel to deter withdrawal; bolts were sometimes made without heads, the head being formed by pounding; they could be used with or without roves (washers); (g) clench bolt, often designated as "bolt" in contemporary documents (see figs. 3-28 and 4-28 for other forms of clenched fastenings); (h) forelock bolt; (i) eye bolt; (j) hook bolt; (k) fishplate; (l) horseshoe plate; (m) planks being aligned with a rectangular, or block, coak and (n) with a cylindrical coak (dowel); (o) a wedged treenail in a blind hole; (p) a headed treenail in a through hole; it is wedged at its inner end.

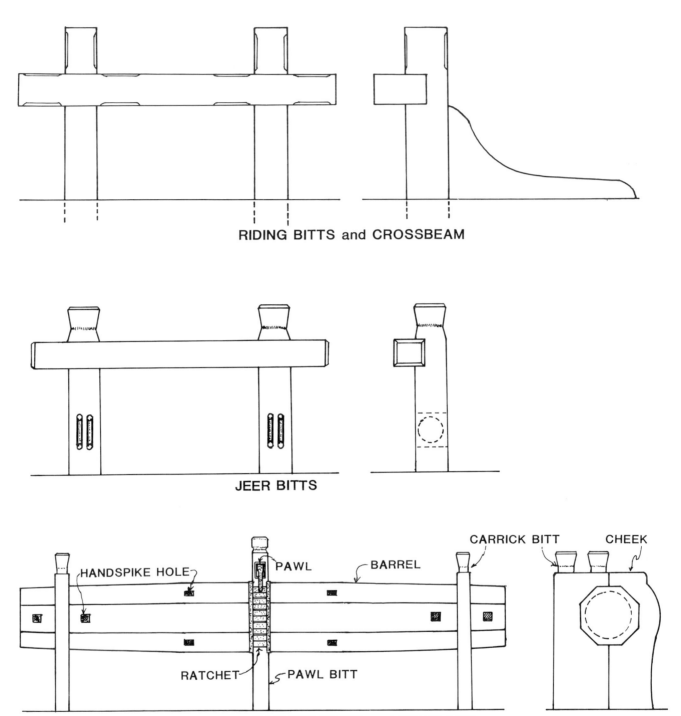

RIDING BITTS and CROSSBEAM

JEER BITTS

HANDSPIKE HOLE   PAWL   BARREL   CARRICK BITT   CHEEK

RATCHET   PAWL BITT

CARRICK BITTS and WINDLASS

FIG. G–10. Bitts.

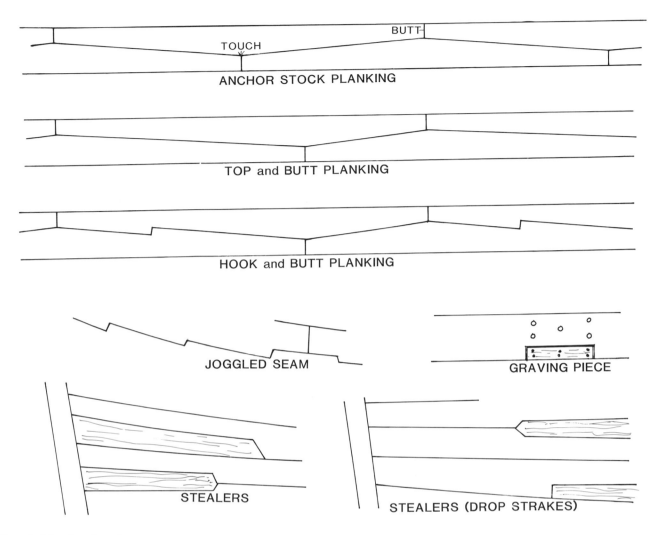

FIG. G–11a. Scarfs and seams.

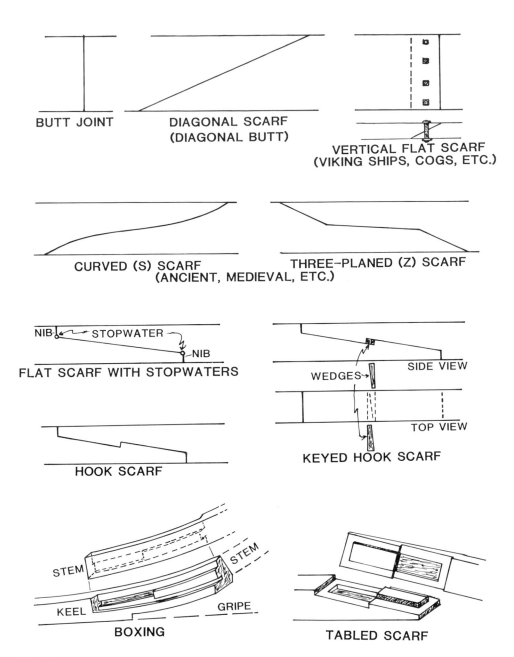

Fig. G–11b. Scarfs and seams.

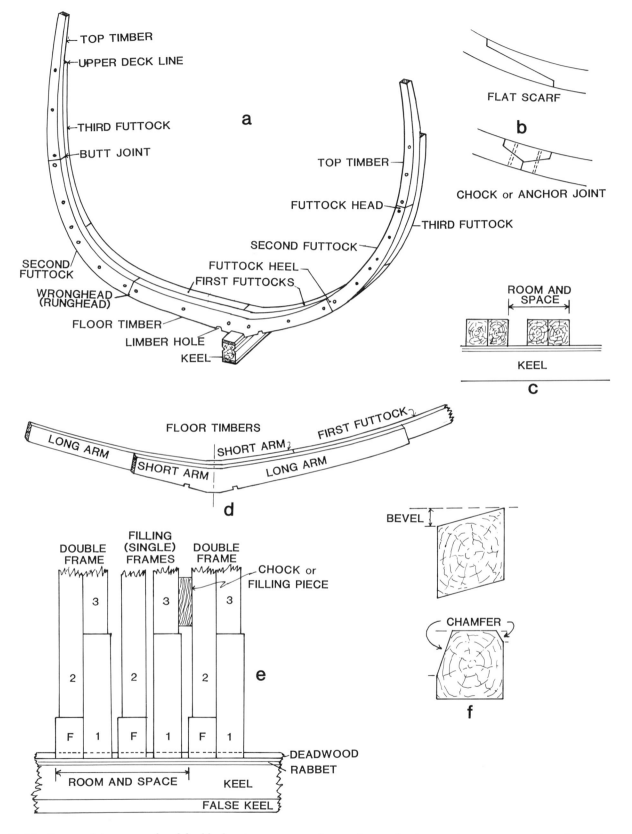

FIG. G–12. Frames: (a) an example of double framing—a square frame of an early nineteenth-century merchant ship; (b) two additional commonly used frame timber joints; (c) room and space of a popular framing plan; (d) some vessels were framed with a pair of overlapping floor timbers having arms of unequal length, resulting in an even number of timbers in each frame; (e) lower side view of the framing plan of a large warship, where a pair of single frames (called *filling frames*) were set between double frames; futtocks, marked F, are shown by number; in such an arrangement, the room and space included the filling frames; (f) bevels and chamfers.

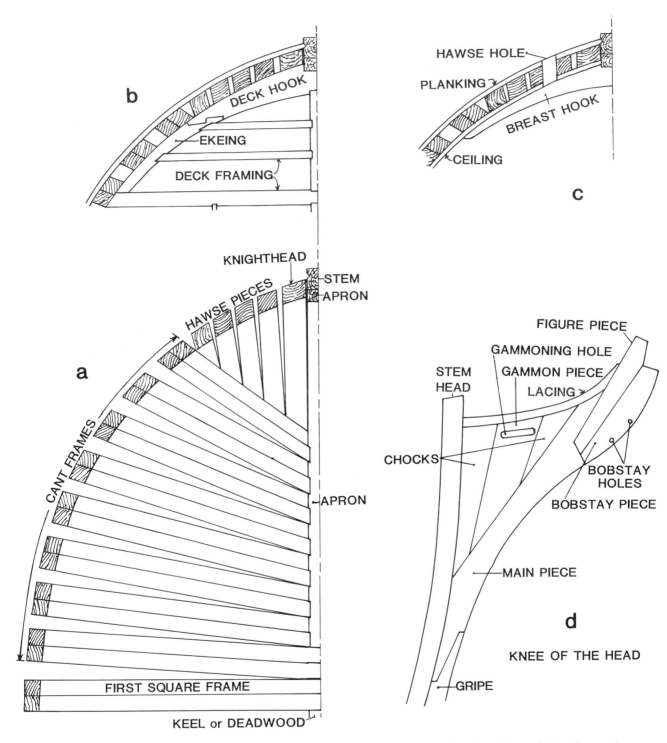

FIG. G–13. Bow construction: (a) top view of port frames; (b) deck hook; (c) breast hook and hawse hole; (d) one of many arrangements used for assembling the knee of the head.

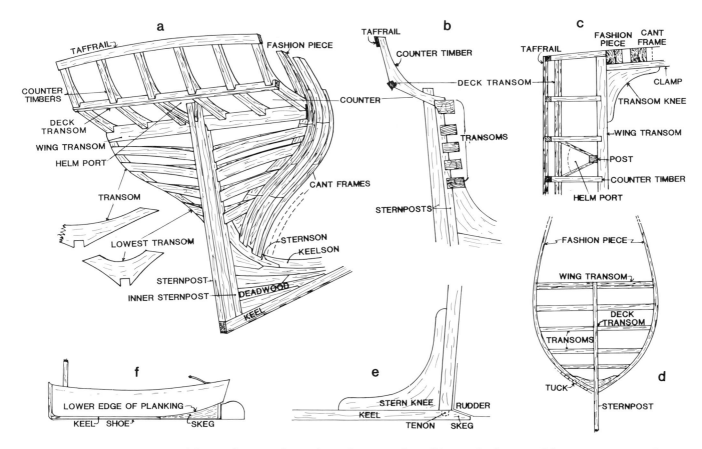

Fig. G–14. Stern construction: (a) stern framing of an eighteenth-century brig; (b) partial side view of the same stern near the post; (c) partial top view of the same stern; (d) lower stern framing of a galleon (see fig. 5-15 for planking and orientation with the rest of the hull); (e) alternate stern details; (f) one form of skeg installation on a small sloop.

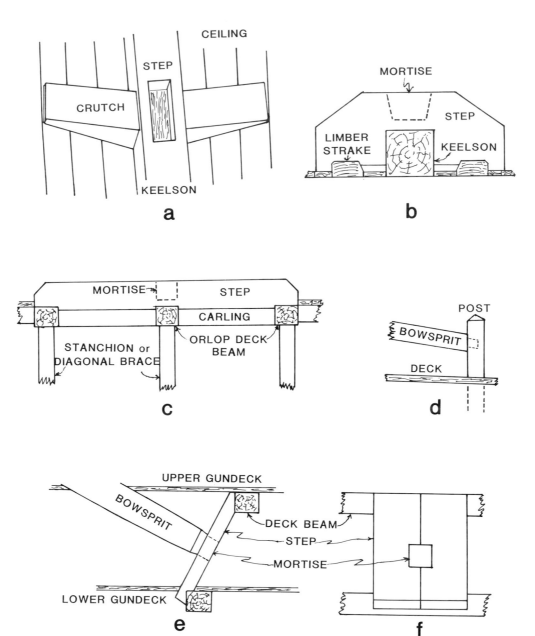

FIG. G–15. In addition to the variety of mast and stanchion steps illustrated in chapters 3, 4, and 5, the following composite sketches, gleaned from a variety of sources, illustrate additional arrangements likely to be encountered on shipwrecks: (a) crutches brace the foremast step on the Revolutionary War privateer *Defence* (see fig. 5-60); (b) a mainmast step of the type used on very large eighteenth-century warships; (c) one of a variety of methods for stepping a mizzenmast; (d) bowsprits of smaller vessels were sometimes stepped above deck in a broad sampson post as illustrated, or between pairs of riding bitts just below deck; (e) the bowsprit of a large eighteenth-century warship and (f) an athwartships view of the forward surface of the same step, showing its two-piece construction.

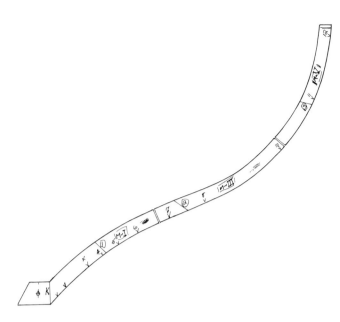

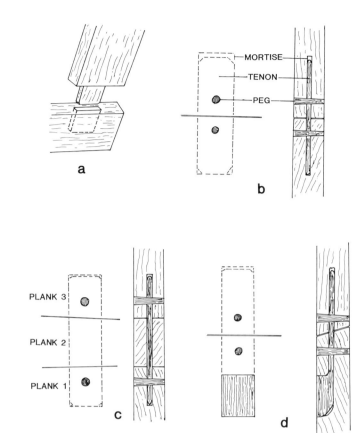

FIG. G–16. Two bend molds and a hollow mold are fitted together to form a compound mold or half of a square frame. Individual molds, probably representing futtocks of frame M, are numbered in Roman numerals. Diagonals taken from the loft are indicated, as are carets which probably denote bevel measurements; the numbers and symbols may refer to degrees of bevel or settings on the shipwright's bevel gauge. K is the side of the keel, ⊕ the centerline, and S probably indicates the sheer line. Redrawn from old notebook sketches. For molds used in whole molding, see figure 5-24.

FIG. G–17. Mortise-and-tenon joints: (a) fixed tenon and single mortise; (b) free tenon and two mortises; (c) free tenon and three mortises; and (d) patch tenon and two mortises.

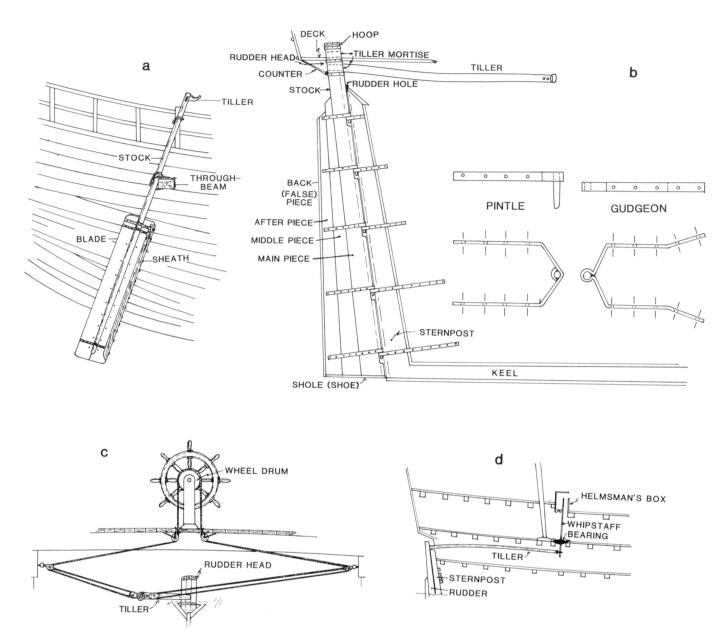

FIG. G–18. Steering devices: (a) a Mediterranean balanced quarter-rudder system, ca. fourth century B.C.; (b) terminology of an eighteenth-century frigate-sized rudder, which includes a mortise for a manual tiller to be used in the main steering gear failed; details of the hinges—the pintles and gudgeons—are also shown; (c) a common steering wheel rig for medium-sized vessels, eighteenth and nineteenth centuries; (d) steering with a vertical lever called a whipstaff (also see Fig. 5–25 as used on the *Vasa*).

SELECT BIBLIOGRAPHY

Ancient Subjects

Basch, Lucien. "Ancient Wrecks and the Archaeology of Ships." *IJNA* 1 (1972): 1–58.

———. *Le musée imaginaire de la marine antique.* Athens, 1987. An iconographic gem; nearly 1,150 illustrations of ancient Mediterranean craft and supporting material, many of them previously unpublished or unknown. Descriptive text and lengthy bibliography covering publications to 1983.

Bass, George F. "The Construction of a Seagoing Vessel of the Late Bronze Age." In *Tropis I.*

Benoit, Fernand. *L'épave du Grand Congloué a Marseille. Gallia* suppl. 14. Paris, 1961.

Bonino, Marco. "Notes on the Architecture of Some Roman Ships: Nemi and Fiumicino." In *Tropis I.*

———. "Notes on the Steering Devices of Ancient Ships." In *Tropis II.*

Casson, Lionel. *Ships and Seamanship in the Ancient World.* Princeton, 1971. First Princeton paperback edition, with addenda and corrigenda, 1986. Excellent scholarly work on ancient ships, shipbuilding, and seafaring.

Casson, Lionel, and J. Richard Steffy, eds. *The Athlit Ram.* Texas A&M University Press: College Station, 1991. Ram and bow details; metallurgy; symbols; naval logistics.

Coates, John, and Sean McGrail, eds. *The Greek Trireme of the Fifth Century* B.C. *Discussion of a Projected Reconstruction.* Greenwich, 1983.

Crumlin-Pedersen, Ole. "Skin or Wood? A Study of the Origin of the Scandinavian Plank-Built Boat. In *Ships and Shipyards, Sailors and Fishermen,* edited by Olof Hasslöf et al. Copenhagen, 1972.

de Morgan, Jean-Jacques. *Fouilles à Dâhchour: Mars–juin 1894.* Vienna, 1895.

Eiseman, Cynthia J., and Brunilde S. Ridgway. *The Porticello Shipwreck: A Mediterranean Merchant Vessel of 415–385 B.C.* Texas A&M University Press: College Station, 1987.

Fitzgerald, Michael A. "The Ship." In *The Harbours of Caesarea Maritima: Results of the Ancient Harbour Excavation Project, 1980–1985,* vol. 2, *The Small Finds and the Ship,* edited by John P. Oleson. BAR-S. Forthcoming.

Frost, Honor. "First Season of Excavation on the Punic Wreck in Sicily." *IJNA* 2.1 (1973): 33–49.

Frost, Honor, et al. *Lilybaeum.* Accademia Nazionale dei Lincei, Notizie Degli Scavi di Antichità, Serie Ottava, vol. 30 (suppl.). Rome, 1981. Marsala ship excavation; recording; hull construction; artifacts.

Gassend, Jean-Marie; Bernard Liou; and Serge Ximénès. "L'épave 2 de l'anse des Laurons (Martigues, Bouches-du-Rhône)." *Archaeonautica* 4 (1984):75–105. Excavation; recording; construction; architectural analysis artifacts; interesting information on second-century deck construction; construction drawings.

Geannette, Mark A. "Mast Step and Keelson: The Early Development of a Shipbuilding Technology." Master's thesis, Texas A&M University, 1985.

Haldane, Cheryl Ward. "Ancient Egyptian Hull Construction." Ph.D. diss., Texas A&M University, 1992. A thorough study of Egyptian hulls and hull remains from a variety of types and periods.

———. "Boat Timbers from El-Lisht: A New Method of Ancient Egyptian Hull Construction, Preliminary Report." *MM* 74.2 (1988): 141–52. Very large, 3,900-year-old timbers found at a pyramid site shed new light on Egyptian hull construction.

———. "The Dashur Boats." Master's thesis, Texas A&M University, 1984. Twelfth-dynasty funerary vessels, hull analysis; history; lines and construction drawings.

———. "A Fourth Boat from Dashur." *AJA* 88.3 (1988):389.

Haldane, Cheryl Ward, and Cynthia W. Shelmerdine. "Herodotus 2.96.1–2 Again." *Classical Quarterly* 40.4 (1990): 535–39.

Haldane, David Douglas. "The Wooden Anchor." Master's thesis, Texas A&M University, 1984. Contains an extensive bibliography for this subject.

Höckman, Olaf. "Zur Bauweise, Funktion und Typologie der Mainzer Schiffe." In *Die Mainzer Römerschiffe,* edited by Gerd Rupprecht. Mainz, 1982.

———. "Late Roman River Craft from Mainz, Germany." In *Local Boats: Fourth International Symposium on Boat and Ship Archaeology, Porto 1985,* BAR Int. Series 438(i), edited by Octavio Lixa Filgueiras. Oxford, 1988.

Jenkins, Nancy. *The Boat beneath the Pyramid.* London, 1980. A popular, well-illustrated account of the excavation and reconstruction of the Royal Ship of Cheops and associated subjects.

Johnston, Paul F. *Ship and Boat Models in Ancient Greece.* Annapolis, 1985.

Joncheray, Jean-Pierre. "L'épave grecque, ou étrusque, de Bon-Porté." *Cahiers d'Archéologie Subaquatique* 5 (1976): 5–36. Details of a vessel whose seams were aligned with treenails and lashed with ligatures.

Kapitän, Gerhard. "Ancient Anchors: Technology and Classification." *IJNA* 13.1 (1984): 33–44.

———. "Greco-Roman Anchors and the Evidence for the One-armed Wooden Anchor in Antiquity." *Marine Archaeology,* Colston Papers no. 23, edited by D. J. Blackman. London, 1973.

Katzev, Michael L. "An Analysis of the Experimental Voyage of Kyrenia II." In *Tropis II.*

Katzev, Michael L., and Susan Womer Katzev. "Kyrenia II: Building a Replica of an Ancient Greek Merchantman." In *Tropis I.*

———. "Voyage of Kyrenia II." *INA Newsletter* 16.1 (1989): 4–10. Describes sailing trials of this fourth-century B.C. merchant ship replica.

Landström, Björn. *Ships of the Pharaohs.* New York, 1970.

Lipke, Paul. "Retrospective on the Royal Ship of Cheops." In *Sewn Plank Boats,* BAR-S276, edited by Sean McGrail and Eric Kentley. Greenwich, 1985.

———. *The Royal Ship of Cheops.* BAR-S225. Greenwich, 1984. Extensive information and drawings on the construction of a large fourth-dynasty funerary vessel.

Marsden, Peter. "The County Hall Ship." *Transactions of the London and Middlesex Archaeological Society* 21.2 (1965): 109–17. Details of a Roman vessel excavated in London.

———. "The County Hall Ship, London." *IJNA* 3.1 (1974): 55–65.

———. *A Roman Ship from Blackfriars, London.* London, 1966.

Meiggs, Russell. *Trees and Timber in the Ancient Mediterranean World.* Oxford, 1982.

Morrison, J. S., and J. F. Coates. *The Athenian Trireme.* Cambridge, 1986. The background material, ranging from ancient pictorial and literary evidence to modern naval architecture, used to develop and build *Olympias,* the modern version of the ancient Greek trireme recently constructed in a Piraeus shipyard.

———. *An Athenian Trireme Reconstructed: The British Sea Trials of Olympias, 1987.* BAR-S486. Oxford, 1989.

Morrison, J. S., and R. T. Williams. *Greek Oared Ships, 900–322 B.C.* Cambridge, 1968. After more than twenty years, it is still a thorough, respected, and oft-consulted source.

Murray, William H., and Photios M. Petsas. *Octavian's Campsite Memorial for the Actium War.* TAPS 79.4. Philadelphia, 1989. An elaborate, well-illustrated description of the ram sockets and possible ship sizes represented by this long-neglected site.

Nour, Mohammad Zaki; Mohammad Salah Osman; Zaky Iskander; and Ahmad Youssof Moustafa. *The Cheops Boats,* part 1. Cairo, 1960. The first and only official scholarly report on the disposition of the contents of the two boat pits before 1960. Well illustrated and thorough.

Patch, Diana Craig, and Cheryl Ward Haldane, *The Pharaoh's Boat at The Carnegie.* Pittsburgh, 1990. A well-illustrated popular account of the excavation, acquisition, construction features, and display of the Pittsburgh Dashur Boat.

Pomey, Patrice. "La coque." In A. Tchernia, P. Pomey, et al. *L'épave romaine de la Madrague de Giens (Var) (Campagnes 1972–1975). Gallia* suppl. 34. Paris, 1978. Drawings and interpretation of a large, well-preserved Roman wine carrier. Excellent example of a double-planked hull.

———. "L'épave de Bon-Porté et les bateaux cousus de Méditerranée." *MM* 67.3 (1981): 225–43.

———. "Le navire romaine de la Madrague de Giens." *Comptes rendus de l'académie des inscriptions* (Jan.–Mar., 1982): 133–54. Supplemental information and revised interpretations.

Pulak, Cemal. "The Bronze Age Shipwreck at Ulu Burun, Turkey: 1985 Campaign." *AJA* 92.1 (1988): 1–37. Stone anchors; cargo; artifacts; examination of one small area of the hull.

Rival, Michel. *La charpenterie navale romaine.* Paris, 1991. An excellent treatise, elaborately illustrated, on Roman ship carpentry. Discusses the qualities and properties of the various Mediterranean shipbuilding wood types, describes the ancient methods of converting trees into timber and then fabricating various hull elements, and relates this methodology to three archaeological finds. A chapter on the carpentry involved in the big Madrague de Giens ship is especially interesting. This book is a must for scholars of ancient construction and of great value to those interested in vessels of other periods.

Rogers, Edward M. "Boat Reliefs in the Tomb of Ti and Mastaba of Mereruka." *INA Quarterly* 19.3 (1992): 8–13.

Rosenberg, G. "Hjörtspringfundet." *Nord Oldtideminder*, vol. 3, part 1. Copenhagen, 1937.

Rosloff, Jay P. "A One-armed Anchor of c. 400 B.C.E. from the Ma'agan Michael Vessel, Israel. A Preliminary Report." *IJNA* 20.3 (1991): 223–26.

Steffy, J. Richard. "The Herculaneum Boat: Preliminary Notes on Hull Details." *AJA* 89.3 (1985): 519–21. Brief construction details of a first-century Roman boat.

———. "The Kinneret Boat Project. Part II: Notes on the Construction of the Kinneret Boat." *IJNA* 16.4 (1987): 325–29.

———. "The Kyrenia Ship: An Interim Report on Its Hull Construction." *AJA* 89.1 (1985): 71–101.

———. "The Role of Three-dimensional Research in the Kyrenia Ship Reconstruction." In *Tropis I*.

Swiny, Helena Wylde, and Michael L. Katzev. "The Kyrenia Shipwreck: A Fourth-Century B.C. Greek Merchant Ship." In *Marine Archaeology*, Colston Papers no. 23, edited by D. J. Blackman. London, 1973. Site information; excavation; artifacts; limited hull details.

Throckmorton, Peter. "The Antikythera Ship." In Gladys Davidson Weinberg et al., *The Antikythera Shipwreck Reconsidered*. TAPS 55.3, pp. 40–47. Philadelphia, 1965.

Tzalas, Harry E. "Kyrenia II in the Fresco of Pedoula Church, Cyprus: A Comparison with Ancient Ship Iconography." In *Tropis II*. A very interesting study

that investigates the values and pitfalls of using iconography as a research source.

Ucelli, Guido. *Le navi de Nemi*. Rome, 1950. Excavation; hull construction; anchors; quarter rudders; design. Detailed account of gigantic pleasure barges.

Vinson, Stephen M. "Boats of Egypt before the Old Kingdom." Master's thesis, Texas A&M University, 1987.

Wachsmann, Shelley, et al. *The Excavations of an Ancient Boat in the Sea of Galilee (Lake Kinneret)*, 'Atiqot (English Series)XIX. Edited by Ayala Sussman and Inna Pommerantz. Jerusalem, 1990. A preliminary report on the excavation, conservation, associated finds, and construction details of a large boat from the classical period.

Wachsmann, Shelley; Kurt Raveh; and Orna Cohen. "The Kinneret Boat Project. Part I: The Excavation and Conservation of the Kinneret Boat." *IJNA* 16.3 (1987): 233–45.

Wild, Henri. *Le Tombeau de Ti, Fascile II: La Chapelle (Première partie)*. Cairo, 1953.

Wright, E. V. *The Ferriby Boats: Seacraft of the Bronze Age*. London, 1990.

———. *The North Ferriby Boats*. NMM Monograph no. 23. London, 1976.

———. "The North Ferriby Boats: A Final Report." In *Proceedings of the Sixth International Symposium on Boat and Ship Archaeology*. Roskilde, Denmark, 1991. Forthcoming.

———. "The North Ferriby Boats: A Revised Basis for Reconstruction." In *Sewn Plank Boats*, BAR-S276, edited by Sean McGrail and Eric Kentley. Greenwich, 1985.

Medieval Subjects

Anderson, R. C. "The Burleson Ship." *MM* 20 (1934): 158–70.

———. "Italian Naval Architecture about 1445." *MM* 11 (1925): 135–63.

Arenson, Sarah. *The Encircled Sea*. An interesting popular account of the maritime contributions the Mediterranean has made to modern civilization. A broad variety of subjects includes history, archaeology, and marine sciences.

———. "Ship Construction in Cyprus, 1325–6." In *Tropis II*. An interesting analysis of shipbuilding through the documentation of labor and material costs.

Bass, George F., and Frederick H. van Doorninck, Jr. "An Eleventh Century Shipwreck at Serçe Liman, Turkey." *IJNA* 7.2 (1978): 119–72.

Bass, George F.; Frederick H. van Doorninck; et al. *Yassi Ada: A Seventh-Century Byzantine Shipwreck*. Texas

A&M University Press: College Station, 1982. The final report on this excavation includes extensive details on the hull remains and their reconstruction.

Bellabarba, Sergio. "The Square-rigged Ship of the *Fabrica di Galere* Manuscript." *MM* 74.2 and 74.3 (1988): 113–30 and 255–39.

Bonino, Marco. "Lateen-rigged Medieval Ships: New Evidence from Wrecks in the Po Delta (Italy) and Notes on Pictorial and Other Documents." *IJNA* 7.1 (1978): 9–28.

Brøgger, A. W., and Haakon Shetelig. *The Viking Ships: Their Ancestry and Evolution*. English translation by Katherine John. Oslo, 1971.

Bruce-Mitford, Rupert, et al. *The Sutton Hoo Ship-Burial*. Vol. 1. London, 1975.

Christensen, Arne Emil. "Viking Age Boatbuilding Tools." In *Woodworking Techniques before A.D. 1500*, edited by Sean McGrail. BAR-S129. Oxford, 1982.

Crumlin-Pedersen, Ole. "Danish Cog-Finds." In *The Archaeology of Medieval Ships and Harbours in Northern Europe,* edited by Sean McGrail. BAR-S66. Oxford, 1979.

Dammann, Werner. *Das Gokstadschiffe und seine Boote.* Heidesheim, 1983. Excellent drawings and sketches of the Gokstad ship.

Dotson, J. E. "Jal's Nef X and Genoese Naval Architecture in the Thirteenth Century." *MM* 59 (1973): 161–70.

Ellmers, Detlev. "The Cog of Bremen and Related Boats." In *The Archaeology of Medieval Ships and Harbors in Northern Europe,* edited by Sean McGrail. BAR-S66. Oxford, 1979.

———. "The History of the Cog as a Ship Type." In *The Hanse Cog of 1380,* edited by Klaus-Peter Kiedel and Uwe Schnall. Bremerhaven, 1985.

Evans, Angela Care, and Rupert Bruce-Mitford. "The Ship." In Rupert Bruce-Mitford et al. *The Sutton Hoo Ship-Burial.* Volume 1, *Excavations, Background, The Ship, Dating, and Inventory.* London, 1975.

Fenwick, Valerie, ed. *The Graveney Boat: A Tenth-Century Find from Kent.* BAR-53. Oxford, 1978.

Goitein, S. D. *A Mediterranean Society.* 5 vols. Berkeley, 1967–88. Vol. 1, *Economic Foundations,* is especially valuable to students of medieval shipbuilding and seafaring.

Green, Jeremy. "The Shinan Excavation, Korea: An Interim Report on the Hull Structure." *IJNA* 12.4 (1983): 293–301.

———. "The Song Dynasty Shipwreck at Quanzhou, Fujian Province, People's Republic of China." *IJNA* 12.3 (1983): 253–61. Interesting double and triple planked hull construction.

Green, Jeremy, and Zae Geum Kim. "The Shinan and Wando Sites, Korea: Further Information." *IJNA* 18.1 (1989): 33–41.

Hocker, Frederick M. "Cogge en Coggeschip: Late Trends in Cog Development." In *Bouwtraditie en Scheepstype,* edited by Reinder Reinders. Groningen, 1991.

Jal, Auguste. *Archéologie navale.* 2 vols. Paris, 1840.

Jézégou, Marie-Pierre. "Elements de construction sur couples observes sur une épave du haut moyen-age decouverte a Fos-sur-mer (Bouches-du-Rhône)." *VI Congreso Internacional de Archqueologie Submarina.* Cartegena, 1985.

Keith, Donald H., and Christian J. Buys. "New Light on Medieval Chinese Seagoing Ship Construction." *IJNA* 10.2 (1981): 119–32.

Kiedel, Klaus-Peter, and Uwe Schnall, eds. *The Hanse Cog of 1380.* Bremerhaven, 1985.

Kreutz, Barbara M. "Ships, Shipping, and the Implications of Change in the Early Medieval Mediterranean." *Viator* 7 (1976): 79–109.

Lane, Frederic C. *Venetian Ships and Shipbuilders of the Renaissance.* Baltimore, 1934.

Lewis, Archibald R., and Timothy J. Runyan. *European Naval and Maritime History, 300–1500.* Bloomington, 1985.

Li Guo-Qing. "Archaeological Evidence for the Use of 'Chu-nam' on the Thirteenth Century Quanzhou Ship, Fujian Province, China." *IJNA* 18.4 (1989): 277–83.

Lopez, Robert S. "The Role of Trade in the Economic Readjustment of Byzantium in the Seventh Century." *Dumbarton Oaks Papers XIII* (1959): 69–85.

Matthews, Sheila D. "The Rig of the Eleventh-Century Ship at Serçe Liman, Turkey." Master's thesis, Texas A&M University, 1983.

McGrail, Sean. "Further Aspects of Viking Age Boatbuilding." In Basil Greenhill, *Archaeology of the Boat.* London, 1976.

———, ed. *The Archaeology of Medieval Ships and Harbours in Northern Europe.* BAR-S66. Oxford, 1979.

———, ed. *Woodworking Techniques Before A.D. 1500.* BAR-S129. Oxford, 1982.

McGrail, Sean, and Eric McKee. *The Building and Trials of the Replica of an Ancient Boat: The Gokstad Faering.* Maritime Monographs and Reports no. 11 (2 parts). London, 1974.

McKee, Alexander. "The Influence of British Naval Strategy on Ship Design: 1400–1850." In *A History of Seafaring Based on Underwater Archaeology,* edited by George F. Bass. London, 1972.

Nicolaysen, N. *Langskibet Fra Gokstad Ved Sandefjord.* Christiana, 1982. See also the English reprint of original publication and drawings: *The Viking Ship from Gokstad.* Westmead, Hants, 1971.

Olsen, Olaf, and Ole Crumlin-Pedersen. *Five Viking Ships from Roskilde Fjord.* Roskilde, 1969.

———. "The Skuldelev Ships. (II)." *Acta Archaeologica* 38 (1967): 75–170. General information on the five late Viking ship reconstructions at Roskilde, Denmark.

Prynne, M. W. "Henry V's *Grace Dieu.*" *MM* 54 (1968): 115–28. Details of a large, triple-layered, clinker-built hull.

Pryor, John H. "The Naval Architecture of Crusader Transport Ships." *MM* 70.2, 70.3, and 70.4 (1984): 171–219, 275–92, and 363–86.

Redknap, M. *The Cattewater Wreck: The Investigation of an Armed Vessel of the Early Sixteenth Century.* BAR-131. Oxford, 1984.

Reinders, Reinder. *Cog Finds from the IJsselmeerpolders.* Flevobericht no. 248, Lelystad, 1985.

Relazione. *Sulla scoperta di due barche antiche nel territorio del comune di Contarina in provincia di Rovigo nel gennaio 1898.* Commissione della R. Deputazione di Storia patria per le Venezie. Venice, 1900. The official report of the Contarina vessels excavated in 1898 in Rovigo. Extensive data and illustrations, said to be accurate in all respects, provide interesting information about these thirteenth- and sixteenth-century wrecks.

Sarsfield, John P. "Mediterranean Whole Moulding." *MM* 70.1 (1984): 86–88.

———. "Survival of Pre–Sixteenth Century Mediterranean Lofting Techniques in Bahia, Brasil." In *Local Boats: Fourth International Symposium on Boat and Ship Archaeology, Porto, 1985.* BAR-S438 (part 1), edited by Octávio Lixa Filgueiras. Oxford, 1988.

Shetelig, Haakon, and H. Falk. *Scandinavian Archeology.* Translated by E. V. Gordon. Oxford, 1937.

Steffy, J. Richard. "The Mediterranean Shell to Skeleton Transition: A Northwestern European Parallel??" In *Carvel Construction Technique: Skeleton-first, Shell-first,* edited by Reinder Reinders and Kees Paul, 1–9. Oxford, 1991. Describes the methods of mensuration and determination of hull shapes for a small, eleventh-century merchant vessel.

———. "Reconstructing the Hull." *INA Newsletter* 15.3 (1988): 14–21. Construction and reconstruction information for an eleventh-century Mediterranean merchantman.

———. "The Reconstruction of the Eleventh Century Serçe Liman Vessel: A Preliminary Report." *IJNA* 11.1 (1982): 13–34.

Throckmorton, Peter, and Joan Throckmorton. "The Roman Wreck at Pantano Longarini." *IJNA* 2.2 (1973): 243–66. Study of the stern of a sixth-century vessel in Italy.

Tinniswood, J. T. "English Galleys, 1272–1377." *MM* 35 (1949): 276–315.

Udovitch, Abraham L. "Time, the Sea, and Society: Duration of Commercial Voyages on the Southern Shores of the Mediterranean during the High Middle Ages." *La navagazione mediterranea nell'alto medioevo (1977 Settimane),* 2:503–63. Spoleto, 1978.

Unger, Richard W. *The Ship in Medieval Economy, 600–1600.* Montreal, 1980.

Van de Moortel, Aleydis M. *A Cog-like Vessel from the Netherlands,* Flevobericht 331, Lelystad, 1991.

van Doorninck, Frederick H., Jr. "The Anchors: A Limited Technology, a Sophisticated Design." *INA Newsletter* 15.3 (1988): 24, 25. Details of eleventh-century anchor fabrication.

———. "The Fourth-Century Wreck at Yassi Ada: An Interim Report on the Hull." *IJNA* 5.2 (1976): 115–31.

Postmedieval Subjects

Adams, Jonathan. "*Sea Venture:* A Second Interim Report, Part I." *IJNA* 14.4 (1985): 275–99. Floor structure details of a large, early seventeenth-century ship.

Adams, Robert M. "Construction and Qualitative Analysis of a Sewn Boat of the Western Indian Ocean." Master's thesis, Texas A&M University, 1985. Study of *mtepe's.*

Albright, Alan B., and J. Richard Steffy. "The Browns Ferry Vessel, South Carolina: Preliminary Report." *IJNA* 8.2 (1979): 121–42. Excavation, cargo, artifacts, and hull construction of an eighteenth-century riverine vessel.

Amer, Christopher F. "The Construction of the Brown's Bay Vessel." Master's thesis, Texas A&M University, 1986.

Andersen, R. C. *The Rigging of Ships in the Days of the Spritsail Topmast 1600–1720.* London, 1982.

Baker, William A. *The Mayflower and Other Colonial Vessels.* London, 1983. Excellent discussion of the construction, rigging, and fitting out of various seventeenth-century vessel types, including the building of the *Mayflower* replica.

Bankston, J. *Nautical Instruction, 1587, by Dr. Diego García de Palacio.* Bisbee, Ariz., 1986.

Barker, Richard A. "Design in the Dockyards, about 1600." In *Carvel Construction Technique: Skeleton-first, Shell-first,* edited by Reinder Reinders and Kees Paul. Analysis of the earliest English documents on ship design.

———. "Fragments from the Pepysian Library." *Revista da Universidade de Coimbra* 32 (1986): 161–78. New and interesting perspectives on the document known as "Fragments of English Shipwrightery."

Bass, George F., ed. *Ships and Shipwrecks of the Americas.* London, 1988. A popular history of shipbuilding and seafaring in the New World, based on underwater archaeology and written by twelve nautical archaeologists and historians involved in the research.

Blake, Warren, and Jeremy Green. "A Mid–Sixteenth Century Portugese Wreck in the Seychelles." *IJNA* 15.1 (1986): 5–7.

Boudriot, Jean. *The Seventy-four Gun Ship.* 4 vols. English translation by David H. Roberts. Annapolis, 1986–88. Just about everything you need to know concerning the construction, fitting out, rigging, and handling of French seventy-four gun ships.

Broadwater, John D.; Robert M. Adams; and Marcie Renner. "The Yorktown Shipwreck Archaeological Project: An Interim Report on the Excavation of Shipwreck 44YO88." *IJNA* 14.4 (1985): 301–14. Excavation and structural features of a double-ended British vessel sunk in 1781.

Burlet, René, and Eric Rieth. "Outils et Démarches." *Histoire et Mesure* III.4 (1988): 463–89. A report on an interesting developmental research project wherein a hull of four hundred tons described in Diego García de Palacio's publication of 1587 is reconstructed. Enlightening conclusions result from the use of mold-and-batten and solid half-models and a lot of ingenuity.

Burwash, Dorothy. *English Merchant Shipping, 1460–1540.* Toronto, 1947.

Cederlund, Carl O. "Shipbuilding in the Seventeenth and Eighteenth Centuries: The *Wasa* as a Product of Dutch Shipbuilding." In *The North Sea: A Highway of Economic and Cultural Exchange*, edited by A. Bang-Andersen, B. Greenhill, and E. H. Grude. Stavanger, 1985.

———, ed. *Postmedieval Boat and Ship Archaeology.* BAR-S256. Oxford, 1985. Papers presented at the Third International Symposium on Boat and Ship Archaeology, Stockholm, 1982.

Chapelle, Howard I. *American Small Sailing Craft.* New York, 1951. Describes over a hundred types of small craft; lines and sail drawings.

———. *The Baltimore Clipper.* New York, 1930. A study in nautical beauty.

———. *The History of American Sailing Ships.* New York, 1935. Plenty of sketches, sail and construction plans, and lines drawings.

———. *The History of the American Sailing Navy.* New York, 1949.

———. *The National Watercraft Collection.* Second edition. Washington, 1976. Drawings, photos, and information about models in the watercraft collection at the Smithsonian Institution.

———. *The Search for Speed under Sail, 1700–1855.* New York, 1967. A study of fast hull designs.

Chapman, Frederik H. af. *Architectura Navalis Mercatoria.* Stockholm, 1768. Facsimile edition, London, 1971. Reprint of the 1768 collection of ship and boat drawings by one of the greatest contributors to naval architecture and shipbuilding technology.

Crescentio, Bartolomeo. *Náutica Mediterránea.* Rome, 1607.

Crisman, Kevin J. "The Construction of the *Boscawen.*" *The Bulletin of the Fort Ticonderoga Museum* 14.6 (1985): 356–70. Details of a vessel from the French and Indian War.

———. *The Eagle: An American Brig on Lake Champlain during the War of 1812.* Annapolis, 1987. History, excavation, construction details; elaborate construction and lines drawings.

———. *The History and Construction of the United States Schooner Ticonderoga.* Alexandria, 1982.

———. "The *Jefferson*: The History and Archaeology of an American Brig from the War of 1812." Ph.D., University of Pennsylvania, 1989.

———. "The Lake Brigs *Jefferson* and *Eagle.*" *Seaways* 2.4 (1991): 5–9.

Cutler, Carl C. *Greyhounds of the Sea.* 3d. ed. Annapolis, 1984.

Davis, Andy. "Double-Sawn Framing." *Wooden Boat* 82 (May/June 1988): 48–59.

Doran, Edwin, Jr. "The Tortola Boat: Characteristics, Origin, Demise." *MM* 56.1 (1970) Suppl.

Evans, Cerinda W. *Some Notes on Shipbuilding and Shipping in Colonial Virginia.* Charlottesville, 1957.

Falconer, William. *Falconer's Marine Dictionary (1780).* Reprint. New York, 1970. A descriptive record of subjects ranging from shipbuilding and seamanship to naval discipline; predominantly eighteenth-century English subjects written by an English seafarer, but contains a glossary of French sea terms and phrases. In my opinion, the best of the contemporary marine dictionaries.

Fennis, Jan. *Un Manuel de Construction des Galères, 1691.* Amsterdam, 1983.

Fincham, John. *History of Naval Architecture.* London, 1851.

———. *A Treatise on Masting Ships and Mast Making.* 1854. Reprint. London, 1982.

Fleetwood, Rusty. *Tidecraft.* Savannah, 1982. A study of the coastal and riverine vessels of lower South Carolina, Georgia, and northeastern Florida from 1650 to 1950.

Franklin, Carol A. "Caulking Techniques in Northern and Central European Ships and Boats: 1500 B.C.–A.D. 1940." Master's thesis, Texas A&M University, 1985.

Franklin, John. *Navy Board Ship Models, 1650–1750.* Annapolis, 1989.

Franzen, Anders. *The Warship Vasa.* Stockholm, 1962.

García de Palacio, Diego. *Instrucción Náutica para navegar.* Mexico City, 1587.

Goldenberg, Joseph A. *Shipbuilding in Colonial America.* Charlottesville, 1976.

Goodwin, Peter. *The Construction and Fitting of the English Man-of-War 1650–1850.* London, 1987. A very thorough and well-illustrated study of warship construction.

———. *The 20-gun Ship Blandford.* Annapolis, 1988.

Green, Jeremy, Rosemary Harper; and Vidya Intakosi. "The Ko Si Chang One Shipwreck Excavation 1983–1985. A Progress Report." *IJNA* 15.2 (1986): 105–22.

Grenier, Robert. "Basque Whalers in the New World: The Red Bay Wrecks." In *Ships and Shipwrecks of the Americas*, edited by George F. Bass. London, 1988.

Griffiths, John W. *A Treatise on Marine and Naval Architecture.* New York, 1853.

Guérout, Max; Eric Rieth; Jean-Marie Gassend; avec le concours de Bernard Liou. "Le navire génois de Villefranche: un naufrage de 1516 (?)" *Archaeonautica* 9.

Paris, 1989. An interesting study of a large, well-preserved Genoese ship from the sixteenth century.

Harris, Daniel G. *F. H. Chapman: The First Naval Architect and His Work.* Annapolis, 1989.

Hawkins, Clifford W. *The Dhow: An Illustrated History of the Dhow and its World.* Lymington, Hants, 1977.

Hocker, Frederick M. "The Brown's Ferry Vessel: An Interim Hull Report." In *Underwater Archaeology Proceedings of the Society for Historical Archaeology Conference, Kingston, 1992,* edited by Donald H. Keith and Toni Carrell.

———. "The Lelystad *beurtschip:* Preliminary report on the hull construction." In *Scheepsarcheologie: prioriteiten en lopend onderzoek,* Flevobericht 322, edited by Reinder Reinders and Rob Oosting, n.p. Lelystad, 1991.

Hoving, A. J. "A Seventeenth-Century Dutch 134-foot *Pinas:* A Reconstruction after *Aeloude en Hendendaegse Scheepsbouw en Bestier by Nicolaes Witsen 1671.*" *IJNA* 17.3 (1988): 211–22 and *IJNA* 17.4 (1988): 331–38.

Howard, Frank. *Sailing Ships of War, 1400–1860.* London, 1979.

Hundley, Paul F. *The Griffon Cove Wreck: A Case Study in Archaeological Reconstruction of Timber Hull Remains.* Australian Institute for Maritime Archaeology, special pub. no. 2, Freemantle, 1984. Study of the remains of a large boat from Lake Huron.

Keith, Donald H. "Shipwrecks of the Explorers." In *Ships and Shipwrecks of the Americas,* edited by George F. Bass. London, 1988.

Lane, Frederic C. "Tonnages, Medieval and Modern." *The Economic History Review,* Second Series 17.8 (1964): 213–33.

———. "Venetian Naval Architecture about 1550." *MM* 20 (1934): 24–49.

Lavery, Brian, ed. *Deane's Doctrine of Naval Architecture, 1670.* London, 1981.

———. *The Royal Navy's First Invincible.* Portsmouth, England, 1988.

———. *The 74-gun Ship Bellona.* Annapolis, 1985.

———. *The Ship of the Line.* 2 vols. Annapolis, 1983–84. History, design, construction, rigging, and fitting of British vessels larger than fifty guns between 1650 and 1850. Very thorough.

Lees, James. *The Masting and Rigging of English Ships of War, 1625–1850.* 2d ed. London, 1984.

Lovegrove, H. "Remains of Two Old Vessels Found at Rye, Sussex. *MM* 50.2 (1964): 115–22.

Lyman, John. "Register Tonnage and Its Measurement, Part I." *The American Neptune* 5.3 (1945): 223–34.

———. "Register Tonnage and Its Measurement, Part II." *The American Neptune* 5.4 (1945): 311–25.

———. "Tonnage—Weight and Measurement." *The American Neptune* 8.2 (1948): 99–113.

MacGregor, David R. *Fast Sailing Ships, 1775–1875.* Lausanne, 1973. Plenty of good drawings, photographs, and commentary make this large, attractive volume an asset to any library and a necessity for scholars of nineteenth-century sailing ships.

———. *Merchant Sailing Ships, 1775–1815.* Annapolis, 1988.

———. *The Tea Clippers, 1833–1875.* London, 1983.

McKay, John. *The 100-gun Ship Victory.* Annapolis, 1987.

McKay, Lauchlan. *The Practical Shipbuilder.* New York, 1839.

Mainwaring, Henry. *The Sea-man's Dictionary.* London, 1644. Facsimile ed., Menston, England, 1972. Seventeenth-century English terms, phrases, and nautical descriptions; of more value as a research source than as a dictionary.

Martin, Colin J. M. "The *Dartmouth,* A British Frigate Wrecked off Mull, 1690; 5. The Ship." *IJNA* 7.1 (1978): 29–58.

Morris, John William, III. "Site 44YO88: The Archaeological Assessment of the Hull Remains at Yorktown, Virginia." Master's thesis, East Carolina University, 1991. Details of the construction of an eighteenth-century British collier.

Murray, Mungo. *A Treatise on Ship-Building and Navigation.* London, 1765. A rare but marvelous treatise on the methodology of shipbuilding; many foldout plates illustrate merchant ship details, the beveling of timbers, and dozens of seldom-discussed subjects.

Myers, Mark D. "The Evolution of Hull Design in Sixteenth-Century English Ships-of-War." Master's thesis, Texas A&M University, 1987.

Oertling, Thomas J. "The Highborn Cay Wreck: The 1986 Field Season." *IJNA* 18.3 (1989): 244–53. Hull structure analysis of the remains of possibly the two oldest European wrecks yet excavated in the Americas.

———. "The History and Development of Ships' Bilge Pumps, 1500–1840." Master's thesis, Texas A&M University, 1984.

———. "The Molasses Reef Wreck Hull Analysis: Final Report." *IJNA* 18.3 (1989): 229–43.

Oppenheim, M. *A History of the Administration of the Royal Navy and of Merchant Shipping in Relation to the Navy from 1509 to 1660.* London, 1896.

Paris, Edmond. *Souvenirs de marine.* 6 vols. Paris, 1886–1910. An elaborate study of ships from ancient times to the date of publication. Drawings, specifications, and more than 350 plates.

Redknap, M. *The Cattewater Wreck.* BAR-131. Oxford, 1984. Information on the remains of a sixteenth-century wreck in England.

Rees, Abraham. "Naval Architecture." *Cyclopaedia.* London, 1820.

Riess, Warren C. "Design and Construction of the Ronson Ship." In *Carvel Construction Technique: Skeleton-first, Shell-first.* Oxford, 1991.

———. "The Ronson Ship: The Study of an Eighteenth Century Merchantman Excavated in Manhattan, New York in 1982." Ph.D. diss., University of New Hampshire, 1987.

Rieth, Eric. "Les écrits de Fernando Oliveira." *Neptunia* 165 (mars, 1987): 18–25.

———. "La question de la construction navale à franc-bord au Ponant." *Neptunia* 160 (décembre, 1985): 8–21. Comparison of the Mediterranean and Atlantic transitions from plank-first to frame-first methods of construction.

———. Remarques sur une série d'illustrations de l'*Ars Nautica* (1570) de Fernando Oliveira. *Neptunia* 169 (mars, 1988): 36–43. Interpretive series of articles analyzing the architectural philosophies of Oliveira and others.

———. "Un système de conception des carènes de la seconde moitié du XVI siecle." *Neptunia* 166 (jui, 1987): 16–31.

Rosloff, Jay P. "The Water Street Ship: Preliminary Analysis of an Eighteenth-Century Merchant Ship's Bow." Master's thesis, Texas A&M University, 1986. As above, the study of a large merchantman dating to the first half of the eighteenth century.

Rosloff, Jay P., and J. Barto Arnold III. "The Keel of the *San Esteban*: Continued Analysis." *IJNA* 13.4 (1984): 287–96. Lower stern construction of an early Spanish colonial vessel.

Rule, Margaret. *The Mary Rose: The Excavation and Raising of Henry VIII's Flagship.* London, 1982.

Salisbury, William. "Early Tonnage Measurement in England." *MM* 52 (1966): 41–51, 173–80, 329–40 and *MM* 53 (1967): 251–64.

———. "The Woolwich Ship." *MM* 47.2 (1961): 81–90.

Salisbury, William, and R. C. Anderson. *A Treatise on Shipbuilding and a Treatise on Rigging Written about 1620–1625.* The Society for Nautical Research Occasional Publications no. 6, London, 1958.

Sands, John O. *Yorktown's Captive Fleet.* Charlottesville, 1983.

The Shipbuilder's Repository; or, A Treatise on Marine Architecture. London, 1789.

Simmons, Joe John, III. "The Development of External Sanitary Facilities aboard Ships of the Fifteenth to Ninteenth Centuries." Master's thesis, Texas A&M University, 1985.

Smith, Roger C. *Vanguard of Empire: Ships of Exploration in the Age of Columbus.* New York, 1992.

Staalkart, Marmaduke. *Naval Architecture or Rudiments and Rules of Shipbuilding.* 2 vols. London, 1781. One volume in text, the second in superb drafting; Staalkart was one of England's best marine draftsmen.

Statens Sjöhistoriska Museum. *Drawings. Wasa 1628.* Stockholm, 1982. Elaborate lines, construction, rigging, and detail drawings and photographic illustrations of this large, intact warship.

Steel, David. *The Elements and Practice of Naval Architecture.* 2 vols. London, 1822.

———. *Elements of Mastmaking, Sailmaking, and Rigging.* 1794 edition. Reprint. New York, 1932.

Steffy J. Richard, et al. "The *Charon* Report." In *Underwater Archaeology: The Challenge before Us,* edited by Gordon P. Watts, Jr. San Marino, 1981. Details of the remains of a British 44-gun ship sunk in 1781.

Stevens, John R. *An Account of the Construction, and Embellishment of Old Time Ships.* Toronto, 1949. Construction details, drawings, and scantling lists of large wooden ships, mostly from seventeenth- and eighteenth-century sources; also photos of contemporary models.

Sutherland, William. *Britain's Glory or Ship-Building Unvail'd.* London, 1717.

———. *The Shipbuilder's Assistant or Marine Architecture.* London, 1711. Various editions to 1794.

Switzer, David C. "Nautical Archaeology in Penobscot Bay: The Revolutionary War Privateer *Defence.*" In *New Aspects of Naval History,* edited by Craig L. Symonds. Annapolis, 1979.

Thompson, Bruce F. C. "The Rigging of a Seventeenth-Century Frigate at Mombasa, Kenya. Master's thesis, Texas A&M University, 1988.

Unger, Richard W. *Dutch Shipbuilding before 1800.* Amsterdam, 1978.

van Yk, Cornelius. *De Nederlandse Scheepsbouwkonst Opengesteld.* Amsterdam, 1671. See description in chapter 5.

Waddell, Peter J. A. "The Disassembly of a Sixteenth-Century Galleon." *IJNA* 15.2 (1986): 137–48. Details of the timbers of a Basque whaler.

Webb, William H. *Plans of Wooden Vessels Selected as Types from One Hundred and Fifty Various Kinds . . . Built by William H. Webb in the City of New York from the Year 1840 to the Year 1869.* 2 vols. New York, 1895.

White, David. *The Frigate Diana.* Annapolis, 1987. One of the Anatomy of the Ship series; a complete account of the construction, rigging, and fittings of this 38-gun British frigate of 1794.

Wingood, Allan J. "*Sea Venture.* An Interim Report on an Early Seventeenth-Century Shipwreck Lost in 1609." *IJNA* 11.4 (1982): 333–47.

Witsen, Nicolaes. *Aeloude en Hedendaagse Scheepsbouw en Bestier.* Amsterdam, 1671. Facsimile edition, Alvin on the Rhine, 1979. See description on this elaborate work in chapter 5.

Wood, Virginia Steele. *Live Oaking: Southern Timber for Tall Ships*. Boston, 1981. An excellent account of the procurement of live oak for American shipbuilding.

Worcester, G. R. G. *The Junks and Sampans of the Yangtze*. Annapolis, 1971.

General Subjects

Abell, Sir Wescott. *The Shipwright's Trade*. Cambridge, England, 1948.

Anderson, Richard K., Jr. *Guidelines for Recording Historic Ships*. Washington, D.C., 1988. An excellent publication of the Historic American Buildings Survey/Historic American Engineering Record divisions of the National Park Service for taking off lines and recording hull and rigging components.

Bass, George F., ed. *A History of Seafaring Based on Underwater Archaeology*. London, 1972.

Bathe, Basil W., and Alan J. Villiers. *The Visual Encyclopedia of Nautical Terms under Sail*. New York, 1978. Covers a wide range of subjects, but most definitions (especially construction subjects) apply to England in the last couple of centuries of working sail.

Chapelle, Howard I. *Boatbuilding: A Complete Handbook of Wooden Boat Construction*. New York, 1969.

———. *Yacht Designing and Planning*. New York, 1971.

Department of the Environment (United Kingdom). *Handbook of Hardwoods* 2d ed. Revised by R. H. Farmer. London, 1981.

———. *A Handbook of Softwoods* 2d ed. London, 1981.

Filgueiras, Octavio Lixa, ed. *Local Boats: Fourth International Symposium on Boat and Ship Archaeology, Porto, 1985*. BAR-S438, 2 vols. Oxford, 1988.

Forest Products Laboratory, U. S. Dept. of Agriculture. *The Encyclopedia of Wood*. New York, 1980.

Gianfrotta, Piero A., and Patrice Pomey. *Archeologia Subacquea*. Milan, 1980. Popular account of shipwreck excavations around the world.

Gillmer, Thomas C., and Bruce Johnson. *Introduction to Naval Architecture*. Annapolis, 1982.

Goodman, W. L. *The History of Woodworking Tools*. London, 1964.

Greenhill, Basil. *Archaeology of the Boat*. London, 1976.

Greenhill, Basil, and Sam Manning. *The Evolution of the Wooden Ship*. New York, 1988. A brief history of ship construction, but deals mostly with the construction of a late nineteenth-century schooner.

Hamilton, D. L. "INA Enters the SHARPS Era." *INA Newsletter* 15.2 (1988): 6, 7.

Hasslöf, Olof; Henning Henningsen; and Arne Emil Christensen, Jr., eds. *Ships and Shipyards, Sailors and Fishermen*. Copenhagen, 1972. A collection of papers by a distinguished group of Scandinavian maritime historians on a wide range of historical, archaeological, and ethnographic subjects.

Hocker, Frederick M. "The Development of a Bottom-based Shipbuilding Tradition in Northwestern Europe and the New World." Ph.D. diss., Texas A&M University, 1991. An excellent analysis of the construction of flat-bottomed vessels of all periods that were built by a technique that varied from shell-first and skeleton-first methods.

Hornell, James. *Water Transport: Origins and Early Evolution*. Cambridge, England, 1946.

Horsley, John E. *Tools of the Maritime Trades*. Camden, Maine, 1978.

Jal, Auguste. *Archéologie navale*. 2 vols. Paris, 1840. A pioneering effort in the literary analysis of historical watercraft.

Kemp, Peter, ed. *The Oxford Companion to Ships and the Sea*. London, 1976. An encyclopedia of seafaring and the sea.

Landström, Björn. *The Ship*. London, 1961.

Lavers, Gwendoline M. *The strength properties of timbers*. Forest Products Research Bulletin no. 50, 2d ed. London, 1969.

Lipke, Paul, ed. *Boats: A Field Manual for Their Documentation*. Forthcoming. Highly detailed descriptions and illustrations dealing with the recording, drawing, and documentation of small craft; includes a short chapter on boat archaeology.

McEwen, W. A., and A. H. Lewis. *Encyclopedia of Nautical Knowledge*. Cambridge, Md., 1953. An exhaustive compendium of nautical information; enumerates and clarifies a multitude of terms and phrases relating to the sea.

McGrail, Sean. *Ancient Boats in N.W. Europe: The Archaeology of Water Transport to A.D. 1500*. London, 1987.

———. *The Ship: Rafts, Boats, and Ships from Prehistoric Times to the Medieval Era*. London, 1981.

———, ed. *Sources and Techniques in Boat Archaeology*. BAR-S29. Oxford, 1977. Highly recommended to anyone interested in recording or studying hull remains. Most of the methodology described in this series of papers by leading scholars is still timely and reliable.

McGrail, Sean, and Eric Kentley, eds. *Sewn Plank Boats*. BAR-S129. Oxford, 1982. A collection of papers on a variety of watercraft employing ligatures or lashing techniques in their construction.

Mott, Lawrence. "The Development of the Rudder, A.D. 100–1600: A Technological Tale." Master's thesis, Texas A&M University, 1991.

Muckelroy, Keith, ed. *Archaeology under Water.* New York, 1980.

Oddy, W. A., ed. *Problems of the Conservation of Waterlogged Wood.* London, 1975.

Perlin, John. *A Forest Journey. The Role of Wood in the Development of Civilization.* New York, 1989.

Phillips-Birt, Douglas. *The Building of Boats.* New York, 1979. Historical analysis of small vessel construction.

Pomey, Patrice. *Recherches sous-marines.* Marseilles, 1987–88. Brief descriptions of all nautical archaeology projects along the coasts of France.

Reinders, Reinder, and Kees Paul, eds. *Carvel Construction Technique: Skeleton-first, Shell-first.* Oxford, 1991. Thirty-one papers presented at the Fifth International Symposium on Ship and Boat Archaeology, Amsterdam, 1988, cover construction subjects from antiquity to the eighteenth century.

Rule, Nick. "The Direct Survey Method (DSM) of Underwater Survey, and Its Application Underwater." *IJNA* 18.2 (1989): 157–62.

Singer, Charles, et al. *A History of Technology.* 2d ed. 5 vols. Oxford, 1954–58.

Spectre, Peter and David Larkin. *Wooden Ship.* Boston, 1991. An interesting popular account of wooden shipbuilding, beautifully illustrated with more than two hundred color photographs.

Throckmorton, Peter, ed. *The Sea Remembers: Shipwrecks and Archaeology.* New York, 1987.

Vaitses, Allan H. *Lofting.* Camden, Maine, 1980. A description of modern methods of mold lofting, as well as techniques for taking lines off small craft.

Waddell, Peter J. A. "Electronic Mapping of Underwater Sites." In *Underwater Archaeology Proceedings from the Society for Historical Archaeology Conference (1990)*, edited by Toni Carrell. Tucson, 1990.

INDEX

(Italicized page numbers refer to illustrations. For specific vessels or excavations, see ships and boats *entries.)*